RESCUING SOLDIERS
OF MISFORTUNE

RESCUING SOLDIERS
OF MISFORTUNE

A Full-Spectrum Approach to Veterans in the
Criminal Justice System from Arrest to Reentry

By

EVAN R. SEAMONE, LL.M., J.D., M.P.P.

Attorney, Veterans Legal Clinic
Harvard Law School
Major, U.S. Army Reserve

CHARLES C THOMAS • PUBLISHER, LTD.
Springfield • Illinois • U.S.A.

Published and Distributed Throughout the World by

CHARLES C THOMAS • PUBLISHER, LTD.
2600 South First Street
Springfield, Illinois 62704

© 2019 by CHARLES C THOMAS • PUBLISHER, LTD.

ISBN 978-0-398-09249-8 (paper)
ISBN 978-0-398-09250-4 (ebook)

With THOMAS BOOKS *careful attention is given to all details of manufacturing and design. It is the Publisher's desire to present books that are satisfactory as to their physical qualities and artistic possibilities and appropriate for their particular use.* THOMAS BOOKS *will be true to those laws of quality that assure a good name and good will.*

Printed in the United States of America
MM-C-1

Library of Congress Cataloging-in-Publication Data

Names: Seamone, Evan R., author.
Title: Rescuing soldiers of misfortune : a full-spectrum approach to veterans
   in the criminal justice system from arrest to reentry / by Evan R. Seamone,
   LL.M., J.D., M.P.P., Major, U.S. Army Reserve.
Description: Springfield, Ill. : Charles C Thomas, Publisher, Ltd., [2019] |

   Includes bibliographical references and index.
Identifiers: LCCN 2018039280 (print) | LCCN 2018051324 (ebook) | ISBN
   9780398092504 (ebook) | ISBN 9780398092498 (paper)
Subjects: LCSH: Veterans--Services for--United States. |
   Criminals--Rehabilitation--United States. | Criminal justice,
   Administration of--United States.
Classification: LCC UB357 (ebook) | LCC UB357 .S43 2019 (print) | DDC
   365/.661086970973--dc23
LC record available at https://lccn.loc.gov/2018039280

This book is dedicated to the veterans of our nation's wars who gave all they had only to be redeployed to prisons and jails because those battles never ended. These warriors are not forgotten, but rather owed the nation's most urgent support for that very sacrifice.

PREFACE

This is not a book in search of a disorder. Nor is it an attempt to explain away every veteran offender's crimes as the result of military insensitivity, combat trauma, or a rough homecoming experience. Veterans, like civilians, commit crimes for a number of reasons, many of which may have nothing to do with combat, training, or trauma—even if these are salient features within their personal histories. Neither does this book view the veteran offender as victim even though the media may sometimes portray them this way.

Rather, as military historian Clive Emsley observes, "Crime is one element of any society. If service personnel commit crime it is essentially because they are members of a society and it would be surprising if membership in the armed forces changed them in such a manner as not to reflect that society" (Emsley, 2013, p. 200). In line with the recommendations of the National Center for Post-Traumatic Stress Disorder and other mental health experts, it is difficult to make accurate generalizations about veteran offenders because they constitute a very diverse population, necessitating case-by-case examination.

Despite individual differences, far too many incarcerated veterans fall into a similar pattern: they were transformed by their military service, had no prior history of offending before enlistment, performed their duties loyally and faithfully, and have current mental health needs. To ignore them on the possibility that some nefarious inmates might lie about their service, might not truly need help, or might be motivated solely by the prospect of secondary gain completely defies the magnitude of their collective and individual sacrifice to the nation. Many in this group willingly endured a reality that included the most harrowing conditions and no promise of even surviving them. At the time of enlistment, most were not thinking about how they might benefit from disability compensation or other benefits in the future. This book concerns those veteran inmates who have failed to complete the readjustment process and who continue to wage their own personal wars to regain a sense of normalcy—those veterans who have not yet redeployed home from combat even though they have relocated to the inherently traumatizing confinement setting.

The literature on the criminalization and overrepresentation of individuals with mental illness makes an important distinction. While the criminal justice system should rightly hold those responsible for crimes that are "unrelated to symptomatic mental illness," it should not adopt a punitive posture with inmates who suffer from mental illness "simply because of their mental disorder or lack of access to appropriate treatment" (Munetz & Griffin, 2006, p. 544; Edelman, 2018).

Jails and prisons have a tremendous opportunity either to prevent or to induce negative symptoms among incarcerated veterans with legitimate mental health needs. In the establishment of veteran-specific interventions, good screening systems, solid eligibility criteria, and stringent participation standards will help reduce the possibility of fraud, waste, and abuse. Additionally, veterans have their own laser-like precision in detecting the fakers in their midst.

Aside from identifying factors that will help those seeking to be aware of the unique problems of incarcerated veterans and those advocating for these veterans, this book will attempt to help these individuals as well as correctional professionals to understand veteran inmates and their "unique" needs, which stem from military service (Tsai, Flatley, Kasprow, Clark, & Finlay, 2017, p. 376). This book refrains from a singular blueprint for all veterans and for all modes of incarceration including jails, prisons, and alternatives to incarceration altogether. What this book shows through much research—including a historical study of past programs—is that programs must be implemented flexibly despite operational and budgetary challenges. Instead, the author draws on the forgotten past and presently obscured lessons from the few jurisdictions that have developed targeted responses to the special needs of veteran inmates.

This book should help elected officials, law enforcement, the legal system, and veterans' advocates to develop relevant programs that do far more than simply warehouse some troublesome individuals. Eventually, more than 90 percent of individuals, including incarcerated veterans, leave prison (James, 2015, p. 1). However, if they do not have programs that are capable of meeting their needs while they are incarcerated, these returning convicts risk being recidivists and can cost their jurisdictions far more than what effective programming would have cost (James, 2015). Thus, this book provides ideas that public administrators and other leaders can use to strengthen the fabric of our society—often at a surprisingly low cost.

The approach in this book spans the post-World War I period to the present to show programs that promote successful readjustment from military service and treatment of combat and operational stress injuries *during confinement*. To strike a proper balance, the author also considers responses to the leading objections about veteran-specific interventions. At its core, this publication seeks to eliminate the guesswork from the formulation of responses to a special population. The aim is to identify responses that are verifiable and can be replicated by others.

One of the major challenges facing correctional institutions has been identification of inmates who are veterans (Edelman, 2018). Because many veterans conceal their identities for fear of losing benefits or shame at the fact of arrest (Rosenthal & McGuire, 2013), the inability to quantify this group with any degree of certainty has traditionally limited options for addressing the problem of incarcerated veterans. Requests for military records could take months to obtain, if they were even available. Correctional administrators had to contend with the possibility that "fakers" would attempt to gain benefits if they offered programs without the capability of verifying veteran status.

In 1990, during congressional hearings on the readjustment and mental health needs of incarcerated veterans, J. Michael Quinlan, Director of the Federal Bureau of Prisons, emphasized the need for a system to conduct computer matching of inmates with databases at the Department of Veterans Affairs (Quinlan, 1990, p. 20). The hearings underscored the fact that it was difficult to identify veterans and their needs for veteran-specific services because of the lack of methods to confirm the veteran status of inmates.

After decades of concern and confusion, as a part of the Department of Veterans Affairs (Veterans Administration) intensified outreach efforts, on April 25, 2012, personnel at the Homeless Program Office developed a computerized system to quickly scan their own systems for confirmation of veteran status. The program, called the Veterans Reentry Search Service (VRSS), requires only a Social Security number to access basic information about veterans' military records. To protect the information, prison administrators obtain basic confirmation of veteran status while Veterans Administration personnel simultaneously receive a more detailed output including the character of the veteran's discharge and other facts about the nature of an inmate's military service and experiences (U.S. Department of Veterans Affairs, 2015).

The Veterans Administration fielded the VRSS in the state correctional systems of California, Iowa, and Maryland to determine how accurately the system could account for veterans within the institutions. Surprisingly, while California prisons had estimated their veteran population at 2.7 percent based on inmate self-identification, the results of the VRSS computer matching revealed more than double the amount—roughly 7.9 percent (J. McGuire, personal communication, December 30, 2013). In California's example, the computerized search identified more than 5,000 previously not accounted for veteran inmates.

In the Middlesex County House of Correction, use of VRSS revealed more than 50 incarcerated veterans when most thought only a handful existed (Edelman, 2018, p. 67). Identification of this substantial population led the sheriff to develop a support group, then a separate Housing Unit for Military Veterans (HUMV) dorm to respond to these inmates' service-related needs (Edelman, 2018, pp. 67–68). The VRSS program is now available in several correctional systems, and VA specialists have encouraged correctional professionals to use the system to provide services that will assist veterans in their readjustment to society.

While the VRSS program offers a relatively new capability for jails and prisons to identify veteran inmates, it poses a more daunting question—***what do to with them once identified!*** Based on research on the topics of military service, combat, and criminal behavior, inevitably some portion of veterans in the offender population—perhaps quite small but still very significant—have dire needs to complete the process of readjusting to society after discharge from the military. Others—in another distinct subpopulation—have legitimate needs for treatment to address lingering operational stress injuries such as Posttraumatic Stress Disorder (PTSD) and mild Traumatic Brain Injury (TBI).

For these combat-traumatized veterans, especially, there is a lingering question of how suitable correctional facilities are to address their specific needs. While the VRSS program offers new ability to confirm inmates' veteran status, it does not provide any means for the Veterans Administration to overcome 38 C.F.R. § 17.38, a regulatory ban against offering any in- or outpatient medical treatment services to an inmate (Schaffer, 2016). Undoubtedly, with the use of the VRSS program, there will be new pressure on correctional professionals to address the population of "forgotten warriors" who occupy their cells and dorms, but there is little Veterans Administration corresponding assistance in addressing these inmates' needs during the period of incarceration, aside from transitional planning for the period of reentry.

E.R.S.

INTRODUCTION

Since 2008 when I developed a specialized court for military veterans after seeing increasing numbers making appearances in my mental health court, many developments have occurred across the nation. After ten years, it is estimated that 461 veterans treatment courts exist with many others in the planning stages. Although not all 50 states and territories have a dedicated program, well over 40 states do. Even in those jurisdictions which lack veterans treatment courts, they may have other programs tailored to the special needs of this population. As only one example, research by Major Evan Seamone reveals a veterans dorm in the state of Nebraska, as one of at least 80 similar dorms operating nationally (likely more by the time of this publication), even though Nebraska does not have a dedicated veterans treatment court.

With a novel perspective on criminal justice, Seamone suggests that nationwide veteran-specific programs in the criminal justice system—including first-responders trained in crisis communication with former military personnel and the nascent veterans traffic court operating as a first of its kind in Suffolk County, New York—represent a compromise between the military and civilian society. It is a tacit agreement that civilian society, while lacking expertise in the nuances of veteran culture and mental health needs, has shouldered the responsibility of aiding in the readjustment process. Seamone argues that, sometimes, veterans may require aid from the criminal justice system for completing the readjustment process when stubbornness, stigma, delayed onset of symptoms, or any number of other factors leave the veteran unable to recognize maladaptive methods he or she has adopted to cope with trauma symptoms or impaired perception of potential threats. Seamone makes the point, as I regularly witness along with other Veterans Treatment Court judges, that it often takes the back seat of a police car for a veteran to understand the need for help and the ineffectiveness of self-initiated responses.

Seamone's book, *Rescuing Soldiers of Misfortune: A Full-Spectrum Approach to Veterans in the Criminal Justice System from Arrest to Reentry,* presents the most comprehensive evaluation to date of the manner in which military veterans and active duty service members find themselves in conflict with the law and, correspondingly how the entire justice system can function as a seamless web to address the underlying conditions that contribute to veteran offending. Drawing on vital but obscured lessons from the past to supplement current innovative practices, Seamone demonstrates that many precedents exist for the civilian criminal justice system to respond to veterans in a manner that stresses accountability while offering opportunities for treatment and adjustment that had not been available before justice involvement.

This book, which represents years of research and experience serving as a military lawyer in both prosecution and defense, is an important reference for a variety of readers, including: law enforcement and first responders, corrections professionals, mental health providers, lawyers, judges, and anyone who desires to understand the challenges faced by military veterans in conflict with the law. Seamone provides expert information to assess individual veteran offenders who may have identical records, but very, very different personal experiences related to their service. Whether a given veteran is still in the military, left only days ago, or has been separated for decades, this book considers various factors that will promote veterans' recovery and aid in their readjustment to civilian society.

While some have criticized veteran-specific programming, Seamone clarifies the major differences between former military members and nonmilitary offenders who may have their own pressing mental health needs. First, having gone through basic training, which totally transforms a recruit from a civilian into a warrior, the veteran's military experience cements very different cultural values and assumptions that will stay with veterans for their lifetimes. Justice involvement may result from the conflict between these military values and civilian society's divergent expectations and cultural norms. Seamone provides a roadmap demonstrating how justice involvement offers unmatched opportunities for veterans to evaluate the manner in which deeply-held beliefs have contributed to or shaped behavior. Second, the vast majority of justice-involved veterans (roughly 80%) will have eligibility for benefits administered by the Veterans Administration even though many may have never used such benefits. Connecting veterans to benefits they rightfully earned, and helping veterans obtain upgrades of their discharge characterizations if they were separated less-than-honorably, can raise the quality of a veteran's life through housing and healthcare while reducing recidivism.

I will turn to this volume as a ready resource for the practical knowledge it imparts and salute Major Seamone for mightily enriching the limited scholarship in this area. The book delivers on its objective to make the justice system smarter along all points of the spectrum of justice involvement from arrest to reentry. While we may never reach every veteran entangled in the criminal justice system, the guidance in this volume will amplify current attempts to finally end veterans' personal wars that rage on after their return to the community.

> Honorable Robert T. Russell, Jr.
> *Presiding Judge*
> *Erie County Veterans Treatment Court*

DISCLAIMER

The views expressed in this book are solely those of the author and do not represent the positions of, and are not endorsed by, the Department of Defense, the Department of Veterans Affairs, or any other public agency.

ACKNOWLEDGMENTS

This book would not have been possible without the unmatched generosity of many individuals from a variety of professions: social workers, administrators, political scientists, correctional professionals, judges, Department of Veterans Affairs (Veterans Administration) employees, mental health clinicians, and community veterans' advocates who have been innovative in their work with and for veterans. This same group is targeted in this book so that we can complete the loop by providing information for the many people involved in helping incarcerated veterans succeed in rejoining our democratic processes.

In particular, my heartfelt thanks extend to Jim McGuire, Sean Clark, Joel Rosenthal, and Jessica Blue-Howells of the Veterans Health Administration Justice Programs, an organization responsible for forging new and vital connections between incarcerated veterans, the courts, and various service providers. Thank you as well to Dr. Shoba Sreenivasan for insights on the readjustment of veteran offenders. I owe special gratitude to Ruthanne Gordon, who assisted me in obtaining the original court records from the litigation that led to the development of the Pennsylvania Department of Corrections' ground-breaking Vietnam Veteran Combat PTSD treatment program, after the files had been lost at the National Archives. For their historical perspectives on Pennsylvania's program, I appreciate the help of Otis Nash and Dr. Edward Flournoy.

A necessary component of this book was the current state of Crisis Intervention (team) Training programs to prepare first-responders (including correctional staff) for engagements with veterans in crisis. To this end, I am grateful for the unique insights of Dr. Amy Watson, retired Chicago police lieutenant Jeff Murphy, and Memphis Veterans Administration psychologist Thomas M. Kirchberg. Beyond this, the book's insights on the establishment of veterans' organizations and veterans dormitories in jails and prisons would not have been possible without the assistance of those who have been integral in the development and operation of such programs.

During the research for this book, I was extremely fortunate to benefit from the insights of Susan Verbecke and Jim Strollo, who innovated for decades within the New York Department of Correctional Services Veterans Residential Therapeutic Program, shortly after the program was established. No other veteran-specific programs such as theirs has managed to survive for so long. Their determination and dedication to the program surely explains why the program serves as a virtual center of excellence for other programs wishing to gain priceless insights on correctional programming. In addition, my gratitude also extends to Gregory Crawford and his team from the National Institute of Corrections (NIC), including Mr. Bernard Edelman, who offered me an unparalleled opportunity to contribute to NICs efforts to promote the development of specialized housing units in jails across the nation.

For their insights on the establishment of the Muscogee County Veterans Dorm, I give my sincere thanks to former Sheriff John Darr and Reverend Neil Richardson, both of whom have demonstrated the benefits of developing targeted housing programs for veterans. To Gary Cranor and Sandra Womack of Texas' Mark W. Stiles Unit, you have my unending appreciation for insight on the fifteen-year evolution of the Vietnam Veterans of America chapter there. I also thank Warden Greg Hershberger of the Roxbury Correctional Institution for allowing me to visit the facility and Corporal John Worgul for his priceless insights on sponsorship of the Incarcerated Veterans of Roxbury, an exceptional organization that has found a new way to channel the energies of incarcerated veterans in continued service to the community.

I also thank Sheriff Ross Mirkarimi, Sunny Schwartz, Leslie Levitas, Ida McCray, Ron Perez, Lieutenant Stephanie Colmenero, Mel Jarrett, and Sergeant Robert Taylor. I am also grateful to Mrs. Susan Fahey of the Community of Veterans Engaged in Restoration (C.O.V.E.R.) at San Francisco County Jail (No. 5) for the privilege of visiting and learning about their program, which is the standard-bearer for effective coordination of a variety of community agencies devoted to the unique needs of veteran inmates. Thanks also to Sheriff Glenn Boyer of Jefferson County, Missouri, for sharing his insights on the development of a veterans dormitory for vets during periods of extremely brief jail incarceration.

CONTENTS

RESCUING SOLDIERS
OF MISFORTUNE

Chapter 1

COMPONENTS OF
VETERANS' READJUSTMENT

Renewed Concern for Veteran Offenders

On August 17, 2017, a watershed moment occurred for veterans across the United States. Under Secretary of Defense Anthony M. Kurta issued a memorandum and accompanying guidance for the special boards that decide on petitions to upgrade military discharge characterizations (Kurta, 2017). The full five-page document, including its enclosure, appears in the Appendix to this chapter. The Kurta Memorandum articulated, for the first time, factors that would mitigate less-than-honorable military discharge characterizations based on misconduct where a veteran suffered from Posttraumatic Stress Disorder (PTSD), Traumatic Brain Injury (TBI), other "mental health condition[s]," or had experienced sexual assault or sexual harassment while in Service (Kurta, 2017, p. 1, ¶ 6).

The significance of Under Secretary Kurta's memorandum was open to debate. For many veterans who had attempted to upgrade their discharges for decades to no avail, Kurta's guidance seemed well-intentioned, but little different from previous efforts to recognize the impact of "invisible" war wounds. In the 1970s, President Jimmy Carter attempted to grant discharge upgrades for Vietnam veterans as a form of a Special Discharge Review program. These efforts failed because Congress enacted legislation to prevent this act of mercy from impacting VA benefit determinations. Congress, in fact, further forbade advertising of the program and optimal outreach (Kidder, 1978).

In 2014, in response to lawsuits premised on statistics demonstrating a trend of denials of PTSD-afflicted Vietnam veterans' discharge upgrade requests (Paznoikas, 2014), Defense Secretary Chuck Hagel issued guidance inviting the boards to exercise more meaningful consideration of these claims. The basis was that PTSD diagnoses did not exist until the 1980 *DSM III* and available military records from the war years often lacked "substantive information concerning medical conditions" (Hagel, 2014, p. 2). Secretary Hagel instructed that discharge review boards should give "special consideration" to later PTSD diagnoses as well as service-related records revealing "one or more [PTSD] symptoms" (Hagel, 2014, Attachment, p. 1).

Evident in the filling of additional class action law suits against the Department of Defense (DoD), the boards apparently did not take this guidance to heart (McCarthy, 2017). In 2016, Under Secretary Brad Carson formalized Secretary Hagel's guidance and reminded boards that the Hagel Memorandum's standards "remaine[d] exceptionally important" and directed that the boards "renew and re-double . . . efforts" to apply Secretary Hagel's standards (Carson, 2016, p. 1). Given this chain of failed policies, for some veterans, there were few guarantees that Kurta's Memorandum would be any different.

Other commentators recognized important differences in Kurta's new standards. Homeless Rights Attorney Neha Chiaramonte (2018), for example, hailed the Kurta Memo as a "monumental shift in the law [that] has dramatically changed the lives of many service members." The Connecticut Veterans Legal Center, which authors a popular discharge upgrade manual, recently updated its guidance to reflect Kurta's standards. It indicates how the Memorandum "expands the liberal consideration protections stated by the Hagel and Carson Memos, broadening the pool of applicable veterans to those suffering from 'mental health conditions' rather than just PTSD or TBI," accounts for symptoms of military sexual trauma and sexual harassment, and "expand[s] all three memos' coverage to all discharge characterizations, not just other than honorable" (2018, p. 3). Kristofer Goldsmith, a veterans' advocate who practiced for a decade in the area of veterans' benefits after his own tour, marveled that the Kurta Memorandum is "filled with signals that there may yet be hope for veterans who have been unfairly suffering the effects of [stigmatizing less-than-honorable discharges]" (Wentling, 2017). Undoubtedly, another important difference was Under Secretary Kurta's expansion of the guidance beyond Secretary Hagel's focus on Vietnam-era veterans (2014) to *all* veterans (Kurta, 2017; Chiaramonte, 2018).

The Kurta Memorandum is monumental for a different reason entirely. Less-than-honorable discharges, especially those falling in the categories of Undesirable or Other-Than-Honorable, arise from the military's finding that the veteran engaged in unlawful behavior. The Kurta Memo thus represents the clearest and most direct official recognition of the connection between traumatizing events occurring during military service and subsequent criminal offending while in the military.

The sixth paragraph of the Kurta Memorandum observes: "Evidence of misconduct, including any misconduct underlying a veteran's discharge, may be evidence of a mental health condition, including PTSD; TBI; or of behavior consistent with experiencing sexual assault or sexual harassment" (2017, Attachment p. 1 ¶ 6). It condemns traditional skepticism of self-serving diagnoses long after military service and directs the boards to give liberal and favorable consideration to private and Veterans Affairs' mental health diagnoses made "years" after military service because "[i]nvisible wounds . . . are some of the most difficult cases to review and there are frequently limited records for the boards to consider" (Kurta, 2017, p. 1).

"Evidence of misconduct, including any misconduct underlying a veteran's discharge, may be evidence of a mental health condition, including PTSD; TBI; or of behavior consistent with experiencing sexual assault or sexual harassment."

Under Secretary of Defense A. M. Kurta (2017, p. 1, ¶ 6)

The combined effect of this new guidance marks not only the recognition, but codification of a presumption that military misconduct is attributable to service-connected mental health conditions. At the most general level, Under Secretary Kurta's presumption can properly be considered part of a broader consensus—a "paradigm shift" (Schaffer, 2016, p. 293; Trojano, Christopher, Pinals, Harnish, & Smelson, 2017, p. 409), a "sea change" (Seamone et al., 2018a, p. 140), and an "emergent nationwide effort to reduce mass incarceration and better address the root cause of criminal behavior through treatment and supervision" (Robinson & Tate, 2016, p. 26)—that has grown since attacks of 9/11 and in response to America's longest wars.

The Kurta Memorandum represents the DoD's adoption of the same principles that underlie veteran-specific responses across the range of civilian criminal involvement, from specially trained police officers to veterans treatment courts, specialized housing units for veterans in prisons and jails, and veteran reentry courts. Collectively, all of these innovations, endorsed most prominently during America's present "forever wars" in Iraq and Afghanistan (*New York Times* Editorial Board, 2017), recognize the instrumental value of treating the underlying mental health condition and aiding in post-service readjustment rather than using a traditional punitive approach.

With the exception of a single federal veterans treatment court at Fort Hood, Texas, that has enrolled military members (Robinson & Tate, 2016, p. 24), the active duty military has largely rejected the civilian justice system's successful approach to its own offenders (Seamone, 2011; Seamone et al., 2018a). The recent innovations in the civilian sector have occurred at such a widespread and accelerated pace across the nation that off-the-shelf models now exist to assist law enforcement, correctional administrators, prosecutors, judges, and other members of the civilian criminal justice system to develop effective veteran-specific interventions that improve communities by linking veterans to much-needed benefits and resources that they rightfully earned (Seamone et al., 2018a). Although some have criticized the lack of evidence-based and longitudinal data regarding these different models, current trends, combined with historical lessons provide a firm enough foundation for planning and implementation (Edelman, 2018).

The Critical Role of Military Culture in Criminal Offending

During different periods of war in society, scholars concluded that military service transformed veterans into very different people when they returned from combat (e.g., Bryant, 1979). However, family members, spouses, partners, and significant others who knew the veterans prior to their entry into the military have routinely observed the dramatic and all-encompassing transformation of civilian into warrior after the completion of basic combat training and before exposure to the horrors of war. As Blum, the brother of an Army Ranger trainee, observed, "[t]he moment the infantry recruit walks down the cinder-block path from his childhood home at 0430 hours and enters a recruiting sergeant's car via the passenger-side door, he crosses over into a new plane of existence" (2017, p. 34). In the process of "making" a marine, sailor, soldier, or airman, recruits are taught by drill instructors to despise and doubt their prior civilian routines, ambitions, and behaviors, and to embrace a new military culture that prioritizes entirely different values that are necessary to meet the military's purpose (Holyfield, 2011).

Blum correctly identifies that basic training is "a carefully calibrated process" in which "[r]ecruits are both habituated to violence and acculturated into a new family with radically different standards of behavior" (2017, p. 44). The book *Khaki-Collar Crime,* written by a former Army combat veteran, alludes to the manner in which

> [c]ivilian value systems and military value systems are often antithetical, and the average civilian may well be disaffected to the point of immobility at the prospect of violence and mayhem, killing and/or being killed, and the necessity for blind obedience to orders from superiors. The civilian must be converted into that which he was not—a warrior with warlike proclivities. (Bryant, 1979, p. 55)

This new military culture indoctrinates a sense of "violent and aggressive behavior" in which "'[t]oughness' and aggressiveness are highly favored characteristics and are often equated with 'leadership'" (Bryant, 1979, p. 53).

Unfortunately, many of the skills inculcated in the warrior through training, repetition, and peer pressure are tremendously useful during military service, but highly detrimental in civilian society after the veteran's departure (Zogas, 2017).

Culture can be described as a passed on "set of behaviors, values, and ways of assessing circumstances. . ." (Kirkland, 2003, p. 159). In some cases, the implicit or explicit values fostered by military culture may provoke, attenuate, and aggravate the veteran's aggressive responses to different stimuli. For example, attitudes promoting use alcohol as a sleep-aid, to relax after stressful experiences, or to self-medicate in avoidance of prescriptions that result in unwanted side-effects, can enable dysregulated episodes of anger and rage (Tharp, Sherman, Holland, Townsend, & Bowling, 2016). Another example of culture may be likened to the promotion of hypermasculinity that makes it acceptable to objectify women to gain acceptance among peers in tight-knit and competitive military teams (Seamone, Brooks-Holliday, & Sreenivasan, 2018).

Contemporary concerns over veterans' combat experiences and the additional cultural phenomenon of avoidance of help-seeking behavior due to military values (Harding, 2016), led to the realization that some veterans would inevitably become involved in the criminal justice system upon their return from combat, either from the lack of efforts to deprogram their lethal warrior mentality or mental illnesses they had before joining the military that were exacerbated by combat conditions, or symptoms of the invisible wounds of war that were first sustained during combat deployments (Seamone et al., 2018a).

In the search for answers, the public and policymakers turned to the nation's past experiences with PTSD-afflicted Vietnam veterans, nearly half of whom (45.7%) were confined for criminal behavior following their military service (Kulka et al., 1990, pp. 186–187). Formerly, organizations such as the Vietnam Veterans of America had been advocating on behalf of these "forgotten warriors" (Boivin, 1986), but this new consciousness embraced incarcerated veterans from all of the country's wars, raising concerns about their well-being and whether they ever had the opportunity to successfully integrate back into society.

In this decade after combat operations commenced in Afghanistan, and later Iraq, the American criminal justice system has responded to incarcerated veterans with an increasing and unprecedented sense of urgency—despite simultaneously shrinking budgets. The Department of Veterans Affairs (Veterans Administration) has created the position of Veterans Justice Outreach Specialist to identify and facilitate access to benefits for incarcerated veterans, who chiefly depend on cooperation from correctional administrators to meet their objectives (Schaffer, 2016). The Veterans Administration has likewise placed federal employees in more than 461 state veterans treatment courts to help defer veteran offenders from confinement into community-based treatment programs with ongoing judicial oversight (Tsai, Flatley, Kasprow, Clark, & Finlay, 2018).

Besides the Veterans Administration, some state legislatures have instituted measures to help alert law enforcement officers to traumatized veterans with the development of drivers' licenses that indicate a diagnosis of PTSD in Georgia or of honorably discharged veteran status in Utah (Seamone, 2011). Many law enforcement officers attend training to become familiar with symptoms of PTSD and how to de-escalate these symptoms in high-conflict environments. Some police departments have also instituted programs to divert veteran offenders from jail into treatment facilities during pre-booking stages of arrest when responding to high-stress events (Gambill, 2010).

Other Important Aspects of Military Culture

To better equip correctional professionals with the knowledge-base to innovate for effective and institution-sensitive solutions, this chapter also includes a brief introduction to military culture and its effects on service members and their families. A reason for this preliminary investigation is to help explain the otherwise puzzling behavior observed in corrections settings. Correctional professionals may, for example, wonder why veterans would purposely conceal their status during initial entry into the criminal justice system. Why would the veterans avoid seeking help for ongoing PTSD symptoms despite constant reminders of their horrific combat experiences? Why would veterans withdraw from the affection of their family members, and why would the veteran not desire to obtain monetary or health benefits despite full VA eligibility? Answers to these queries stems from knowledge of the veteran population and its shared experiences, which demonstrate what makes veterans different from other groups of inmates.

Understanding the nature of the distinct military culture in the United States is essential. The first point to recognize is a tremendous cultural divide. There has been a declining trend in military participation with less than 1 percent of the population having served the Nation (e.g., Zuchinno & Cloud, 2015) (estimating "less than one-half of 1 percent of the U.S. population"). While, overall, there may be approximately 24 million living veterans, the decline in military participation has produced an unmistakable distancing effect. A Pew Research Center report, titled *The Military-Civilian Gap*, reveals:

> **In a sample, 84 percent of post-9-11 veterans and 71 percent of the general public agreed with the statement "the public does not understand the problems faced by those in the military" (2011, p. 2).**

Part of this can be explained by the fact that the military exists outside of the public eye, living and training, for the most part, in bases that are large enough to constitute small cities.

On balance, the three major factors contributing to this noticeable "cultural divide" include the following: (1) the fact that military bases largely operate separately from the community with their own schools, hospitals, supermarkets, and so forth; (2) the fact that service members work on military installations that are frequently closed to the general community; and (3) the fact that military training for advancement in career fields largely occurs at military schools. There may be some exceptions, such as advanced degree programs at civilian universities or families who live off-base. But these stark differences make it more difficult for Americans to understand the realities facing military members and veterans—especially the magnitude of combat operations—and the other multiple demands that military culture places on its members and its families. These differences also explain what has been called a "cross-cultural transition" when a service-member returns to civilian life, for whatever the reason.

Volumes are available on military culture, which are many times the size of this book, which already has much ground to cover. Hence, the following summary provides a snapshot of some key demographics on military membership and military family cycles. The two most important are the career cycle and the deployment cycle. Recognizing that one cannot understand incarcerated veterans without appreciating distinguishing characteristics of the military culture (Rosenthal & McGuire, 2013) or the total institution framework that the military uses to achieve its demanding mission (Brown, Stanulis, Theis, Farnsworth, & Daniels, 2013), this book will attempt, in every chapter, to continue weaving in important cultural considerations.

1. The Military and Its Members

Despite the fact that immediate retirement benefits after twenty years of service is a retention incentive, most service members leave after an initial tour. The relatively young and mostly married parents who constitute the ground forces (Hall, 2008; U.S. Department of Defense, 2016) are likely to have deployed to combat and been exposed to the sorts of traumatic events known to result in psychological wounds of war (Hoge, 2010). What is clear to an observer with experience in corrections is that veterans are largely more educated than the average inmates and were likely more successful in a highly demanding and stressful environment. Their success is evident because the overwhelming majority of incarcerated veterans (80 percent) received honorable discharges from the service (Rosenthal & McGuire, 2013).

In contemporary times, service members who constitute the combat arms in the ground forces of the Marines and the Army are relatively young. The average age of a Marine is twenty-five (with 36.9% of its forces aged eighteen-to-twenty-four), and the average age of an Army soldier is twenty-nine (with 18.3% of its forces aged eighteen-to-twenty-one). The Air Force constitutes an older force with only 14.4 of its members in the eighteen-to-twenty-one age category (Defense Manpower Data Center, 2011).

Among the many young service members in the combat forces, most are married (53.5% of the Active Forces in 2016) to relatively young spouses and a substantial number have children (35.6% of the Active Forces, with 4.3% additional single parents with children) (U.S. Department of Defense, 2016, pp. iv, vi). With the military's provision of additional compensation and off-post housing privileges for married service members, some suggest an incentive, even "inducement," to marry young and have children (Hogan & Seifert, 2010).

2. The Single Service Member

The military has a distinct culture that envelopes all of its members for as long as they remain within its ranks (Savitsky, Illingworth, & Dulaney, 2009, pp. 328–329). This culture has both positive and negative elements, which can influence the veteran's readjustment to civilian life after leaving the military. Reliance on teams rather than individuals to accomplish objectives is largely a positive factor when group performance is desired. However, the "warrior mentality," which tends to reject help-seeking, is particularly concerning when it comes to the treatment of mental conditions, their symptoms, or other crises that the individual is unable to handle. Enlisted service members are 85 percent of the Armed Forces and only 15 percent constitute officers. Most new recruits join straight out of high school. Many of these troops have come to the military from rough circumstances, which may include physical or sexual abuse prior to enlistment.

The military continues to offer a means to join a new family of motivated individuals and to break local ties, which can be extremely important for individuals who have already suffered some degree of trauma in their lives. With many recruits being teenagers in their late period of adolescence, the impact of basic training and indoctrination into the military is profound because the military is a total institution, which governs nearly every aspect of their existence (Brown et al., 2013). Within this massive American subculture, youthful warriors will obtain several services that eliminate more traditional civilian stressors, such as obtaining housing, paying rent, preparing meals to eat, buying clothing, paying utility bills, and so forth. These forms of direct assistance are of great benefit because they permit the troop to focus on warrior tasks, which are stressful and overburdening in their own right.

Yet, these benefits are also part of a "double-edged sword" for youthful service members because—*for some*—the burdens they remove are an essential part of the process of adult development (Ray, Haines, & Longo, 2013, p. 291). Dr. Susan L. Ray and her colleagues convincingly describe how "difficulties developing an autonomous adult identity can be interrupted by military training that precludes *independent decision-making,* which is a required adult coping ability" (2013, p. 291). Accordingly, the military's act of thinking for the service members often results in a form of stunted development impairing their ability to exercise independent judgment following discharge from the Service, making it more difficult to succeed in the civilian world without the same supports. While this certainly explains many problems in readjustment, it also contributes to veteran homelessness and offending in the civilian population.

Many veterans who entered the military in their younger years leave the service feeling as though they have lost their place in the world. They are no longer part of the institution that provided for many of their needs, and many feel as though they are not ideally suited for civilian lifestyles that operate under different rules, which might be to slow-paced, compared to their former service. A major underlying problem appears to be a common belief in the myth of self-sufficiency—essentially that the military provided them with the skills to survive in any type of adversity and prevail.

While, indeed, veterans are better equipped to survive in the streets and the jails as result of their training, and some are able to simply disappear and live off the land if they wanted to, this does not mean that they will live their lives peacefully or productively. The double-edged sword emerges here as well because many become reluctant to ask for assistance until it may be simply too late.

Unfortunately, veterans can easily become overly confident. Later parts of this book explore the impact of combat training on threat-perception. However, training has a different aspect that relates to the veteran's existence after discharge. A large aspect of survival training in the military hinges upon the notion of self-sufficiency and invincibility because warriors must be bold to survive in combat (Moore, Hopewell, & Grossman, 2009). With the support of a band of brothers and sisters, it is easy to be confident.

Tragically, this element falls away, when the veteran is no longer a member of the service. Some veterans, who are convinced, based on their training, that they can overcome any conditions, will stay in a disconnected mode of existence permanently. They will often perceive that they are capable of handling all aspects of survival, including symptoms of any mental or physical health disorders. The reliance on distancing or openness to others prevents the veterans from obtaining assistance with public services, and pushes them further into adverse conditions that might eventually place the veterans in conflict with the law (Ray et al., 2013).

3. The Military Family Experience

Like the service member, military spouses and family members also exist in a world of unspoken expectations (Hall, 2008, p. 57). Military family members often refuse to request assistance for similar reasons as the uniformed member; they do not want their problems reflecting poorly on the service member's reputation (Truscott, 1989, p. 4). Their lives are often said to be shrouded in secrecy and "denial" (Hall, 2008, p. 57).

As an increasing number of military families experience incidents of interpersonal violence, especially when the family includes a member with PTSD (Teten et al., 2010; Taft et al., 2005). The cultural practices of the family will often lead them to wait until a situation has become intolerable before they obtain help. Within this "fortress," demographics demonstrate the difficulties in the way families are influenced by multiple deployments and the invisible wounds of war.

In the Army, the largest military service, most soldiers have deployed more than once, with some on their seventh or eighth deployment (Bonds, Baiocchi, & MacDonald, 2010). What we currently know is that each new deployment generates a greater likelihood of psychological injury, and that each deployment for a mentally wounded warrior increases the chances of aggravated symptoms (Newhouse, 2008, pp. 27–28). Commentators say that military service is not like a standard civilian job, not even comparable to more demanding and dangerous professions such as law enforcement (Truscott, 1989, p. 3). Unlike police work, the military promotes lethality and extended deployments in harm's way. This, combined with a highly-transient existence, has subjected military families to tremendous amounts of strain and transformation (Everson & Camp, 2011). While these salient characteristics have surely brought families closer together (Karney & Crown, 2007), they have the power to change the dynamics of mutual support in ways that can outlast military service and affect rehabilitation in confinement and eventual community reentry.

The "warrior mentality" often encourages both service members and their families to conceal weakness, appear stable in the face of chaos, and deny help-seeking behavior (Hall, 2011). This common mindset can explain why it is difficult to detect mental disorders that can only be identified through self-disclosure, and sometimes why the veteran has been incarcerated in the first place.

Two different cycles are important for corrections officers to know. First, the deployment cycle, depicted in Figure 1, visually captures the common family responses from pre-deployment to combat, through the service members' absence, and their eventual return (Everson & Camp, 2011, p. 23, Fig. 1.4). The deployment cycle leaves many opportunities for families to be adversely affected, sometimes to the point where the family becomes so used to the parent's absence that the other family members grow used to—and prefer—it (Rosen & Durand, 2000).

The second cycle that will assist corrections officers is the military career development cycle, shown in Figure 2. Notably, most young service members will move on to a different career following their military service, rather

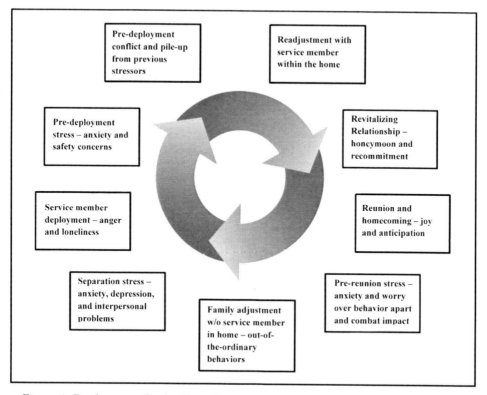

Figure 1. Deployment Cycle. Note: Reprinted with Permission of Taylor & Francis.

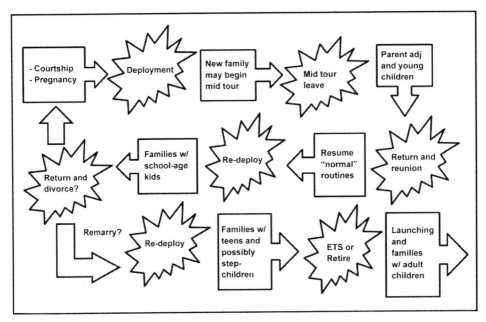

Figure 2. Military Career Development Cycle. Source: Everson & Camp (2011, p. 15, Fig. 1.1). Reprinted with Permission of Taylor & Francis.

than serving a full twenty years, after which they would be eligible for a reduced pension the moment that they retire. For those who endure the two decades of service, a military family's existence is best described as nomadic, with some families moving geographic locations more than twenty times in the course of a career (Truscott, 1989, p. 3). This highly transient lifestyle brings additional complications for the development of relationships and feelings of security for all of the military family members. These confusions often contribute to divorce and separation, which may explain why the creators of Figure 2, have provided for multiple marriages in the career life course. Possibly military members and their families have been forced to choose between the military and the family on different occasions, which can complicate the already delicate calculus of preserving family bonds during the course of incarceration (Martin & McClure, 2000, p. 15). The intense family tradeoffs that occur over the military career—however long or short—may influence communications. Children may have to become caretakers for parents with mental health conditions through shifted roles and responsibilities.

Spouses may need to make crucial decisions in the household and may not desire to share that responsibility after having to do it independently in the military spouse's absence. These dynamics are ever so important because, if a veteran has PTSD or another invisible wound, family support or lack thereof may make the crucial difference in the veteran's potential for recovery. Consideration of these cultural influences will likewise assist in planning comprehensively for the family components of reentry.

The Veteran as a "Special" Offender with Unique Needs

Within confined settings, special concern exists over treatment programs for veterans during the course of their incarceration. At the most basic level, many think that veterans are better-suited than other inmates to respond to authority based on their military conditioning. The director of the Federal Bureau of Prisons echoed this point during the Korean War after assessing veteran inmates across the nation: "All of the 29 federal prison wardens and camp superintendents agreed that by and large the ex-GI made a better adjustment, profited more by the rehabilitation program, and generally found it easier to adjust than the man who had no military experience" (Bennett, 1954, p. 42).

When a prison or jail inherits a combat veteran, these inmates have essentially undergone the same basic training, drill and ceremony, and disciplinary orientation that has made incarceration programs appealing in several correctional systems over the years (Edelman, 2018; Tsai & Goggin, 2017).

Although it is reasonable to expect that the veterans have inherited some engrained qualities of order and discipline from years of experience that would help prepare them for better outcomes in being supervised, combat trauma is an important exception. When an inmate has an untreated, undiagnosed, or misdiagnosed combat-induced condition—as is often the case with returning Iraq and Afghanistan veterans—confinement aggravates symptoms of mental illness, especially anxiety disorders. In 2009, mental health professionals became extremely concerned about the fact that the incarcerated veteran "sits at the intersection" of two groups that independently show increased risks of suicide (Wortzel, Binswanger, Anderson, & Adler, 2009, p. 82). They warned that this overlapping status, especially for mentally ill veterans, increased the likelihood of self-destructive behavior and called for urgent intervention, even without hard numbers or direct connections (Frisman & Griffin-Fennell, 2009).

Veteran well-being in confinement is an issue that poses special considerations for correctional administrators and officers, aside from reentry or diversion. The major reason is a statutory bar that prohibits the Veterans Administration from duplicating health services when a different agency is primarily responsible for the veteran's housing and subsistence (Schaffer, 2016). Diminished Veterans Administration benefit payments during incarceration further limit the veterans' options because they are prevented from using those payments to fund treatment. With the sole responsibility for treatment falling on the shoulders of the jail or prison, correctional officers, correctional psychologists, and correctional administrators face unique obstacles and the very real possibility that invisible war wounds will show up in ongoing psychological battles while veterans are confined, unless they institute effective and meaningful treatment interventions.

The Value of Historical Precedents

Historical lessons are vital because they remind us that this is not the first-time society has contended with criminal involvement of veterans and military members. In fact, experienced mental health clinicians who have treated veterans for decades make a compelling case that the military has intentionally resorted to punishment over treatment of symptoms of predictable service-related mental health conditions so as to avoid recognizing the magnitude of combat trauma (Russell, Schaubel, & Figley, 2018). They identify "10 approaches aimed at avoiding learning from [the military's] war trauma lessons by punishing, eliminating, and/or concealing its mental health problem," three of which include "legal prosecution, incarceration, and executions," "bad paper discharges," and "cruel and inhumane handling" (Russell et al., 2018, pp. 39–50).

In the last few years, some jails and prisons have instituted special programs to address the unique needs of incarcerated veterans. Whether the Veterans Administration's limitations motivated the change or these institutions independently desired to offer more comprehensive services to the veterans, the programs signify a sea change in the provision of jail and prison services. Two types of programs have emerged. On the one hand, the San Francisco Sheriff's Department's Community of Veterans Engaged in Restoration (COVER) program represents a "modified therapeutic community," in which veterans can obtain treatment together and work through their issues, helping to challenge destructive combat-related thoughts that have impeded their reasoning since they sustained combat trauma (Schwartz & Levitas, 2011, p. 55; Edelman, 2018).

On the other hand, the Florida Department of Corrections' veterans dormitory program, like similar programs now operating in California and Illinois, draws on engrained military discipline to accomplish its goals and uses formations and other military formalities as the backdrop for individual service delivery (Alvarez, 2011). While, these programs are often considered to be developing, first-of-their-kind, and in their infancy, they are, in fact, hardly new. Instead, they bring to mind an important lesson underscored by historians of correctional programs who have observed that corrections is constantly reinventing past programs, making it vital to revisit historical lessons and perspectives (Burkhead, 2007).

Innovation in the correctional treatment of veterans dates back to at least the aftermath of the Civil War, where state veterans' homes dealt with veterans' readjustment problems by adjudicating their disciplinary issues in protected communities, rather than in the courts of the state, specifically because of their special needs (Cetina, 1977). Soon, other programs developed within courts and confinement facilities. After noting instances of concern for veterans who were offenders over the centuries, the Supreme Court's *Porter v. McCollum* (2009) case recognized that the nation has a "long tradition of according leniency to veterans in recognition of their service, especially for those who fought on the front lines" (p. 43, n.8).

Indiana's 1946 program of "short-term incarceration" at the State Farm in Greencastle reveals the value of treatment in confined settings, especially when it is accomplished in a way that allows veterans to work with one another, helps them obtain benefits, and addresses issues unique to their uncommon shared experiences in combat (Evigil & Hawkins, 1946). Equally reminiscent of today's veterans treatment courts, the military has also instituted similar measures for incarcerated combat-traumatized veterans in its Service Command Rehabilitation Centers and other correctional institutions since World War II (Seamone, 2011; Russell et al., 2018).

The combination of past lessons with contemporary concern over criminally involved veterans clarifies an important point. Rather than turning to studies and posing the same questions from decades and centuries past, sheriffs and wardens are starting to understand that jails and prisons are a necessary part of the readjustment process for many veterans returning from wars, in any society. This point is echoed in the correctional systems of the United Kingdom, where, in response to a rise in crime committed by Iraq and Afghanistan veterans, correctional administrators are again relying on treatment models that were used to treat war-traumatized veterans generations ago (Brookes, Ashton, & Hollis, 2010).

When the military or civilian criminal justice systems turn a blind eye toward past experiences, especially in the aftermath of the First World War, it is easy to dismiss important trends on the basis that more systematic study is needed. In this respect, Snowden and his colleagues (2017) suggest that "our understanding of the involvement of military personnel in criminal behaviors and the criminal justice system continues to be in its infancy" (pp. 605–606). However, this remains true only if we do not take stock of historical examples and if we avoid looking in the right locations. This book aims to remove the veil of ignorance.

Flexibility in Programming Options for Incarcerated Veterans

In addressing an inmate's mental health needs, any correctional facility is faced with very clear challenges. Although there are many standards and guidelines from professional organizations and the courts, too often they lack specific measures for implementation: "Basically [the planner] is left with a whole set of prescriptions, without any guidance as to how to fit them together into a coherent program, how to initiate the program, and how to finance the program" (Steadman, McCarty, & Morrisey, 1989, p. 38). Furthermore, with decreased spending on mental health in general, this trend in state and local budgeting has led to a fiscal "crisis" in correctional programming for mental health services (Sieleni, 2011).

However, more and more jails and prisons have embraced a "new world for corrections" in the mental health field (Sieleni, 2011, p. 10). Successful facilities realize that collaboration must occur "outside the walls and into the community" and that their greatest assets are concerned members of a diverse interdisciplinary correctional staff (Aufderheide, 2011, p. 40). In a very important way, the absence of finite requirements allows for a greater degree of innovation in both funding and collaboration. When correctional professionals and those outside of confinement facilities such as civic planners and sociologists start to view confinement as part of the readjustment process—as a necessary phase for the veteran's successful reintegration into society—many doors open. This book is organized in a manner that will best prepare professionals from a variety of disciplines to meet the demands of a growing population of offenders with unique treatment needs.

The Structure of This Book

One of the main ways that the military is able to achieve its goal is by making discipline—and punishment when necessary—a central component of its distinct culture. Given the necessity and prominence of "good order and discipline" in military culture (Russell et al., 2018), Chapter 2 distinguishes between civilian and military justice systems and punishments. While judges largely implement sanctions for criminal conduct in civilian settings, individual unit commanders assume control over the military justice system from the inception of the investigation through sentencing and clemency, with some exceptions (Seamone et al., 2018a). In fact, when the military judge or jury reaches a verdict or adjudges punishment, these pronouncements have only the weight of recommendations, which may sometimes be reduced or entirely disapproved after the fact (Seamone, 2011). While commanders have wide latitude in deciding on potential punishments and an arsenal of intermediate administrative tools ranging from corrective counseling to administrative non-judicial punishment (Article 15 or Captain's

Mast), they have something with no civilian parallel: the ability to pursue a stigmatizing discharge, at a court-martial or administrative separation. Administrative discharges can have similar effects as a court, but without the hassle of assembling witnesses, juries, or a judge.

The difference between systems of punishment might not seem significant at first blush. However, correctional professionals must understand the nuances of discharge characterization because these labels can foreclose the opportunity to obtain VA benefits. This is crucial because many VA programs will not accept a veteran without first establishing entitlement to their resources—in both the near term for reentry and in the long term for disability compensation, pension benefits, or healthcare.

Whereas Chapter 2 describes the nuances of the military's disciplinary system, Chapter 3 moves to the civilian criminal justice system's response to returning veterans who have committed criminal offenses. Following all major wars, there have been perceived upsurges in crimes committed by veterans. While supporters and skeptics have both weighed-in on the debate (Holbrook & Anderson, 2011; Scurfield, 2004), history has documented certain indisputable trends. Even though a very small percentage of returning veterans actually commits criminal misconduct, some veterans inevitably do. Admittedly, it is difficult to identify statistics related to arrest, conviction, or incarceration of these veterans because the nation has consistently provided some of them with a "second chance" to evade the criminal consequences of their behavior. Yet, the inevitable question emerges regarding the appropriate posture for society to assume when it inherits the veteran offender with a history of combat trauma.

The RAND Corporation's estimate that 300,000 veterans of the Iraq and Afghanistan campaigns would return with PTSD or major depression (Schell & Marshall, 2008) underscored the dire need for comprehensive mental health services in both the VA and community mental health providers. To a large extent, the nature of counterinsurgency in these campaigns along with lengthier and recurring deployments is blamed for the rise in PTSD, Traumatic Brain Injury (TBI), and recent invisible wounds of war (Hafemeister & Stockey, 2010). Chapter 3 emphasizes how no two incarcerated veterans experience their symptoms in the same predictable way, and how it is important to recognize and avoid generalizations on either side of the spectrum, from those suggesting that nearly every veteran will commit an offense to those suggesting that veterans who offend are so minor a presence that they are insignificant.

After distinguishing between common myths and misperceptions about mental health conditions, Chapter 4 examines those connections from several perspectives. The chapter not only focuses on the most popular issues, including PTSD, TBI, and major depression, but it looks at the broader context of combat and operational stress injury, which includes many more mental health manifestations. For example, the chapter considers the newer concept of Moral Injury, which may result in PTSD symptoms as severe as a traditional life-threat in combat even though the injury was caused by a less threatening act that violated one's deeply held moral convictions. Although veterans may experience symptoms differently, first-responders, including correctional professionals, have begun training with an eye toward common reactions in crisis situations. Although "suicide watch," isolation, and intensive observation are traditionally sound ways to de-escalate mental health symptomology in confined settings (Correia, 2001), the arsenal for PTSD-response is necessarily expanded.

For situations where the inmates show signs of an active stress response, veteran-specific interventions exist within the framework of Psychological First Aid (PFA). Although PFA has different connotations (Jacobs & Meyer, 2006), its unifying theory permits non-psychologists to intervene during a psychologically volatile time to stabilize the condition (Edelman, 2018). In this way, while the helpers are not conducting therapy, they are paving the way for a licensed mental health professional to apply more advanced psychological techniques. Upon implementation of standard Crisis Intervention Training (CIT) models and PFA-based interventions, corrections officers will have a better understanding of their potential to respond to a PTSD stress reaction and identify additional possibilities for effective intervention.

Progressing from immediate and individual interventions, Chapter 5 looks at the VA as a potential source of assistance in treatment of the incarcerated veteran. Evident from the VA's emphasis on reentry, many commentators overlook the benefits for which veterans may still be eligible during the period of incarceration. The chapter begins by discussing the bars to treatment, such as a federal regulation which prohibits the VA from duplicating any health care services that are the primary responsibility of the confinement facility. Consequently, while some prison and jail mental health services are criticized as failing to meet even an inmate's most basic treatment needs (Pfeiffer, 2007), and mental health staff are routinely occupied with multiple competing duties that hamper the ability to provide sustained individual treatment (Correia, 2001), these programs will bar the veterans from receiving the state-of-the-art care they earned through military service.

Also impacted by incarceration are VA disability benefits and pensions. Depending upon the nature of the offense and the length of the sentence, the VA will discontinue or substantially reduce payments. Incarcerated veterans are still often eligible for some VA benefits, however. They retain certain educational benefits, and they may be able to apportion lost funds to their needy family members. Most importantly, the VA's appellate boards and benefits court has recognized the VA's continuing obligation to assist

incarcerated veterans in filing for benefits, obtaining their records to substantiate claims, and obtaining medical evaluations (Hager, 2009). The chapter considers each of these nuances and concludes with a discussion of the
original intent behind the Veterans' Bureau's outreach to war traumatized
veterans to provide a sorely needed historical perspective.

Chapter 6 examines the various points of intersection during which the
criminal justice system links veteran offenders with treatment services. Using
the popular Sequential Intercept Model (Edelman, 2018), the chapter briefly
reviews some of the key interventions developed specifically for justice-involved veterans from the point of initial law enforcement encounter through
the interaction with the courts, the jails, and the prisons. With 461 veterans
treatment courts (VTCs) in operation, a number that grows practically by the
week, the chapter identifies some of the ways that these courts might impact
a given jail or prison and why correctional staff should not reach any
assumptions about why a given inmate may not have been accepted for
diversion. Beyond this, the chapter also considers common criticisms against
veterans treatment courts, and the courts' responses to such criticisms so that
correctional professionals will be better able to consider potential objections
and responses to their own development of a veteran-specific program. Although there are surely differences between community-based and correctional interventions, many similar ideological points might still arise.

Even if community-based treatment programs are the *sin qua non* of programming for veteran offenders, Chapters 8, 9, and 10 approach the task of
programming within jails and prisons, especially in the absence of VA
healthcare. Chapter 7 begins by identifying key characteristics of veterans
programs within correctional institutions. Many of these features emulate
some aspect of the military culture including the pride that the veteran once
felt serving the nation (Edelman, 2018). While each feature may have no
meaning to a non-veteran, the chapter explores the intrinsic value of each
element, from military-themed monuments and wall art to participation in a
color guard at institutional ceremonies. The intent of the chapter is to provide an assortment of options that a given institution may want to implement
within budgetary and resource constraints, which enables a desired effect.
This chapter also surveys the evolution of self-governed veterans' organizations within prisons to the point where their collective experience also highlights aspects of this subset of inmates who have very special experiences
and capabilities.

Separate from jail and prison self-governing groups are veteran-specific
programs instituted by the correctional institution. Chapter 8 provides a historical perspective on these programs as well. Scholars emphasize the importance of past lessons in corrections, specifically because "[w]e keep repeating
ourselves, recycling old ideas as if they were brand new, and then discard-

ing them before we have found out if they are effective or not, only to bring them up later" (Burkhead, 2007, p. 3). This chapter reveals a very rich history of programs for combat-traumatized veterans, most notably in the advent of WWII where the Indiana State Farm at Greencastle first recognized the need for a comprehensive veteran-specific program (Evigil & Hawkins, 1946). Through the ensuing years of the nation's combat involvement, various programs came in and out of existence, often as a direct result of the needs perceived by the corrective staff who were themselves veterans (e.g., Sigafoos, 1994). Regardless of the source or underlying motivation for these recurring treatment experiments, each offers important lessons that are vital to any correctional professional who is considering options for currently incarcerated veterans. This review will compare and contrast the key attributes of programs, including the manner in which each program resolved universal dilemmas.

Perhaps the biggest issue in the development of an effective treatment program for incarcerated veterans is whether to allocate a separate geographic space in which they can interact on a daily basis. Fortunately, there are no less than eighty-one veterans' dormitories in twenty-seven states as of the writing of this book (National Institute of Corrections, 2018).

While these specialized housing units are unique to veterans, the idea is catching on. In Muscogee County, Georgia, for example, the sheriff operates a faith-based dorm, a fatherhood dorm, a G.E.D. dorm, and a veterans' dorm. These programs are beginning to emerge for different inmates because they provide an efficient way of targeting services and facilitating the assistance of volunteer community organizations. With continued public support for veterans of the nation's wars, especially those with combat trauma, the dorm is becoming a method to maintain order in the facility, promote officer safety, and to improve the quality of the institutional community.

Chapter 9 carefully examines the current trends in the operation of these programs offering correctional staff the benefit of valuable lessons learned. Ultimately, the most salient lesson to emerge from all veteran-specific programs is that the confinement facility likely already has the three components that still make their veteran population an asset rather than a liability:

- Other veteran inmates with shared experiences who can support one another in achieving treatment goals;
- corrections officers and administrators who are themselves veterans and who can thus foster more support and trust from inmate participants; and
- a population of inmates who are considered a national resource for their collective sacrifices to the nation (Vitello, 2011; Edelman, 2018).

Programs that succeed largely for these three reasons can save as much as $3 for every $1 spent in obtaining treatment, which is significant under any view (Frakt, 2017).

Chapter 10 concludes the book by examining the current landscape for veterans in the correctional system. With the unveiling of the Veterans Reentry Search Service (VRSS) in late 2013, the VA has enabled computerized-identity matching to confirm a given inmate's military status in a privacy-protected but effective manner. In a short time, the program has already been successful in detecting thousands of lost veterans, ensuring that they are truly not forgotten warriors. Before VRSS, incarcerated veterans' needs were purely hypothetical because there was little evidence of a certain population to be assisted. Today, the major question is: What now? The issue requires a harder look, beyond the esoteric to the practical. But this will be a harder task because planning will require specific objectives and purpose for attaining them.

As evident in the debates surrounding veterans' treatment courts, a philosophical tension often surrounds treatment programs tailored to veteran offenders in the criminal justice system. At one level, critics voice concern over unequal treatment. They claim that the justice system gives special consideration to veterans at the expense of other nonveterans with similar mental health needs, resulting in a lower quality of care. Other critics suggest that veteran inmates might falsely claim mental illness to manipulate justice officials, evade responsibility, and ultimately improve their own circumstances. Undeniably, because PTSD can only be diagnosed based on a person's self-reports, spectators have dubbed it a "designer disorder," a "diagnosis of choice," and even "post-*dramatic* stress" (Slovenko, 2004).

A key theme throughout this volume is that incarceration of the veteran offender, though less optimal when compared with community treatment, still provides a tremendous window of "opportunity to seize the moment by providing comprehensive programs that address the underlying causes of [veteran] crime and violence" (Schwartz & Levitas, 2011, p. 59). If the incarcerated veterans are ones who never yet obtained the cognitive tools to readjust to societal demands—never activated the "off-switch" for their hyper-aggressive instinct—confinement creates a captive audience and the opportunity to "at least assess the impact of past trauma and start to provide a framework for effective intervention" (Rogers & Law, 2010, p. 172).

The recent groundswell of innovation in veteran-specific programs both in and out of confined settings, despite a budgetary crisis and the lack of statistical data on effectiveness, signals more than mere patriotism. Rather, it signals what some would recognize as a public health and safety *mandate* to assist in the final stage of veteran readjustment. Fortunately, as demonstrated by the variety of jail and prison initiatives, there are nearly infinite ways that correctional institutions can meet this special obligation.

Appendix

PERSONNEL AND
READINESS

OFFICE OF THE UNDER SECRETARY OF DEFENSE
4000 DEFENSE PENTAGON
WASHINGTON, DC 20301-4000

AUG 2 5 2017

MEMORANDUM FOR SECRETARIES OF THE MILITARY DEPARTMENTS

SUBJECT: Clarifying Guidance to Military Discharge Review Boards and Boards for
Correction of Military/Naval Records Considering Requests by Veterans for
Modification of their Discharge Due to Mental Health Conditions, Sexual Assault,
or Sexual Harassment

 In December 2016, the Department announced a renewed effort to ensure veterans were
aware of the opportunity to have their discharges and military records reviewed. As part of that
effort, we noted the Department was currently reviewing our policies for the Boards for
Correction of Military/Naval Records (BCM/NRs) and Discharge Review Boards (DRBs) and
considering whether further guidance was needed. We also invited feedback from the public on
our policies and how we could improve the discharge review process.

 As a result of that feedback and our internal review, we have determined that
clarifications are needed regarding mental health conditions, sexual assault, and sexual
harassment. To resolve lingering questions and potential ambiguities, clarifying guidance is
attached to this memorandum. This guidance is not intended to interfere with or impede the
Boards' statutory independence. Through this guidance, however, there should be greater
uniformity amongst the review boards and veterans will be better informed about how to achieve
relief in these types of cases.

 To be sure, the BCM/NRs and DRBs are tasked with tremendous responsibility and they
perform their tasks with remarkable professionalism. Invisible wounds, however, are some of
the most difficult cases they review and there are frequently limited records for the boards to
consider, often through no fault of the veteran, in resolving appeals for relief. Standards for
review should rightly consider the unique nature of these cases and afford each veteran a
reasonable opportunity for relief even if the sexual assault or sexual harassment was unreported,
or the mental health condition was not diagnosed until years later. This clarifying guidance
ensures fair and consistent standards of review for veterans with mental health conditions, or
who experienced sexual assault or sexual harassment regardless of when they served or in which
Military Department they served.

 Military Department Secretaries shall direct immediate implementation of this guidance
and report on compliance with this guidance within 45 days. My point of contact is Lieutenant
Colonel Reggie Yager, Office of Legal Policy, (703) 571-9301 or reggie.d.yager.mil@mail.mil.

A. M. Kurta
Performing the Duties of the Under Secretary of
Defense for Personnel and Readiness

Attachment:
As stated

cc:
Chairman of the Joint Chiefs of Staff
General Counsel of the Department of Defense
Assistant Secretary of Defense for Legislative Affairs
Assistant to the Secretary of Defense for Public Affairs

Attachment

Clarifying Guidance to Military Discharge Review Boards and Boards for Correction of Military/Naval Records Considering Requests by Veterans for Modification of their Discharge Due to Mental Health Conditions; Traumatic Brain Injury; Sexual Assault; or Sexual Harassment

Generally

1. This document provides clarifying guidance to Discharge Review Boards (DRBs) and Boards for Correction of Military/Naval Records (BCM/NRs) considering requests by veterans for modification of their discharges due in whole or in part to mental health conditions, including post-traumatic stress disorder (PTSD); Traumatic Brain Injury (TBI); sexual assault; or sexual harassment.

2. Requests for discharge relief typically involve four questions:

    a. Did the veteran have a condition or experience that may excuse or mitigate the discharge?
    b. Did that condition exist/ experience occur during military service?
    c. Does that condition or experience actually excuse or mitigate the discharge?
    d. Does that condition or experience outweigh the discharge?

3. Liberal consideration will be given to veterans petitioning for discharge relief when the application for relief is based in whole or in part on matters relating to mental health conditions, including PTSD; TBI; sexual assault; or sexual harassment.

4. Evidence may come from sources other than a veteran's service record and may include records from the DoD Sexual Assault Prevention and Response Program (DD Form 2910, *Victim Reporting Preference Statement*) and/or DD Form 2911, *DoD Sexual Assault Forensic Examination [SAFE] Report*), law enforcement authorities, rape crisis centers, mental health counseling centers, hospitals, physicians, pregnancy tests, tests for sexually transmitted diseases, and statements from family members, friends, roommates, co-workers, fellow servicemembers, or clergy.

5. Evidence may also include changes in behavior; requests for transfer to another military duty assignment; deterioration in work performance; inability of the individual to conform their behavior to the expectations of a military environment; substance abuse; episodes of depression, panic attacks, or anxiety without an identifiable cause; unexplained economic or social behavior changes; relationship issues; or sexual dysfunction.

6. Evidence of misconduct, including any misconduct underlying a veteran's discharge, may be evidence of a mental health condition, including PTSD; TBI; or of behavior consistent with experiencing sexual assault or sexual harassment.

7. The veteran's testimony alone, oral or written, may establish the existence of a condition or experience, that the condition or experience existed during or was aggravated by military service, and that the condition or experience excuses or mitigates the discharge.

8. Cases falling under this guidance will receive timely consideration consistent with statutory requirements.

Was there a condition or experience?

9. Absent clear evidence to the contrary, a diagnosis rendered by a licensed psychiatrist or psychologist is evidence the veteran had a condition that may excuse or mitigate the discharge.

10. Evidence that may reasonably support more than one diagnosis should be liberally considered as supporting a diagnosis, where applicable, that could excuse or mitigate the discharge.

11. A veteran asserting a mental health condition without a corresponding diagnosis of such condition from a licensed psychiatrist or psychologist, will receive liberal consideration of evidence that may support the existence of such a condition.

12. Review Boards are not required to find that a crime of sexual assault or an incident of sexual harassment occurred in order to grant liberal consideration to a veteran that the experience happened during military service, was aggravated by military service, or that it excuses or mitigates the discharge.

Did it exist/occur during military service?

13. A diagnosis made by a licensed psychiatrist or psychologist that the condition existed during military service will receive liberal consideration.

14. A determination made by the Department of Veterans Affairs (VA) that a veteran's mental health condition, including PTSD; TBI; sexual assault; or sexual harassment is connected to military service, while not binding on the Department of Defense, is persuasive evidence that the condition existed or experience occurred during military service.

15. Liberal consideration is not required for cases involving pre-existing conditions which are determined not to have been aggravated by military service.

Does the condition/experience excuse or mitigate the discharge?

16. Conditions or experiences that may reasonably have existed at the time of discharge will be liberally considered as excusing or mitigating the discharge.

17. Evidence that may reasonably support more than one diagnosis or a change in diagnosis, particularly where the diagnosis is listed as the narrative reason for discharge, will be liberally

construed as warranting a change in narrative reason to "Secretarial Authority," "Condition not a disability," or another appropriate basis.

Does the condition/experience outweigh the discharge?

18. In some cases, the severity of misconduct may outweigh any mitigation from mental health conditions, including PTSD; TBI; sexual assault; or sexual harassment.

19. Premeditated misconduct is not generally excused by mental health conditions, including PTSD; TBI; or by a sexual assault or sexual harassment experience. However, substance-seeking behavior and efforts to self-medicate symptoms of a mental health condition may warrant consideration. Review Boards will exercise caution in assessing the causal relationship between asserted conditions or experiences and premeditated misconduct.

Additional Clarifications

20. Unless otherwise indicated, the term "discharge" includes the characterization, narrative reason, separation code, and re-enlistment code.

21. This guidance applies to both the BCM/NRs and DRBs.

22. The supplemental guidance provided by then-Secretary Hagel on September 3, 2014, as clarified in this guidance, also applies to both BCM/NRs and DRBs.

23. The guidance memorandum provided by then-Acting Principal Deputy Under Secretary of Defense for Personnel and Readiness Brad Carson on February 24, 2016, applies in full to BCM/NRs but also applies to DRBs with regards to de novo reconsideration of petitions previously decided without the benefit of all applicable supplemental guidance.

24. These guidance documents are not limited to Under Other Than Honorable Condition discharge characterizations but rather apply to any petition seeking discharge relief including requests to change the narrative reason, re-enlistment codes, and upgrades from General to Honorable characterizations.

25. Unless otherwise indicated, liberal consideration applies to applications based in whole or in part on matters related to diagnosed conditions, undiagnosed conditions, and misdiagnosed TBI or mental health conditions, including PTSD, as well as reported and unreported sexual assault and sexual harassment experiences asserted as justification or supporting rationale for discharge relief.

26. Liberal consideration includes but is not limited to the following concepts:

a. Some circumstances require greater leniency and excusal from normal evidentiary burdens.

b. It is unreasonable to expect the same level of proof for injustices committed years ago when TBI; mental health conditions, such as PTSD; and victimology were far less understood than they are today.

c.   It is unreasonable to expect the same level of proof for injustices committed years ago when there is now restricted reporting, heightened protections for victims, greater support available for victims and witnesses, and more extensive training on sexual assault and sexual harassment than ever before.

d.   Mental health conditions, including PTSD; TBI; sexual assault; and sexual harassment impact veterans in many intimate ways, are often undiagnosed or diagnosed years afterwards, and are frequently unreported.

e.   Mental health conditions, including PTSD; TBI; sexual assault; and sexual harassment inherently affect one's behaviors and choices causing veterans to think and behave differently than might otherwise be expected.

f.   Reviews involving diagnosed, undiagnosed, or misdiagnosed TBI or mental health conditions, such as PTSD, or reported or unreported sexual assault or sexual harassment experiences should not condition relief on the existence of evidence that would be unreasonable or unlikely under the specific circumstances of the case.

g.   Veterans with mental health conditions, including PTSD; TBI; or who experienced sexual assault or sexual harassment may have difficulty presenting a thorough appeal for relief because of how the asserted condition or experience has impacted the veteran's life.

h.   An Honorable discharge characterization does not require flawless military service. Many veterans are separated with an honorable characterization despite some relatively minor or infrequent misconduct.

i.   The relative severity of some misconduct can change over time, thereby changing the relative weight of the misconduct to the mitigating evidence in a case. For example, marijuana use is still unlawful in the military but it is now legal in some states and it may be viewed, in the context of mitigating evidence, as less severe today than it was decades ago.

j.   Service members diagnosed with mental health conditions, including PTSD; TBI; or who reported sexual assault or sexual harassment receive heightened screening today to ensure the causal relationship of possible symptoms and discharge basis is fully considered, and characterization of service is appropriate. Veterans discharged under prior procedures, or before verifiable diagnosis, may not have suffered an error because the separation authority was unaware of their condition or experience at the time of discharge. However, when compared to similarly situated individuals under today's standards, they may be the victim of injustice because commanders fully informed of such conditions and causal relationships today may opt for a less prejudicial discharge to ensure the veteran retains certain benefits, such as medical care.

k.   Liberal consideration does not mandate an upgrade. Relief may be appropriate, however, for minor misconduct commonly associated with mental health conditions, including PTSD; TBI; or behaviors commonly associated with sexual assault or sexual harassment; and some significant misconduct sufficiently justified or outweighed by the facts and circumstances.

Chapter 2

MILITARY DISCIPLINE AND MILITARY DISCHARGE: A DIFFERENT CONCEPT OF PUNISHMENT COMPARED WITH THE CIVILIAN JUSTICE SYSTEM

Renewed Concern for Veteran Offenders

The prior chapter reviewed some salient aspects of military culture, which emphasized the importance of shared military values. The military disciplinary system is vital to understand because it enforces and maintains the military culture (Bryant, 1979; Seamone et al., 2018a). Beyond this, military justice is vital for correctional professionals to understand because it is the system that accounts for the stigmatizing discharge characterizations that often preclude eligibility for Veterans Administration benefits (Veterans Legal Clinic, 2016).

Military discharges come in many variations. Some discharges can be uncharacterized, such as the recruit who is deemed unsuitable for further military service during initial entry training. Other discharges can be based on an individual's hardship request and signify no criminal activity or unsuitability on the part of the person discharged. The purely Honorable Discharge is given when "the quality of the [service member's] service generally has met the standards of acceptable conduct and performance of duty" within the respective branch of service (U.S. Department of Army, 2011, ¶ 3-7(d)).

It has often been suggested that any discharge that is not fully honorable is stigmatizing to an individual because it suggests substandard performance (Jones, 1973, p. 15, n.71). Researchers consequently refer to the "less-than-honorable discharge" as a single class (Baskir & Strauss, 1978, p. 114), which includes discharges like the General Discharge, which basically notes conduct that is "satisfactory but not sufficiently meritorious to warrant an honorable discharge" (U.S. Department of Army, 2011, ¶ 3-7(d)(3)b.1). While

Issued through
nonpunitive
administrative
procedures that do not
result in conviction.

Issued only as a result of
a sentence following
conviction at court-
martial by military judge
or jury.

Summary of Sigmatizing Discharge Types

1. The Administrative "Blue" Discharge (1916-
    1947)
2. The Administrative Undesirable Discharge
    (1947-1976)
3. The Administrative Under Other Than
    Honorable Conditions Discharge (1976-
    present)

4. The Court-Martial Adjudicated Bad-Conduct
    Discharge
5. The Court-Martial Adjudicated Dishonorable
    Discharge
6. The Court-Martial Adjudicated Officer
    Dismissal

Figure 3.

the General Discharge may have stigmas of its own (Lunding, 1973, p. 35), and will disqualify one from G.I. Bill benefits, its impact is limited because it leads to most other Veterans Administration benefits (Wilde, 2007, p. 139; Custis, 1971, p. 875 n.4). Among the variations of discharges, the most stigmatizing ones are traceable to misconduct, and they are distinguishable from other discharge types because they signify "blame on the part of the veteran" for engaging in misconduct (Bitzer, 1980, p. 308). Figure 3 categorizes the major stigmatizing discharges.

Importantly, there is a distinction between the first and last three types of stigmatizing discharges. The first three come exclusively from an administrative process, which means that they do not reflect a court conviction by the standard of guilt beyond a reasonable doubt. Accordingly, their purpose is not supposed to be punitive. The last three discharge types can only be adjudicated by a court-martial, which means that either a military judge or a panel of military members (military jury) considered the various types of penalties available at sentencing and adjudged a specific discharge type as a form of punishment.

Accordingly, the last three types are intended to be more severe. For example, the laws applicable to the Veterans Healthcare Administration prohibit veterans from receiving Veterans Administration healthcare if they receive a Bad-Conduct Discharge, even if their service is considered to be sufficiently meritorious as not to be under dishonorable conditions (38 C.F.R. § 3.360(b)). Also evident in Figure 3, some of these discharges are specific to certain timeframes. For example, the Blue Discharge existed until 1947, when the military divided it into the General Discharge and the Undesirable Discharge to further distinguish it from a broad range of behavior (Jones, 1973, p. 2). In 1976, the military changed the name of the Undesirable Discharge to the "Other-Than-Honorable Conditions" discharge to convey the fact that its purpose was administrative and not punitive (Baskir & Strauss, 1978, p. 110 n.*). Insofar as the distinction between the Bad-Conduct and Dishonorable Discharge is concerned, the former was originally considered to be less severe and reserved for purely "'military offenses' or common law crimes not involving moral turpitude," while the Dishonorable Discharge was intended for the most depraved felonies (Bednar, 1962, pp. 6, 10).

On balance, this book considers the six discharges in Figure 3 as the most stigmatizing because any of them could prevent the ex-service member from meeting the statutory definition of a "veteran." As reflected in 38 U.S.C. § 101(2), veteran status for the purpose of Veterans Administration benefit eligibility is accorded to one whose service was "under conditions other than dishonorable." It is important to consider what this phrase automatically includes and what it automatically excludes. The Honorable and General (Under Honorable Conditions) Discharges have been traditionally considered to be under honorable conditions, so they are both normally binding on the Veterans Administration because they are not dishonorable (Brooker, Seamone, & Rogall, 2012, p. 26).[1] On the other hand, a dishonorable discharge is clearly dishonorable, as is the officer dismissal, which is "equivalent" to the dishonorable discharge for enlisted service members, and signifies "dishonorable expulsion of an officer from the service" (Bednar, 1962, p. 7).

Both the dishonorable discharge and the dismissal preclude their holders from benefit eligibility (38 U.S.C. § 101(2)); 38 U.S.C. § 3103).[2] But the law here does not merely exclude those receiving "dishonorable" discharges from benefits. Rather, the phrase "conditions other than dishonorable" enlarges the scope to potentially any type of discharge that is not under honorable conditions, including, but not limited to a Dishonorable Discharge. This

1. A notable exception are the individuals who were discharged as conscientious objectors who refused to wear the uniform or perform their duties. Even with an honorable discharge, these individuals are statutorily barred from VA benefit eligibility by the provisions of 38 C.F.R. § 3.12(c)(1).
2. The slim exception to this rule is the ex-service member with the dishonorable discharge or dismissal who can demonstrate that the acts that constituted the basis for the discharge were due to insanity, as defined by the VA. This exception is beyond the scope of this book, but addressed in more detail in Brooker, Seamone, and Rogall's article (2012).

means that, in the case of any of the six stigmatizing discharge characterizations, the Veterans Administration must conduct an independent analysis to determine the ex-service member's character of service (Brooker et al., 2012).

I. Current Military Discharge Trends

A. *Cost Efficiency of the Administrative Discharge*

Courts-martial and punitive discharges resulting from them have great historical significance in promoting good order and discipline for the most serious offenses (Seamone, 2011). Military justice historians describe elaborate rituals in the 1800s. During these ceremonies punitively discharged service members would have their buttons and decorations stripped from their uniforms, their enlistment contracts torn to shreds, their swords broken over their heads, and be forced to march to the accompaniment of the band's "rogue's march" as they were ejected from the camp in disgrace, banished from the area in the presence of their former unit members (Lance, 1978, pp. 1–2).

During times of war, when it is necessary to provide deterrents to impressionable service members who might not enjoy their duties, disciplinary actions substantially rise. In World War II, for example, commanders conducted more than 2,000,000 courts-martial (Generous, 1973). Following World War II, however, reports of widespread abuses of authority in the court-martial process and inconsistent results across commands led to serious changes. This included the institution of a *Uniform Code of Military Justice* in 1950 and substantially more procedural rights for the accused service member, including the right to a qualified defense attorney, a legally trained military judge, a right to appeal decisions to a higher court, and so forth.

Even today, to strike the balance between legal rules applicable to the military and those applicable to society, military law changes on a frequent basis with many of its own unique rules that have no civilian precedents (Russell, 2011, pp. 57–62). In some ways, service members obtain more rights than civilian defendants, such as the requirement of a military member to advise a subject their rights when they are suspected of a crime even if they are not in custody. In other respects, they are disadvantaged, due to the absence of a system to post bail, and the ability of a military jury to convict with a less-than-unanimous verdict (Perillo, 2011).

As the military justice system evolved with increasing protections, it took a longer amount of time to conduct trials, and it required more funding to conduct them. During the Vietnam era, the military revised its system of administrative discharge proceedings to permit commanders more flexibility in eliminating service members from the military based upon misconduct.

These expedited proceedings would not permit a punitive discharge but could result in a discharge characterization that would not only preclude the service member from re-entering the military following discharge, but also would terminate any rights to Veterans Administration benefits.

For these appealing reasons, since Vietnam, the administrative discharge became a primary way for the military to "cleanse" itself (Camacho, 1980, p. 269) and eliminate those who are either unpopular for any number of reasons or perceived to be "troublemakers" (Lunding, 1973, p. 52). The administrative discharge process has also come under attack because it is a process with fewer rights than a court-martial. Under administrative discharge procedure, written statements from non-appearing witnesses may be accepted for consideration, and the government does not have to comply with the traditional Military Rules of Evidence. Additionally, administrative procedures have lower burdens of proof than a court-martial's proof of beyond a reasonable doubt standard.

As former Marine attorney, Patrick Callahan, observes, "Sometimes serious criminal charges that could not be proved at court beyond a reasonable doubt or where the evidence has been suppressed [for law enforcement violations] under the exclusionary rule are sent to administrative forums because it is easier for the military to win at an administrative hearing" (2013, p. 83). Accordingly, administrative separation boards have consistently been criticized on the basis that they allow commanders to exercise bias against service members on grounds of race, gender, ethnicity, sexual orientation, and other improper purposes (Sandel, 1984, pp. 855–856; Callahan, 2013, pp. 97–106).

Even in 2017, careful analysis of punitive actions reveals continued patterns of racial discrimination in these proceedings (Editorial, 2017). Racial bias may not be the only basis for concern. Law professor Kyndra Rotunda, who runs a clinic to assist veterans in upgrading discharges has observed how, "[i]n some instances the unfavorable discharge is a form of unlawful reprisal to punish victims for complaining about sexual harassment or assault, and to discourage other complaints" (Rotunda, 2013, p. 22). Military retaliation against sexual assault survivors was explored in two recent publications by Human Rights Watch, *Embattled* (2015) and *Booted* (2016), both of which indicated trends in punishment labeling as "misconduct" the survivor's traumatic responses to their assaults.

B. Court-Martial Trends

The cost and resource efficiency of administrative separation boards have not entirely eliminated the need for courts-martial. Thus, commanders, who must pay out of unit funds for defense expenses, transportation of witnesses, and the hefty fees of expert witnesses, must necessarily conduct a cost-benefit analysis to determine whether the offense is worth pursuing in any given case (Feldman, 2011, p. 8). Even though courts-martial are generally declining due to cost (Russell, 2011, p. 56), commanders have increasingly prosecuted specific types of offenses. For example, the epidemic of sexual assault has led to almost a default decision to send those cases to court, even when the evidence is highly questionable. As Attorney Charles E. Feldman notes, "It is very unlikely in today's political climate that a convening authority would put their career on the line by not referring a sexual assault allegation to a trial" (2011, p. 9). A former military prosecutor adds:

> I have had multiple convening authorities [commanders who send cases to trial] tell me that they would rather refer any case they think is close to trial and let the members [military jury] do what they feel is just with the case rather than make the difficult decision not to send a case to trial. This especially occurs in rape cases where it is one person's word against another. (Callahan, 2013, pp. 104–105)

Yet, the pressure to convict sexual predators does not explain all current courts-martial. Separate from highly politicized sex crimes cases, attorney Greg T. Rinkey notes a distinct recent trend of increased prosecution of military-specific crimes, such as desertion and absence without leave for the purpose of maintaining order by deterring such conduct within the ranks (2011, p. 38).

While the total number of courts-martial has declined over the years of the Global War on Terrorism, the cases that have been tried highlight some key points, especially when they are juxtaposed with statistics from the Vietnam era. In the comparison in Figure 4, it is clear that commanders have sent proportionately more cases to trial during the Global War on Terrorism than during Vietnam, when military offending and disciplinary problems were indisputably much greater. Vietnam, after all, was a time of various wartime atrocities and rampant drug use. The term "double veteran" was used to signify a troop who killed a woman after raping her (Bourke, 1999, p. 175), and many officers carried a sidearm when they ventured into the enlisted barracks aware of an estimated 788 incidents—and hundreds more attempted incidents—of fragging, where subordinates used grenades or other weapons to kill their own superiors (pp. 197–198). This distinction makes current court-martial rates noteworthy, especially considering the military has issued more Dishonorable Discharges in the current era than during the Vietnam era.

Numbers of Courts-Martial, Bad-Conduct Discharges, and Dishonorable Discharges for Vietnam War and Global War on Terrorism Eras

Period of Active Service	Courts-Martial Charges/Cases Tried No.	Bad-Conduct Discharges No.	Dishonorable Discharges No.
Vietnam War Era (July 1, 1964–June 30, 1974)	164 000	31 800	2200
Global War on Terrorism Era	41 715	23 315	3200

Figure 4. Source: Seamone et al. (2014, p. 1808, tbl. 1).

C. The "Military Misconduct Catch-22"

Whether through court-martial or administrative separation proceedings, recent discharge practices reflect another trend involving service members who engage in military-specific offenses. The military has a number of offenses that govern nearly all facets of work behavior from showing up late to rolling one's eyes (Seamone, 2013a). While these same acts might provide the basis for a civilian employer to fire an employee, the military is unique in the criminalization of such behaviors. Attorney Edward Reddington explains how the military culture itself is responsible for the punitive response:

> Perhaps no difference is more important than the cultural backdrop of the US military. . . . The purpose of the military justice system . . . reflects the organizational emphasis on prioritizing the group over the individual. The military's core values also reflect the organization's emphasis on two important priorities that sometimes are in tension: completing the mission and taking care of soldiers. (2011, p. 72)

Service members who violate the law (for any reason) often suffer harsher penalties as a result of the "cultural context—a tendency toward homogeneous decision makers, prioritization of group goals over individual goals, and an emphasis on good order and discipline and mission success" (Reddington, 2011, p. 73).

Unfortunately, the problem for many recent service members who have deployed on multiple occasions is the manner in which their combat and operational-stress injuries frequently result in deceased duty performance and the full range of behaviors specifically targeted for discipline by the military (for example, concentration and attention deficits, impulse-control problems, outbursts, late and missed workdays, and so forth) (Seamone, 2013a; Seamone et al., 2014; Seamone et al., 2018a). Some civilian and military attorneys who provide services to discharged military personnel observe what they call a "Military Misconduct Catch-22," in which former troops are ultimately ineligible for needed treatment because their mental health symptoms were military offenses that led to a stigmatizing discharge from the service (Seamone, 2013a; Seamone et al., 2018a).

While there has been recent growing attention to the plight of combat-traumatized military members with "bad paper" discharges linked to their untreated service-related mental health conditions (Seamone et al., 2018a; U.S. Government Accountability Office, 2017; Veterans Legal Clinic, 2016; Lawrence & Penaloza, 2013; Carter, 2013; Phillips, 2013; Bernton, 2012), the military has largely been unsympathetic, on occasion refusing to follow-up even on service members known to be suffering from mental health conditions at the time of their stigmatizing discharge (e.g., Government Accountability Office, 2017). Much of the trouble is the military's historic position on combat-related mental illness.

Prior to World War II, the military responded punitively to attempts to invoke mental health conditions on the battlefield (Russell et al., 2018). Consequently, many service members suffering from combat and operational stress injury were executed as shirkers and deserters in prior wars (Russell et al., 2018). This was evident in General George Patton's notorious act of striking a soldier for seeking treatment for combat trauma rather than fighting, as there still remained concern over "goldbrickers," who would feign or exaggerate illness to save themselves from the harsh conditions on the line (Kennedy & Jeffrey, 2006, pp. 6–7).

During the Vietnam era, military mental health providers were directed to treat criminal offenders' mental conditions in a uniformly unforgiving manner: "[service-connected mental illnesses] in mild to moderate form do not prevent the individual from 'recognizing the difference between right and wrong' or from 'adhering to the right.' Hence, they do not absolve the individual from criminal accountability" (Bitzer, 1980, p. 307) (citation omitted).

Today, similar positions are evident in sanity board determinations by panels of military mental health providers, which routinely find that service members were responsible for their criminal offending even when they suffered from severe PTSD and other combat-related conditions at the time of the offending (Seamone, 2012, p. 9, n.14). Largely attributable to distinct military cultural influences, Figure 5, depicts six leading reasons why commanders and military members may be ambivalent about the treatment needs of military offenders, leading to a situation in which "military misconduct trumps the demonstrated need for mental health treatment," and the offender's mental health needs are essentially written-off as unimportant (Seamone, 2012, p. 27).

While, ultimately, individual commanders are the ones who decide whether and how to punish an offender, many *are* concerned for the well-being of their subordinates. Current practices reveal some continuation of

Six Common Justifications for Ambivalence about the Treatment of Active Duty Offenders with Operational Stress Injuries
1. Preservation of good order and discipline is paramount in the military; exceptions weaken the ability to provide a deterrent to young and impressionable troops.
2. There is a lack of research demonstrating a direct causal link between PTSD and other operational stress injuries and aggression or other types of offending.
3. In an all-volunteer-force, the service member has assumed the risk that he or she may be traumatized by combat. Asking for help is an obligation. Hardship stemming from misconduct is well-deserved.
4. The military justice system does not allow judges or juries to include terms of probation in their sentences. The system provides for temporary courts and boards that cannot spare personnel to provide ongoing oversight of treatment compliance and progress.
5. The diagnosis of PTSD is the easiest to fake; there is no way to tell if it is legitimate in a given case.
6. The military is not the type of organization that can afford to rehabilitate offenders. If it did, this expanded role will limit the ability to meet mission demands. It also places offenders' needs above those who did not violate the law and served honorably.

Figure 5. Source: Seamone (2013a).

these unsympathetic trends. In response to concerns over the court-martial of a special forces operator with PTSD who had deployed multiple times, representatives for the Army's Special Operations Command remarked, "Nowhere in our four major criteria for PTSD does it allow for breaking the law" (Carpenter, 2010, p. A1). Likewise, some commanders have pursued courts-martial for service members with mental illnesses who have attempted suicide and have charged the offense as self-injury without intent to avoid service (Seamone, 2013a).

Another major difficulty with the military misconduct Catch-22 is the failure of the military to maintain or publish accurate statistics on the number of service members who are administratively discharged for misconduct. Based upon a variety of scattered reports obtained through Freedom of Information Act requests and other investigations, we can begin to appreciate

Some Statistics on Other-Than-Honorable (OTH)/Undesirable (UD), Bad-Conduct Discharges (BCDs), and Dishonorable Discharges (DD)			
Vietnam Era Active Duty	OTH/UD	BCD	DD
	224,000	31,800	2,200
FY 2000 to FY 2005 Active Duty	55,111	13,549	1,545
FY 2005 to FY 2011/12 Active Duty	20,000	9,766	1,655

Figure 6. Source: Seamone (2013a; Brooker et al., 2012).

the size of an entire class of ex-service members who were discharged with "bad paper" and who subsequently faced extremely limited options in their lives for social mobility, health care, employment, and meaning in their lives.

While Figure 6, is not entirely representative of the total numbers, even this partial estimate suggests that Vietnam and the Global War on Terrorism produced a population of at least 359,626 stigmatizing discharge recipients, many of whom are now living in society with these profound consequences.

Certainly, service members may commit crimes unrelated to mental health conditions even if they have mental illness (Elbogen, 2012, p. 1101), and not all of those who have been discharged with "bad paper" have mental illnesses.

Separate statistics from the Veterans Legal Clinic at Harvard Legal Services Center, depicted in Figure 7, below, reveal that the post-9/11 era represents the greatest number of stigmatizing administrative discharges issued by the military since the WWII era.

Even though different services may have varied rates, with the Marine Corps discharging wholly 10 percent of its troops with Other-than-Honorable Discharges in FY11 alone (Veterans Legal Clinic, 2016, p. 12), these trends result in palpable post-discharge consequences.

The observable "sharp spike" (Tayyeb & Greenburg, 2017, p. 1) in stigmatizing discharges also mirrors the greatest number of VA benefit denials

	Sum of Army, Navy, Marine Corps & Air Force					Percentage of Army, Navy, Marine Corps & Air Force				
	HON	GEN	OTH	BCD	DD	HON	GEN	OTH	BCD	DD
World War II Era	6,762,863	12,979	70,686	24,394	23,247	98.1%	0.2%	1%	0.4%	0.3%
Korean War Era	3,882,013	122,381	78,335	37,760	21,414	93.7%	3.0%	1.9%	0.9%	0.5%
Vietnam War Era	8,549,660	354,484	229,357	35,334	3,508	93.3%	3.9%	2.5%	0.4%	0.0%
Cold War Era ('76-'90)	6,737,316	439,501	291,455	66,145	6,155	89.3%	5.8%	3.9%	0.9%	0.1%
First Gulf War ('91-'01)	2,171,286	128,315	117,297	20,114	2,034	89.0%	5.3%	4.8%	0.8%	0.1%
Post-2001 Era ('02-'13)	1,518,392	150,434	103,581	16,720	1,189	84.8%	8.4%	5.8%	0.9%	0.1%

Figure 7. From: Veterans Legal Clinic (2016, p. 48, App. C). Reprinted with permission.

by the Department of Veterans Affairs related to discharge characterizations, as reflected by Figure 8.

These numbers translate to the equivalent of several divisions of discharged service members.

Even though there are not currently reliable statistics on the size of the population of combat-traumatized veterans with stigmatizing discharges that prohibit their treatment, the military misconduct Catch-22 suggests that a substantial enough portion of the population of Vietnam discharge recipients, and *at least* "125,000 . . . Post-2001 veterans who cannot access basic

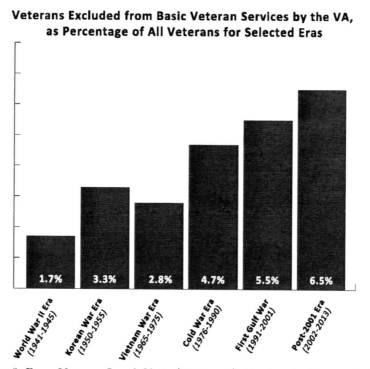

Figure 8. From Veterans Legal Clinic (2016, p. 9). Reprinted with permission.

VA services" (Veterans Legal Clinic, 2016, p. 7) likely fall into this category because individuals with combat-related operational stress injuries are more likely to be at risk of aggression and impulse control behaviors (see Chapter 4).

More recently, a comprehensive study of Department of Defense misconduct discharges between FY11 and FY15 revealed that, "62 percent, or 57,141 of the 91,764 service members separated for misconduct . . . had been diagnosed within the past 2 years prior to separation with [PTSD, TBI] or certain other [mental health] conditions that could be associated with misconduct" (U.S. Government Accountability Office, 2017, Executive Summary). While the Veterans Administration does not collect or maintain easily accessible statistics, various reports on the rate of benefits denials suggest that:

> **The vast majority of applicants for Character of Service determinations result in denials, even where the ex-service member possesses a Bad-Conduct Discharge, Undesirable Discharge, or Under Other-Than-Honorable Conditions Discharge that could potentially still be considered honorable.**

Supporting this conclusion, "90 [percent] of Post-2001 veterans with bad-paper discharges have not been reviewed for eligibility by the VA," and of those who are denied benefits and appeal to the Board of Veterans Appeals, "3 out of 4 veterans with bad-paper discharges who have PTSD or TBI . . . are denied eligibility for benefits. . ." (Veterans Legal Clinic, 2016, pp. 10, 14). Different reports indicate that Veterans Administration adjudicators denied eight-out-of-ten applications from recipients of stigmatizing discharges between 1990 and 2006, that there is an overall 93 percent denial rate for all applicants with "bad paper," and that Veterans Administration records indicate at least 100,781 determinations that discharges were dishonorable for Veterans Administration purposes—for those few ex-service members who actually did apply for Veterans Administration benefits (Brooker et al., 2012, pp. 157–158).

Data consistently reveal that different regional offices can evaluate the same misconduct under identical circumstances and reach different determinations, signaling confusing and ambiguous adjudicatory standards (Brooker et al., 2012). As a result of these factors, most ex-service members with stigmatizing discharges assume that they are ineligible for benefits and refuse to apply. For a host of reasons, it is painfully clear that the ideal time to prevent adverse outcomes is while the service member is still on active duty and before the commander finalizes a discharge determination.

II. The Tacit Agreement Between the Military and Civilian Law Enforcement

Retired Connecticut Supreme Court Justice Barry Schaller, in considering the problem of veterans in the criminal justice system following their release into the community, suggests that the military has unfairly placed a tremendous burden on the civilian criminal justice system whenever it has failed to treat veterans' underlying mental health conditions. According to Schaller, veterans with mental health conditions "need appropriate support *before* transitioning to civilian life. The failure of current [military] support systems has left it to states and cities to fill in the gaps" (2012, p. 208) (emphasis added). This problem of inheritance often reflects military commanders' failure to consider potential "loss to members of society as a result of criminal behavior and other consequences of PTSD" (Schaller, 2012, p. 197). Given common stigmas to help-seeking and delayed onset of symptoms, many local sheriffs and judges have identified a moral obligation and responsibility to assist in the reintegration of veterans who become entangled in the criminal justice system as a result of their military service-related conditions.

The nation's more than 461 veterans treatment courts exist as a testament to this position, with nearly all of them functioning under the assumption that the military failed to provide the tools or treatment necessary for a successful and productive readjustment to civilian life (Tsai et al., 2018). The implicit agreement between the military and the nation's criminal justice system is that, in order to fight the nation's wars, the military cannot be primarily responsible for healthcare and readjustment because it would detract from mission accomplishment.

In the context of individuals eliminated for misconduct, the military functions optimally as long as it can promptly eliminate its misfits and negative influences and replace them with new recruits without the burden of follow-on responsibilities: "The lack of concern for treatment [of military offenders with operational stress injuries] is troublesome because of its inherent assumption that *somebody else,* outside of the military, will someday be responsible for dealing with aggravated psychological symptoms," even though the individual with "bad paper" is ineligible for most Veterans Administration services (Seamone, 2011, pp. 27–28).

Schaller's criticism focuses upon the military's ability to provide the offender with a support system and a framework for treatment delivery that is unparalleled in the civilian sector, which, despite increased efforts to prepare for a groundswell of veterans with mental health needs, lacks sufficient training in military-specific combat trauma. Although Schaller does not focus specifically on military offenders with mental illness, his position is compelling. It relates to these individuals because their predicament creates even greater limitations on the ability of civilian courts and corrections systems to assist inmates with special military-connected needs.

Russell and colleagues have addressed punitive handling of war-traumatized offenders. They conclude that the military, through its insensitive and ambivalent misconduct discharges of combat traumatized service members, perpetuates an "unethical revolving door" of future recidivism in the civilian community (2018, p. 46). They also note how "the present-day policy disavows responsibility for provision of mental health treatment and rehabilitation of veterans in the criminal justice system and foists the responsibility on the VA and private sector" (Russell et al., 2018, p. 47).

Veterans treatment courts and diversion programs largely depend on the treatment services provided by Veterans Administration and federal mental and physical health providers. As long as the criminally involved veteran is eligible for federal benefits, the local agencies do not have to pay for specialized services or divert local funds from other nonveteran inmates. However, ex-service members with stigmatizing discharges are barred from participating in these programs unless and until the Veterans Administration has determined that they meet the definition of a qualified veteran. While a few veterans treatment court programs have pledged to enroll and treat (apart from the Veterans Administration) ex-service members with "bad paper" discharges, this is not the case for most programs because they are forced to develop the capability to treat combat- or service-related conditions apart from the Veterans Administration (Seamone, 2011). "Bad Paper" thus complicates matters by distancing ex-service members from the resources they require the most and keep conditions destabilized in their lives.

In the early 1990s, after the country was learning about severe readjustment problems faced by Vietnam veterans, legislators and mental health providers lobbied for reform on the basis of increased risks of homelessness and other risks related to reliance on emergency rooms for medical care, inability to maintain employment, and factors normally necessary for successful reentry into the community (Waters & Shay, 1994). In 2000, some of the growing data revealed that "the relative risk for homelessness among veterans with [stigmatizing discharges] is . . . 9.9 times as great as among veterans without such discharges" (Gamache, 2000).

Recent, post-9/11 studies are even more compelling in this regard. In 2015, medical providers published an article in the *Journal of the American Medical Association,* emphasizing that "[t]he psychosocial challenges faced by veterans who receive any discharge beside Honorable may contribute to mental health concerns, substance use, and a sense of self-stigma—potentially above and beyond symptoms that were present prior to discharge" (Brooks-Holliday & Pedersen, 2017, p. 429). They focused specifically on the risks that emerge for recipients of Other-than-Honorable Discharges, including criminal justice involvement (Brooks-Holliday & Pedersen, 2017, p. 433).

A 2017 examination of data from 443,360 veterans who had deployed to Iraq and Afghanistan between 2004 and 2013 revealed that "[c]ompared with routinely discharged Veterans, odds for nearly all diagnostic outcomes were significantly greater among Veterans . . . discharged for misconduct . . ." (Brignone et al., 2017, p. 557). This translated to 2.3 times higher odds of "any mental health or substance use disorder," 3.4 times higher odds of "bipolar/psychotic disorders," 2.8 times higher odds for "suicidal ideation," and 2.1 times higher odds of "depressive disorders" (Brignone et al., 2017, p. 561). Similar results emerged from the research of Brooks-Holliday and Pederson (2017). These "indicators of adverse post-discharge outcomes" coincided with recent findings that such veterans "are at greater risk for several reintegration outcomes of significant public health concern including unemployment, incarceration, homelessness, and suicide" (Brignone et al., 2017, pp. 558, 562).

Regarding homelessness, specifically, a study of 448,290 veterans who had deployed to Iraq or Afghanistan revealed that, "Although only 5.6 percent (n = 24,992) separated for misconduct, they represented 25.6 percent of homeless veterans at first [Veterans Health Administration (VHA)] encounter . . . 28.1 percent within one year . . . , and 20.6 percent within five years" (Gundlapalli et al., 2015, p. 832). Likewise, the "[i]ncidence of homelessness was significantly greater for misconduct vs. normal separations at first VHA encounter (1.3 percent versus 0.2 percent) . . . , within one year (5.4 percent versus 0.6 percent . . . , and five years (9.8 percent versus 1.4 percent) . . . of first VHA encounter" (Gundlapalli et al., 2015, p. 832). The researchers used these data to conclude that "[m]ilitary misconduct may be a proxy indicator for a variety of risk factors associated with homelessness among veterans" (Gundlapalli et al., 2015, p. 832).

Active Duty and Reserve Service Members in Prisons and Jails

The military operates under a military justice principle of universal jurisdiction, which means that it has the power to prosecute and pursue its own service members for offenses committed anywhere at any time. Some attorneys who practice in the military courts suggest that the military is now pursuing more cases involving domestic disputes that it did not pursue as aggressively in the past (Wheelock, 2011, p. 84). Despite the military's long reach, local authorities still have an interest in prosecuting military offenders who commit crimes within their own jurisdictional limits.

With stricter standards of performance in the face of withdrawal of forces from Iraq and Afghanistan, the military has increasingly targeted civilian offenses as the basis for ejection from the service. Whether the issue is drug possession, interpersonal violence, driving while intoxicated, bar fights, or resisting an officer, violations of civilian law on off-duty time commonly form the basis for stigmatizing administrative discharges that will prevent a person from receiving benefits such as healthcare in the future.

Obtaining statistics on the number of actively serving military members who are confined in jails and prisons is extremely difficult. However, books such as David Philipps's *Lethal Warriors* highlight the reality of routine jail booking within towns close to military installations following service members' recent redeployment from combat (2010). Further, any worker in the military justice division of an installation's legal office will be able to share the daily experience of receiving military police blotter extracts reporting numerous civilian arrests of active duty service members.

Chapter 6 describes the notion of the Sequential Intercept Model, which is used by many law enforcement agencies and courts to divert veterans from confinement and conviction to facilities and services that can meet their mental health treatment needs. The primary theory of this model is that the earliest point of intervention provides the best chances for addressing the problem and limits the chances recidivism. For active duty and reserve service members who are in contact with the civilian criminal justice system for civilian offenses committed off duty or off the installation, the sequential intercept model applies in a different but vital manner:

> **The optimal intercept for active duty and reserve offenders in jails and prisons is to divert the military members from stigmatizing administrative or punitive discharges so that they will retain benefits that will enable future care following separation from the service.**

Beyond the objective of releasing the offender back to the military to obtain health care through military services, which may be another important intercept for the service member with an untreated combat or operational stress injury, the objective to prevent punitive discharge takes precedence because the military justice process is one area where the civilian criminal justice system is unable to intervene after the fact, even though it shoulders the greatest consequence when it inherits a punitively discharged ex-service member.

This is not a suggestion for jails or courts to study the military justice system and adopt a role within it. Nor is this a suggestion that all active duty or reserve offenders should be retained in the military if they have mental health treatment needs. Very often, a troop's symptomatic behavior *does* detract from the cohesion of a military unit, *does* consume an inordinate amount of the leadership's time, and, most importantly, *does* impair the ability to accomplish the mission as a result of these factors. In a given case, it may be very wise to initiate the swift removal of a service member from active military service because of the person's inability to contribute to the mission.

The objective is simply to ease removal from the service with a discharge characterization that permits retention of key Veterans Administration benefits, especially health care. The flexibility of the military justice system and the commanders' discretion provides a variety of methods to achieve retribution with deterrents that are lacking in the civilian justice system. Through creative disciplinary arrangements, that can be aided through pretrial agreements, a service member might serve time in jail through an administrative proceeding known as the summary court-martial and then be discharged administratively with a general discharge that would preserve most benefits.

Alternatively, through the court-martial or administrative separation board proceedings, the service member and commander might arrange for a suspended sentence of discharge and or confinement, which would be remitted upon the service member's successful completion of a civilian veterans' treatment court or a military treatment program with similar sanctions and rewards (Seamone, 2011). In 2016, a former Deputy Judge Advocate General of the Army, Major General (ret.) Clyde "Butch" Tate, noted the development of a veterans' treatment court on the Fort Hood Military Installation, which accepted soldiers into the program for certain federal offenses. Recognizing the novelty of this approach, Robinson and Tate concluded, "Federal VTCs on and around military installations . . . have the potential to augment military justice processing in ways that promote good order and discipline and provide better care for service members transitioning due to misconduct" (2016, p. 30). They even suggest that a civilian judge or prosecutor could "draft a memorandum . . . in support of upgraded characterization of service based on the Veteran[']s substance use disorder or other mental health diagnosis and subsequent completion of a VTC program" (Robinson, & Tate, 2016, p. 31, n.100).

For jail administrators and for veteran activists, specifically, the major role in this earliest intercept is to effectively communicate with the individual's command and the military justice office that will inevitably initiate action in response to the civilian justice system involvement. The Appendix of this chapter features a generic template for a memorandum of agreement that can aid in the necessary coordination between military justice and local law enforcement entities. It addresses the scenario in which active duty

---

Attributes of Law Enforcement Diversion from the Stigmatizing Discharge for Active Service Members

- Local jails screen for active-duty military status
- Local jails notify installation military justice liaison upon intake
- Service members voluntarily participate in treatment program
- A signed release permitting release of military personnel, medical, and *disciplinary* records to local authorities
- For admitted military personnel, commanders identify objectives to retain, separate with preservation of benefits, or separate with "Bad Paper" following successful completion of treatment
- Mutual reporting requirements for noncompliance or misconduct
- Command recommends sanctions to a veterans' treatment court judge, but retains independent ability to punish misconduct during participation
- Pre-discharge transition counseling for all "bad paper" recipients
- Funding considerations addressed with particularity

Figure 9.

offenders who commit local offenses are being considered for placement in a local veterans' treatment court, as originally proposed (Seamone, 2011). Figure 9, summarizes the key attributes of such agreements.

Even in cases where commanders are determined to separate the service member with as stigmatizing a discharge as possible, increased coordination between the civilian and the military entities during this period of overlapping response to criminal behavior can yield significant returns. One gain is the ability to target different services toward military members at the earliest point, such as transitional counseling from veterans' service organizations and other entities that can assist the exiting military member in perfecting discharge upgrade and Veterans Administration character of service application *prior* to separation when the possibility of obtaining evidence and witness statements significantly diminishes. Moreover, the time when any service member is pending adverse military justice action has proven to be a leading risk factor for suicide, often topping the charts as a contender for the greatest suicide risk factor (U.S. Department of Navy and U.S. Marine Corps, 2010, p. L–1).

The status of pending investigation, punishment, or separation for military misconduct has been recognized as a risk factor for suicide of military members. The need to develop alternatives prior to discharge becomes clearer when one considers suicide attempts. One study of service members showed that those who attempted suicide were pending "at least one administrative or legal issue" and 15.9 percent (142) had "more than one [such] issue" (National Center for Telehealth and Technology, 2012).

While numerous factors combine in an individual case to influence suicidal ideation and behavior, it is understandable that the uncertainty of pending criminal action by the military will aggravate any underlying mental disorders. Accordingly, efforts to provide some structure and predictability will help to lessen the potential for self-harm or recidivism during the often-lengthy time period between arrest and disposition of a military case. Local law enforcement can play a significant role in this intervention to their own benefit as well.

Take-Home Points

This chapter described a number of reasons why the military justice system is important for correctional professionals to understand. Foremost, it is responsible for making at least 20 percent of incarcerated ex-service members ineligible for Veterans Administration benefits due to their discharge characterization (Rosenthal & McGuire, 2013), with some estimating greater numbers, such as 23 percent (Bronson, Carson, Noonan, & Berzofsky, 2015, p. 1), closer to 38 percent (Noonan & Mumola, 2007, p. 1), or even "most" of a specific jail's veteran inmates (Levitas & Schwartz, 2011, p. 53). Because the military must necessarily enforce good order and discipline among its fighting forces, its criminal code has different aims from the civilian criminal justice system.

> **Unintentionally, the military justice system criminalizes mental illness at rates far greater than the civilian sector based on its premium for efficient performance of military duties.**

Military criminal law disproportionately targets the types of behavior that emerge as symptoms of PTSD, TBI, and other operational stress injuries, leading the patient to be seen as the perpetrator of a pattern of misconduct. Too often, it takes criminal involvement and discharge proceedings to recognize the underlying causes of these behaviors. Then, it is too late to provide effective treatment because the service member's discharge will preclude quality mental health treatment (Seamone et al., 2018a).

While wardens and sheriffs cannot alter the character of a military discharge that may have been issued years or decades before incarceration, they can encourage inmates with stigmatizing discharges to obtain help in either upgrading their discharges through the military's own review process, initiating a Character of Service review through the Veterans Administration, or both (Edelman, 2018).

The Kurta Memorandum represents a renewed opportunity for discharge upgrade among veterans with mental health conditions (2017). Similarly, those who advocate for veterans should recognize that while the Veterans Administration representatives might often recommend the inmates' first attempt to upgrade their discharge through a military board prior to applying for Veterans Administration benefits, the processes do not depend upon one another, and the Veterans Administration is obligated to review the case even if the ex-service members have never petitioned the military for an upgrade. Furthermore, the military's process for upgrading is based upon entirely different standards than the Veterans Administration's Character of Service review. In its independent review, the Veterans Administration does not even use the military's definitions for key terms such as "dishonorable" (Morris, 2003, pp. 139–140). These multiple layers of bureaucracy would be a fitting case study for those interested in examining political and administrative systems and streamlining procedures.

In some prisons, inmates are prohibited from participating in veterans' dorms or veterans' organizations unless they have an honorable conditions discharge (see Chapters 7-9). For those inmates who were convicted of heinous crimes while in the military, there may be good reason for this policy. But, the wide variety of circumstances surrounding military misconduct discharges makes it unwise to treat all inmates' discharges in the same manner or preclude correctional services or opportunities solely based upon discharge characterization. To this end, when considering the relationship between veteran offenders with "bad paper" and society, it is worthwhile to revisit President Johnson's christening of a Department of Labor program called the "Certificate of Exemplary Rehabilitation." Upon signing the bill on October 16, 1966, he noted how it "offers new hope to persons discharged from the Armed Forces under conditions other than honorable":

> This new law recognizes a basic principle of American justice: A man who has acknowledged his past mistakes and overcome his weaknesses, deserves a chance to overcome his past failures. . . . The underlying principle of this measure is both simple and important: It recognizes the fallibility of man— and also his capacity for rehabilitation. (Johnson, 1966)

Although the certificate, depicted in Figure 10, had strict requirements, such as letters of recommendation from local law enforcement officers and attestations to faithful employment for a period of years, in the end, it merely entitled the bearer to obtain special assistance from the Department of Labor and did not restore any of the benefits that the veteran would have earned before being branded as other than honorable (Hadley, 1968).

With a lack of publicity, the program died (Jones, 1973, p. 7). But, its very existence officially recognized the need to avoid the military discharge from being so crippling that it ruined the veteran's chances of rejoining society in a productive way.

If the inmates' court-martial were based on purely military offenses, it is important to recognize that the military assigns greater weight in its own disciplinary process to behavior that would not be treated similarly in the civilian justice system. Especially for those inmates who are recipients of the administrative Other-Than-Honorable or Undesirable Discharges, it is also important to consider how susceptible administrative boards are to bias and discrimination on the part of the initiating commander, and that future stig-

United States Department of Labor

EXEMPLARY REHABILITATION CERTIFICATE

—this is to certify that—

has under the provisions of Public Law 89-690 established since separation from the Armed Forces of the United States a record of good character and exemplary conduct, activities, and habits for a period of not less than the three years preceding this date.

In witness of this, I hereby issue this Exemplary Rehabilitation Certificate on this   day of   19

W. Willard Wirtz
SECRETARY OF LABOR

Figure 10. Source: Hadley (1968, p. 80).

matizing treatment on the basis of an improper discharge only serves to magnify the underlying injustice. Most importantly, an ex-service member's discharge characterization should not preclude the opportunity for veteran-specific programming in a prison or jail because that designation may have resulted directly from injuries sustained through faithful service to the nation.

Another important take-home point is the value of coordinating with active duty military organizations to address underlying mental health conditions prior to the time of discharge, while there may still be a way to prevent permanent impediments. When cognized in the context of the Sequential Intercept Model, interface with the civilian criminal justice system immediately after arrest is the best time to intervene and develop solid channels of communication between law enforcement and the command to provide richer information to civilian law enforcement and the courts to improve their own classification and adjudication purposes. Such intervention may ultimately help to prevent the service member from becoming a frequent flyer through the courts and jails following discharge.

Appendix

Template for Memorandum of Understanding Between Local Justice Entities and Nearby Military Installation Commanders

Draft Active Duty/Veterans Treatment Court Memorandum of Agreement

Purpose: Fort Davis wishes to enter into a memorandum of agreement with the Blake County Veterans Treatment Court to standardize the disposition of cases involving active duty military personnel assigned to Fort Davis.

General: After more than a decade of sustained combat operations, an increasing number of servicemembers has sustained mental health conditions connected to their service, including Posttraumatic Stress Disorder, Traumatic Brain Injury, and Major Depression. While statistics vary, a conservative estimate is approximately 20% of all deployed personnel. Independently, many of the servicemembers who have entered active duty service will experience mental health conditions during their initial term because the average age when conditions generally materialize is between eighteen and twenty-five years. Although not all servicemembers, or combat veterans, will suffer from mental conditions, a substantial portion of the Service may require treatment. Because untreated mental illness often materializes in symptoms and behavior that can be characterized as criminal, it is foreseeable that some of the active duty military offenders apprehended and confined in the Blake County Jail on State charges will require mental health treatment and planning.

Authority: At present, the Court Rules and statutory authority for instituting the Blake County Veterans Treatment Court has enabled it to enroll Active Duty offenders, regardless of whether the servicemember/offender's chain of command supports enrollment or not. From the perspective of military law, Article 14 of the *Uniform Code of Military Justice* requires the military to surrender active duty personnel to State authorities for the purpose of criminal prosecution. Although the military retains worldwide jurisdiction to prosecute servicemembers for civilian offenses, the military cannot direct the state regarding when or how to prosecute its case and often must wait until the State has had the opportunity to prosecute before taking independent court-martial action. Numerous observers of incidents of such "concurrent" jurisdiction highlight the need for coordinated responses between civilian and military authorities. Successful completion of suspended sentences will permit active duty offenders to remain in the military. Moreover, certainty regarding the disposition of a case would allow the military units to better plan for replacements and/or other organizational modifications for those who will be discharged from the military.

Identification and Classification of Eligible Participants and Related Responsibilities: Active duty offenders, like all veterans considered by the Blake County Veterans Treatment Court program, will be eligible to participate in the treatment program only if they have a qualifying mental health and/or co-occurring substance abuse condition. Traditionally, active duty offenders have been referred to the program through law enforcement agencies, military members, outreach efforts, and other impromptu efforts. To improve the chances that truly needy active duty offenders will be identified as quickly as possible for an eligibility determination, Blake County will take the following steps:

1) The Blake County Jail will inquire during the intake process if an individual is stationed at Fort Davis or currently serving in the military. Jail personnel will further attempt independent verification, such as an inventory of personal effects for a Military Identification Card.

2) Upon identifying an offender as an active duty member of the military, the Veterans Court Administrator will further attempt to identify the offender's unit of assignment and contact the Military Justice Primary Point of Contact to relate the fact that the servicemember is in custody and is under consideration for eligibility in the Blake County Veterans Treatment Court.

3) The Veterans Court Administrator will determine whether the offender has the desire to voluntarily enroll in the treatment program if they meet the prescribed criteria. If the servicemember does not desire to participate, this relieves the parties from further obligations respecting treatment planning through the Blake County Veterans Treatment Court program.

4) The Veterans Court Administrator will obtain a signed release of information that authorizes the transfer of military medical, personnel, and disciplinary records to the State authorities. Such information will provide a more extensive history of the offender's deployment experience, disciplinary history, and prior treatment attempts, if any.

5) For all servicemembers accepted into the program, the offender's company commander will indicate his or her preference regarding the offender's successful completion of a treatment plan and graduation from the Blake County Veterans Treatment Court, as follows:

   a. Track 1: Designates all servicemembers desired for continued service on active duty following rehabilitation with the expectation of adherence to a treatment plan following release.

   b. Track 2: Designates all servicemembers desired for elimination from the military following rehabilitation with the expectation of use of community services following release from local custody. Here, despite the involuntary separation of the offender, the commander will agree to initiate a discharge under honorable conditions to preserve the offender's benefits following separation from the service. This includes a General Under

Honorable Conditions Discharge, which will act as an incentive for the offender to successfully complete the treatment program.

c. Track 3: Designates all servicemembers who have an acute mental condition and who require stabilization and potential commitment in a long-term institution for extensive treatment.

d. Track 4: Designates all servicemembers desired for elimination from the military following rehabilitation with the expectation of administrative elimination Under Other Than Honorable conditions.

6) For all offenders falling within Tracks 1 and 2, above, commanders will agree to provide updates to the designated Blake County Veterans Treatment Court Point of Contact[3] to report any violations of treatment plans developed through the program. Such notice will be timely, and in any event not more than 72-hours following the commander's knowledge of the violation. Likewise, the Blake County Veterans Treatment Court will promptly report all known treatment plan or criminal violations occurring outside of the military setting to the Military Justice Primary Point of Contact.[4]

7) When an offender in any track commits minor misconduct in violation of the treatment plan, which normally includes any type of civilian or federal offense—including *Uniform Code of Military Justice* Offenses under Title 10 of the *United States Code*—the preference will be for the command to recommend a proper remedial measure for implementation by the Veterans Treatment Court Judge. Nothing prohibits the command from acting independently in response to the misconduct.

8) For all offenders within Track 4, where a stigmatizing discharge is expected, the command will assist in providing pre-discharge counseling that includes information on discharge upgrading through Discharge Review Boards, Boards for Correction of Military Records, and the Department of Veterans Affairs Character of Service determination process. Efforts will be made to coordinate post-release counseling services with veterans service organizations, such as the Disabled American Veterans and the local Vet Center. The command will facilitate these outreach efforts to the extent practicable pending the finalization of the administrative action.

---

3. The Blake County Veterans Treatment Court Point of Contact is a State employee who works with the Veterans Treatment Court. This employee is designated as the point of contact for military personnel at Fort Davis with duties related to a State case involving an active duty servicemember.

4. The Military Justice Primary Point of Contact is a military member who works with the Fort Davis Office of the Staff Judge Advocate with duties related to a case involving an active duty servicemember. This military member is designated as the primary contact person for members of the Blake County Veterans Treatment Court.

Tricare Billing and Compensation: Under current practice, depending on the needs of a particular participant, the costs of program participation per day will vary by the nature of services provided. The following rates are generally applicable for treatment services rendered:

- Case Management: 97.44 per hour
- Transitional Planning: 83.68 per hour
- Crisis Intervention: 250.00 per hour
- Group Therapy: 105.60 per session
- Residential Substance Abuse Treatment: 400.00 per day
- Residential Mental Health: 175.00 per day (room, board medication maintenance and supervision)

Under the terms of this agreement, for each servicemember considered for enrollment in a Blake County Veterans Treatment Court program, representatives from the County will contact Tricare and determine whether an individual's expenses will be covered. If Tricare does not commit to funding the servicemember's treatment expenses, Blake County Veterans Treatment Court personnel will attempt to determine whether the Department of Veterans Affairs will cover the costs or provide its own services under liberalized provisions that permit treatment of active duty offenders by Department of Veterans Affairs entities. If the Department of Veterans Affairs is not able to facilitate treatment requirements through Blake County, the servicemember will be responsible for paying all associated treatment costs.

Anticipated Endstate: The following benefits of this Memorandum are anticipated:

1) Assuring the safety of Blake County and Fort Davis;

2) Retaining Soldiers in the military where there is a chance for effective rehabilitation;

3) Instituting a reliable treatment plan even if the offender is separated from the military;

4) Enabling offenders to be discharged with a characterization of service that permits continued receipt of federal entitlements, even if they are separated involuntarily;

5) Stabilizing high-risk offenders before their return to military control.

Effective Date: This Memorandum of Agreement will become effective upon completion of all signatories.

Periodic Review: This Memorandum of Agreement will be reviewed annually by the appropriate authorities.

Miscellaneous: The original of this Memorandum of Agreement will be maintained by the Fort Davis Office of the Staff Judge Advocate, who shall provide copies thereof to all signatories.

Signatories

_____

Blake County Veterans Treatment Court Judge

_____

Blake County Sheriff

_____

Blake County District Attorney

_____

Fort Davis Garrison Commander

Chapter 3

VETERAN CRIME WAVES, WHACKO-VETS, AND OTHER STEREOTYPES: THE RELATIONSHIP BETWEEN MILITARY SERVICE AND CRIME

Renewed Concern for Veteran Offenders

All members of the uniformed services are trained to be warriors first, even if they have duties that may be comparable to the civilian sector (Bryant, 1979). For example, military lawyers, doctors, dentists, and psychiatrists, who are burdened with various professional duties, must still have familiarity with basic combat skills. Proficiency in soldier tasks and physical conditioning are nonnegotiable because these skilled personnel all wear the same uniform as an infantryman or woman when deployed, and enemy forces do not discriminate by occupational specialty in their attacks.

For years, commentators have seized on this distinction and tried to demonstrate a link between this basic duty description of waging war and criminal offending in society. The connection might seem appealing on its face because no other profession has a similar duty, not even those law enforcement professionals who are authorized to use force in certain limited situations.

In other words, "[t]he only profession that explicitly trains its employees to harm, disable, and destroy another human being is the profession of the warrior—the soldier, sailor, airman, and Marine" (Moore et al., 2009, p. 307). Researchers have historically attempted to explain connections to criminal offending either with the "Violent Veteran" model, which attributes violent crime to military service in general, or the "whacko-vet" myth, which attributes violent crime to combat-traumatized service members. These models are important to explore because, while neither one is valid, politicians, the media, and veterans' advocacy groups have interjected these models into the discourse on programs for criminally involved veteran offenders.

1. The Violent Veteran Model

Historically, there have been upticks in crime following most wars, in most countries, which has led many to question whether returning veterans are responsible for these results. Vietnam was the most evident one, with the homicide rate rising from 4.5 per 100,000 in 1963 to 9.3 per 100,000 in 1973 (Archer & Gartner, 1984, p. 68). Accounting for scholars' interest throughout the centuries, historians Dane Archer and Rosemary Gartner offered up the theoretical "Violent Veteran" model as one of many possible explanations. This model states that "the experience of war resocializes soldiers to be more accepting of violence and more proficient at it" (Archer & Gartner, 1984, p. 75).

Over the years, the media's interest in veteran offending has provided support for the theory by raising the public consciousness of veteran offenders. In the 1920s, following World War I, newspapers frequently portrayed veterans as a criminal class, with headlines such as "Ex-Soldier Kills Wife and Self," "Vet Loots Till," "Homestead Hotel Man Slain; War Veteran Blamed After Firing Shots into own Body" (Painton, 1922, p. 5). In 1947, illustrator Bill Mauldin created a comic illustration to criticize the manner in which the media presented a misleading picture of veteran criminality through overreporting. The scene depicted a husband and wife sitting on the living room couch reading a newspaper appropriately titled *The Daily Dirt.* Large headlines indicated, "Veteran Kicks Aunt," "Combat Veteran Argues with Cop," and "Jealous Vet Sees Judge." The wife notes with interest, "There's a small item on page 17 about a triple ax murder. No veterans involved" (Mauldin, 1947).

In his book, *Back Home,* Mauldin observed how "CRAZED VET RUN AMOK" headlines "gave added impetus to the rumor that always appeared in every country after war—that the returning soldiers are trained in killing and assault and are potential menaces to society" (1947, p. 55). His criticisms echo concerns over the manner in which the media portrayed Vietnam veterans as ticking "time bombs" waiting to explode in violence at the slightest provocation (Burkett & Whitley, 1998, p.150). Some have argued that similar sensationalism exists in coverage of homicides committed by Iraq and Afghanistan war veterans (Holbrook & Anderson, 2011) or exaggerations of the number of "unstable" violent veterans returning from those wars (Moore et al., 2009, p. 312).

Despite anecdotal support for the violent veteran theory, Archer and Gartner's very careful research concluded that it was completely insufficient, and that large-scale crime waves following most wars are more likely attributable to poor economic conditions and other social forces, rather than the behaviors of ex-service members. Contrary to the violent veteran model, research has shown that military service actually reduces overall rates of crime, not only in the United States, but across the globe. Because young men are the most likely to commit violent offenses, the military, by recruiting from the same at-risk population, is credited with providing a more constructive outlet. Professor Ivan Y. Sun and his colleagues conclude that military service has a distinctive crime-prevention role, in which the Armed Forces minimize social "strain by providing many young individuals an opportunity to achieve self-sufficiency and other social values and goals, which in turn make crime involvement or the seeking of illegitimate means unattractive" (Sun, Sung, & Chu, 2007, p. 602).

Because the violent veteran model focuses on military service in general, a permutation of it suggests that combat is *the* crucial factor. In other words, because even the strongest soldier will reach a breaking point in sustained combat operations (Gabriel, 1987, p. 4; Blum, 2017), exposure to combat conditions transforms the veterans and make them more likely to offend once back in civilian society. Research has similarly debunked this permutation of the violent veteran model. Even though combat veterans frequently experience significant and life-altering negative experiences, the vast "majority of warriors return from the battlefield, resume normal lives, adjust, and often succeed better than their non-serving peers and are never unusually violent" (Moore et al., 2009, p. 314).

2. The Whacko-Vet Myth

Commentators have offered the whacko-vet myth as an explanation for criminal offending in the community, attributing violent crimes to war-traumatized veterans whose training in the art of war makes them a particularly high risk to the community upon the activation of stress triggers. In the context of interpersonal violence, the myth claims "that having been in combat turns a man into a woman or child beater" (Matsakis, 2007, p. 235). This belief may stem from an incident in 1949, when a World War II veteran with sniper training reportedly "snapped" and went on a shooting spree with a souvenir pistol killing twelve victims in Camden, New Jersey (Archer & Gartner, 1984, p. 75).

Based on fears like these in the aftermath of World War II, some influential New York socialites argued for special "identification patches" to designate veterans in public and pushed for their isolation at "reorientation camps" where they could be deprogrammed for the safety of the community (Bourke, 1999, p. 352). As in the case of the "violent veteran" model, media portrayals also fueled the myth, especially fictional stories such as World War II era soap operas that depicted veterans as "perhaps the greatest threat domestically" because many "returned from the war stripped of all social restraints" (Shuker-Haines, 1995, p. 157). Later, following Vietnam, a commentator noted the "Kojack Syndrome" in which television plots routinely concluded, "If there is a bizarre crime, check out all the recently discharged Vietnam veterans" (Camacho, 1980, p. 270). He examined the *TV Guide* listings and cited the following entry from 1975 as a representative example of recurring weekly programming: "A psychotic Vietnam veteran is terrorizing hostages in a remote island hotel" (Camacho, 1980, p. 270).

The major problem with any stereotypes is that they usually hold some small element of truth, even though the ultimate assertion is a baseless generalization. The whacko-vet myth is such a stereotype. The partial truth is that some portion of veterans who return from combat are forever transformed by the experience, and, among them, some will experience symptoms that contribute to or cause them to behave in a manner that is both symptomatic of their mental condition and criminal (Seamone et al., 2014; Seamone et al., 2018a). Inevitably, some combat veterans will engage in such extreme violence as a result of their illness that they will be sentenced to death for capital crimes (Wortzel & Arciniegas, 2010).

In fact, for *some* combat-traumatized veterans, criminal offending will necessarily be a form of readjustment to civilian society (Brown, 2010; Seamone, 2011; Seamone, 2013a). As Veterans Administration clinicians Bruce Pentland and James Dwyer observed early on, some "Viet Nam veterans come home via criminal behavior and incarceration" (1985, p. 405). The problem with the whacko-vet myth is the exaggeration in which *all* is substituted for *some*. Persons with mental illnesses—across the board—are unfairly stigmatized as being more dangerous and violent simply because of their mental condition.

Ultimately, mental illness, alone, does not increase the risk of violence (Elbogen & Johnson, 2009). Simply having PTSD or another combat-related condition does not make a veteran more likely to be violent. Nor does combat experience predispose veterans to become more physically abusive to their spouse and/or children. Compared to the population, veterans are less likely to commit criminal offenses than members of the civilian community. Veterans in prisons and jails are not exclusively combat veterans. Considering the estimates of significant numbers of Vietnam veterans and Iraq and Afghanistan veterans who suffer from PTSD, it remains the case that these veterans, even with mental illness, are not only largely capable of, but largely successful at, regulating their behavioral impulses.

The Problem of Unwarranted
Assumptions and Associational Leaps

The whacko-vet myth suffers from the inability to distinguish risk factors from actual mental states: "It is overly simplistic to say that a veteran with

PTSD is at risk for violence despite PTSD being a validated risk factor" (Elbogen et al., 2010, p. 601). Combat veterans, especially those who have killed in combat (Maguen et al., 2012) or experienced events that challenged their deeply-held moral beliefs (Litz et al., 2009), are at greater risk of developing PTSD and combat and operational stress injuries that could potentially result in violent symptoms. However, this hardly explains all combat experiences. The jump from combat trauma to violent or criminal acts skips several steps that could be affected by a wide range of variables. Criminologists and psychologists suggest at least five major considerations that severely limit the association:

1. *Personal Thresholds.* Not all individuals will develop the same mental conditions based on similar traumatic combat experiences. If individuals have experienced prior trauma or other adversity, they might be more vulnerable to the types of symptoms that commonly result in violence (Matsakis, 2007). However, a number of protective factors mitigate the risk, such as one's level of social support.

2. *Trauma Types.* Some types of combat experiences are more likely to result in violent behaviors than others. For example, individuals whose PTSD resulted from the loss of someone close to them in combat are less likely to engage in aggressive behaviors. Contrarily, "specific combat-related variables, such as atrocities exposure . . . and perceived threat during war service . . . predict violence, rather than general combat exposure itself" (Elbogen et al., 2010, p. 598). Thus, the nature of combat trauma is often context-specific and cannot be generalized to an entire population.

3. *Symptoms of Anger Do Not Automatically Equate to Symptoms of Aggression.* PTSD is a mental condition with symptoms that often result in anger. Similarly, the veteran will often experience anger in response to other combat and operational stress injuries related to guilt and shame because the state of rage helps to provide a temporary sense of control. Importantly, anger does not automatically lead to aggression, which is a behavior rather than a feeling: "It is possible to be angry without becoming verbally or physically violent" (Matsakis, 2007, p. 191).

4. *Posttraumatic Stress Disorder and Other Mental Health Conditions Are Often Temporary.* Some say that individuals with combat trauma are forever transformed by their experiences. This may lead to adjustment difficulties where they will need to learn how to adjust their experience of symptoms like a dial, rather than an off-switch (Hoge, 2010). But, it is misleading to believe that all invisible injuries from combat are permanent. Recovery from PTSD is possible. In many cases, the condition will resolve over time, even without treatment from a clinician. Effective evidence-based treatments, such as cognitive-behavioral therapies and exposure therapies can assist the great major-

ity of veterans in their recovery even when conditions persist. Generally, complete remission occurs in approximately 30 to 50 percent of the instances of PTSD (Seamone, 2012, p. 322). Granted PTSD can become chronic in another 10 percent who will "never recover" (Seamone, 2012, p. 322). However, symptoms should never be assumed consistent and permanent in the entire population of combat-traumatized veterans. The myth of the whacko-vet entirely ignores the potential for recovery.

5. *Violence Often Results from the Combination of PTSD Symptoms with Other Psychosocial Factors.* In many cases, combat trauma alone is not responsible for violence, but rather becomes amplified by conditions such as unemployment and homelessness. Without these different aggravating factors, the veteran might not offend, even in the face of significant symptoms (Olusay-naya, 2012, p. 692).

While the five reasons above describe severe limitations to the whacko-vet myth, there are additional ones. Ultimately, each offender's behavior necessarily depends on the individual's specific combat experiences and personal history, making it difficult to draw connections between combat trauma and offending. In a study, international researchers highlighted three reasons why there is not yet a reliable model of the relationship, including the failure of corrections systems to account for veteran status and inconstancies in application of diagnostic criteria (Taylor, Parkes, Haw, & Jepson, 2012). Other researchers have rejected the possibility of research links between PTSD and violence committed by veterans based on the "complex number of pathways to violence" (Grieger, Benedek, & Ursano, 2011, p. 208). The section below describes how, in debunking the violent veteran and whacko-vet myths, other commentators have spawned new myths, on the opposite end of the spectrum.

Mythology Among Those Defending Veterans' Honor

The sections above highlight the weaknesses of common attempts to connect criminal offending to veteran status or combat trauma. Although the media has portrayed these connections and anecdotal cases might lend support, we cannot conclude that serving in the military or experiencing combat trauma necessarily makes a given veteran more likely to commit a criminal or violent act. The violent veteran and whacko-vet theories are myths as applied to veterans at large. These popular theories, however, have contributed to a larger fable that is far more devastating than unfair prejudice and an assault on the pride of the veteran who has peacefully adjusted following service: Based on the fact that veteran status and combat trauma do not *automatically* lead to offending, other commentators may assume that the number of veteran offenders is too small to matter on a grand scale and that those veterans who do offend engage in criminal behavior based on factors unrelated to the military.

The Myth of Insignificance

According to researcher Myra MacPherson, a major reason explaining a lack of interest in incarcerated veterans is a commonly held position that incarcerated veterans constitute so "miniscule" and "insignificant" a population that they do not matter (1992, pp. 582–583). This theory contends, it is an insult to the vast majority of law-abiding veterans to focus attention on the smaller population. This theory distorts the other myths by suggesting that *any* shift in focus to veteran offenders unfairly promotes the myth of the whacko- or violent vet and further confirms the exaggerated media portrayals that pervade society (McCormick-Goodhart, 2013). This was a way in which conservative veterans from the "greatest generation" and prior wars were able to distance themselves from Vietnam veterans, whom they believed would tarnish their reputations through associations as veterans (MacPherson, 1992). The position permeates literature on veteran offenders even today, with authors adopting an apologetic stance when discussing these issues—if they dare. As Clive Emsley explains, "there can be hostility to anyone who addresses criminal offenses by service personnel, even in a serious academic fashion" (2013, p. 6). He offers the following simple reason.

> **Particularly in countries on the winning side in war, or where the military is held in high regard, focusing on the criminal behavior of soldiers can be seen as tarnishing the memory of tough, ordinary soldiers (Emsley, 2013, p. 2).**

In an environment of concern over media portrayals of Iraq and Afghanistan War veterans, some may inevitably criticize any concern over veteran criminality as an overexaggeration.

The "Bad Apple" Myth

Separate from the idea that attention would unfairly magnify a small population of offenders, another reason some may be ambivalent to the plight of the incarcerated veteran is the notion that the offender was already prone to crime prior to entry into the military. There is certainly evidence that a number of recruits engaged in criminal behavior prior to entering the military. Some came to the military under a program of moral waivers, which relaxed eligibility standards prior to the economic crisis when recruiters had trouble meeting their benchmarks (Alvarez, 2007).

Other studies reveal recruits who admitted that they had engaged in attempted or completed rape or sexual assault prior to their entry into the service. One revealed that 12 percent of Navy recruits in a sample admitted to committing a completed rape, while 3 percent admitted to perpetrating an attempted rape (Stander, Merrill, & Thomsen, 2008, p. 9). In other instances, members of gangs and child predators may purposely join the military for easier access to money or victims. In fact, very recently, researchers have developed actuarial models to predict which recruits are at risk of committing "non-familial major physical violent crime perpetration" (Rosellini et al., 2016), and "sexual assault perpetration" (Rosellini et al., 2017). These predictions have been based upon "administrative data," such as prior behavioral problems (Rosellini et al., 2016, p. 662).

While elevated risk suggests the need for preventive measures, none of these facts support the generalization that all veteran offending is attributable to factors unrelated to the military. Instead, there are varied reports of military veterans entering the criminal justice system as first-time offenders following their discharge or return from a deployment. Additionally, statistics suggest that military members are more likely to be first-time offenders than the general population (Bronson et al., 2015; Noonan & Mumola, 2007).

In 1975, the president of a court-martial panel shared this view, which explained the military jury's own collective opinion of how the military can uniquely contribute to mental conditions that result in criminal offending. After commenting on the convicted airman's absence of a prior record and clean upbringing, the major explained: "I felt strongly, and still do, that the military environment in South East Asia brought about Airman McBride's change of attitude, and that the Air Force was therefore at least partially obligated to provide him medical or psychiatric treatment" (*United States v. McBride*, 1975, p. 134, app. A). These comments represent the experiences of a great many justice-involved veterans.

Chapter 4, in fact, describes the military's own recognition of how combat stress can directly result in mental health disorders and offenses falling under the umbrella of "misconduct stress behaviors." Perhaps former Chairman of the Joint Chiefs of Staff, Admiral Michael Mullen, put it best in a letter to the Secretary of Veterans Affairs: "Many of our returning veterans and service members experience life-changing events, some of which may cause them to react in adverse ways and get in trouble with the law" (Mullen, 2011, p. 1). Secretary Kurta's guiding conclusions also highlight the same relationship (2017). Accordingly, while the barrel of offenders may include a number of bad apples, these spoils hardly account for all violent offenders.

Take-Home Points

In recognizing both extremes of the whacko- and violent vet myths on the one hand, and the insignificant and bad-apple vet myths on the other, it is vital to remember that legitimate connections between combat trauma and offending inevitably do exist among some portion of veterans, even if that subset is much smaller than the entire veteran population. Some combat-traumatized veterans will be at greater risk of offending based on particular experiences. To entirely ignore factors that would help distinguish between myth and realty in this most important area is not only illogical, but dangerous for the veterans who are truly at greatest risk of reoffending without intervention. Not only are they at risk, but so are their families and communities. The following chapter thus illustrates the manner in which military service and combat influences that smaller subset of veterans for whom there is a connection to their criminal offending.

Chapter 4

CRIMINAL MANIFESTATIONS OF MILITARY SERVICE, WAR ZONE DEPLOYMENT, AND COMBAT TRAUMA

Renewed Concern for Veteran Offenders

The prior chapter described the reality that a small, but nonetheless substantial, portion of veterans is at risk of criminal offending based on specific military or combat experiences. This group of offenders draws from three subpopulations of military members: (1) those whose offenses are related to the training they received, regardless of whether they deployed to combat; (2) those who faced deployment conditions on a day-to-day basis; and (3) those who experienced trauma during service, whether in combat or in garrison. It is vital for justice and correctional professionals to understand different pathways leading from military service to criminality because this variance requires differentiated approaches to treat the veterans and reduce recidivism.

The first part of this chapter discusses the impact of training on the military member and how it often results in instantaneous responses to perceived threats, which can easily lead to certain types of violent offenses in the civilian community. The second part focuses on the wear-and-tear effect of survival in a combat zone, which can lead to increased risk-taking behavior and specific types of criminal offenses, even if the veteran does not suffer from a diagnosable disorder, and even if the veteran did not engage in direct hostility with enemy forces.

The third part provides insight on a range of conditions that may be related to combat, specifically. Although, PTSD, TBI, and major depression are usually considered to be the most common "invisible injuries" stemming from combat (Seamone et al., 2014), combat and operational stress injuries include a broader range of mental conditions, sometimes subclinical, that appear in larger numbers of service members and which may increase risks of criminal offending. The fourth part considers factors from military service and combat trauma that uniquely contribute to sexually based offenses and interpersonal violence. The fifth part concludes with a brief discussion of cumulative trauma and the special concerns that arise when pre-enlistment mental health conditions are aggravated by service-related traumas. We should understand the interactive effects of different trauma types over time because these situations may require targeted approaches for more than one underlying cause, and to pursue for such treatment requires an understanding of what it entails.

This chapter assumes that sociologists, correctional professionals, and others concerned with veterans have a basic understanding of common mental health disorders, including substance abuse and dependence, depression, PTSD, anxiety, and so forth. Researchers now commonly label prisons and jails as the "new asylums" because of the disproportionately high number of incarcerated offenders with mental illness (Gideon, 2013, p. 8). For example, inmates suffer from a full range of disorders including traditional serious mental illnesses to panic and anxiety disorders. Some indicate that approximately 26 percent of inmates suffer from PTSD (Baillargeon, Hoge, & Penn, 2010, p. 362). Other texts suggest that more than two-thirds of inmates have experienced substance dependence (Gideon, 2013, p. 2). The National Institute of Corrections and others have promoted corrections-specific crisis-intervention training in recognition of the need for greater correctional staff familiarity with the symptoms of commonly encountered mental illness.

There are two important caveats for readers. First, while this chapter may briefly introduce a given disorder, the main purpose here is to address military-specific factors that are often missed, even in the clinical approaches that target the disorders among the general population. A major objective of this chapter is to share the scales and tools that help to summarize complex clinical terms and processes. Given a groundswell of public and professional interest in PTSD since the 9-11 attacks, there is currently a state of information overload with conflicting and contradictory studies on the same topic and little means of quality control among non-clinicians. The purpose for including these simplified approaches is not for correctional professionals or other nonmedical individuals to "diagnose" inmates, but rather to help them conceptualize several moving pieces that would otherwise be difficult to comprehend and apply.

The second caveat is to understand that many mental illnesses may arise during military service that would have emerged regardless of whether the individual had been in the military. Notably, the age during which most service members enlist and serve overlaps with the time when other mental conditions might first surface in individuals who suffer from the condition at a level where they are able to recognize the influences of the disorder. Consequently, there may be certain cases where a given veteran's criminally connected symptoms may not totally be explained by military service, even if military service may have exacerbated or influenced the manner in which the symptoms manifested following discharge.

I. Criminal Offending Related to Military Training, Regardless of Combat Experience

Conditioned Responses to Perceived Threats

Regardless of a veteran's branch of military service, all have participated in some form of basic training and indoctrination into military culture. The purpose of this training is to eliminate civilian habits and replace them with a warrior orientation that will best serve the military. In essence, from the time they join the military service, members are "taught that aggression and the ability to kill without hesitation are part and parcel of being a warrior" (Moore et al., 2009, p. 310). Following World War II, the military totally revamped its methodology for this acculturation process, making the training as realistic as possible and developing the mentality that will put a service member at ease about killing the enemy.

Psychologist David Grossman explains that such changes were necessary because a great many service members were opposed to engaging the enemy in combat when they had the opportunity due to fear and moral considerations (Grossman, 2009). Basic training is a pivotal experience because it has been engineered to remove the types of ethical constraints that would weigh against the use of force in favor of nonviolent alternatives. As evident in the accounts of many combat veterans, military basic training and other experiences in preparation for combat made them want to kill the enemy. Many fantasied about it and longed for it like an unquenchable thirst—until it finally happened (Moore et al., 2009, p. 311). Scholars who recognize the profound effects of combat training emphasize that "[t]here is nothing wrong with those who are not disturbed by the killing or who may even derive joy from the act during combat [and who] find peace and satisfaction in killing on the battlefield" (Moore et al., 2009, p. 311). The experience will affect individuals in a different manner.

Aside from basic combat training, military units engage in additional follow-on training over the course of assignments. The amount and nature of such training will be dictated largely by one's occupational specialty. However, it is not uncommon for service members in combat arms positions, such as the infantry, to spend weeks or months at a time in the field rehearsing various battle drills. Essentially, training for combat promotes certain instinctive and aggressive behaviors because decisiveness on the battlefield can save lives. In urban combat and other close-quarters environments, instinctual reactions often relate to anticipating attacks from behind, eliminating rapidly approaching objects or individuals, and other responses to short-or-no-notice physical threats. Combat operations require immediate responses. The quicker the individual service member is able to respond to a threat without the delay of thought, the greater the capability to accomplish the mission. For this reason, "critical warrior training, so absolutely essential in combat, requires extensive overlearning and makes use of procedural/motor learning" (Moore et al., 2009, p. 320).

The conditioned responses that result from military training can explain certain types of criminal offenses perpetrated by veterans. Often, family members are warned—or learn through experience—not to suddenly approach a veteran, or approach from behind (Seamone, 2012). This is common to other professions, such as law enforcement officers—or correctional officers—who also receive training that can lead them to respond to perceived threats at an instinctual level. The major problem with training in this regard, whether for the responding police officer, corrections officer, or the veteran of the armed forces, is that training often eliminates response times and the chance to assess a situation. In these common scenarios involving potential threats, the responders are unable to make an accurate assessment because of the danger cues they have learned as shortcuts in threat response.

Others describe the reliance on military training as "survival mode," and reason that the veteran will resort to training as a result of all human beings' fight-or-flight response to a perceived threat, which, as a matter of survival, precludes the opportunity for careful consideration of alternative courses of action (Matsakis, 2007, pp. 191–192). Dr. Matsakis concludes, "[b]ecause of their prolonged exposure to life-threatening situations, combat veterans can enter a state of alarm and terror more quickly than civilians, especially those who have never been traumatized" (2007, p. 192). Importantly, such instinctual survival responses may come in response to any type of event that would make veterans feel vulnerable and less able to defend themselves. This commonly extends beyond perceptions of purely physical threats to feelings of emotional vulnerability (Matsakis, 2007, p.192). In other words, "when a veteran experiences the first glimmer of sadness or guilt internally, he or she may panic, thus setting the stage for an aggressive act" (Matsakis, 2007, p. 192).

II. Criminal Offending Related to the Wear-and-Tear of Deployment Conditions, Regardless of Participation in Direct Hostile Engagements

Military service is the most stressful occupation known, as echoed in 2013 surveys of various professions, finding "American Soldier" tops other first-responders such as police or emergency medical personnel (Kensing, 2013). While doctors and law enforcement personnel face tremendous stress, the realities faced by the enlisted man and woman are unique and especially burdensome. This form of military operational stress is specific to service members largely because of the "lack of reprieve time and competing demands" (Rubin & Weiss, 2013, p. 72). Perhaps the major reason for this result is the nature of stressors one experiences while deployed in a hostile fire zone.

For families and their deployed service members, the foremost stressor related to deployment is the knowledge of the potential that the troop may never return home. This weight is heavy to bear, whether the service member participates in intense combat or none at all. However, it is vital to recognize that enemy forces are only one of many stressors that coexist during a combat tour.

Researchers Caroline Carney and her colleagues compiled a list of thirty-one potential war zone stressors endured by service members who deployed during the Gulf War. While nine of the stressors directly related to combat, more than twice that number related to other characteristics, including exposure to: "smoke, solvents/petrochemicals, pesticides, infectious disease, neurotoxins, psychological stress, heat stress, trauma, radiation, and lead" (Carney et al., 2003, p. 655). The variation in stressors underscores how much the military occupation can generate its own unique and quite extensive detractors, aside from hostile fire from enemy forces.

Depending on their occupational specialties, service members may be forced to spend countless hours in demanding battle briefings at a tactical operations center; they may have to interface with citizens of the host nation who do not appreciate their presence; they may be exposed to atrocities committed by local armed forces and police of the host nation; and they may suffer from various deficits in leadership from superiors who have control over every facet of their existence, including where they are assigned and the amount of danger they face. On patrols, infantrymen and women often endure minimal sleep on repeated missions and may require medication to stay awake. Despite differences in occupational specialties, the multiple stresses of combat take their toll in a process that the Navy and Marine Corps describe simply as "wear and tear," or "the accumulated effects of smaller stressors over time, such as those from nonoperational sources or lack of sleep, rest, and restoration" (U.S. Department of Navy and U.S. Marine Corps, 2010, pp. 1-11).

This wear-and-tear can predispose a veteran toward greater levels of distress and easily manifest in other diagnosable disorders. However, exposure to the stresses of combat, alone, even without direct enemy engagement, can independently result in behaviors that place a veteran at greater risk of criminal offending. As Dr. Wiliam D. S. Killgore and his colleagues conclude:

> **Based entirely on combat experience alone, "[s]ome veterans may have an elevated propensity for risk-taking that may emerge independently from any diagnosis of major clinical psychiatric syndromes such as PTSD, anxiety or major depression" (Killgore et al., 2008, p. 119).**

A family of related consequences may emerge, including "thrill-seeking" behavior, "risk-taking" behavior, and "invincibility." Thrill-seeking behavior basically relates to the idea that the veteran desires to replicate the rush experienced from living on the edge in combat conditions (Strom et al., 2012).

Although it is common among those who survived close calls in firefights and those diagnosed with PTSD, neither combat engagement nor mental diagnosis are necessary for this condition. Upon returning from a hostile fire zone, civilian life may appear exceedingly boring and consequently meaningless for some. Thrill-seekers, who have sometimes been called "action junkies" (Wilson & Zigelbaum, 1983), often will attempt to replicate the rush they experienced during earlier times, as if the excitement and feelings of unpredictability were drugs.

Rather than attempting to replicate conditions from the war zone, risk-takers will commonly engage in dangerous behavior as a result of acclimation to combat conditions, which are extremely different from civilian life. For example, the risk-taking veteran may drive far more carelessly, speed at high rates, and barrel through stop signs as a consequence of repeated survival driving in commonly mined roads overseas frequented by attackers who would target stopped U.S. vehicles. The notion of "post-combat invincibility" builds on this paradigm of risk-taking in general (Killgore et al., 2008).

With an entirely different cost-benefit analysis for one's behavior, veterans who perceive that they have been face-to-face with death—and survived it—may become more tolerant of risk in different areas of life, as if their survival proved that they are immune to consequences for their behavior. All three of these manifestations of deployment to a combat zone will increase a veteran's risk for contact with the criminal justice system.

III. Criminal Offending Related to Operational
Stress Injuries from Combat Exposure

A. PTSD

At times both PTSD and TBI have been called *the* signature injury of the wars in Iraq and Afghanistan. Other studies of invisible injuries routinely conclude that the three major conditions stemming from the global war on terror included PTSD, TBI, and major depression. PTSD is an anxiety disorder that is distinguished from other mental diagnoses in the *Diagnostic and Statistical Manual of Mental Disorders* (*DSM*) by its unique requirement for a precipitating causal event. Traditionally, the underlying trauma has been conceived as a "life-threat" type incident, consisting of actual or threatened death or serious injury (Gold, Marx, Soler-Baillo, & Sloan, 2005). The PTSD diagnosis has undergone many changes since its creation in the 1980 *DSM-III*. The current edition of the *DSM* has expanded qualifying stressor events to include "sexual violence" and recognizes that PTSD may arise from learning about a threat to a close person or "experiencing repeated or extreme exposure to aversive details of the traumatic event" (American Psychiatric Association, 2013, p. 271). Upon a glance at the diagnostic criteria, a reader will see various categories of symptoms.

As evident in Figure 11, which is a rough summary for purposes of illustration, a patient must experience a certain mixture of symptoms from different clusters. Even after the publication of the Fifth Edition of the *DSM*, the recipe generally includes a causal event of sufficient magnitude, avoidance

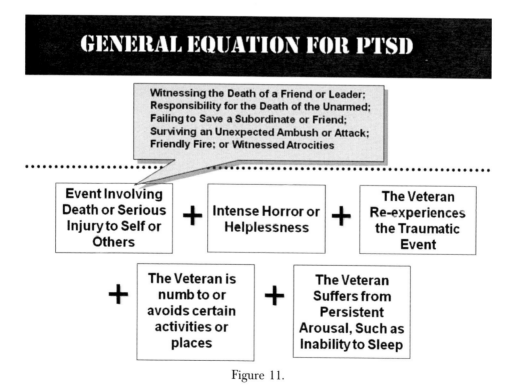

Figure 11.

behaviors, unwanted recurring reminders of trauma, and emotional arousal for a certain period of time to be diagnosed with full-blown PTSD (American Psychiatric Association, 2013, pp. 271–280).

Some have criticized the PTSD diagnosis on the basis that so many different possible permutations of the disorder make treatment of a specific series of symptoms inherently more difficult. Others note that, at best, a PTSD diagnosis represents a "simplified communication device" for discussing a variety of symptoms (Young, 2007, p. 148). The criteria depend entirely upon the patient's own self-report, which gives rise to concerns of exaggeration of symptoms and other unintentional errors that would impair the possibility of an accurate diagnosis, even where conscious malingering is not present.

Beyond this, any number of mental health professionals might consider the same patients' self-report of symptoms and diagnose them differently based upon the inherent subjectivity of the diagnostic criteria. As Dr. Andrew Kane notes, "It is not unusual for a clinician or forensic expert to indicate a diagnosis of [PTSD] when the individual's experience and/or symptoms do not meet the full diagnostic criteria" (2007, p. 283). This may explain why "[w]hat the U.S. Army refers to as chronic combat stress reaction is essentially synonymous with PTSD" (Ritchie, Schneider, Bradley, & Forsten, 2008, p. 39).

Despite its potential for problems, the PTSD diagnosis is still extremely relevant to military members in the criminal justice system for two primary reasons. The first reason is the sheer number of service members who have experienced the types of causal events that are classically known to manifest in PTSD. It helps to consider statistics that capture the effect of multiple and prolonged deployments that continued through the last decade, resulting in a situation where a substantial number of service members have deployed more than once, with some deploying three to five times, and some members of the special forces deploying more than ten times. For example, in a study of 670 service members who deployed to Iraq between 2003 and 2006, some of whom likely had multiple deployments at the time, 97.9 percent of the respondents endorsed having "[r]eceived hostile incoming fire from small arms, rockets, mortars, or bombs," 67.6 percent experienced these events "[a]t least a few times per week," causing 64.5 percent to agree or strongly agree that they "felt [they were] in great danger of being killed or wounded" during their service (Vasterling et al., 2010, p. 47, tbl. 2)

Other studies suggest measurable rates of more direct hostile engagements, such as 86.3 percent receiving incoming artillery rocket or mortar fire; 70.3 percent knowing someone seriously injured or killed; 66.3 percent working in areas that were mined or had IEDs; and 66.6 percent having a member of their own unit become a casualty (Killgore et al., 2008, p. 1113).

When we consider the effects of repeated exposure to these same sorts of precipitating events during subsequent deployments, it is no wonder that that the chance of a PTSD diagnosis increases with each additional deployment.

Rates of combat PTSD have been estimated across the board, suggesting a high level of inaccuracy. Clinical psychologist Aphrodite Matsakis makes the compelling point that, "[i]n truth, we do not actually know how many veterans suffer or suffered from some form of combat trauma," owing to a host of reasons that include differences in diagnostic standards, the fact that multiple disorders coexist, mental health professionals do not all use consistent measures, stigma against seeking help prevents timely intervention and the onset of symptoms may be delayed for years (2007, p. 41). Despite this considerable margin of error, combat PTSD rates are usually diluted to the point that they minimize the impact of exposure among those who engaged in the most intense combat.

Too often, statistics include the deployed service member who lived on a well-fortified forward operating base, who commonly exhibits the same PTSD rates as individuals who have never deployed to combat (Castro, 2009, p. 252). This inclusion heavily skews overall rates for those who may have engaged in direct hostilities with the enemy on a daily basis over the course of hundreds, if not thousands of missions, during a year-long—or longer—deployment. Psychologist Carl Castro highlights the vital distinction that PTSD rates for moderate-intensity combat veterans commonly reach 30 percent and 50 percent for veterans who engaged in high-intensity combat, resulting in the following conclusion:

> **"I'm beginning to believe that after multiple deployments and high combat intensities, developing mental health symptoms becomes the norm, rather than the exception to the norm, when you look at the soldiers who are at greatest risk"** (Castro, 2009, p. 252).

These rates of combat PTSD are relevant to criminal offending because certain common PTSD hyperarousal symptoms increase chances of violent behavior, such as "anger and irritability" (Elbogen et al., 2012, p. 1099). Specifically, "domains of anger problems include:

- Inaccurate perception and processing of environmental cues;
- Heightened physiological and emotional activation; and
- Behavioral inclinations to act in antagonistic and confrontative ways" Source: Grieger et al. (2011, p. 207).

If veterans suffer from all three deficits simultaneously, myths may transform into realities, making them appear as a "ball of rage," even to trained clinicians (Grieger et al., 2011, p. 207). Apart from anger, PTSD often results in criminal complications because veterans commonly self-medicate their symptoms with alcohol and controlled substances, with a substantial portion of combat veterans diagnosed with PTSD also suffering from a co-occurring substance abuse disorder (Matsakis, 2007).

Perhaps the most important thing that those who work with veterans, including correctional professionals, should keep in mind about PTSD is the fact that violence and other criminal behavior can result in individuals who suffer from one or some symptoms of PTSD, but not enough to qualify for the full-blown diagnosis. Among these "sub-threshold" PTSD veterans, research has shown that these individuals often experience PTSD symptoms at a greater level of intensity than those diagnosed with the full-blown disorder, thus increasing their risk of offending (Grieger et al., 2011, p. 212).

Because PTSD symptoms in isolation may represent significant risk, clinicians have created some tools to address different manifestations of the symptoms. A popular instrument is the PTSD Checklist-Military Version (PCL-M), developed by the National Center for PTSD. The PCL-M is often used as a measure of veterans' symptoms during the course of therapy visits to monitor mental health improvement over time. It is a self-report tool that simplifies symptoms in an easily understood manner, removing some of the technical jargon. The PCL-M, which is based upon the *DSM-IV,* is included in Appendix A of this chapter to assist readers in considering the manner in which common PTSD symptoms manifest in veterans.

The PCL-M is not the only measure that traces one's symptoms, feelings, and behaviors to combat experiences. In 1996, Psychiatrist Jonathan Shay developed the Combat Stress Barometer specifically to assist combat veterans in gauging the intensity of their stress reactions (Shay, 1996, pp. 117–122). This scale, which is reproduced with permission in Appendix B of this chapter, is far more detailed than the PCL-M and covers forty-six different indications of behavioral links to combat trauma. A review of the instrument along with the PCL-M will help readers understand different reactions to military trauma as time passes.

B. Moral Injury and Non-Life-Threatening Causal Factors

The traditional life-threat stressor has been cognized as a Criterion A1 traumatic event based upon the *DSM*'s diagnostic taxonomy. Over time, clinicians have come to accept the fact that trauma falling outside of Criterion A1 can be as, if not more, impactful than a traditional life threat. For example, the loss of a close friend or sight of human remains is often the basis for

PTSD symptomatology even though these experiences may not involve threatened death or severe injury to the military witness (Stein et al., 2012, p. 788). This is important for those working with veterans to realize because many combat situations that do not involve traditional life-threat trauma nevertheless result in PTSD (U.S. Department of Navy and U.S. Department of Marine Corps, 2010).

One of the foremost non-life-threat traumatic experiences facing combat veterans is the morally injurious experience. *Moral injury* is best defined as a situation in which a veteran must violate deeply held moral beliefs. Combat produces many more opportunities for ethical dilemmas, which may help explain the results of a 2008 study of deployed troops in which "27 percent of soldiers faced ethical situations during deployment in which they did not know how to respond" (Litz et al., 2009, p. 696). Moral injury has existed perhaps since the beginning of armed conflict but was expansively defined by psychologist Brett Litz and his colleagues as:

> **"Perpetrating, failing to prevent, bearing witness to, or learning about acts that transgress deeply held moral beliefs and expectations" (2009, p. 700).**

Many different situations may result in moral injury, including:

- "Participating in or witnessing inhumane or cruel actions";
- "Failing to prevent the immoral acts of others";
- "Engaging in subtle acts or experiencing reactions that, upon reflection, transgress a moral code"; and
- "Bearing witness to the aftermath of violence and human carnage"
  Source: Litz et al. (2009, p. 700).

Since 2009, Litz and his colleagues have pushed for more expansive analysis of veterans' combat experiences beyond the traditional life-threat versions of trauma. In 2013, Litz and his colleagues developed a Moral Injury Event Scale to capture the full range of such experiences, which appear along nine different dimensions rated on a six point variable scale, including:

(1) "I saw things that were morally wrong"; (2) "I am troubled by having witnessed others' immoral acts"; (3) "I acted in ways that violated my own moral code or values; (4) "I feel betrayed by leaders who I once trusted; and (5) "I feel betrayed by fellow service members who I once trusted" (Nash et al., 2013).

The complete scale is useful for identifying different military events that have the potential to cause moral injury. According to Nash and colleagues, the scale measures "exposure to events in a military context with the potential to contradict deeply held moral beliefs" (2013, p. 650). Given that moral injury often involves more than participation in or witnessing of atrocities and killing, and might encompass many different types of events, this scale is useful because it identifies factors that can apply across the varied contexts. The authors emphasize how the scale does not measure moral wrongdoing, but rather only measures morally injurious events: "The [scale] indexes only perceived contradictions between remembered behaviors and post hoc moral expectations in the necessarily complex moral context of modern warfare; it does not index wrongdoing in any form" (Nash et al., 2013, p. 650).

In 2010, the U.S. Navy and Marine Corps officially recognized moral injury as a separate pathway to PTSD in its doctrine on combat and operational stress. They describe it as an "Inner Conflict," in which "[s]tress arises due to moral damage from carrying out or bearing witness to acts or failures to act that violate deploy held belief systems (U.S. Department of Navy and U.S. Marine Corps, 2010, pp. 1–11). The manual further explains that the inner conflict is a separate pathway to PTSD and other psychiatric disorders, and that it may be as potent an influence as the life-threat category. In an effort to better understand the separate types of events that lead to PTSD and other mental health conditions, researchers developed six "proposed categories of traumatic events," that should assist researchers and correctional professionals in recognizing how inmates with different experiences in the military may still have had the opportunity to sustain a stress injury. The categories include: (1) Life Threat to Self; (2) Life Threat to Others; (3) Aftermath of Violence; (4) Traumatic Loss; (5) Moral Injury by Self; and (6) "Moral Injury by Others" (Stein et al., 2012, p. 802, app.).

The developers of the above framework underscore how the categories aftermath of violence, traumatic loss, and committing or observing morally injurious acts each can independently lead to "the most distressing and haunting events experienced by active duty service members" (Stein et al., 2012, p. 799). Within their framework, "Moral Injury by Self" was the best predictor of re-experiencing symptoms (Stein et al., 2012, pp. 799–800), and "Moral Injury by Others" was the category most associated with anger and threat of violence to others (Stein et al., 2012, p. 800). The researchers theorize that attention to and assessment of trauma types will permit mental health providers to develop more effective treatments that are tailored to "the primary source of the distress" (Stein et al., 2012, pp. 788–789).

Drone-Operator Stress as a Window to Moral Injury

As an applied example of moral injury and its relationship with criminal offending, recent concern has emerged regarding the psychological impact experienced by crew members and intelligence analysts who are responsible for coordinating and observing the aftermath of targeted killings by Unmanned Aerial Vehicles (UAVs) or drones. Following the attacks of 9/11, the Bush, Obama, and Trump Administrations increasingly adopted Unmanned Aerial Vehicles (UAVs or drones)[5] to augment traditional ground forces in combat operations (Purkiss, Serle, & Fielding-Smith, 2017). For example, the Obama Administration carried out more than ten times the number of drone attacks than the Bush-Cheney Administration, and the Trump Administration has engaged in even more widespread strikes (McDonnell, 2017, p. 46). This intensified use led to an estimate of at least 4,705 strikes between January 2002 and January 2018 (Bureau of Investigative Journalism, 2018).[6]

With increasing pressure to bring a swift end to America's longest wars in Asia and the Middle East, targeted killings began to replace and eclipse the use of infantry forces and special operations teams as the preferred method of preserving young American lives. Whereas the Air Force was flying approximately one dozen drones a day in the mid-2000s, by 2010, the number increased to sixty (Schmidt, 2016). This Islamic State, in fact, began to deploy explosives-laden drones to enhance their lethality after suffering so many drone attacks from the United States (Schmidt & Schmitt, 2016).

Along with the increase in targeted killings, the U.S. military designated an increasing number of drone operators to perpetrate such acts. Targeted killings had become so pervasive in countries like Syria, Yemen, Pakistan, and Afghanistan, with attendant loss of civilian lives, that human rights organizations have raised concerns that drone warfare was violating international law principles based on the expediency of killing rather than detaining or even confirming the target's identity (e.g., Shane, 2016).

As drone operations increase exponentially with time, one of the biggest justifications for their use has been the savings in American lives, to include fewer casualties of war in terms of both physical injuries and mental health consequences of traditional manned combat operations. As author Richard

---

5. Other common names for drones include Remotely Piloted Aircraft (RPA). Predators and the MQ-9 Reapers refer to drones that are commonly used in remote warfare when they are equipped with laser-guided missiles and bombs. Other drones might include the Sky Warrior and the RQ-4 Global Hawk UAV (Trustam, 2017).

6. These numbers are limited to the strikes confirmed by the Bureau of Investigative Journalism from the time they began collecting data on each country. This includes drone strikes in Yemen from January 2002, Afghanistan from January 2015, Pakistan from January 2004, and Somalia from January 2007 (Bureau of Investigative Journalism, 2018).

Whittle explained, "When a Predator goes to war and dies for its country, no one has to knock at a family member's front door to deliver the bad news and no one plays Taps" (R. Whittle, Speech at the George Washington University Law School, September 22, 2014). Although UAVs do have human crew members, none of these individuals are required to be physically located in a theater of operations. In fact, most drone operators conduct their operations with the aid of live video feeds to stateside locations at well-fortified air bases in Nevada, California, and other installations. In the confines of well-guarded domestic facilities, drone crew members can avoid blast injuries, return fire, or the fear of impending death or injury that has typically led to the greatest increase in VA benefits observed during any period of war.

This "qualitatively distinct [activity] from ground combat" (Ogle, Reichwald, Rutland, & Thurman, 2017, p. 2) has led to a rift within military and veteran populations that wish to accord more respect and honor to those who remain in the fight, rather than conduct "armchair warfare" (Olson & Rashid, 2013). The longstanding basis for objection has been rooted in "the ancient idea that warfare is about physical [valor] and skill at close quarters[;] that [k]illing with lance and sword was considered chivalric, while doing so from a distance was ignoble and cowardly" (Hambling, 2017).

Most notably, widespread opposition to a proposed "Nintendo" military medal for drone warfare participants led the Pentagon to reject the medal on the grounds that it was an affront to ground combat forces, especially since it would have been ranked higher than the Bronze Star in order of precedence (Tighman, 2016). However, very recently, the U.S. military did permit the addition of the golden "R" device for existing medals (excluding the Bronze Star) to "recognize achievements which directly impact combat operations" (U.S. Army Human Resources Command, 2017).[7]

Despite many protections accorded to drone crew members, their activities are not entirely free of consequences. Multiple service members are impacted by drone operations, considering that for each drone in the air, there "is a need for up to four dozen analysts who can look at the many hours of footage to assess targets and other intelligence" (Schmidt, 2016). With the rise in targeted killing, many in the military, the mental health profession, and Congress have questioned whether this new form of warfare puts drone operators at risk for mental health consequences. Using the vernacular of "drone stress" "screen trauma," "distant trauma," or "traumatic media exposure" psychologists have defined this unique risk as akin to "per-

7. The creation of the device was "in response to requests for a way to distinguish [traditional] awards as having been earned . . . for directly contributing to combat" (U.S. Army Human Resources Command, 2017).

petrator-induced traumatic stress[:] a form of PTSD caused not by being a victim of trauma but by being an active participant in producing trauma" (Pincheviski, 2016, pp. 52, 64, 67). In many published peer-reviewed articles, Air Force professionals have addressed remote trauma in a guarded way using gentler terms like "burnout," distancing the discussion from the vernacular of PTSD, and suggesting that more research is necessary before reaching any generalizable conclusions based on the nascent stages of the phenomenon (Pincheviski, 2016, p. 65).

Even without significant longitudinal studies, the existing research has still concluded that drone crew members' "cumulative exposure to remote combat and graphic media, as well as exposure to specific types of events (e.g., witnessing U.S. casualties, civilian casualties, atrocities committed by the enemy) was related to increased symptoms of Posttraumatic Stress and other negative psychological outcomes" (Ogle et al., 2017, p. 2). They hypothesize that this consequence may even be amplified by the fact that, "[u]nlike fighter pilots, who fly thousands of feet away from the target, drone operators have a real-time, high-resolution view of the strike—and its aftermath" (Pinchevski, 2016, p. 65). Recognizing the significant number of drone crews facing these risks from often round-the-clock combat operations, in June 2015, Senator Claire McCaskill, a member of the Senate Armed Services Committee, demanded information on "the Air Force's plan to deal with this unique form of combat stress" from the Air Force's top brass:

> I want to take this opportunity to note my concern about the effect of Airmen being "deployed on station." It is unprecedented in warfare for our men and women to fly combat missions, engage and kill our enemies, and a short while later go home to their families. An RPA pilot could be sitting down to a meal with his or her family less than two hours after killing Islamic State or Taliban fighters on the other side of the world. They could be playing with their children shortly after witnessing up close and in graphic detail the effects of a 500-pound bomb or Hellfire missile on a soft target. I am not sure we fully understand the consequences this has for our men and women in uniform, or on their families (McCaskill, 2015)

To date, while there has been no public response to the inquiry, in the same year as Senator McCaskill's letter, Air Force Secretary Deborah Lee James confided that, with regard to the high demand for drone operations, the Air Force "cannot sustain this pace indefinitely" (Schmidt, 2016). Recent studies of drone crews in the Intelligence, Surveillance, and Reconnaissance (ISR) Wing by Air Force psychologists have placed remote trauma "squarely within proposed moral injury frameworks (responsibility versus loss of control, guilt, and perceived culpability over immediate and/or second and third-order consequences, and wrestling with the consequences of imperfect intelligence or imperfect operations" (Ogle et al., 2017, p. 7). Furthermore, research from embedded work with these crews has led to the conclusion that, "The challenges of 'combat to cul-de-sac' life can be very jarring, and if not navigated successfully—can leave airmen in a perpetual combat posture [on] high idle . . ." (Ogle et al., 2017, p. 32). This is likely why the Air Force classifies all of the ISR members on drone crews as "'at-risk' due to historically elevated rates of attempted and completed suicides across the community" (Ogle et al., 2017, p. 6).

The link to misconduct symptoms of Drone Stress is also becoming clearer. In the case of one drone sensor operator with PTSD caused by his remote exposure to targeted killings, the Air Force released him from confinement and dropped court-martial charges for "domestic violence, drug use, and disobeying orders" (Rogers, 2015). The alternative disposition of an administrative separation came after his attorney had requested the production of internal studies regarding the Air Force's knowledge of the risks to which he was exposed (Rogers, 2015). With the high rates of remote trauma facing drone crews, it is likely that he represents a larger population that has been addressed in the solitude of highly secure military bases. The recent passage of legislation known as *The Honor Our Commitment Act* also recognizes the relationship between drone operations and misconduct. This law, which is now in effect, extends VA mental health treatment to recipients of Other-Than-Honorable discharges for misconduct when it can be established that the veteran with the discharge "deployed to a combat zone, zone of hostilities, or operated a drone in a combat zone" (Press Release, 2018).

C. Depression and Guilt

Depression is a mental health condition characterized by a persistent state of disinterest in activities and a lack of enjoyment and fulfillment in life. Although there are numerous forms of depression, which include psychotic depression or atypical depression, major depression relates to "[m]arked, sustained unhappiness or darkness of mood" (Nydegger, 2013, pp. 167–169). Individuals who experience depressive states are more likely to relapse in the future and that depression substantially raises the risk of suicidal ideology, attempts, and completed suicides. Depression is common among veterans who have served in combat because hostile fire zones give rise to variations of guilt that are not easily encountered in civilian environments.

Psychologist John P. Wilson further demonstrated how guilt commonly resulted from the "inability to fulfill warrior role and authority-based-killing" and even "repeated loss of territory," in an intricate set of behavioral consequences commonly resulting from different types of experiences in Vietnam.

For example, the "[g]uerilla nature of war" commonly resulted in "[m]istrust, time confusion, shame-doubt (lack of control and predictability)," while "[d]eath of buddies and atrocities" commonly resulted in the "sense of existential guilt, search for meaning; [and] [i]deological confusion" (Wilson, 1980, p. 136, tbl. 7.2).

Although some have identified at least nine ways that combat in Iraq and Afghanistan is different from combat in Vietnam, suggesting that "today's veterans are experiencing far more physical and especially mental problems upon their return from the war zone than veterans of previous wars" (Korb, 2009, pp. 1, 1–7), there are a number of similarities, evident in this account, which describes many virtually indistinguishable characteristics:

> A much higher proportion of combat deaths were due to small arms fire, booby traps, and mines than in either of America's other major 20th Century wars. . . . The nature of combat (frequently at close range), the type of wounds . . . especially multiple wounds, combined with excellent medical care resulted in a higher incidence of complicated disabilities, including multiple amputations, paraplegia, and hemiplegia. The percentage of Vietnam veterans who suffered crippling wounds was 300 percent higher than in World War II and 70 percent higher than in Korea. (DeFazio, 1984, pp. 24–25)

Whether the campaign is the Korean War, Vietnam, the Gulf War, or the global war on terror, combat can lead to at least fourteen manifestations of guilt among combat veterans based upon specific situations. Figure 12, describes these variants of guilt, many of which naturally result in depressed states.

There are several distinctions between these guilt types. For example, as opposed to "Competency Guilt," which involves "feelings of guilt for not having acted as efficiently or wisely as one thinks one should have" (Matsakis, 2007, p. 186), "Negligence Guilt" results from the perception that one actually "made a mistake in the execution of assigned duties" (Matsakis, 2007, p. 187). Alternatively, "Catch-22 Guilt" occurs when the veteran faced "lose-lose situations where all the choices available [were] unacceptable or involve[d] a violation of personal ethics" (p. 188). "True Guilt" signifies the perception that one has failed to measure up to his or her own personal standards as a result of a military experience (Matsakis, 2007, p. 189). When guilt is persistent and intense over time, it can result in any number of effects that might contribute to combat and operational stress injuries, symptoms aggravation, and even criminal behavior, certainly at an indirect level if not directly (Matsakis, 2007, pp. 190–191).

1. Survivor Guilt

2. Failure to Meet Parental Expectations

3. Failure to Meet Societal Expectations

4. Childhood Omnipotent Guilt

5. Superman/Superwoman Guilt

6. Existential/Religious Guilt

7. Guilt of Being

8. Shadow Guilt

9. Moral or Atrocity Guilt

10. Competency Guilt

11. Negligence Guilt

12. Catch-22 Guilt

13. Responsibility Guilt

14. True Guilt

Figure 12. Fourteen Variations of Guilt Related to Military Service. Source: Matsakis (2007, pp. 175–189).

D. *mTBI*

In brief, TB, also referred to as Mild TBI (mTBI) for our purposes, is "a brain injury caused by a blow or jolt to the head or a penetrating head injury that disrupts the normal function of the brain" (U.S. Department of Navy and U.S. Marine Corps, 2010, Glossary 5). Synonymous with a concussion, TBI is defined clinically as an injury "to the head that results in brief loss of consciousness (LOC) <30 minutes), alteration of consciousness (AOC), or posttraumatic amnesia" (Wilk, Herrell, Wynn, Rivere, & Hoge, 2012, p. 249).

A number of mental health professionals have criticized the common use of the term as an overbroad representation that obscures the difference between a brief post-concussive state and a lasting physiological impairment. According to Psychiatrist Charles Hoge and his colleagues, "'Mild TBI' is often misused to refer to post-concussive symptoms, conveying a present-tense state of an incompletely healed brain injury, (brain 'damage'), where a 'concussion' refers to a past event. . ." (Hoge, Goldberg, & Castro, 2009, p. 1589). Not all TBIs are permanently debilitating. In fact, clinicians suggest that most TBIs will not typically lead to criminal offending (Moore et al., 2009, p. 316). Even though numerous service members have sustained head trauma in a variety of combat settings, the majority of these injuries are in a category of minor impairment.

Criminal offending is likely in those instances where a veteran suffers serious frontal lobe damage from a blast or puncture. Because those areas regulate impulse control, some brain damage may lead one to misperceive threats, or lack the ability to control anger or excitability (Moore et al., 2009, p. 317). Indirectly, a combination of TBI symptoms, which commonly include difficulty maintaining concentration and organizing information can combine with co-occurring PTSD to amplify PTSD symptoms or irritability in general, which may lead to emotional dysregulation.

E. Other Mental Health Conditions Resulting from Combat Trauma

While it is logical to focus on prevalent mental health conditions among combat veterans, there has arguably been an overemphasis on PTSD and TBI to the exclusion of other conditions that still result in problematic symptomatology. With an eye toward combat, Australian General Peter Cosgrove explains "the range of other problems that can develop or be aggravated, as a result of traumatic experiences, include acute stress reactions, depression, hostility, substance abuse, family violence, anxiety disorders, antisocial behavior and adjustment disorders" (2003, p. xv). Dr. Andrew Kane (2007, p. 284) further provides this list of overlapping "diagnostic categories of PTSD and other mental conditions":

- Panic Disorder;
- Social Phobia (Social Anxiety Disorder);
- Specific Phobia;
- Generalized Anxiety Disorder;
- Major Depressive Episode;
- Somatoform Disorder;

- Antisocial Personality Disorder;
- Substance-Related Disorders;
- Some Organic Mental Disorders; and
- Some Adjustment Disorders

Interestingly, in the many studies that reveal low-to-moderate rates of PTSD in deployed personnel, the same studies often reveal much higher numbers of individuals who suffer from the collective category of "other mental health conditions." In recognition of this overemphasis of PTSD to the exclusion of different conditions that may contribute to negative symptoms, military agencies have developed more inclusive terms for the full array of invisible war wounds.

The Canadian Forces refer to operational stress injuries as "any persistent psychological difficulty that has resulted from military service" (Ray et al., 2013, p. 292), which the U.S. Navy and Marine Corps distinguish further between combat stress and operational stress (2010). Regardless of the term used, these approaches recognize that combat results in a wide range of mental health conditions, including some that may not rise to the level of any official diagnosis, even if they are likely to result in criminal symptoms.

F. Combat and Operational Stress Injuries and Criminal Offenses

The academic debates over the degree to which combat trauma influences criminal offending are divorced from the reality of warfare. Common problems in academic circles might arise because the aim is to develop some type of predictive model that will enable policymakers to predict criminal involvement within a certain margin of error. However, if the goal is simply to confirm whether combat trauma can and does result in criminal offending, the military itself formally recognized this at least since the 1940s during World War II.

Historically, military psychiatry existed to benefit commanders not service members. The major desire was to repair battlefield psychiatric casualties to the degree that they were capable of being placed back on the field as quickly as possible with military efficiency. As a consequence, heavily traumatized warriors who were incapable of fighting were often treated as disciplinary problems, charged with desertion or other offenses against military order, and even executed for confession to the tolls of combat trauma. During World War II, when many of the battlefield casualties were due to psychiatric causes, military policy changed.

The concept of mental hygiene grew from efforts to provide direct treatment to service members (Seamone, 2011). Through an intensified effort to treat the underlying psychiatric disorders of combat-traumatized military personnel, military psychiatrists became aware of certain types of warriors who committed crimes as a direct result of their combat trauma. Army psychiatrist Major Harry L. Freedman championed the concept of the "Soldier-Patient" as a result of this recognition, promoting treatment and medical discharge with benefits in lieu of harsh punishment and punitive discharges for combat-traumatized veterans who committed offenses (Seamone, 2011, p. 94).

Over time, this formal recognition of criminal behavior as a manifestation of combat trauma took the form of a theory of *misconduct stress behavior.* This theory, which is espoused in a number of official combat-stress publications, recognizes that the strains and pressures of combat have the potential to enhance military efficiency but also result in violations of military discipline. "*Misconduct Stress,*" is accordingly defined as a "maladaptive stress reaction" occasioned by military operations (U.S. Department of Army, 2006, p. 1–5). Elspeth Cameron Ritchie, of the Army Surgeon General's Office, and other experienced military colleagues defined the concept in some detail:

> "*Maladaptive stress reactions,* which may be transient or persistent, include misconduct or behavioral disorders (e.g., depression or anxiety) that develop or are exacerbated as the result of deployment or combat stress. Stress-related misconduct is usually characterized by rule breaking or criminal behavior . . ." (Ritchie et al., 2008, p. 30).

Within combat and operational environments, misconduct stress can manifest itself in several ways, which are depicted in Figure 13, reproduced from the *Army Field Manual* 4-02.51 (FM 8-51), the *Combat and Operational Stress Control* manual:

The 2006 manual emphasizes that "Soldiers, however good and heroic, under extreme combat stress may also engage in misconduct" (pp. 1–5). The Army's 1994 Field Manual 22-51, *Leader's Manual for Combat Stress Control,* elaborates on each type of "misconduct stress," and cites "using excessive force," "fighting with [other] United States Forces," in addition to allies," and "refusing to obey an order" as additional examples of misconduct stress resulting from military operations (U.S. Department of Army, 1994, pp. 4–2 to 4–11, ¶¶ 4–5 to 4–18). As evident in the Figure, not only does the military recognize that combat conditions can and do directly result in atrocities, murder, and other acts of aggression and violent behavior, it further establishes that the precipitating combat conditions can manifest in

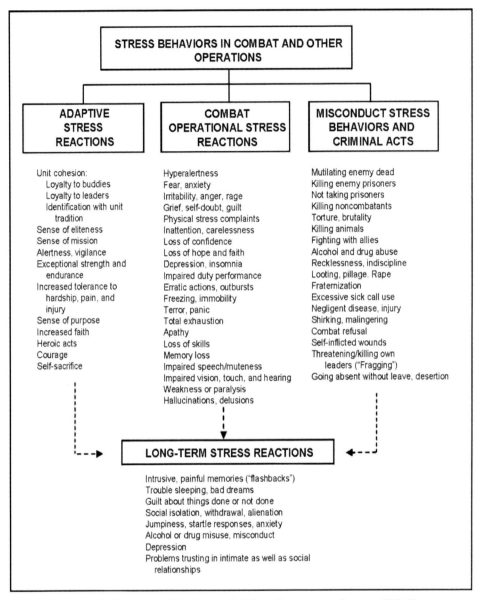

Figure 13. Stress Behaviors in Combat and Other Operations. Source: U.S. Department of the Army (2006, p. 1–6, fig. 1-3).

"long-term" disorders, including PTSD following the return to civilian society.

Along the lines of the Army's various manuals, in 2011, a military task force further recognized connections between crime and "complex dis-inhibitory behaviors" from mental health conditions sustained in combat occurring "months after the battlefield injury or trauma" (for example, "[d]ifficulty controlling one's emotions, including irritability and anger . . . , [s]elf-medica[tion] with . . . illicit drugs in an attempt to return to 'normalcy,' [and] reckless/high risk behaviors" (Task Force on Mental Health, 2007, p. 22). The Army published a detailed study of discipline called the *Goldbook,* in which the vice chief of staff explained that military leaders "cannot simply deal with health or discipline in isolation" because "these issues are interrelated and will require interdisciplinary solutions" (Chiarelli, 2012, Second Introductory Page).

Further, the Navy and Marine Corps' 2010 *Combat and Operational Stress Control* guide identified specific types of behaviors resulting from combat and other military experiences. Similar to the Army's conception of misconduct stress, the guide used different color bands to denote the category of behavior that characteristically results from "losses of control," including "violent images or thoughts that keep popping into awareness and can't easily be pushed aside," "intense and uncharacteristic anger," and "sudden outbursts of rage" (U.S. Department of Navy and U.S. Marine Corps, 2010, pp. 4–18). Collectively, these military sources support former Chairman of the Joint Chiefs of Staff Michael Mullen's position that, military service can propel a service member into conflict with the law based on the nature of his or her combat trauma transformation (Mullen, 2011).

Figure 14 depicts a variety of conditions related to combat and operational stress injuries that might ultimately contribute to criminal offenses by active duty service members and veterans, either alone or in combination.

While combat hardly accounts for all veterans' criminal offenses, and combat-traumatized veterans surely are capable of committing offenses as the result of conscious deliberation and behavior that has no connection to their disorders, the reality of combat and operational stress injuries underscores a number of unique factors that distinguish veteran offenders from the population of civilian offenders.

The experience of Sergeant Dwight Johnson is instructive on the reality of offending that relates to combat trauma as well as its manifestation of "depression-suicide" syndrome. At the age of twenty-one years, Specialist Dwight Johnson was serving as a member of a tank crew in the Vietnam's Kontum Province. His platoon came under attack from a battalion-size enemy force and erupted in flames after a firefight. Outgunned and overwhelmed by these forces, Johnson lost a number of his fellow soldiers in the attack. His struggles to return fire and rescue his severely burned comrades resulted in a condition of extreme combat stress. At one point, Johnson entered a state of pure, uncontrolled rage, during which he charged the enemy forces on his own, and repelled the attack, killing between five and

- • Self-Medication (Mainly for the Purpose of Sleeping or Relaxing)

- • Dissociative Episodes (Mistakenly Believing a Threat is Present)

- • Shattering of the Assumption that a Moral Order Exists (Right and Wrong)

- • Thrill- or Sensation-Seeking Behavior

- • Self-Punishment, including Depression-Suicide Syndrome

- • Moral Injury (Specifically the "Strike First" Mentality from Lack of Trust)

- • Revenge (Usually on Society or Symbols/Figures of Authority)

- • Decrease in Duty Performance (Missed Appointments, Outbursts)

- • Violent Behavior Occurring in Sleep or in Response to Vivid Nightmares

- • Adverse Reactions to Psychotropic Medications or Dosage Change

Figure 14. Nonexhaustive List of Operational Stress Injury Symptoms Often Related to Criminal Offending. Source: Brooker et al. (2012, pp. 251–260).

twenty of the enemy. Johnson was promoted to the rank of Sergeant and awarded the Congressional Medal of Honor, depicted in various photos of President Johnson placing the medal around his neck.

His story did not end in the White House. Upon his return to metropolitan Detroit, Johnson suffered from a severe case of the condition then known as post-Vietnam Syndrome. He was extremely conflicted over the fact that he earned the nation's highest award "for the one time in his life when he lost complete control of himself" (Lifton, 1992, p. 39, n.). He shared personal fears, "What would happen if I lost control of myself in Detroit and behaved like I did in Vietnam?" (Lifton, 1992, p. 39, n.). At the age of twenty-four, in April of 1971, Johnson died not by the bullet of an enemy soldier, but the bullet of a store clerk defending himself against a robbery Johnson perpetrated. In Johnson's *New York Times* obituary, his mother opined on the cause of her son's death, noting how, "Sometimes I wonder if [Sergeant Johnson was] tired of his life and needed someone else to pull the trigger" (Lifton, 1992, p. 39, n.). Although not all combat-traumatized veterans receive the Medal of Honor or engage in the same level of hostility, many fear what they might do as a result of their combat experiences, and a number of combat veterans end up in stand-offs with police as a result of their combat trauma (Etter, McCarthy, & Asken, 2011).

The Function of Help-Seeking Stigma as a Contributor to Criminal Conduct

As a special note, merely having suffered combat trauma and having an operational stress injury is not the major contributor to criminal offending. Instead, the real problems arise from the lack of diagnosis, and more importantly, the lack of effective treatment, which leads to aggravation of symptoms over time (Brown, 2010, p. 10). This is suggested by many criminally involved veterans who commit offenses years after their discharge. Failure to obtain treatment can result from a host of factors including denial, stigmas against seeking help, and the delayed onset of symptoms.

Many veterans who would otherwise qualify for benefits do not take advantage of them. In many instances, it is too painful for veterans to revisit traumatic experiences. Other times, it is the culturally instilled warrior ethos that makes veterans believe that they should be able to handle their symptoms on their own. While a number of veterans revealed the belief, "It's up to me to work out my problems" as a basis for not seeking treatment, those veterans who were recently arrested endorsed this opinion at a level 24 percent greater than non-arrested veterans (Elbogen, n.d., p. 23). Among the small population who do seek treatment, many commence it specifically because they fear the potential consequences of their own violent symptomatology. In fact, some veterans will distance themselves from spouses and children, literally retreating in isolation to the basement as a mechanism to protect their own family members from their violent impulses (Matsakis, 2007, p. 232).

Some of the same help-seeking stigmas exist during active military and the time period following discharge, such as the perception that the military or an employer will not provide the time to obtain necessary treatment. However, the realities of civilian life impose some different barriers, such as the lack of insurance to cover the costs of mental health treatment in the civilian sector (Elbogen, n.d., p. 22). For those on active duty, the stigmas of being seen as weak and the potential harm to one's career are so widespread that they arise in a nearly identical manner in the militaries of the United States, the United Kingdom, Canada, Australia, and New Zealand (Gould, Adler, & Zamorski, 2010). These factors all support estimates of an increasing number of veterans returning from combat with mental health concerns and subsequently becoming involved in the criminal justice system, as well recognition that many veterans will inevitably engage in criminal conduct.

G. Sexually-Based Offending and Interpersonal Violence Directly Related to Military Service and Direct Hostile Engagements

A substantial number of incarcerated veterans owe their sentences to sexual violence to the point where veteran offending has soared over three times the rate of civilian offending, marking violent sexual offenses as the only crimes that veterans commit at greater levels than civilians (Seamone et al., 2018b). In the population studied for the Bureau of Justice Statistics' 2007 report, 23 percent of veteran prisoners were sex offenders, compared to 9 percent of the general population (Noonan & Mumola, 2007, p. 1). Later, in a study of veterans incarcerated between 2011 and 2012, the Bureau found a variance of 35 percent compared to 23 percent, respectively (Bronson et al., 2015, p. 5). Interestingly, recent studies of incarcerated veterans in the United Kingdom reveal similar proportions of sex offenders in their prisons: "In England and Wales, 25 percent of ex-servicemen are in prison for sexual [offenses], compared to 11 percent of the civilian prison population" (Howard League for Penal Reform, 2011, p. 31).

These statistics might naturally lead one to question whether there are aspects of military service that contribute to sexual offending. The U.S. military's ongoing epidemic of sexual assault perpetrated by service members against fellow service members lends support to the existence of a connection. The year 2013, for example, marked another year in which sexual assault reports increased despite targeted and widespread efforts to prevent such acts. Accordingly, on May 17, 2013, the Army's Chief of Staff declared, "It is time we take on the fight against sexual assault and sexual harassment as our *primary mission*" (Odierno, 2013, p. 1). Sadly, it appears that in the years since that time, reporting of sexual assault has continued to rise, leading Defense Secretary Jim Mattis to characterize sexual assault as a metastasizing "cancer" in the military, which must not spread further (Gibbons-Neff, 2018).

The few studies of the effects of combat trauma on veterans' sexual behaviors focused upon Vietnam veterans and prisoners of war who reintegrated back with their families. Although there are consistent reports of major problems related to sexual functioning, including erectile dysfunction and premature ejaculation, the studies were limited in scope (Matsakis, 2007, p. 139).

In her comprehensive book, *Back from the Front: Combat Trauma, Love, and the Family,* clinical psychologist Aphrodite Matsakis provides significant insight on the connection between combat trauma and specific sexual behaviors, including those which are highly degrading and nonconsensual. The intention of this book is not to suggest that combat trauma should excuse sexual offending. However, like Matsakis, this chapter seeks to identify connections to criminal offending to help provide insight that will explain specific patterns of behavior that can be directly related to combat trauma. Without distinguishing these differences, it is far more difficult to address underlying causes of offending behavior both within the walls of the institution and following release.

Self-Medication with Sex

Sexual intercourse is a form of tremendous physical release that necessarily results in relaxation. For the combat veteran who experiences severe guilt, depression, or anxiety as symptoms of a combat or operational stress injury, the physical release from sexual activity can have a "sedative" effect and act as a temporary "tranquilizer" or "mood altering drug" (Matsakis, 2007, p. 153). Aside from physical relaxation, intercourse provides feelings of control, relief from personal insecurities, affirmation of a sense of agency and manhood, and relief from anxiety (Matsakis, 2007, p. 154). It essentially allows the veteran to regain much of what he lost on the battlefield. Sadly, these benefits are fleeting for those veterans who do not have other means of effective treatment. This often leads veterans who are capable of having sexual relationships to engage in relationships of sexual convenience or anonymity, or prostitution, as emphasized in one combat veterans' anonymous poem:

> Come here, lie with me
> And take away the pain
> Then go away
> I never want to see you again

> (Matsakis, 2007, p. 137)

Combat veterans experience a full range of sexual effects as a result of their wartime trauma. While many avoid sex altogether, others demand it as frequently as possible based on the nature of one's symptoms. Based on her many years of counseling combat veterans, Dr. Matsakis observes "sexual urgency" as a common result of combat trauma in which "the veteran rushes sex . . . wants to strictly control every sexual move, or in other ways enters into 'combat mode'" within the bedroom (2007, p. 152). Importantly, she acknowledges that many veterans can enter a survival and combat-ready mode in the bedroom based upon intimate situations. Combat-traumatized veterans may become "hypervigilant in the bedroom" (Matsakis, 2007, p. 150) because intimate scenarios often trigger the same types of fears that prompted the combat-ready mode while deployed (for example, "fear of being attacked or losing control") (Matsakis, 2007, p. 151).

The Legion of Charlies (Veitch & Irons, 1971), an underground comic produced during the Vietnam War, depicted this phenomenon. During the
course of an intimate moment in the bedroom with a prostitute named
Ronette, she protests, "Hey! Ease up! You're hurting me!" The veteran
responds, "Urg! I can't help it, Ronette! Every time I [engage in intercourse]
I find myself back at that ditch in My Lai, M-16 cocked and loaded!" (Veitch
& Irons, 1971, p. 263). As the flash-back intensifies, the veteran screams over
her protestations until eventually he has smashed and slammed her into
unconsciousness (Veitch & Irons, 1971, pp. 263–264). It is unclear whether
this fictional account was based on the writers' own experiences or representative accounts of veterans relayed to the writers.

Because sexual intimacy necessarily involves elements of vulnerability
with one's partner, combat-traumatized veterans frequently attempt to protect themselves in the bedroom by exerting physical and mental control over
their sexual partners. Methods may vary from directing the partner's every
move during sexual acts, limiting the amount of conversation and displays of
affection during physical contact, making the partner face away from the veteran, and other behaviors that easily include verbal and physical humiliation
and degradation of the sexual partner, including nonconsensual physical
aggression (Matsakis, 2007, pp. 151–163). While these factors do not account
for all veterans' sexual offenses, some sex crimes may be explained by the
veteran's maladaptive response to an "intense need . . . to combat depression
or anxiety or to forget not only war experiences but also current problems"
(Matsakis, 2007, p. 163).

While Dr. Matsakis' observations are based upon years of her treatment
of veterans and their families, systematic study of the phenomenon of compulsive sexual behavior by combat veterans with PTSD has begun to offer
empirical support (Seamone et al., 2018b). Compulsive sexual behavior (CSB)
can be defined broadly as "problematic sexuality," "sexual compulsivity,"
and "impaired self-control" which has components of: "1) a pattern of abnor-
mally frequent paraphilic (e.g., fetishism, sadism, pedophilia) or normaphilic
(e.g., sexual fantasies, sexual urges, intercourse, masturbation) thoughts and/
or actions, and 2) significant distress and/or life problems associated with
these thoughts and behaviors" (Krauss et al., 2017, p. 144).

Albeit the definition is broad and includes behaviors not associated with
sexual assault, the definition can encompass violent sexual assault (Seamone
et al., 2018b, p. 214). An initial study in 2014 revealed that PTSD afflicted
combat veterans are at elevated risk—"several fold higher"—for compulsive
sexual behavior compared to the general population (Smith et al., 2014, pp.
217, 219). Then, in 2017, an examination of 820 veterans who had deployed
to combat in the past revealed greater than expected levels of CSB among
those who suffered from anxiety and impulse-control disorders that ulti-

mately inhibited their ability to control their sexual behavior (Kraus et al., 2017, pp. 148, 153). The consequence of this research is clear: standardized methods to treat sex offenders may not address the underlying cause of the offending if the sexual assault resulted from combat-related trauma (Seamone et al., 2018b, p. 215).

Seamone and colleagues (2018b) have recommended reentry courts for veteran sex offenders to operate separate from veterans treatment courts but in a manner that enables connection to VA treatment for combat trauma.

Objectifying Attitudes

Combat trauma is not the only factor tied to military service, which may explain the high number of veteran sex offenders. British historian Clive Emsley recently described another contributing cause in his examination of military criminal offenses *Soldier, Sailor, Beggarman, Thief* (2013). Emsley observes that, especially within the combat infantry units, common experiences of retraining in combat-like conditions are often punctuated by periods of extreme boredom, during which troops are known to engage in a great amount of banter about sexual fantasies and sexual exploits (2013, p. 197). Within infantry units, particularly, which glorify brute force and other traits of hypermasculinity, sexual objectification of women, typecasting, and conquest is frequent. Psychologist Mic Hunter similarly observes:

> Certain attitudes related to masculinity have been found to be associated with increased propensity to sexual assault. A view of masculinity that emphasizes dominance, aggression, self-sufficiency, and willingness to take risks, combined with a rejection of compassion and empathy, is correlated with rape. These are the very values that have been promoted in military training. (2007, p. 42)

In the United Kingdom, members of the Royal Army often use the "decent" versus "dog" scale to determine their interests in women: "Decent girls were still sex objects but were treated and described differently. 'Dogs' were suitable for one-night-stands and their only positive attribute was the granting of more or less instant sexual access" (Emsley, 2013, p. 197). Regardless of the country, the end result is a desire to prove oneself to other male service members by the ease with which the troop can bed and take advantage of a potential sexual partner (Seamone et al., 2018b).

Emsley points to a sex crimes trial, in which the perpetrator, who was a paratrooper, acknowledged the significant effects of his and his unit's attitudes toward women and his resulting offense. The offender commented how it was not necessarily the military that encouraged this result, but rather how "that was done mostly by ourselves to ourselves" (2013, p. 196). Degrading attitudes like the ones exhibited by some members of the infantry and combat arms can promote a philosophy that "no" means "yes" and that the service member is entitled to obtain sexual gratification from a partner who is unwilling or unable to engage in intercourse either due to her conscious choice or her inability to consent as a result of intoxication.

Interpersonal Violence

Statistics suggest that military families experience interpersonal violence at a much greater rate than civilian families (Matsakis, 2007). However, the numbers still may underestimate the true incidence of these acts based upon family members' reluctance to report interpersonal violence for a host of reasons. These may include, for example, fear of retaliation or fear of the loss of military benefits for spouses and children that may discontinue following legal action. Inevitably, some military families suffer interpersonal violence as a result of a combat-traumatized veteran who suffers from PTSD or other psychiatric disorders that increase the risk of aggression (Elbogen et al., 2010, p. 598).

Common batterer-intervention models focus upon power, control, and sexism to eradicate biased assumptions and encourage acceptance of personal responsibility for adopting a more balanced approach (Kravetz, 2012, p. 195). With greater understanding of combat trauma, many courts and clinicians have recognized how some interpersonal violence may relate to symptoms of combat trauma rather than the desire to control and humiliate a partner or spouse (Seamone, 2012; Matsakis, 2007).

Through her work with countless military couples over the past decades of various wars, Dr. Matsakis has identified the traits and characteristics that distinguish "combat-related versus noncombat-related battering" (2007, p. 230). In the first example of combat-related battering, she explains, "In some cases, woman battering is the direct result of the vet's confusing his partner with enemy soldiers in the midst of a flashback or a paranoid state resulting from an extreme state of hyperarousal due to being severely triggered" (Matsakis, 2007, p. 230). In the second example, she observes, "In other cases, a wife or girlfriend may be assaulted because—without prior warning—she approached her veteran from behind, thus stimulating his startle response, which puts him into 'combat mode'" (Matsakis, 2007, pp. 230–231).

On a related note, domestic violence courts sometimes encounter a scenario in which the veteran struck his wife or girlfriend while awaking from a disturbed sleep state. Each of these assaultive behaviors is a "direct result of combat trauma" where the veteran, for any number of reasons, "automatically goes into 'survival mode,'" leaving "his abilities to accurately assess the situation, as well as . . . to control his verbal and physical aggressiveness . . . severely compromised" (Matsakis, 2007, p. 231).

Figure 15 depicts the first page of the pamphlet *Coming Home: What to Expect, How to Deal When You Return from Combat,* a publication produced under government contract to aid service members in understanding how combat can influence their family relationships and perceptions of threats at home (Jacobson & Colón, 2009, p. 1). It depicts the common scene of a mil-

Figure 15. Coming Home Pamphlet.

itary husband sleeping on the ground as he did in a combat environment with a bat within reach while his wife sleeps in the bed. Attuned to the slightest movement, the husband approaches the window expecting enemy contact in his own neighborhood. Common experiences like these substantially increase the risks that spouses, partners, and children will inadvertently become additional "casualties of the war" (Matsakis, 2007).

In response to the stark differences between forms of aggression, Dr. Matsakis highlighted the following four hallmarks to help identify combat-related battering (2007, p. 239):

Common Hallmarks of Combat-Related Battering

1. "Violence is infrequent";
2. Violence "is usually followed by prolonged periods of guilt, self-blame, and withdrawal from the partner";
3. Violence "is usually restricted to physical and emotional abuse and rarely involves economic, social, or other forms of abuse";
4. Violence "typically occurs during certain flashbacks to combat-related experiences in times of family loss or injury, or when the vet is feeling powerless over his emotions, his finances, his personal relationships, or some other aspect of his life."

These characteristics stand out in contrast to the controlling veteran batterer who "takes no responsibility for his actions and blames the victim for provoking them" (Matsakis, 2007, p. 239). While some argue that it is not worth the effort to distinguish between combat- and noncombat-related battering on the basis that such evaluation requires expertise that is not easily obtained and for fear of the message conveyed to victims (Kravetz, 2012), this chapter highlights the above points to place the issue in proper perspective by confirming that some battering is a direct result of combat trauma and has its roots in specific experiences that may require specialized attention to abate, beyond the treatment reserved for civilian offenders without similar experiences.

Criminal Offending Related to Cumulative Trauma

A final consideration in the connection between military service and criminal offending is the concept of cumulative trauma. Many recruits enlist in the military to escape a dangerous and abusive home life rife with physical, sexual and emotional abuse and exploitation (Seamone & Traskey,

2014). Service members who join to escape the gang life, may have seen relatives or friends gunned down in front of them. Cumulative trauma represents the effect of adding different forms of trauma over one's lifespan. It has been called "complex trauma" because it may be very difficult to disentangle different causes for the purpose of linking them to one's present symptoms (Seamone & Traskey, 2014).

Cumulative trauma can best be described with the following account: "[A] seasoned officer did not develop symptoms of PTSD until his third round of combat duty when he saw the corpse of a five-year-old girl lying on the side of the road." The trigger for the officer was that the dead child assumed a position that was identical to the final resting position of the officer's sister when she was killed in a drive-by-shooting that he witnessed at the age of four (Matsakis, 2007, p. 52). This is a primary example of the manner in which different stress triggers may be activated by events that do not, at least on their face, seem to have a direct connection to a given trauma type. Just as combat can intensify past child abuse (Matsakis, 2007, p. 52), a car accident might trigger suppressed combat trauma:

> A man who experienced abuse as a child and then served in a combat zone in war can start experiencing traumatic symptoms by witnessing a car accident years later. If none of his previous traumas were resolved, they may have been bubbling below the surface, waiting for one more traumatic event to occur before the symptoms exploded. (Catanese, 2010, p. 36)

There are two main lessons from cumulative trauma. First, it is definitely possible for criminal offending to result from the interaction of different trauma types, which still might relate to some element of military service. Second, when a combat veteran has experienced multiple types of trauma, each may need to be addressed separately using specific trauma-focused interventions to fully abate the types of symptoms that have contributed or can potentially contribute to criminal offending. This lesson is most evident in the Veterans Administration's efforts to treat military sexual trauma in veterans who were also separately traumatized by combat experiences. These "multiple trauma" veterans have significant needs that make their treatment much more challenging for mental health clinicians specifically because of the manifestations of symptoms and different triggers owing to one type of trauma versus the other (Matsakis, 2007). Treatment must be carefully planned to account for different trauma types over the veteran inmate's lifecourse, even if its scope is limited by the special constraints on mental health services within confinement facilities.

Treatment, Malingering, and Forensic Evaluation

Forensic psychologists and especially correctional professionals know better than most that inmates are often manipulative and that many may attempt to use supposed mental health conditions for personal gain, whether it means extra individualized attention from a sympathetic ear, removal from an unwanted work detail, or a sense of importance and control over correctional staff. Some might desire to second-guess an inmate's self-identified or presenting symptoms to prevent such secondary gain. It is vital to recognize that malingering comes in different forms. The term, in general, which coincidentally emerged from the military context, defines false presentation of mental illness (Nicholson & Martelli, 2007, p. 379).

Many correctional professionals may estimate that the great majority of inmates who profess mental health symptoms are malingering about their conditions, and numerous studies suggest incentives for criminal defendants to malinger to avoid responsibility for their crimes or severe penalties; yet, nearly all of the stories are anecdotal. In fact, when rigorous scientific protocols have been used, they reveal far fewer cases of malingering than expected. For example, Dr. Gerald Young observes, "[t]he assumption that litigation is a context that 'substantially' increases the likelihood of feigning is not supported by the data" (Young, 2007, pp. 145–146).

Beyond the fact that malingering is overestimated throughout the domains involving forensic mental health analysis, it is equally important to recognize that there are four major variants of malingering, only one of which relates to an entirely concocted account (Nicholson & Martelli, 2007, p. 380):

1. Fabrication of nonexistent symptoms;
2. Exaggeration of actual symptoms;
3. Extension of symptoms that have actually improved or resolved; and
4. Misattribution of or fraudulent attribution of symptoms to an injury or accident when they actually preceded or are otherwise unrelated to the accident/injury

Within mental health settings, a general rule is to err on the side of caution in addressing reports of symptomatology specifically because the presentation of mental illness likely represents some level of symptoms that should be addressed, even if they are not as severe as claimed. As the researchers explain, there may commonly be "exaggeration or accentuation of symptomatology due to other psychological or biological factors" besides intentional calculated misrepresentations (Nicholson & Martelli, 2007, p. 380).

Incarcerated veterans, as a collective group, face heightened risks of self-harm and suicide when compared to inmates in the general population (Wortzel, Binswanger, Anderson, & Adler, 2009). Veteran status adds yet another layer of risk as do any combat and operational stress injury symptoms that they may be experiencing while incarcerated. This is enough reason to address an incarcerated veteran's symptoms with more urgency.

Ironically, veterans with mental health needs often engage in a form of malingering called "dissimilation" or "faking good" whereby they purposely conceal or downplay the actual symptoms that they are experiencing (Budd & Harvey, 2006, p. 49). While many in corrections believe it is those inmates who need help the most who do not ask for it and those who do not need it who request it the most, this is particularly likely in the context of incarcerated veterans, providing a basis for more interest and effort to identify symptomatology. Surely, there is a more compelling reason to treat any self-identified mental health concerns as legitimate ones.

Concluding Remarks

This chapter's exploration of connections between military service, combat trauma, and offending highlights the fact that there are numerous pathways to violent and other unlawful behavior. Even without a full-blown PTSD diagnosis, if a veteran is experiencing just one of the many PTSD symptoms, this can significantly enhance risk, enough to the point where further evaluation should be undertaken. Additionally, risks may present simply based upon experiences with moral challenges, regardless of combat exposure. Correctional professionals should consider assessing inmates not only for military service but, for the types of experiences that frequently cause operational stress injuries. This includes participation in combat, intensity of combat operations, and other factors addressed above. While it may not be the optimal time to explore deployment history on the first moments of intake given the circumstances of arrest, these issues should be considered as part of classification and continued risk assessment over time.

The Veterans Administration Center for Health Care Evaluation conducted a comprehensive examination of various treatment programs in the 2013 Veterans Administration publication *A Structured Evidence Review to Identify Treatment Needs of Justice-Involved Veterans and Associated Psychological Interventions*. Although the review is not exclusively tailored to confinement-based programs, the publication is helpful for identifying a range of trauma-focused interventions and comparing their aims and capabilities. With incarcerated veteran inmates' mental health and readjustment needs in mind, the following chapter explores the evolution of corrections-based interventions and the hallmarks that distinguished them. The following chapters will discuss the nature of treatment programs developed specifically for veterans within correctional institutions. Of course, all the information in the previous chapters and the ones that follow will be useful for those who work with or wish to understand veterans both those inside and those outside of incarceration facilities.

Appendix A

PTSD Checklist-Military (PCL-M)
Government Work in the Public Domain

Patient's Name: _____

> Instruction to patient: Below is a list of problems and complaints that veterans sometimes have in response to stressful life experiences. Please read each one carefully, put an "X" in the box to indicate how much you have been bothered by that problem *in the last month*.

No.	Response	Not at all (1)	A little bit (2)	Moder-ately (3)	Quite a bit (4)	Extre-mely (5)
1	Repeated, disturbing *memories, thoughts, or images* of a stressful military experience from the past?					
2	Repeated, disturbing *dreams* of a stressful military experience from the past?					
3	Suddenly *acting* or *feeling* as if a stressful military experience *were happening* again (as if you were reliving it)?					
4	Feeling *very upset* when *something reminded* you of a stressful military experience from the past?					
5	Having *physical reactions* (e.g., heart pounding, trouble breathing, or sweating) when *something reminded* you of a stressful military experience from the past?					
6	Avoid *thinking about* or *talking about* a stressful military experience from the past or avoid *having feelings* related to it?					
7	Avoid *activities* or *situations* because they *remind you* of a stressful military experience from the past?					
8	Trouble *remembering important parts* of a stressful military experience from the past?					

No.	Response	Not at all (1)	A little bit (2)	Moder -ately (3)	Quite a bit (4)	Extre- mely (5)
9	Loss of *interest in things that you used to enjoy*?					
10	Feeling *distant or cut off* from other people?					
11	Feeling *emotionally numb* or being unable to have loving feelings for those close to you?					
12	Feeling as if your *future* will somehow be *cut short*?					
13	Trouble *falling* or *staying asleep*?					
14	Feeling *irritable* or having *angry outbursts*?					
15	Having *difficulty concentrating*?					
16	Being *"super alert"* or watchful on guard?					
17	Feeling *jumpy* or easily startled?					

Appendix B

Combat Stress Barometer
© 1996 Jonathan Shay
Reprinted with Permission
(Shay, 1996, pp. 117–112)

Combat Stress Barometer—Recording How Bad and How Often

[Filled in examples are on the next page]

To give you the best possible advice on medications, we need to know what you have been going though. The Combat Stress Barometer is a monthly monitor of the things that often cause suffering to Vietnam combat veterans. Please read each item carefully, and then tag each one with the code for *how bad* each was for you *at its worst* in the last month, and *how often* in the last month it has been a problem for you at all. Make two passes through each item.

The **first pass** is for how bad each problem was at its worst, use the letters—N, M, I, S, E—to code how bad each item was at its worst:

N = Never, In the last month this never bothered you at all. If you mark "Never" in the first box go on to the next item, skipping the second pass. Leave "Never" items blank on the second pass.

M = Mild, it was there, but it didn't cause much distress or get in the way of whatever you were doing or wanted to do. This is something you feel you can live with and maybe are even used to it, but you know your life would be better if it were gone.

I = Intermediate, it caused definite distress or got in the way of what you were doing or wanted to do, but you could deal with it. When this has happened you were able to manage, using your *regular* resources of strength, self-respect, nerve, self-control, sense of reality, endurance, control of your own mental functions, or ability to relax and sleep.

S = Severe, it caused great distress or badly upset what you were doing or wanted to do. Overcoming it called on all your resources just to stay even with where you were in your life this last month.

E = Extreme, it caused overwhelming distress and for a time totally crippled what you were doing or wanted to do. Your ability to deal with rage, fear, guilt, and to be sure of what was real was overwhelmed. You did real harm to your relationships, to yourself or your own best interests, or to someone else—or avoided these purely by luck. You don't know if you can get through it again without hurting yourself or someone else.

Here is a filled-in example for *how bad* the following item was *at its worst* for a veteran.

		How Bad Bad (or Never)	1-2 Per Month	Weekly	1-2 Per Week	Daily Or Almost Daily
A.	"Superalert," or watchful or on guard?	1				

Example A: Pretty much every day in the last month you were careful about your surroundings, walking your perimeter every night before you lock up and noticing every person on the street with you in front and behind on both sides of the street, even on your own block, which you think is not quite safe. This is what you're used to, but

> you'd like to be able to let down when it's safe. One night this month was pretty bad, getting no sleep at all because you felt you had to keep yourself awake in a corner of your room where you can scan the door and windows at a glance. You were wired for days after that.

This instrument, by Jonathan Shay, may be reproduced without charge and freely distributed, as long as no funds are exchanged.

The **second pass** through each item is for how often you have suffered from that sort of thing in the last month. "How often" means how often that happened to you *at all*, without looking at whether it was mild, intermediate, severe, or extreme—the second pass is just for how often it has happened in any intensity or severity. If you marked "Never" on the first pass, leave this item blank.

Here is Example A again, with *both* how bad and how often filled in:

		How Bad Bad (or Never)	1-2 Per Month	Weekly	1-2 Per Week	Daily Or Almost Daily
A.	"Superalert," or watchful or on guard?	1				X

The Combat Stress Barometer is important for your treatment. It helps us keep track of how you are doing over time. You will help us to help you if you complete it thoughtfully and honestly every month. It will take less time as you get more familiar with it. Don't hesitate to ask for help from a group leader or another veteran in the group. More filled in illustrations of the use of the Combat Stress Barometer.

		How Bad Bad (or Never)	1-2 Per Month	Weekly	1-2 Per Week	Daily Or Almost Daily
B.	Thought about people who died when you didn't, and *feeling that you should have died instead?*	E				X

Example B: Not a day goes by that you don't think of your friend who had a fever and asked you to switch his ambush duty for your bunker watch. Out on the ambush, you could see the flashes of rockets hitting the firebase. When you got back in you learned that he had been killed in the bunker. Every day you think, "It should have been me." You've thought this every day for the last 23 years, and the ache is so much a part of every day that you hardly notice it.

		How Bad Bad (or Never)	1-2 Per Month	Weekly	1-2 Per Week	Daily Or Almost Daily
C.	Suddenly acting, feeling, or perceiving (sights, sounds, smells) as if your military experiences *were happening again?*	E				X

Example C: About once a week last month, people all began to look like Vietnamese to you on the bus going home from work. Each time, you broke into a sweat and held it together until your stop by looking closely at each face and realizing that (except for some real Orientals once) this was not so. One time last month it suddenly got so bad that you bolted off the bus past another passenger getting out, and decided to walk home, because you didn't want to get back on a bus just then. The next day was OK.

Be sure to put your name and the date at the top of each page.
Complete your Barometer for this month on the page that follows.

name: date:	How Bad Bad (or Never)	1-2 Per Month	Weekly	1-2 Per Week	Daily Or Almost Daily
1. Felt anxious if someone *got to know you well*?					
2. Trouble remembering important parts of your experiences in the Service?					
3. Avoided situations or activities *because you thought you would not be able to control* angry words or actions?					
4. Felt jumpy or easily startled?					
5. *Involuntary and disturbing* memories of your military service? (Do not count if you *chose* to recall the memories, or if *not* disturbing.)					
6. *Wanted to off yourself* or set someone up to take you out, or looked for danger in the hope of getting lucky?					
7. Thought about people who died when you didn't, and *feeling that you should have died instead*?					
8. Avoided activities or situations *because they reminded you of Vietnam*? (Include preparing yourself ahead of time with alcohol, etc.)					
9. Felt emotionally numb, or unable to have loving feelings for those close to you?					
10. Felt like you no longer had the strength to keep it all together?					
11. Avoided *people who pressure you.* (Include zoning out by replaying combat memories, preparing yourself with alcohol, etc.)					
12. Repetitive *dreams that replay the same way* every time, just like a film?					
13. Avoided *thinking about* military experiences, *or having feelings* about them? (Include using alcohol, etc., or staying too busy to think or feel.)					
14. Felt overwhelmed by all the pressures on you?					
15. Avoided people, situations, or activities *because you were afraid you would begin crying*?					
16. Felt *emotionally upset* when something happened that reminded you of your military experiences? (Include combat anniversaries.)					

17. Felt anxious if someone got to *matter too much* to you, or you mattered too much to the other person?				
18. Loss of interest in activities *that you used to enjoy?*				
19. Avoided situations or activities *because you were afraid you'd "lose it" and go berserk?*				
20. Felt two inches tall or like a piece of shit?				
21. Felt irritable, had angry outbursts, went off on people?				
22. *Wanted to cry*, but were not able to?				
23. Had *bodily reactions* when something reminded you of your military experiences?				
24. *Drove away someone who was getting too close* by scaring, hurting, or picking a fight with the other person?				
25. Disturbing *dreams* of your military experience?				
26. Felt like you wanted to hurt someone badly or kill that person?				
27. "Superalert," or watchful or on guard?				
28. Felt so tired of struggling in a hopeless situation that you thought you'd be better off dead?				
29. Trouble falling or staying asleep?				
30. Avoided pleasures, injured yourself or things you valued *because you didn't deserve them?*				
31. Felt hopeless and despaired that anything can improve or succeed for you?				
32. Felt like nothing meant anything any more, that *nothing mattered enough even to want to do it?*				
33. Had trouble with forgetfulness, couldn't remember things you wanted to do?				
34. Avoided situations or activities *because you knew you wouldn't be able to watch your back?*				
35. Thought about joining the dead, had dreams or visions of the dead beckoning to you?				
36. Suddenly acted, felt, or perceived (sights,				

sounds, smells) as if your military experiences *were happening again?*					
37. Did things to other people *before you even had a chance to think*, like automatic reactions?					
38. Thought about, reproached yourself, or felt *like you deserved to be punished* for things you did or failed to do during your military service?					
39. Avoided going to sleep *to avoid dreams, feelings, or actions that happen while you are asleep?* (Include knocking yourself out w/ alcohol, etc.)					
40. Had difficulty concentrating?					
41. *Felt betrayed* by a person, group, or institution you used to trust and respect?					
42. Felt distant or cut off from other people?					
43. Avoided situations or activities because you thought you or someone else *would do something that would leave you feeling like a piece of shit?*					
44. Felt sad, blue, down in the dumps?					
45. Felt as if *your future will be cut short*, that you will die prematurely, perhaps soon?					
46. *Pumped up with adrenalin*, just like in a firefight.					

Feedback on the Combat Stress Barometer (Use backs if you need more space):

Are these items close enough to your experience that you feel that you've given a good picture of things that have caused you suffering in the last month?

Which items are off-target (use item numbers if you like) and you think should be *dropped?*

What items would you *add* to get closer to the experience of Vietnam combat Veterans?

No printed questions, no matter how good, can get at the heart of an individual's experience, which is always unique. What do we need to know about your experience in the last month that you feel is totally missed in the Barometer?

Chapter 5

GRATITUDE WITH LIMITATIONS: A SUMMARY OF VETERANS' BENEFITS AND OUTREACH DURING PERIODS OF INCARCERATION

I. IMPACT ON VETERANS ALREADY RECEIVING BENEFITS AT THE TIME OF INCARCERATION

Incarcerated veterans face a number of obstacles that are not present for other inmates.

Discontinuation of medical care from the VA during the period of incarceration.

Suspension of VA pension benefits on and after the 61st day of a sentence for a misdemeanor or felony.

Suspension or reduction of VA disability compensation benefits on and after the 61st day of sentence for a felony.

Repayment status for all overpayments occurring during incarceration, severely impeding reentry.

The potential for reduced disability rating during incarceration or the requiement for reevaluation of disability rating following release from confinement.

These special rules have the greatest impact on those veterans who have already established eligibility for benefits, received disability ratings, and were receiving specialized care from the Veterans Administration at the time of their incarceration.

A. 38 C.F.R. § 17.38(c)(5)'s Resulting Discontinuity of Care

Of all concerns related to veterans receiving Veterans Administration benefits, discontinuity of care is paramount. Since 1999, 38 C.F.R. § 17.38(c)(5) is a regulatory provision that has prohibited inpatient or outpatient healthcare that would overlap with services that are the responsibility of the incarcerating entity. The genesis of this rule was a 1986 congressional amendment to 38 U.S.C. § 1710(g), now existing as subsection (h), which confirmed that Veterans Administration hospitals were not required to "furnish care to a veteran to whom another agency of federal, state, or local government has a duty under law to provide care in an institution of such government." However, this was not an outright prohibition and a number of hospitals disregarded it.

For example, in New York, the Canandaigua Veterans Administration Medical Center sent a medical team to the Groveland Correctional Facility to operate a PTSD treatment program for incarcerated veterans that used nearly identical treatment protocols on the inmates at the prison as they did in the treatment of veterans in the community (see Chapter 8). Service delivery varied at this time, based upon a combination of correctional administrators' willingness to allow for transport to medical centers and a given Veterans Administration Medical Center's ability and willingness to divert staff from non-incarcerated veterans to incarcerated veterans.

On balance, during this time, treatment of inmate veterans' mental health conditions was largely "the exception rather than the rule" (Brown, 1989, p. 31). In fact, among the few programs providing direct services, they "tend[ed] to be arbitrary, and/or the initiative of a particular Vet Center counselor and/or team leader" and hardly represented any uniform policy (Smith, 1990, p. 48). The 1999 rule clearly established strict limitations, which led to the hasty withdrawal of many Veterans Administration clinicians from individual and group counseling venues and permitted continued contact mainly for the limited purpose of transitional counseling for periods following release from confinement.

Although prisons and jails have a duty to provide healthcare for psychiatric conditions, investigations, books, and court cases have highlighted the severe budgetary and personnel limitations on the quality of such care (e.g., Dretsch, 2013). Indisputably, jails and prisons are not in a position where they are capable of providing the same quality of resource-and time-intensive mental health care as the Veterans Administration. Regardless of how acute the veterans' symptoms or how successful their treatment was prior to incarceration, the veteran inmates will be ineligible for health care from the Veterans Administration until release, creating a likelihood of unwanted side-effects stemming from a lack of continuity in or discontinuation of health-care during transitions between health care systems (Wortzel et al., 2009, p. 88).

B. Limitation on Monetary Benefits

1. Pension and Compensation Benefits

The Veterans Administration administers numerous benefits programs for veterans, which notably include vocational rehabilitation programs, vehicle allowances, and other vouchers and stipends for any number of reasons (Brooker et al., 2012, pp. 42–51). Two benefits that are directly impacted by incarceration include pension benefits and disability compensation benefits. Even though veterans may be eligible for both of these programs (for different reasons), they must elect between the two and usually receive the one that equates to a greater monthly payment (Conly, 2005, pp. 23–24). These two payments exist for entirely different purposes.

The Veterans Administration pension is intended to assist the veteran who served the nation during a time of war and who either has a very significant non-service related disability that makes it impossible to work or who has attained the age of sixty-five, regardless of disability status. Congress made wartime service the pivotal factor for this benefit on the basis that many veterans were forced to put their careers on hold to serve the nation in a time of war and accordingly lost the opportunity to maximize their financial gain at times when funds are most necessary (Costello, 2012, p. 423). One's Veterans Administration pension will be adjusted based on the veteran's income from other sources, including spousal income if the veteran is married. The veterans will be ineligible to receive pension benefits if they earn more than a given amount within the Maximum Annual Pension Rate category, such as the 2018 rate of $13,166 without a spouse or child and $17,241 with one dependent (U.S. Department of Veterans Affairs, 2018).

As contrasted with the Veterans Administration pension, Veterans Administration disability compensation exists to provide income to the veteran in relation to an injury that was either initially caused by active duty military service or aggravated by such service (Costello, 2012, pp. 423–424). If the veterans are able to meet the hurdles of proving this causation and service-connection, they will be compensated according to a rating scale that compensates for impaired earning potential proportional to the disability rate from 10 to 100 percent.

Veterans Administration disability compensation is unique when contrasted with other federal benefits because it is the only form of compensation that is not impacted by other independent sources of income. Often, the ability to combine these payments with other forms of compensation enables recipients to pay for alternative medical care and achieve a much higher quality of living (Sayer et al., 2011). In 2018, the monthly 10 percent level disability compensation payment for a veteran with or without dependents is $136.24, the 100 percent level payment for a veteran without children is $2,973.86, and the 100 percent level payment for a veteran and spouse and child is $3,261.10. Figure 16, provides some additional examples for further clarification. Importantly, the Veterans Administration can rate PTSD and other combat-related psychiatric conditions up to the 100 percent disability rating level based on the impairment of the symptoms.

Both Veterans Administration pensions and disability compensation payments are severely impacted by incarceration. The Veterans Administration

Examples of 2018 Monthly VA Disability Payments Based on Rating

Rating	30%	50%	70%	100%
Veteran Alone	$417.15	$855.41	$1,365.48	$2,973.86
Veteran with Parent	$456.15	$921.41	$1,458.48	$3,106.92
Veteran with Only Child	$450.15	$910.41	$1,442.48	$3,084.75

Figure 16. Source: Military Benefits Info, 2018.

provides a "grace period" of two months during which a *sentenced* veteran can still obtain benefits while incarcerated (National Coalition of Homeless Veterans, n.d., p 16). This provision has been in effect regarding pensions since the effective date of legislation on June 1, 1957 ("Law Changed on Pension Benefits," 1957, p 3). Importantly, no such limitation exists for veterans held while awaiting sentence or veterans committed as a result of a verdict of not guilty by reason of insanity (Conly, 2005, p. 22). It is unknown how many veterans have been able to use Veterans Administration benefits during the short grace period because many confinement facilities control the manner in which veterans are able to cash checks and use money. The limitation of Veterans Administration benefits over time evolved alongside efforts to curtail or terminate other federal benefits during incarceration, such as those administered by the Social Security Administration, and likely gained momentum as correctional approaches shifted from a rehabilitative to a punitive model (Beeler, 2007, p. 62). In this light, a popular position endorsed by many veterans and correctional officers is that criminally involved veterans do not deserve any compensation because it would be an undeserved reward (May, 1979, p. 12).

Over time, the Veterans Administration policy resulted in different results with more severe limitations on Veterans Administration pension benefits than on the Veterans Administration disability compensation. Following the two-month grace period, on the sixty-first day of a sentence for a felony or a misdemeanor, the Veterans Administration is supposed to suspend all pension benefits. Likewise, on the sixty-first day of a *felony* sentence, the Veterans Administration is supposed to reduce all disability compensation benefits. Importantly, disability "[c]ompensation benefits are not reduced if one is imprisoned for a *misdemeanor*" (Veterans Administration Benefits Assistance Service, 2012, p. 1).

For the felons who are disability recipients, if they are compensated at a rate above the 10 percent level, payment is reduced to the 10 percent rate. Alternatively, if the veteran has a 10 percent disability rating at the time of incarceration, payments are halved, since the Veterans Administration does not have a 5 percent disability payment rate (Addlestone & Chaset, 2009, p. 341). In either case of pension or disability compensation limitations, it is vital to understand that these effects are temporary in nature. Too often, due to one's own misunderstanding about the rules, misinformation from other inmates, or misinformation from correctional professionals, veterans frequently believe that their benefits are terminated for good after they have been incarcerated (May, 1979, p. 9).

There are special considerations regarding the process by which benefits cease and by which they resume. Many recipients of Veterans Administration benefits purposely do not reveal their veteran status to corrections personnel in hopes that their benefits will continue (Rosenthal & McGuire, 2013, p. 358). In fact, this is one factor why statistics on incarcerated veterans in the nation's prisons and jails are severely underestimated. Even if veterans are successful in concealing their status, various safeguards are supposed to identify veterans in prisons and jails.

After the Social Security Administration collects incarceration data, it is responsible for transmitting such information to the Veterans Administration's Benefits Delivery Center, which is then responsible for notifying the respective Regional Office that is responsible for administering an incarcerated veteran's benefits (Conly, 2005, p. 24). Evident in the multitude of entities that are involved in this process, a number of factors may prevent the Veterans Administration from obtaining or acting on information if the veteran does not take independent action to provide prompt notice of incarceration status. Inevitably, the incarcerated veteran faces overpayment status, which results in forfeiture of owed benefits upon release until the debt is fully recouped: "If the VA continues to pay after 61 days, the VA should be told to stop so the vet can avoid an overpayment, which will be recouped by the VA from payments made after the vet's release from prison" (Addlestone & Chaset, 2009, p. 342). This overpayment status effectively eviscerates the opportunity for meaningful and effective reentry following release, and forces many families to go on public assistance, including welfare and food stamps (Woods, 1990, p. 57).

2. Apportionment of Reduced or Discontinued Benefits for Family Members or Dependents

One of the major justifications offered for reduced or discontinued Veterans Administration benefits is that the veteran essentially has no living expenses while incarcerated and is provided with all of the essentials that monetary payments were intended to provide for (Pentland & Scurfield, 1982, p. 23). This theory of "double-dipping" does not provide a complete explanation for disability compensation limitations because such funds are paid without respect to other sources of income—even if a veteran is able to pay for all of life's essentials from a separate pot of money (Pentland & Scurfield, 1982, p. 23). Even if the motivation for substantial reduction of benefits is explained more by the desire to punish a criminal, the Veterans Administration has created an important allowance specifically to provide for the financial needs of family members or dependents who are negatively impacted by the reduction of the incarcerated veteran's payments. Qualifying individuals are able to receive whatever portion of the veteran's pension or compensation benefits are suspended or discontinued as a result of incarceration past the grace period.

The caveat here is that this apportionment is not automatic (Addelstone & Chaset, 2009, p. 341). Whether the request originates from the incarcerated veteran or the intended recipient, the family member or dependent will be required to demonstrate that they depend on the veteran's income and will further be required to provide substantiating financial records to establish such need (National Coalition for Homeless Veterans, n.d.). This information is vital for social workers who work with families with incarcerated veterans.

3. Reinstatement of Reduced or Discontinued Benefits

Veterans Administration pension or disability payments are normally reinstated and backdated to the first day of one's release from confinement as long as the veteran applies for reinstatement within a year of release. For Veterans Administration purposes, entry into a half-way house, parole, and participation in a work-release program are considered to terminate one's sentence of incarceration (Veterans Administration Benefits Assistance Service, 2012, p. 2). In theory, the Veterans Administration should approach reinstatement with the same fervor as reduction or suspension of benefits. However, experience cautions against reliance on the Veterans Administration to take action independent of a certificate of release (Addlestone & Chaset, 2009, p. 343) or other confirmations of a pending release date from prison officials (Veterans Benefits Administration, Benefits Assistance Service, 2012, p. 2).

Some factors may prevent swift reinstitution of benefits even where the notice is received in a timely manner. For example, depending on the length of one's incarceration, the Veterans Administration may require the veteran to undergo a medical evaluation to determine whether the injury still exists or whether it became less severe over time. While some commentators note that it is theoretically possible for such evaluations to reveal aggravation of a compensable injury leading to an increase in one's rating (Beeler, 2007, p. 62), others highlight that the process may delay benefits or substantially reduce them following release from incarceration (Addlestone & Chaset, 2009, p. 342). Furthermore, if there is a valid arrest warrant from another jurisdiction, this may prevent any benefit reinstatement from the Veterans Administration (Beeler, 2007, p. 62).

4. G.I. Bill Educational Benefits

The G.I. Bill remains one of the major incentives for new recruits to join the military. With rapidly rising costs of higher education, this benefit provides an unparalleled means of social mobility, and represents the only way that many Americans will be able to afford the high costs of college if they are not independently wealthy. G.I. Bill benefits not only include the cost of tuition, but they also provide monetary stipends to cover the costs of living. Even though these cash payments are supposed to further one's education, veterans routinely used these funds to assist their families, especially when unemployed and especially when incarcerated.

Unlike the limitations on pension and disability payments, G.I. Bill benefits remained unscathed through the 1970s. Opponents offered a number of reasons to strip incarcerated veterans of their cash stipends, including fears that the payments would fund illegal enterprises in jails and prisons (May, 1979), or misplaced concerns that the families who receive surplus money may already be collecting welfare benefits from the state to cover living expenses arising from imprisonment of a spouse ("Claims 'rip-off' in G.I. Bill benefits," 1976, p. 13).

In the face of these attacks, Senator Robert Dole sponsored a bill to strip incarcerated veterans of educational payments on the basis that "the amendment would correct the 'blatant discrimination' of jailed veterans getting higher [educational stipends] than active duty personnel" using their G.I. Bill benefits prior to discharge (Veterans Benefits, 1980, p. 4). In February 1980, a majority of senators (66 to 28) resisted the temptation largely in recognition that "[v]eterans who have been imprisoned continue to receive G.I. Bill educational aid, on the rationale that any surplus payment can be set aside to help the prisoners' dependents or ease their transition back to society and curb recidivism" ("Veterans Benefits," 1980, p. 4). Senator Alan Cranston and others based their rejection of the amendment on the basis that "the amendment added punishment by taking benefits earned though meritorious service of men and women who later ran afoul of the law" (Veterans Benefits, 1980, p. 4).

The tide began to shift, however. According to historian Myra MacPherson, incarcerated veterans soon became "peculiarly" targeted for elimination of federal benefits as part of "the public's rage" over the fact that convicted serial "Son of Sam" murderer David Berkowitz was receiving federal benefits while incarcerated (1992, p. 582). In the early 1980s, legislators mobilized with various bills to cut all federal aid to prisoners soon after it was reported that Berkowitz applied for veteran's aid above and beyond the Social Security benefits he was already receiving (Pienciak, 1980, A10). It took little impetus for them to seize on the pervasive whacko and violent veteran myths enveloping recently returned Vietnam veterans (see Chapter 3). For this combination of reasons, the bow broke and educational stipends for incarcerated veterans ceased a short time later.

"The VA will pay only for tuition, fees, necessary books, equipment, and supplies not otherwise paid for by a government agency" (Addlestone & Chaset, 2009, p. 344).

Beyond the serious reduction in Veterans Administration educational benefits, the new legislation inspired by Berkowitz further imposed additional duties on the Veterans Administration and other federal agencies to monitor incarcerated veterans and other beneficiaries solely for the purpose of shutting-off payments (Brigham, 1989, p. 41).

The instrumental role of Veterans Administration pension, compensation, or educational benefits should not be underestimated. Oftentimes, these payments are indelibly linked with child support payments and other obligations that extend far beyond the veteran. While the rules often appear simple and certain on their face, they are inherently complex to understand in practice due to various factors, such as sporadic legislative and regulatory changes in policy, the failure to update other provisions in the face of new and different wars and types of injury, and inconsistent application of adjudicatory standards by adjudicators in different Veterans Administration regional offices (Reed, 2009). As a result of this combination of factors, Veterans Administration benefits experts warn that no case is ever easy. Most require assistance from an experienced veterans service officer or lawyer (National Coalition for Homeless Veterans, n.d., pp. 17–18), and they caution that veterans are not best served by approaching benefits issues alone because of the almost inevitable temptation to see the "forest" at the cost of the "trees" due to "incomplete and often conflicting information received by the veterans in their own dealings" (Waite, 2008, p. 14).

II. Prospective Veterans Administration Benefits for New Applicants

While the veteran already in receipt of Veterans Administration benefits faces significant hardships as a result of incarceration, the prospective applicants are not as limited and they benefit substantially from a term of incarceration, during which they can perfect an application and pass time with fewer detrimental effects given the basic amenities provided by incarceration, such as housing and meals.

> **Incarcerated ex-service members are not prevented from: (1) obtaining information to inform them about benefit eligibility; (2) from initially applying for benefits; or (3) from applying for physical disability evaluations; (4) from requesting an apportionment of benefits; or (5) from applying for an increase in existing disability ratings (Addlestone & Chaset, 2009, p. 342).**

Each of these actions may be severely complicated by particular challenges that include:

Seven Nuances Complicating VA Benefit Eligibility and Ratings Determinations

1. The requirement for service in a time of war for pension applicants;
2. Expert opinion on the veteran's inability to work and extent of impairment;
3. Establishing service-connected injuries for disability compensation applicants;
4. Delays in processing of applications;
5. Character of discharge determinations for ex-service members separated with any discharge other than Honorable or General (see also Chapter 2 of this book);
6. Injuries relating to the veteran's own willful misconduct;
7. Lost or destroyed military records.

Source: Costello (2012, pp. 424–429).

In pursuing these privileges, prospective applicants who are incarcerated are at an advantage for two major reasons. The first reason is legal in nature and takes the form of a unique "duty to assist rule," which obligates the Veterans Administration to take active measures in assisting veterans in perfecting their applications in some very important respects, such as communicating with the veteran, providing adequate notice, and assisting the veteran in obtaining records that might substantiate the claim (Hager, 2009). The veterans' benefits courts have even provided suggestions for regional offices to assist incarcerated veterans if the confinement facility will not permit the veteran to obtain a health assessment at a Veterans Administration Medical Center (Hager, 2009). Other related rules also help veterans, such as the "benefit-of-the-doubt" rule in which "reasonable disagreements are resolved in favor of the veteran" when decisions are close (Berenson, 2009, p. 23).

For initial VA benefit applications, it is essential to ensure that an application is complete and thoroughly supported with the type of documentation and corroborating evidence requested by the VA. While it may take months to process the application, appeals of denied benefits commonly require three-to-five years' time (Underhill, 2011, p. 27).

Even with the extra assistance and deference owed to Veterans Administration applicants, the truth remains that the practical reality of confinement will limit the amount and quality of assistance that the Veterans Administration and a prison or jail can provide to an incarcerated veteran versus one who is not incarcerated. As a former Director of the Veterans' Assistance Service once observed, "Benefits programs to veterans who are incarcerated are limited by law, as well as by the circumstances of incarceration" (Brigham, 1990, p. 36).

To a large extent, the Veterans Administration's ability to assist incarcerated applicants in obtaining medical evaluations depend in great part upon the correctional institution's capacity to provide security during transport to and from the facility and during the interface with Veterans Administration medical personnel (Cleland, 1979, pp. 463–464). In some cases, inmates seeking evaluations apparently had to go out-of-pocket paying exorbitant fees to hire private security personnel to accompany them because Veterans Administration rules limited any service to an inmate unless there were personnel on hand to ensure responsibility for oversight of the offender (Brown, 1990, p. 31). In the advent of videoconferencing and other arrangements over time, greater opportunities exist to provide veterans with a sufficient amount of assistance for the Veterans Administration to meet its various obligations (Hager, 2009). However, any interface with other governmental agencies will inevitably be subject to a given institution's operational realities and requirements.

III. Secretary Shinseki's "Surge" and Incarcerated Veterans: Outreach Reentry Planning to Decrease Veteran Homelessness

The second reason the prospective applicant for Veterans Administration benefits currently fares better than the established recipient owes to intensified outreach efforts to assist incarcerated veterans. The intensity of outreach efforts to incarcerated veterans has varied substantially over the years with a magnificent start in the 1920s, a minimal effort following the Second World War, an abysmal response in the advent of Vietnam, a brief peak of interest through the early 80s, and a second retreat from incarcerated veterans until 2004 through the present, which can be classified as a revival of ingenuity. Collectively these periods reveal major shifts in priorities and other social forces.

While present efforts to assist veterans represent tremendous strides in effective community reentry, an incarcerated veteran still must survive the period of incarceration and remain free from significant mental degradation to benefit from transition services.

- Being incarcerated ranks alongside being tortured or exposed to combat as a potential cause of persistent psychological dysfunction (Richardson, Thompson, Boswall, & Jetly, 2010, p. 430).
- "[T]he incarceration experience is a significant, stressful life event, even for those who do not have mental illness" (U.S. Department of Defense & U.S. Department of Veterans Affairs, n.d., p. 1).
- Therefore, the effect of incarceration on the combat-traumatized veteran requires even more emphasis on treatment during confinement than in the time following eventual release.

While reentry counseling is helpful, it is entirely insufficient to respond to the demonstrated needs of incarcerated veterans. The Veterans Administration's major justification for withholding direct healthcare services from incarcerated veterans has been the fear that these services would detract from the ability to serve the treatment needs of unincarcerated special-needs veterans. Ironically, the inevitable aggravation of mental health conditions during incarceration without effective treatment capabilities generates substantially greater burdens on Veterans Administration service providers upon the veterans' release, inevitably detracting from those other unincarcerated special-needs veterans. For this reason, specifically, this chapter concludes on an optimistic note from the 1920s, when the original intention of the Veterans' Bureau regarding outreach to veterans was crystal clear.

A. The Inception and Evolution of Veterans Administration's Outreach Efforts for Incarcerated Veterans

1. Post-World War II to 1960 (Minimal and Ineffective Outreach)

Veterans Administration representatives suggest that the roots of efforts to assist incarcerated veterans can theoretically be traced to 1910, when the federal government initiated efforts to conduct outreach to underserved populations of veterans in rural areas (Cox, 1990, p. 25). World War II was the first time that the Veterans Administration made any type of organized efforts to conduct outreach to incarcerated veterans (Cox, 1990, p. 25). This post-war period witnessed a number of recent war veterans in conflict with the criminal justice system, though perhaps not as many as the media would suggest (Mauldin, 1947, p. 55).

While the Veterans Administration apparently made some outreach efforts following World War II, its policies highlighted various limitations on the delivery of benefits to incarcerated veterans. A January 1946 *Racine Journal Times* article reported that the Veterans Administration planned to "send field men to jail to advise imprisoned veterans of benefits under the G.I. Bill." However, at the same time, there was lack of clarity on the scope of those very benefits. The article further noted that "[t]he Veterans Administration was cautious about what rights a veteran might expect while in jail," demonstrating the potential for conflicting and unclear guidance ("Veterans Administration to furnish data to jailed veterans," 1946, p. 5).

As one example of limitations on the Veterans Administration's services, in 1949, the Utah state legislature asked the governor of the state to appoint a panel look into "the problem of obtaining adequate treatment for psychotic veterans imprisoned for felonies." Utah's Chief Justice, Eugene E. Pratt, lamented the fact that "the Veterans Administration will not treat any veteran who is under sentence for committing a felony," and there were no clear answers regarding alternatives or other treatment options ("Psychotic Vet Care," 1950, p. 2B). As a result of incomplete guidance and lacking alternatives, elected representatives took matters into their own hands trying to devise ways to bypass the Veterans Administration's limitations. In the absence of effective outreach and in the face of limited federal assistance to incarcerated veterans, the 1940s marked a time when local jurisdictions hired their own veterans' counselors in prisons and jails to make up for federal shortfalls.

The same year that Utah's issues came to surface, a *Prison World* editorial observed that institutions had begun to implement veterans' counselor positions in larger American correctional facilities as "one of the newer innovations in the modern correctional institution." The editorial applauded how the creation of such positions performed a threefold service "to the prisoner, to the administration, and to society" at large ("Editors' Note," 1949, p. 14). Thomas Lunney, a World War I veteran who held a veterans' counselor position at Riker's Island, explained the nuances of his special role. This function included not only educating inmates on their benefit eligibility, but participating in veteran inmate classification determinations and responding to veterans' major concerns, which primarily related to support for their families during the period of incarceration (Lunney, 1949).

2. 1960-1974 (Abysmal Outreach Efforts)

While a policy of organized prison outreach continued through the 1950s, changes at the Veterans Administration ushered in an era of the on-call prison visitation model due to "declining workloads, the expiration of delimiting dates for certain benefits, and reductions in Veterans Administration manpower resources" (Cox, 1979, p. 25). For more than a decade, no formalized programs were in place to ensure comprehensive and accurate information was relayed to incarcerated veterans about their benefits. This led to a situation where more than half of the incarcerated veterans responding to a General Accounting Office study reported that they believed they lost all their Veterans Administration benefits at the time of incarceration and more than 80 percent received no information regarding the status of their Veterans Administration benefits since being incarcerated (General Accounting Office, 1974). Unless the state departments of correction continued their own veterans' liaison offices, veteran inmates were forced either to rely on responses to individual requests they made to the Veterans Administration or the inconsistent assistance from local veterans' organizations (Cranston, 1979, p. 2).

3. 1974–1980 (A Period of Renewed Interest in Outreach)

Involvement in the Vietnam War generated congressional concern over the plight of veterans, especially those suffering from what was then known as *Post-Vietnam Syndrome.* In addition to the development of Vet Centers throughout the nation originally devoted to the special mental health concerns of Vietnam veterans, Congress shored up the Veterans Administration's outreach obligation in 1970. It mandated that the Veterans Administration's administrator "seek out and offer a wide range of assistance to recently discharged veterans to aid and encourage such veterans to apply for and obtain benefits to which they were entitled as veterans" (Cranston, 1979, p. 1; P. L. 91-219 (1970)). Inevitably, this mandate encompassed those recently discharged Vietnam veterans.

In 1974, during a period when the criminal justice system witnessed an influx of veterans, there was still no uniform program requiring routine visits to prisons and jails (Cranston, 1979, p. 2). In response to the growing veteran criminal demographic, the General Accounting Office (GAO) investigated the effectiveness of the Veterans Administration in meeting its outreach objective respecting incarcerated veterans. The study, *Need for Improved Outreach Efforts for Veterans in Prison or on Parole,* shared alarming statistics revealing how veterans were largely misinformed about their benefit eligibility.

In response to these findings, the Veterans Administration instituted a policy of semiannual visits to federal and state prisons to provide inmates with counseling on their benefits. Those employees who conducted the visits included vet reps, veterans' benefits counselors, counseling psychologists, community services specialists, and other employees (Cox, 1979, p. 27). Among the various benefits that outreach personnel covered during this period, including disability and educational benefits, they also offered guidance regarding the process of discharge upgrading. The Veterans Administration also developed an informational pamphlet for incarcerated veterans (Cox, 1979, p. 28).

In the late 1970s, President Jimmy Carter signaled that incarcerated veterans belong to a group that "warranted special attention so as to help them complete their readjustment back into society following their military service" (Cranston, 1979, p. 2). In his October 10, 1978 address to Congress, later printed as the *Presidential Review Memorandum on the Status of Vietnam-Era Veterans,* President Carter also stressed the need to obtain accurate information regarding the status of incarcerated veterans so that the Veterans Administration could plan accordingly and target those for outreach who needed the most assistance and would otherwise be unreachable (Carter, 1979, p. 9). The President highlighted eight major obstacles to outreach efforts, indicated in Figure 17.

Eight Major Obstacles to Incarcerated Veteran Outreach Observed by President Jimmy Carter

1. Lack of accurate data on the scope and nature of the incarcerated veteran population;
2. Limited access of inmate veterans to programs and services by virtue of incarceration;
3. Lack of programs exclusively for [incarcerated] veterans as distinguished from all other veterans;
4. Concern of corrections officials about distinguishing a particular group of inmates for special services, programs, and benefits;
5. Limited access of inmate veterans to discharge upgrade and review;
6. Lack of information and training for court, probation and correctional officials concerning veterans benefits;
7. Lack of comprehensive interagency planning; and
8. Limited manpower to provide special services to incarcerated veterans.

Figure 17. Source: Carter (1979, p. 33).

In 1979, Senator Allan Cranston, as Chair of the Senate Committee on Veterans' Affairs, instituted a congressional hearing to evaluate the Veterans Administration's progress and to determine to what extent the Veterans Administration was able to offer readjustment counseling to incarcerated veterans who ostensibly needed such services as much, if not more, than those living in society (Cranston, 1979, p. 3). In his testimony at the 1979 hearing, the GAO's Associate Director of Human Resources shared his opinion that the Veterans Administration treated its prison outreach efforts as "a low priority" among Veterans Administration programs, that it lacked emphasis within the Veterans Administration, and that the Veterans Administration officials adopted the position that it would not be worth the investment of time to inform veterans of their eligibility for educational assistance because of the short time they stayed confined (Lauve, S. Comm. on Veterans' Affairs, 1979, pp. 5–6).

The urgency to ramp-up outreach efforts at the time during the 1979 hearing was the rapidly approaching delimiting date for Vietnam veterans' eligibility for educational benefits. With the recognition that education would improve veterans' chances of readjustment to meaningful and productive futures, Senator Cranston emphasized how, "Each day, thousands of veterans reach their delimiting date and their opportunity passes to effect a satisfactory readjustment and rehabilitation" (Cranston, 1979, p. 26).

A major impetus for increased outreach in the late 1970s was the fact that many incarcerated veterans had stigmatizing discharges that made them ineligible for the G.I. Bill. Outreach efforts were initiated to beat the approach of many veterans' delimiting date for G.I. Bill entitlement.

As important as the Senate hearings were to the issue of educational benefits, they were even more crucial to the issue of healthcare delivery to incarcerated veterans. Although the Veterans Administration counseling psychologists were visiting prisons, it was unclear to Senator Cranston precisely how the Veterans Administration would meet its mission of readjustment counseling with incarcerated veterans. He therefore pressed the issue by noting how such counseling would "be particularly useful with the problems of some incarcerated Vietnam-era veterans" (Cranston, 1979, p. 30).

At the time, perhaps offering one of the first of few glimmers of hope for a Veterans Administration mental healthcare presence in jails and prisons, Veterans Administration's Director of Mental Health and Behavioral Sciences, Dr. Jack R. Ewalt, explained that although there had been no formal counseling program for incarcerated veterans, he had discussed the vital importance of Veterans Administration collaboration in such efforts. He further noted that, despite no uniform policy, the *Veterans in Prison* program operated in Brentwood, California could serve as pilot program and was "one of the models that we planned on using around the country" (Ewalt, 1979, p. 130). In considering this possibility of collaboration with jails and prisons, Veterans Administration officials apparently gave thought to modeling the program on existing efforts to divert drug offenders into treatment programs in coordination with the local police.

The hearings sparked a number of questions, which resulted in a prompt retreat from the optimism that Dr. Ewalt exhibited regarding the prospect of readjustment counseling by the Veterans Administration for incarcerated veterans. Upon examination of the issue, Dr. Ewalt's response had changed to reflect the position that there was "a lack of specific legal authority" to provide counseling services to inmates during the course of their incarceration (1979. p. 131). He further explained that there were concerns about the Bureau of Prison's lack of support for cooperative in-prison efforts:

> [A]s part of our implementation of plans for a readjustment counseling program for incarcerated veterans, we have met with the appropriate staff of the Federal Bureau of Prisons. Unfortunately, our discussions with them have not been entirely satisfactory, and we do not believe we have their full cooperation. They would prefer to limit our access to the incarcerated veterans only to those who have been released to halfway houses. We believe that our counseling endeavors would be more successful if begun at an earlier stage of incarcerated veterans' rehabilitation programs. (Ewalt, 1979, p. 131)

Although, Dr. Ewalt's position changed over time, there was recognition of a desire to reach veterans at an earlier stage than release from incarceration. Combined with recognition of the *Brentwood Veterans in Prison* program as ideally suited for a pilot program, the discussions with the Bureau of Prisons confirm that the Veterans Administration gave very serious consideration to the possibility of in-prison mental health treatment, even recognizing how it could be valuable for the veterans themselves.

4. The 1980–2002 (Stifled Revival of Outreach Efforts)

The new decade began with the prompt elimination of educational stipends for incarcerated veterans and a more hostile attitude toward jailed offenders in general. Because the G.I. Bill was the basis for increased outreach efforts to incarcerated veterans, the severe limitations on it led many Veterans Administration outreach personnel to believe that their counseling services were no longer necessary. As a result, some regional offices provided standing orders to stop visiting jails and prisons. In 1990, the Director of Veterans Administration's Veterans' Assistance Service shared his observation "that the [Veterans Administration's] Veterans' Services Outreach efforts had declined steadily over a five-year period" below where it had already been since the early-to-mid- 1980s (Brigham, 1990, p. 36). When the Veterans Administration all but abandoned its prison outreach efforts due to monetary concerns, incarcerated veterans either had to rely on each other or state employees to navigate the choppy waters of benefit eligibility and post-release planning as they had following World War II.

In 1989, concern for incarcerated veterans' mental health needs and the ineffectiveness of existing outreach efforts prompted the *Incarcerated Veterans Rehabilitation and Readjustment Act of 1989*. This proposed legislation sought to identify incarcerated veterans, provide them with information about their benefit eligibility, and, most importantly to extend vet centers into federal prisons to meet veterans' mental health treatment needs *during confinement.* The Committee's proposed congressional findings for the bill appear in Figure 18.

To remedy shortfalls in the state of outreach to incarcerated veterans, the bill further sought to mandate specific protocols for the manner in which the Veterans Administration accounted for and counseled veterans and their family members (U.S. House Judiciary Committee, 1989, p. 8). The proposed legislation failed largely because the Veterans Administration opposed

---

Congressional Findings for the *Incarcerated Veterans Rehabilitation and Readjustment Act of 1989*

   (1) There are rehabilitation needs unique to incarcerated veterans which, because of their incarceration, need to be addressed;

   (2) The Readjustment Counseling Program of the Department of Veterans' Affairs could be an effective part of efforts to rehabilitate incarcerated veterans;

   (3) Veterans' Benefits that incarcerated veterans are entitled to are not being provided on a consistent basis;

Incarcerated veterans treated for psychological readjustment problems can be expected to have lower recidivism rates than such veterans who do not receive such treatment.

Figure 18. Source: U.S. House Judiciary Committee (1989, p. 3).

it. The following position statement in response to the Act highlights persistent philosophies that still prevent treatment services to incarcerated veterans:

> **VA is not indifferent to the concerns of the incarcerated veteran. We recognize clearly that more resources could be diverted to . . . assist incarcerated veterans. But mandating that VA establish specific programs would inevitably conflict with both existing statutory priorities and VA's ongoing efforts to assist other veterans who enjoy no specific mandate, including the homeless, the elderly, the chronically mentally ill, Native American veterans, and others residing in rural areas remote from VA medical centers. All have a claim to VA assistance. We cannot support enactment of legislation which would have the effect of requiring VA to take resources away from one group of veterans to augment services to incarcerated veterans (Brigham, 1990, p. 38).**

With the defeat of the Act, incarcerated veterans became more invisible than they had already been. The Veterans Administration's philosophy coincided with a massive drawdown in the military forces following Operation Desert Shield and Desert Storm and the end of the Cold War, marked at a time when many believed that there would be "a period of sustained peace" and no further need for a standing military (Pavlicin, 2003, p. xxii). Lack of interest in the active force, let alone incarcerated veterans may have may have contributed to the institution of the eventual ban on Veterans Administration inpatient or outpatient care to incarcerated veterans that took effect in 1999.

5. 2002–Present (The Most Innovative and Effective Outreach Efforts since the 1920s)

Following the attacks of 9-11, Americans quickly reappraised the need for a standing and strong military force. America was again a nation at war, with the expectation of much longer hostilities, and had renewed interest in veterans' issues, including concerns about veterans with mental illness and especially homeless veterans, who constituted up to 33 percent of America's homeless population, according to some studies (McGuire, 2007, p. 389). While most states' Veterans Administration offices were conducting some level or reentry outreach efforts in 2000, the Veterans Administration began to formally track outreach efforts in 2002. In 2003, the year that marked the commencement of Operation Iraqi Freedom, the U.S. Department of Labor instituted an Incarcerated Veterans Transition Program, which aimed to facilitate improved community reentry (McGuire, 2007, p. 393).

The year 2006 marked a major turning point when the Veterans Administration combined forces with correctional associations and the Federal Bureau of Prisons to initiate the Health Care Reentry for Veterans (HCRV) Program. This initiative created an interagency framework in which the Veterans Administration employees had greater access to incarcerated veterans for identifying them, counseling them on transitional services and benefits, and developing plans for effective community reentry (Rosenthal & McGuire, 2013, p. 365). Today, the program achieves its goals through the dedicated work of forty-nine full-time Health Care Reentry for Veterans specialists (U.S. Department of Veterans Affairs, n.d.). Recent studies indicate that a "majority [of veterans who use the services] entered mental health treatment [upon release] and more than half entered needed substance use disorder treatment within a year" (Finlay et al., 2017, p. 185).

On January 21, 2009, General Eric Shinseki assumed responsibility as the Secretary of Veterans Affairs and quickly developed a targeted plan for the elimination of homelessness among the nation's veterans. The new sense of urgency was rightfully called "Shinskei's Surge" based on its widespread application, which is similar to the military's 2008 "Surge" to combat the insurgents in Iraq and subsequent surges (Scott, 2010). Secretary Shinseki's robust five-year plan to end veteran homelessness would "attack the entire downward spiral that ends in homelessness." This requires the Veterans Administration to "offer education and jobs that treat depression and fight substance abuse, prevent suicides and provide safe housing" (Carden, 2009). While the Health Care Reentry for Veterans program attempted to address incarcerated veterans' reentry needs on the backend of their involvement with the justice system, part of this "surge" included the development of a Veterans Health Administration (VHA) Veterans Justice Outreach Program to intervene with veterans at their initial point of entry into the justice system.

Because arrest and appearance in the court offer ideal opportunities to identify veterans with acute financial, medical, and psychiatric needs, interception of veterans and diversion to intensive therapeutic programs could have an even greater impact in preventing homelessness than interventions following incarceration (Stovall, Cloninger, & Appleby, 1997, pp. 311–312; Clark, 2010, p. 3). Accordingly, approximately 260 Veterans Justice Outreach specialists across the nation play a very different role than the Health Care Reentry for Veterans' reentry specialists (U.S. Government Accountability Office, 2016, Executive Summary). The Veterans Justice Outreach specialists appear in court, obtain residential placements, interface with short-term detention facilities, serve as members of veteran treatment court treatment teams, transport veterans from court to necessary appointments, and have even been instrumental in the development of veterans treatment courts in jurisdictions where there were none (E. Brett, personal communication, December 18, 2013).

In San Francisco County, a Veterans Justice Outreach specialist, Elizabeth Brett developed the first Justice Clinic at the Downtown Medical Center, which is designed as a single location where veterans exiting confinement can obtain health services, peer mentoring, and legal assistance. It operates much like a veterans treatment court by devoting a day when the medical staff can devote their time exclusively to similarly situated veterans who have recently been released (Mendonca, 2012; E. Brett, personal communication, December 18, 2013).

The Health Care for Reentry Veterans and Veterans Justice Outreach website feature three brief videos that showcase the different programs for justice-involved veterans and the manner in which they collectively aim to reduce homelessness among the significantly at-risk group:

- Suits: Support for Incarcerated Veterans
- Assisting Justice Involved Veterans
- A Second Chance for Justice Involved Veterans

To access these videos and for more information, visit:

http://www.va.gov/homeless/vjo.asp

Perhaps the greatest aid in outreach to veterans is the recent development of the Veterans Reentry Search Service (VRSS), a web-based computer program that enables participating prisons and jails to confirm the veteran status of inmates through an electronic identify match with official military records. The system provides basic information through Veterans Administration outreach personnel as intermediaries to prevent disclosure of protected information. To date, the Veterans Reentry Search Service has already proven effective in identifying veterans who have not been asked, concealed, or otherwise failed to share their prior military status, as evident in the experience of institutions in Middlesex, Massachusetts. In July 2013, just after local correctional administrators signed an agreement with the Veterans Administration to use the program, the facilities identified more than two times more veterans than had been identified without it (nineteen versus sixty-eight) (McCabe, 2013; Edelman, 2018).

Secretary Shinseki wrote to each of the nation's governors encouraging their use of the program, and he observed how the number of prisons and jails enrolling in the service doubled in three short months with twenty enrolled and thirty more in the process of enrolling (E. Shinseki, Keynote Address to the General Session of the 143rd Congress of Corrections, American Correctional Association, National Harbor, Maryland, August 12, 2013). The very existence of the Veterans Reentry Search Service answers a twenty-four-year-old need that was identified for independent and reliable "computer matched" confirmation of veteran status, demonstrating how Shinseki's Surge has achieved, and in many cases surpassed, objectives for outreach efforts (Quinlan, 1989, p. 20). Yet, to date, 38 C.F.R. § 17.38 remains a major impediment to the full attainment of effective outreach and assistance to incarcerated veterans. The next section identifies the historical precedent for elimination of Section 17.38 and, moreover, the most compelling reasons for prison and jail administrators to develop programming that will fill the gap in veteran-specific services *during the period of incarceration* (Schaffer, 2016).

IV. A Lost Chapter in American History: The Roaring Twenties and the True Origin of Outreach to Incarcerated Veterans in America's Prisons and Jails[8]

If one follows the media attention paid to veterans treatment courts, criminal diversion programs for veterans, and the establishment of veterans dorms, it may seem that the mid-to-late 2000s marked the nation's greatest interest in and efforts to assist incarcerated veterans. While there is, indeed, a groundswell of interest in this cause far greater than during the Vietnam-era, the most magnificent and robust efforts began almost a century ago in the state of Wisconsin following the First World War. They culminated in what was popularly described as a nationwide "prison clean-up" of incarcerated veterans with mental illness and physical disability traceable to their service.

While World War II is cited as the origin of incarcerated veterans' outreach, careful examination of the 1920s reveals a level of nationwide interest and partnership that sheds important light upon the dilemmas facing both correctional professionals and the Veterans Administration, even today. While the Supreme Court in 2009 mentioned historical efforts to accord veterans leniency for crimes "especially for those who fought on the front lines" (*Porter v. McCollum,* p. 43, n.8), and contemporary legal scholars have point-

---

8. Portions of this chapter originally appeared in *The Nebraska Lawyer* (Seamone, 2013b), and are reprinted with permission of the Nebraska State Bar Association.

ed to a number of scholarly studies focusing on past criminal trends (Holbrook & Anderson, 2011, pp. 8–9), there are numerous buried lessons from the post-World War I period in source materials from the archives of the various states, the records of the U.S. Veterans' Bureau, as well as the publications of the American Legion. This section begins by paying considerable attention to the period of the 1920s because the Veterans' Bureau adopted a robust national policy that has yet to be paralleled, and which exists in contrast to the Veterans Administration's policies after Vietnam—and even today.

At a time when courts and commentators have returned to early conceptions of veterans' rights to promote their interests, we can learn much from the 1920s historical example. This is especially true because many of our current Iraq and Afghanistan war veterans, who volunteered to fight after the 9/11 attacks, have unfairly absorbed residual criticisms and attitudes, which were leveled at veterans of the Vietnam era and represented a new brand of hostility that had never reached veterans from prior conflicts (MacPherson, 1993). A return to founding ideals is needed to dislodge a misplaced perspective. Although there have been stand-outs for innovative jail and prison-based programs in later times, such as Indiana's short-term program for incarcerated veterans in the mid-1940s and Pennsylvania's statewide PTSD treatment program in the early to mid-1980s (see Chapter 8), the combined effort of the Veterans' Bureau, Wisconsin's Governor, and the American Legion in the 1920s is quite unique in its impetus for a nationwide movement.

The Roaring Twenties: The Dawning of a National Movement to Identify and Treat Incarcerated Veterans with Mental Health Conditions

A. Invisible Wounds Among Returning World War I Veterans

When the First World War ended after just over a year of U.S. involvement, approximately 5,019,874 veterans returned to their communities. These communities, while lacking the creature comforts of modern times, still featured mass transit with the Ford Model-T and motion pictures, which had managed to captivate the nation. Approximately one in every five men between sixteen and forty-four years of age had served in the military, as evident in the 1920 census (Painton, 1922, p. 6). Roughly 9,000 had to be institutionalized for the mental effects of the combat trauma they suffered (Woollcott, 1922, p. 5).

Yet, countless more returned with numerous indications that something just wasn't right. In a 1922 *American Legion Weekly* article titled "Invisible

Injuries," the author made the case for compassionate treatment of service members with shell shock (Wollcott, 1922). An inlaid article pointed to numerous signs of the condition. Though there would be no diagnosis of Posttraumatic Stress Disorder (PTSD) for the next fifty-eight years, many of the symptoms were indistinguishable, including fear of sudden noises, premonitions of death, the choice to live in isolation in the dark, inability to maintain concentration in civilian occupational tasks where one had excelled prior to the War, and an inability to deal with people in general ("Welfare Worker," 1922, p. 6). As a commentator remarked in March 1922: "You could hardly blame a nerve-twisted soldier if . . . he were to settle his status by chopping off his hand or foot. He may have come back whole from France, with no wound visible to the unpracticed eye, and yet carry with him an injury as disabling, for the time being, as any mere lost leg" ("The Mental Aftermath," 1922). Little was different then, including popular media concerns that returning veterans were entangled in the civilian criminal justice system at significant, even startling, numbers.

B. The First Studies of Veteran Criminality

Although he served as a Captain in the Medical Corps during World War I, Frank L. Christian dedicated much of his life to the study of criminology. After the War, he served as the Superintendent of the New York State Reformatory at Elmira. He became skeptical of the widespread media focus on veteran criminality, which began shortly after the Armistice and only grew more entrenched over the coming years, as a wave of violent crime subsumed the nation. The following newspaper titles resembled countless more: "Ex-Soldier Kills Wife and Self," "Vet Loots Till," "Homestead Hotel Man Slain; War Veteran Blamed After Firing Shots into Own Body," and "Charge Veteran Stole $3,500 from Widow." In this period, the media engaged in "constant repetition of the terms 'ex-service man' and 'veteran' when reporting the arrest of some criminal who claimed to have a discharge" (Painton, 1922, p. 5). Although no other institutions had collected data on their veteran inmates immediately following the War, Christian began a careful study of those veterans in his own institution with the goal of testing the media's hypothesis.

While Christian was meticulously collecting his data on Elmira Reformatory's veteran inmates, a reporter in Galveston, Texas, had heard estimates that five out of every nine inmates in the Texas penal system were veterans ("Changes in Texas," 1920, p. 2). He contacted J. R. Jordan, Chief Clerk of the Criminal Record Department for the Texas Prison System, to investigate the accuracy of the numbers. Prior to that time, Texas made no inquiry into veteran status. Although Jordan was unable to make a "definite statement" on the exact number of incarcerated veterans, he was "positive" that the prevailing figure was highly exaggerated. Considering the number of veterans confined in Huntsville Prison (30/260), the true number was closer to "one in every nine inmates of the state prisons." If the number was accurate and generalizable, this demonstrated that, in contrast to the ratio of one in four civilians locked away, "relatively fewer ex-service men are in prison than are non-service men." The positive finding was thus "creditable to the men who went to fight for their country." In little time, Minnesota Municipal Court Judge Frank C. Barnes echoed this conclusion after examining his own court's statistics involving 46 veteran offenders out of 160 misdemeanants tried in Fergus Falls: "The ex-service man is no more of a criminal than the average citizen. He has not been made a criminal by service but on the contrary, his attitude toward mankind is better for having been in the service" (1922, p. 22).

After three years of study, Christian revealed the results of his Elmira Reformatory study in New York, which was the most comprehensive empirical study of its time. It similarly rebuffed the media's widespread accounts of veteran incarceration and the corresponding theory "that when the Government put a gun in the hands of its young men, taught them to use it, placed them amongst scenes of carnage and of sudden wholesale death, many of the veterans shed their skin of civilization and lost their respect for life and property" (Painton, 1922, p. 5). His multi-year investigation, which included intelligence testing of each veteran inmate, indicated that, in total, 318 out of 1,900—roughly one out of six inmates—had former military service (with 220 in the Army, 86 in the Navy, 2 in the Marines, and 10 in the armies of Allied Forces). In his study,

1. More than half of the veteran offenders had at least one prior conviction before their initial entry into the service.
2. Out of 318, 224 were working when arrested on the current charges.
3. On the Binet Intelligence Test, at least one-half received scores that would have made them ineligible to serve, reducing the number of incarcerated veterans to one out of every nineteen, if one discounted for those who should have been prevented from enlistment to begin with.
4. While the American crime wave was at its height in 1922, the number of incarcerated veterans had either been holding steady—even dropping—suggesting that veteran status was not a contributor to it.

Mirroring the Clerk's conclusion in Galveston, Christian revealed that "the average soldier was a pretty good sort" during the War, and after returning from combat.

As is still the case today, it was difficult then to tell whether veterans with prior criminal records would have gone on to commit crimes even if they had not been in the military. A conclusion, echoed since that period, was that "[n]o uniform ever turned a man into a criminal; if he was a criminal in uniform, he was a criminal before he got into it" (Shepherd, 1923, p. 7). Others who were similarly concerned that the popular "criminal veteran" title of the 1920s was undeserved, but who lacked the ability to study the prison populations, consulted sureties, whose duties included monitoring trends in criminality. There was little doubt that crime had become shockingly more violent following the war with a high degree of murders, shoot-outs with police, and audacious robberies.

However, through this insider knowledge, the Chairman of the National Surety Company, William B. Joyce, concluded that 90 percent of this violent crime wave was attributable to youthful offenders who were too young to enlist and serve during the time of the First World War (Shepherd, 1923, p. 7). As he noted, "The criminals of today, who amaze and shock the land with violent deeds, were mere boys, too young for the army, on the day the war came to an end." Rather than veteran status, the researchers concluded that the major contributors to the post-World War I crime wave were addiction to hard drugs, accessibility of pistols in pawnshops throughout the country, and the empty pursuit of higher education, which made it far easier for students to drift into crime. Indubitably, some veterans did commit violent crimes, and none of the researchers' studies had accounted for whether combat trauma, rather than merely adorning the uniform, might actually produce a different result. Additional studies would soon shed light on this important aspect of veteran criminality.

New Concern Over Combat-Traumatized Veterans in the Criminal Justice System

C. A Nationwide Movement Begins in Wisconsin

On August 9, 1921, the U.S. Veterans' Bureau had recently been established with the aim of building hospitals to care for the numerous veterans with mental and physical war wounds. These efforts had not reached states as quickly as many desired. In Wisconsin, Dr. William F. Lorenz was instrumental in developing a state hospital for mental care with an aim of reaching the veteran population in time to make an impact. After Lorenz observed "revelations of mental collapse in former soldiers treated" under his care at the Wisconsin State Psychiatric Institute, he began to study what many psychiatrists pondered: the extent to which combat-related mental conditions factored into the crimes committed by incarcerated veterans.

The average age of the confined veterans in Dr. Lorenz's initial study involved offenders under twenty-four years-old. Of the 235 veterans he identified at Waupun Prison and Green Bay Reformatory, 62 percent of them were mentally deficient, and more than 20 percent suffered from "disabilities traceable to military service" (Casey, 1923, p. 7). Not only were most (more than 60 percent) of their crimes trivial, but 70 percent of the cases dealt with property and money, and 30 percent emerged out of "economic stresses" suffered by the veterans in their communities. Lorenz observed how combat likely contributed to many of these cases, "Those who actually got into battle and witnessed or took part in the dreadfulness of war, may in later life have committed some overt act, which by comparison with compulsory military duty seemed inconsequential" ("Treatment not punishment is the need of ex-service men in prison board finds," 1923, p. 3). The survey revealed that "[a] majority of the ex-service men in prisons were found to be mentally abnormal and a high percentage were feeble-minded, with less intelligence than a nine-year-old child" ("Advocates survey war veterans in penal institutions," 1923, p. 25). Interestingly, while alcohol was tied to fifty-one of the cases, drug use related to less than five cases ("Treatment not punishment is the need of ex-service men in prison board finds," 1923, p. 3).

Wisconsin Governor J. Johnson Blaine had taken a particular interest in veterans' mental health from the many executive clemency cases he considered. Although the Governor stated, "When I can take these boys out of prison and put them in colleges then I will be satisfied," his favorable consideration mainly extended to those warriors whose crimes were linked "directly or indirectly to causes arising out of the service to his country" ("Governor to Pardon," 1922, p. 1). From his conversations with Lorenz, and upon learning of the study results, Governor Blaine became concerned that he might never learn of the incarcerated veterans with legitimate needs for healthcare, "without friends or relatives and without money" to elevate their claims to his level ("Blaine Orders Survey," 1922, p. 2). He thus appointed Lorenz and Dr. W. S. Middleton, from the University of Wisconsin, to undertake a statewide study in which they would examine each incarcerated veteran's "mental, nervous, and tubercular" condition. The far-reaching and unprecedented executive order provided further direction on those veterans with pressing treatment needs: "In the cases that should receive immediate attention by transfer to the psychiatric institute or some sanitarium, you can report to me from time to time, and under the statutes, I will issue the necessary permit for their transfer as your report and advice suggests."

Aside from the already monumental commitment to transfer psychiatrically afflicted veteran inmates immediately from incarceration, Governor Blaine pledged further to preserve these veterans' benefits under federal law. In the order, he further articulated:

I also desire to suggest that I will prepare a questionnaire for the prison authorities to have filled out after the time of the examination of each man so that I may carry out a plan I have in mind to see that these men are protected in their compensation, vocational training and other civil rights growing out of their war service which because of their incarceration in all probability has been overlooked.

As for the mechanism to bring these claims to the attention of proper authorities, he concluded, "After the survey is completed, I will arrange through some department the necessary legal assistance to take care of the civil rights involving obligations of the state and federal government of those men who have been unable to enforce such obligations" ("Blaine Orders Survey," 1922, p. 2).

The Wisconsin survey concluded a full year after medical examinations of each inmate with "his record taken by a stenographer on the spot." The examinations identified several veterans who required immediate medical attention. Of these inmates, Governor Blaine transferred more than twenty of the men to the psychiatric facility, with plans underway to parole or transfer additional inmates upon the completion of a new hospital (Casey, 1923, pp. 7, 26).

Governor Blaine strongly believed that every state governor should implement a similar survey of its prison population. He "announced that he is attempting to enlist the support of the federal government and of governors of other states in a movement to give special attention to prisoners who saw service in the war" ("Treatment Not Punishment," 1923, p. 3). To this end, he provided forms and materials as a template for "the Governors of the several States and . . . the departments at Washington" and frequently communicated with other governors over the results of their own prison studies (Casey, 1923, p. 7). While Governor Blaine was the impetus for a national movement, two other entities surely sustained it: The American Legion and the national headquarters and districts of the fledgling U.S. Veterans' Bureau.

D. The Involvement of the American Legion

The Veterans' Bureau, the nation's initial version of the federal entity that would evolve into the Veterans Administration, had been in existence for approximately two years when the Wisconsin movement began. Given the youth of the organization and the magnitude of the problem of incarcerated veterans, it was understood that "the problem is of too great scope for the veterans bureau to handle" ("Hospital Instead of Jail," 1923, p. 3). As would be the case in years to come, the nation mobilized to address this issue through the coordinated efforts of the Veterans' Bureau and veterans service organizations (VSOs).

At the same time that Dr. Lorenz was studying veterans incarcerated in the Wisconsin penal system, a Commissioner of a Wisconsin Circuit Court, and a veteran himself, Francis Ryan Duffy, took interest in the issue and shared Governor Blaine's objective to develop national interest in the issue. Duffy had begun to rise to the leadership of Wisconsin's American Legion, attaining the rank of Vice Commander, which provided him with a dual appointment on the Legion's National Committee. He is credited with raising national awareness through the development of the "Survey of Ex-Service Men in Penal Institutes of the States of the Nation." Through the vast infrastructure of this national network, including more than 11,000 posts throughout the world, each with various officers holding some prominent community positions, the Legion helped to collect data that approximated 20,000 veterans incarcerated in the United States by 1922 ("Duffy to Aid," 1924, p. 3). Stemming from Duffy's leadership on the issue, Legion officials presented the issue of incarcerated veterans at the Fifth National Convention in San Francisco between October 15th and 19th of 1923. As a result, "[a] sweeping recommendation was adopted instructing the national Rehabilitation Committee to make a survey of all Federal and State penal institutions and insane asylums for the purpose of ascertaining the number of veterans therein who are suffering from curable mental ailments due to military or naval service" ("The Record of the Fifth National Convention," 1923, p. 10).

Preliminary surveys revealed that, on balance, "60 percent [of the incarcerated veterans] were suffering from some mental defection, one fifth of which is traceable directly to war service" ("American Legion Notes," 1924, p. 7). Accordingly, the ultimate purpose of the national effort was not merely to count veterans, but to go far beyond and "determine if any such men should be treated in medical institutions rather than imprisoned for crimes committed while in this mental condition."

E. Colonel Charles Forbes and the U.S. Veterans' Bureau

While it is unclear how each of the governors and state penal institutions responded to these recommendations, there was a consensus that the efforts had produced measurable and "highly successful" results at the national level ("Duffy to Aid," 1924, p. 3). One irrefutable impact of these efforts was evident in the reaction of the Veterans' Bureau, which was formed on September 31, 1919, to respond to the needs of World War I veterans. The Bureau was organized in the form of a national headquarters and fourteen different semi-independent districts. Colonel Charles Forbes, the Bureau's first Director, was clearly aware of the ongoing efforts to count the number of incarcerated veterans in the nation. From the perspective of the Veterans'

Bureau and its responsibility to America's returned warriors, however, these statistics did not end the analysis. As evident in Governor Blaine's efforts to preserve eligibility for benefits, "[m]any of these imprisoned men have physical disabilities of service origin [but] they are getting little or no compensation and are unable to present their claims because they are in prison" ("Advocates Survey War Veterans," 1923, p. 25). Forbes saw the need to link these veterans with benefits they rightfully earned.

During a meeting with the district managers, Colonel Forbes "personally recommended that all of the offices institute a survey of penal institutions in their jurisdictions with reference to the compensation status of all former service men" ("Will Look After Jailed Veterans," 1922, p. 5). On November 3, 1922, Colonel Forbes translated the tentative plan into an official order, which he transmitted to each state District. Major W. F. Kent, Manager of the New York District, related the text of Forbes' order, which called for "an investigation and survey of all veterans of the World War now confined in penal institutions throughout the state with a view of giving them treatment and compensation where needed." In Forbes' own unambiguous words: "Where we find beneficiaries in penitentiaries and jails you must remember that there is nothing in the law to prevent them from having care, treatment, and compensation, if necessary" ("Will Look After Jailed Veterans," 1922, p. 5).

The initial policy of the Veterans' Bureau on incarcerated WWI veterans in the 1920s was to evaluate incarcerated veterans for service-connected conditions. For those with mental health needs, the policy was to work with states to transfer the inmate to psychiatric care. For those who remained, incarcerated, the policy was to liberally construe medical treatment and compensation benefits, especially since the laws did not discriminate based on inmate status.

F. Allocation of Responsibilities for Rehabilitating Incarcerated Veterans

In a speech delivered at the time of the order in 1922, Colonel Forbes estimated that no less than 25,000 veterans were incarcerated in the nation's prisons ("Prison Cleanup Campaign," 1922, p. 4). Forbes acknowledged, "no doubt there are a number of men in prisons . . . who have been committed because of a weakened mental or physical condition, directly attributed to the man's military service." Thus, the Veterans' Bureau, in its first iteration of a policy for incarcerated veterans, concluded that "it is the government's responsibility to determine [the mental condition of incarcerated veterans,] to acquaint the state authorities with the situation[,] and take the man off the hands of the state and hospitalize him in a government institution, giving him the treatment and compensation that he is duly entitled to."

The Bureau's sentiment regarding incarcerated veterans in the 1920s is best represented by this account: "No expenses will be spared to discover the man who is entitled to the aid of his government, even though he has been so unfortunate as to violate the laws of his state and is now paying with his liberty for his folly" ("Prison Cleanup Campaign," 1922, p. 4). Forbes, in his repeated calls for public action, urged official audiences to ensure that the many incarcerated veterans in the nation would not be "forgotten" ("Would Pardon a Host," 1922, p. 1).

Under Forbes' leadership, the Veterans' Bureau was responsible for effectuating a nationwide "intensive prison clean-up drive" with VSO coordination to identify, evaluate, and assist incarcerated veterans with medical needs traceable to their military service. Like a military operation, the Prison Clean-Up involved "a squad composed of contract officers, a medical examiner and a male stenographer" ("Prison Cleanup Campaign," 1922, p. 4). Media reports suggest that veterans service organizations played a significant role in these visits, as reflected in a resolution adopted at the November 26, 1922, Veterans of Foreign Wars Baby Convention in Boston that requested the Veterans' Bureau medical examiner to "take the necessary steps to provide a doctor and contract men, to be accompanied by a VFW adjutant to visit the ex-service men in jail and make mental examinations" ("Would Reopen Cases," 1922, p. 6). The Sixth District of the Veterans' Bureau, which included the states of Alabama, Louisiana, and Mississippi, commenced its Clean-Up activities on December 1, 1922. In aid of these efforts, members of the Sixth District solicited help from the public in magazines like Mississippi's *Laurel Daily Leader*:

> Parties who have information on ex-service men confined in prison camps or county jails who feel that the crimes they committed are attributed [to] their military service will be conferring a favor on the bureau as well as the unfortunate man if they will correspond with the district office, U.S. Veterans Bureau . . . or any of the . . . sub-district offices.

As evident in this desire to investigate such cases, "[t]he U.S. Veterans Bureau feels that this prison work is part of their job and that their responsibility will not be fulfilled until they have satisfied themselves that there are no men confined in penal institutions in this country who are there as a direct or indirect result of their sacrifices for their country" ("Prison Cleanup

Campaign," 1922, p. 4). Veterans' Bureau personnel, like Dr. Stanley Rinehart, advocated incarcerated veterans' interests beyond merely the federal level, urging the states to provide meaningful clemency or other relief from prison sentences: "The states must see to it that every service man in prison gets an opportunity to have a hearing if he deserves it, or hospital treatment instead of a jail cell, if this is what he needs" ("Hospital Instead of Jail," 1923, p. 2).

> **In the 1920s, members of the Veterans' Bureau solicited help from the public in identifying cases of suspected service-connected injuries and advocated in the clemency process for veterans to be released to medical care and treated where medical examinations confirmed a service-connection.**

By 1923, efforts to identify incarcerated veterans resulted in statistics showing that between 20,000 and 26,000 veterans were incarcerated throughout the nation. With the help of the Veterans' Bureau and veterans service organizations, statistics began to amass regarding each state's incarcerated veteran population. After more than a year of study, Wisconsin's final total, which included the Milwaukee House of Correction, was 352 ("Blaine Orders Survey," 1922, p. 2). In Oklahoma, there were 358 incarcerated veterans ("May Aid Veterans," 1924, p. 12). In Alabama there were 286 ("Prison Cleanup Campaign," 1922, p. 4). In South Carolina, there were 68 ("American Legion Notes," 1924, p. 7).

Unlike the studies of the Elmira Reformatory in New York, which revealed half of the incarcerated veterans to be previous offenders, in Oklahoma, for example, "[o]nly 31 of the 359 confined [were] serving second sentences" ("May Aid Veterans," 1924, p. 12). Upon learning of the statistical trends, members of the Veterans' Bureau even shared their opinion that "it is remarkable that not more of them men are in jail, because so many left army service with shattered nerves and were compelled to adjust themselves to after-war conditions" ("Hospital Instead of Jail," 1923, p. 2). By January of 1923, the Veterans' Bureau identified at least 2,000 cases for further review from these initial efforts ("American Legion and V.F.W. News," 1923, p. 4).

As reflected in the American Legion's position, the campaign to cleanup prisons and jails had a specific focus on service-connected mental illness. They used the "theory that many [veteran inmates] are prisoners as a result of mental illness and not because of any criminal tendencies" ("Legion to Seek Survey," 1925, p. 1); "The organizations will press no claim for clemency where a veteran shows no disability," explained officials ("American Legion Notes," 1924, p. 7). Having developed rough estimates of the number of incarcerated veterans and having commenced widespread evaluations of their mental health, the movement to divert incarcerated veterans to psychiatric care in the community was aided by conservative estimates from Dr. Lorenz's study that "at least 5,000 [inmates were] in dire need of medical aid instead of the usual course in quarrying rock" (Casey, 1923, p. 27).

As it became clear that responsibilities did not end with a mere tally, the clean-up movement generated the impetus to develop solutions for the challenges facing *all* incarcerated veterans. Seeing that these inmates largely did not understand their rights, a component of outreach by the various institutions necessarily included education and efforts to file claims. Beyond merely treating those in need of immediate mental health care, there were additional considerations. Dr. Lorenz recommended a dual-track for jails and prisons with respect to those who remained. While the "mentally unfit" veterans should "be segregated" with one another away from the general population, healthy veteran inmates should be provided occupational training in schools installed in the prisons and jails specifically for this purpose.

The first recommendation stemmed from the fact that "the segregated class could be allowed certain liberties that might be dangerous from the prison point of view if witnessed by the mentally responsible inmates" (Casey, 1923, p. 24). Such liberties in confined settings were necessary to promote these veterans' health. The American Legion's Soldiers' Relief Commission of Oklahoma similarly advocated for "a full-time neuro-psychiatrist expert [to] be assigned to the prisons, that the prisoners may be closely observed and reclassified where necessary [and] construction of a psychopathic ward inside the prison walls, in which should be confined the mental defectives" ("May Aid Veterans," 1924, p. 12). The second recommendation for occupational rehabilitation came in recognition that economic strain was the contributing factor for a great number of the trivial economic crimes that most of the veterans had committed ("Advocates Survey War Veterans," 1923, p. 25).

> **The Prison Clean-Up of the 1920s also led to increased benefits outreach and education efforts for incarcerated veterans, segregation of veterans with mental illness from the general population so they might enjoy greater health-promoting liberties, psychiatric care within jails and prisons for veterans, and occupational training programs in jails for healthier veterans inmates.**

V. Lessons from the National "Prison Clean-Up" of Veterans in 1920s

On July 21, 1930, the Veterans' Bureau would merge into the Veterans' Administration by consolidating its operations with those of other offices that administered veterans' benefits. Despite the eventual development of a national policy on incarcerated veterans, it is vital to consider the lessons from this lost historical chapter. In the 1920s, the states, the Veterans' Bureau, and the American Legion were mobilized to national action on a theory that "the mere presence of 20,000 former soldiers in our jails automatically demands attention" ("War Veterans in Prison," 1923, p. 2). These entities unanimously adopted Dr. Lorenz's perspective that "[t]here can be no answer to the problem in a mere denial that the problem exists" (Casey, 1923, p. 26). The roaring 1920s is a period that is most valuable because of its vision of shared responsibility among federal agencies and the state courts and governors regarding the needs of incarcerated veterans with mental health problems.

From the time closest to the inception of the organization that would become the contemporary Department of Veterans Affairs, this organization recognized a four-fold duty to: (1) identify incarcerated veterans with service-connected treatment needs; (2) secure benefits that the veterans earned and were qualified for; (3) educate state entities about options for treating those with needs; and (4) provide alternatives to incarceration to enable such treatment. As evident in appeals for the exercise of clemency, states and their governors had the corresponding responsibility to apply the criminal laws in a manner so as to enable flexibility for diversion and treatment. Although this period is separated from contemporary veterans treatment courts by nearly a century, it is more than mere coincidence that a similar vision of responsibility allocation now guides many states and the Veterans Administration in modern efforts to address the needs of incarcerated veterans. With the ability to identify incarcerated veterans through the computerized VRSS program, the evolution of the Prison Clean-Up of the 1920s suggests that there will again arise recognition of the need to do something about the problem, seeing that neither the states nor the Veterans' Bureau settled merely on the numbers after gaining awareness of the incarcerated veteran population.

That Colonel Forbes and the Veterans' Bureau liberally granted benefits to incarcerated veterans is also quite noteworthy. It did not matter whether there were no specific authorizing rules for benefits to the incarcerated. Veterans were veterans—whether incarcerated or not. This position exists in stark contrast to later years, especially the late 1970s, when the Veterans Administration interpreted the "lack of specific legal authority" as a reason it was *precluded* from providing mental healthcare services to incarcerated inmates (Ewalt, 1979, p. 131).

In the few congressional hearings on incarcerated veterans and their mental health needs, although the Veterans Administration cited some historical lessons, it entirely omitted the Prison Clean-Up of the 1920s, which stands out as the most robust effort in the nation to address the issue. One reason for this omission may be the fact that Vietnam and the country's rejection of its veterans have unfairly subsumed the issue. Myra MacPherson's extensive research on this point reveals that, during and following the Vietnam period specifically, prison officials, wardens, legislators, and even veterans themselves, did not have a desire to know the magnitude of the problem (1993, pp. 578–579).

Arguably, these jaded attitudes have stayed even though Iraq and Afghanistan veterans have emerged from an entirely different backdrop, in which the bulk of their numbers volunteered to serve the country following the attacks of September 11th. Now that more is known about the effects of combat and operational stress injuries, America has gained a better understanding of the needs and challenges facing Vietnam veterans. Additionally, now that the Global War on Terrorism has introduced an entirely different population to the nation's prisons and jails, the lessons of the 1920s provide a sorely needed alternative viewpoint on the type of innovation that is possible when communities, veterans service organizations, government agencies, governors, and confinement facilities join forces. Chapters 7 to 9 provide veterans' advocates and correctional administrators with the tools to develop effective programs to aid veterans during the course of their incarceration, even in absence of Veterans Administration healthcare.

Chapter 6

PROBLEM-SOLVING JUSTICE:
POPULAR APPROACHES TO DIVERT
VETERANS FROM CONFINEMENT

A revolution is underway in criminal justice today involving problem-solving courts—and problem-solving in general. Chapter 9 of this book describes how sheriffs such as Randall Liberty in Kennebec County, Maine (now Warden of the Maine State Prison), have instituted specialized veterans' dormitories as examples of "Problem-Oriented Incarceration" (Schroeder, 2013). These prison and jail programs for veteran offenders exist as the counterparts to the problem-solving veterans treatment courts. This is especially true where inmates are ineligible to participate in court-sponsored programs for any number of reasons. In any venue, the idea is to address the underlying issues causing the offender to come in conflict with the law, rather than just the criminal symptoms.

Commentators trace the roots of the approach to a number of theories, including comprehensive law, therapeutic jurisprudence, and restorative justice (Seamone, 2011). All of these theories espouse the idea that it benefits society and the individual more to stop the revolving doors of recidivism and focus on root causes of criminality. Due to shorter periods of confinement, jails have a greater opportunity than prisons to facilitate diversion from confinement, but all elements of the justice system, including prisons, play a vital role.

The Sequential Intercept Model is a popular framework for considering potential responses to offenders with mental health treatment needs. Evident in the name, the approach suggests that every sequential phase of advancement in the criminal justice system—from arrival at a crime scene to arrest, booking, initial appearance, and so forth—provides a separate opportunity for diversion to a more effective treatment venue that targets the underlying mental health condition. Specifically, Munetz and Griffin's 2006 five-stage model contains "filters" progressing from "law enforcement and emergency services" through "post-initial hearings" with the "ultimate intercept" existing in "best clinical practices" (Munetz & Griffin, 2006, p. 545).

The Sequential Intercept Model fundamentally recognizes the antitherapeutic and harmful effects of incarceration and promotes diversion at the earliest stages for the most profound effects (Munitz & Griffin, 2006). Research demonstrates that incarceration does not help inmates with mental illness. Rather, it exacerbates symptoms of mental disorders and in many cases leads to increased disciplinary incidents, extended sentences, and placement in solitary holding facilities for high-risk inmates. Legal scholar Allegra McLeod uses the term "decarceration"—the opposite of incarceration—to signify a trend of diversion from confinement across all elements of the justice system, and especially within specialized "decarceration courts" (2012, pp. 1590–1591).

Reflective of the manner decarceration has dramatically influenced all aspects of the justice system, commentators note a "quiet revolution" among American criminal courts and an entirely new "criminal justice paradigm" (McLeod, 2012, p. 1591). The Sequential Intercept Model envisions that, even when it is not possible to intervene prior to arraignment or trial, the courts can still exist as a means to ease the treatment of mental disorders and underlying causes. While there are more than 3,000 different problem-solving treatment courts in the nation (Hughes & Reichert, 2017), many collectively embrace the Sequential Intercept Model in the way that they "conven[e] courts to therapeutically treat offenders" (McLeod, 2012, p. 1594).

The Illinois Criminal Justice Information Authority depicted problem-solving court demographics as of 2015 in Figure 19, recognizing that veterans courts are some of the "most common models," similar to "drug, mental health, [and] domestic violence" courts. Local law enforcement agencies and the courts have quickly adopted the Sequential Intercept Model as the operative framework for addressing the problems of "justice-involved" veterans on the realization that combat deployment and military service create readjustment difficulties for a great portion of veterans, even if they lack a specific mental health diagnosis. With the help of federal grants, private charitable contributions, and an unprecedented network of community support, members of the public have supplemented law enforcement agencies in efforts to divert veterans from arrest, booking, conviction, and sentencing at nearly every step of the criminal justice process.

Figure 20 uses Loveland and Boyle's intercept framework to identify corresponding veteran-specific interventions within the context of the broader model.

More recently, as displayed in Figure 21, the National Institute of Corrections partnered with the Department of Veterans Affairs and the Substance Abuse and Mental Health Services Administration (SAMHSA) to

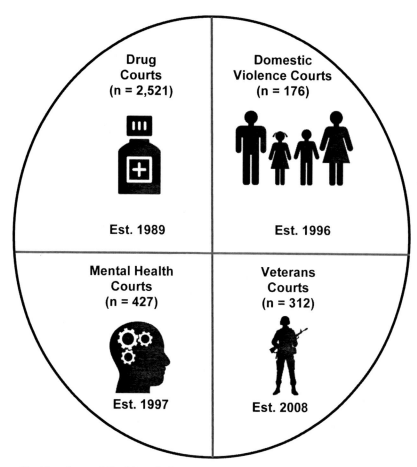

Figure 19. Number of Problem-Solving Courts in the United States by Type, 2015. Source: Hughes & Reichert (2017).

create an interactive web version of the model with links to important re-sources for each intercept point. Each intercept represents a decision point, and opportunity to divert and intervene at the lowest level possible and min-imize the collateral consequences for a veteran getting more deeply involved in the justice system (Edelman, 2018, p. 16). The interactive site can be accessed at the following link: https://info.nicic.gov/jiv/node/113.

To create templates for successful evidence-based interventions and duplicate them throughout the nation, SAMSHA's *Jail Diversion and Trauma Recovery Services for Veterans Initiative* has led to the funding of pilot programs in several states targeting veterans' diversion (Center for Mental Health Services National Gains Center, 2011, pp. 2–4). These and other initiatives have contributed to the development of additional interventions, such as the

Veteran-Specific Modifications of Sequential Intercept Interventions

Range of Interventions*	Veteran–Specific Modifications
1) **Prebooking, police-based** with treatment in lieu of arrest.	--Development of **Specialized Dockets** with Veteran **Mentors**, and treatment from Department of Veterans Affairs rather than the state.
2) **Post-booking, jail-based** with treatment in lieu of incarceration or with reduced incarceration and/or reduced charges.	Coordination with **local veterans groups.**
3) **Post-booking, court-based** with use of adjudication or post-adjudication methods to reduce or forego incarceration or charges.	--Efforts to **identify veterans at the point of entry** into the criminal justice system. --**Coordination** with government to determine veteran status and Entitlements.
4) **Reentry Programs** to link parolees with resources after they have completed their sentence, perhaps in conjunction with early release.	--Veteran counselors embedded with police **during emergency response.**
5) **Combinations of one or more of the above.**	--**PTSD or veteran designations** on license plates and drivers' licenses.

Figure 20. Source: Loveland & Boyle (2006, pp. 131–132); Seamone (2011).

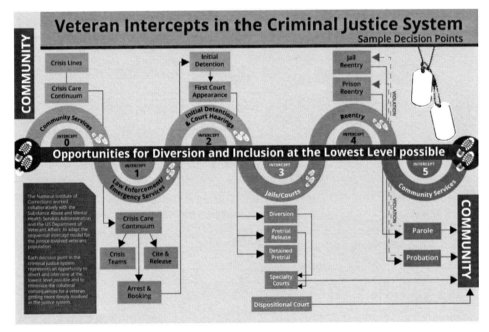

Figure 21. Source: National Institute of Corrections, n.d.

Operation Recovery program piloted in thirteen sites throughout the country, which sends mental health professionals into the jails to identify, interview, and evaluate veteran inmates, and then advocate for classification determinations and other measures that will target treatment needs before veterans go to trial (Bryant, 2012).

II. Veterans Treatment Courts as a Unique Form of Problem-Solving Court

Although there are at least fourteen different types of problem-solving courts, including drug treatment courts, mental health courts, Driving Under the Influence (DUI) courts, and domestic violence courts (Seamone, 2011, p. 35), the veterans treatment court has gained great publicity as the embodiment of the treatment-court movement. One of the main reasons is the rapid expansion of the veterans treatment courts in the short time that they have existed. Compared with all other courts, including more than 2,400 drug treatment courts "Veterans Treatment Courts are one of the fastest growing specialty court types in the U.S." (Tsai et al., 2018, p. 236).

> As of early 2018, there were **461** veterans treatment courts in at least **43** states, with others in the planning stages (Tsai et al., 2018; Justice for Vets, n.d.).

While some researchers have conducted detailed examinations of the differences and similarities between these courts (Tsai et al., 2018; Flatley, Clark, Rosenthal, & Blue-Howells, 2017; Baldwin, 2016), this chapter approaches veterans treatment courts mainly from the perspective of their important lessons for criminologists and other correctional professionals. Consequently, the first part explores the types of veteran offenders who are most likely to be diverted by the veterans treatment courts. The few trends that exist in the veterans treatment courts, given their wide variety, are vital to understand because professionals might otherwise reach faulty assumptions regarding those veteran inmates who are *not* diverted through these programs.

Importantly, for a variety of administrative reasons, veterans treatment courts routinely reject veterans perfectly suitable for participation and who have legitimate treatment needs making it dangerous to assume anything solely because a veteran may have been considered and rejected for participation. The second part highlights some underlying aspects of the veterans treatment courts that are instructive for addressing the needs of veterans in prisons and jails. Finally, despite the significant differences between interventions for veterans living in the community versus interventions for veteran inmates, veterans' advocates and correctional professionals can learn much from how the veterans treatment courts have responded to criticisms of veteran-specific interventions in the courts.

Some Basic Trends in Veterans Treatment Courts

The Veterans Treatment Court Concept

Before examining the veterans treatment court trends, it is vital to recognize what a treatment court is and what it is not. Most treatment courts are not *courts* in the traditional sense. Although they exist in a familiar setting with a bailiff, a judge in a robe, lawyers on both sides of the aisle, and may involve short periods of "therapeutic" incarceration, these outward appearances are deceiving (Seamone, 2011). For example, treatment court participants are commonly called "clients" in these settings, not defendants (McLeod, 2012, p. 1613). Although there is formality in these programs, they lack the adversarial aspect of criminal litigation that is common to criminal courts because the focus is on treatment rather than punishment. Veterans treatment courts are programs designed to aid effective mental health treatment of offenders, largely as a result of combat trauma, and to assist in the readjustment to civilian society following military service (Cavanaugh, 2011, p. 479).

The most salient aspect is the development of a treatment plan tailored to the veteran's unique needs. The plan may include vocational rehabilitation, restitution, and family support components that collectively target the factors that have contributed to instability in the veteran's life. In all treatment courts, teams of interdisciplinary professionals monitor the veteran's adherence to the plan and use the formality of the court and the inherent authority of the treatment court judge to hold the veterans accountable for their progress (Seamone, 2011).

On the one hand, accountability may involve imposing a range of sanctions for noncompliance, which might begin at shaming, additional court appearances to review progress, extend to essays or community service, and end at a day or week in jail. On the other hand, such accountability involves reward, which may take the form of public praise, fewer status hearings, and commemorative coins, hats, shirts, or gift cards. However, normally, when a veteran participant is terminated from a veterans treatment court for failure to comply with the program, the case is assigned to a different judge for sentencing using traditional procedures. Based on these differences, a veterans treatment court is not a court in the traditional sense of the word because it exists for the purpose of keeping veterans out of normal criminal adjudication channels (Seamone, 2011).

While the veterans treatment court has different aims than a traditional criminal court, it does not usually exist as a separate court system apart from the operation of criminal courts. In most cases, the veterans' treatment "court" is nothing more than a specific day when a judge clears the calendar of general offenders and dockets the appearance of similarly situated offenders with prior military service. Within the same courtroom in the same courthouse, a single judge might wear the veterans treatment court judge hat on Monday afternoons, the mental health treatment court hat on Tuesday afternoons, and hear cases involving domestic violence temporary restraining orders on Thursdays. In fact, studies have revealed that most veterans treatment court judges also preside over at least one other specialized court docket in addition to the veterans' docket (Baldwin, 2013, p. 16). While there is certainly room for variation, and some counties may have a large enough veteran population to devote more time, it cannot be overlooked that:

> Veterans treatment courts are ***coordination and consolidation tools*** that enable focused interventions for an easily accessible collection of offenders with similar needs, maximizing the judge's ability to consult with treatment professionals in real-time during court appearances (McCormick-Goodhart, 2013).

Given the fact that offenders would have to make court appearances regardless of whether they were on a specific treatment court's docket, treatment courts represent an effective redistribution of court resources rather than the creation of an entirely different court system.

Researchers have quickly realized that "no two veterans treatment courts are identical" in operation because of a host of factors (McCormick-Goodhart, 2013, p. 909). The quality of individual relationships between members of a treatment team largely determines how these courts function (Seamone, 2011, p. 36). Another significant factor that shapes the operation of these courts is how they came to exist, in other words, whether they were created through a legislative act or through the grass-roots efforts of a treatment court judge or a specific community organization. While a number of states have enacted laws that regulate admissions criteria and other operational considerations (e.g., Clark, McGuire, & Blue-Howells, 2010), most veterans treatment courts—especially the ones that have become the national models—owe their existence to bold judges and interdisciplinary profession-

als who saw the immediate needs for a specially tailored approach to fre-
quent-flyers through their dockets (McLeod, 2012, p. 1607). This was the
case when the first drug treatment court emerged in Miami-Dade County,
Florida, in 1989, when the first mental health court emerged in Broward
County, Florida, in 1997, and when Judge Robert Russell, Jr., developed the
popularized veterans treatment court model in Buffalo, New York in 2008.

While there was a special docket for veterans in Anchorage, Alaska in
2004 (Smith, 2012), Judge Russell charted new territory. He was not directed to create a veterans' court, but rather developed one on his own initiative
because an increasing number of Iraq and Afghanistan veterans were
appearing on his criminal docket with common types of readjustment difficulties (Russell, 2009; Russell, 2015). Then-Chairman of the Joint Chiefs of
Staff, Admiral Michael Mullen, has hailed the effectiveness of the veteran
peer-mentor component that characterizes Judge Russell's Buffalo Veterans
Treatment Court model (Mullen, 2011, p. 1). This distinguishing aspect of
the veterans treatment courts did not come as a result of a peer-reviewed,
double-blinded scientific study. Instead, this essential element arose from
Judge Russell's observation of veterans' reluctance to speak in court without
having the opportunity to share their concerns with another veteran who
shared similar experiences (Salem, 2011, p. 10).

Most importantly, the unprecedented incorporation of Veterans Administration employees into the structure of a local court for coordinating prompt
federal healthcare did not take place as a result of orders from the highest
echelons in Washington, but rather as collaboration between the local court
and the local Veterans Administration. While participants in the veterans
treatment courts range from Korean War veterans to Global War on Terrorism veterans,

> **A 2018 nationwide study of 7,931 veterans treatment court partic-
> ipants revealed that they were mainly white, male, and in their
> forties. Roughly one-third served in Operation Enduring Free-
> dom and Operation Iraqi Freedom. The most common offenses
> were "DUI, public order, and drug offenses," and more than one-
> third of the participants had a PTSD diagnosis (Tsai et al., 2018).**

We can identify some trends in these courts, and a set of ten overarching veterans treatment court principles is reproduced in the Appendix to this chapter. However, most of these courts vary because they have developed with
the support of local organizations and are heavily influenced by local demographics.

Three Noteworthy Veterans Treatment Court Trends

While the Supreme Court has recognized historical efforts to assist veterans in the criminal justice system (*Porter v. McCollum,* 2009), some researchers observe a growing trend of prosecutors desiring to give leniency to combat veterans, especially those who have deployed to combat and sustained PTSD (Wilson, Brodsky, Neal, & Cramer, 2011a). There are, of course, prosecutors who will see it as part of their duty as advocates to demean the veterans, question their status, and oppose any diagnoses or suggestion of combat-related mental health conditions (Seamone, 2011). Where prosecutors do extend favorable consideration, their efforts are largely based on a sense of patriotism and feelings that military service played a role in the circumstances of the offense (Wilson et al., 2011a). Importantly, there does not have to be a veterans treatment court in place for a district attorney or a court to incorporate treatment and diversionary measures. Federal prosecutors, for example, have used pretrial diversion agreements within the federal system to enable treatment for veterans (Seamone, 2011).

With the proliferation of veterans treatment courts in some communities, there is a risk that some individuals including correctional professionals might reach negative opinions about the veteran inmates because they were not favorably considered for diversion. They might, for example, look with suspicion on veterans who were passed over or rejected by the veterans treatment courts believing that all veterans with credible treatment needs will be diverted after thorough evaluation. Such non-selection might possibly suggest: (1) that the veteran does not suffer from a serious enough mental condition to warrant specialized intervention; (2) that the veteran is malingering; (3) that the veteran lacks the ability to successfully complete a treatment-based program; or (4) that the veteran would cause a disruption to other treatment program participants. For the reasons discussed below, none of these assumptions is warranted simply based on affirmative rejection from or non-selection by a veterans treatment court program.

Common Trends in Veterans Treatment Courts

A given offender's participation in a veterans treatment court may be influenced by at least nine major considerations. Accordingly, "significant variability exists across jurisdictions regarding eligibility criteria, with some courts requiring a link between a veteran's service, the illness, and the crime; some permitting violent felonies; and some accepting combat veterans from earlier eras" (Johnson et al., 2017, p. 144).

While the substantial number of veterans treatment courts has permitted a great deal of variety, two common trends are noteworthy because they gen-

---

Major Considerations in Veterans Treatment Court Eligibility

1. Severity of Crime (Felony or Misdemeanor)
2. Type of Crime (Violent or Nonviolent, Vicitm, Sexual Offense, Domestic Violence)
3. Military Experience (Combat or Noncombat)
4. Military Campaign (Global War on Terrorism or earlier)
5. Mental Condition Type (Diagnosable or Nondiagnosable)
6. Mental Condition Origin (Service or Non-service-related)
7. VA Benefit Eligibility (Minimum Active Service Requirement, Character of Discharge)
8. Adjudication Stage (Pre-Plea, Post-Plea, Post-Conviction)
9. Length of Treatment (Months or Years, Continued Probation)

Source: Holbrook & Anderson (2011); Seamone (2011); McCormick-Goodhart (2013); Baldwin (2013).

---

erally lead to the rejection of a substantial number of applicants with significant treatment needs who would benefit greatly from targeted alternatives. First, many veterans treatment courts limit eligibility to nonviolent and misdemeanor offenses. Out of 461 courts, 20 percent considered only misdemeanors and 14 percent considered only felonies. Substantial clusters of courts further differentiated cases, such as the 18 percent of courts that would limit their consideration of violent offenses only to domestic violence cases or the 16 percent who would take no violent offenses whatsoever (Tsai et al., 2018). Any preference to avoid violent offenses is of concern because violent felony offenses are commonly related to untreated combat and operational stress injuries, thus preventing the most effective interventions for those with dire mental health treatment needs (Lithwick, 2010; Kavanaugh, 2011; Seamone, 2011).

The second trend of concern is the requirement for only those with Veterans Administration benefit eligibility to participate in the veterans treatment court program. The 2013 study of seventy-four veterans treatment courts across the nation reveals that "one-third do not allow veterans who are ineligible for Veterans Administration services," with a number categorically barring participation solely by virtue of a Dishonorable, Bad-Conduct, or Other-than-Honorable Discharge (Baldwin, p. 13). The distinction is important because individuals with Other than Honorable and Bad-Conduct discharges may still qualify for various benefits if their service is deemed other than dishonorable (see Chapters 2 and 6).

From a pure budgetary perspective, this requirement makes sense since the Veterans Administration assumes the cost of treating eligible veterans without any significant burden to the state (Seamone, 2011). But, this is a problem for an estimated 20 percent of veteran offenders who are ineligible for Veterans Administration healthcare as a result of their discharge characterization (Rosenthal & McGuire, 2013). The 20 percent figure is only an approximation and is likely an underestimate due to the fact that "[m]any veterans with bad papers won't admit it[,] feel that they are penalized for life," and conceal their discharges because of shame that they were branded as undesirable and less than honorable (MacPherson, 1992, p. 577).

In fact, upon careful examination, some correctional administrators have found far greater numbers of veteran inmates with stigmatizing discharges than they originally believed. Chapter 2 describes the nuances of discharge status. For these purposes, however, remember that a veteran who meets all of a veterans treatment court's other criteria for treatment may be rejected solely as a basis of a discharge, relating to a time when they were still in late adolescence.

Some Key Lessons

Those concerned with the cost of corrections should understand the basis for this variety in the structure and operation of most veterans treatment courts. Those in correctional administration deal with some overlapping populations. Importantly, despite an insatiable appetite for longitudinal data to demonstrate the effectiveness of treatment interventions in criminal justice, veterans treatment courts have erupted without an evidence-based approach or clear answers on the connection between mental illness and offending (see Chapters 3 and 4 for a discussion of veteran offending).

> **First-responders to emergencies are not waiting on definitive statistics on the nature of [causal links between PTSD and offending] to tell them what they already know: Awareness of untreated veteran mental health conditions and de-escalation of their symptoms can save not only the veterans in crisis, but the lives of police officers and innocent bystanders as well (Seamone, 2011, p. 26).**

In addressing untreated combat and operational stress injuries, veterans treatment court judges and treatment teams are first-responders, just like correctional staff. The same forces that have moved many jurisdictions to develop veterans treatment courts affect prisons and jails, as evident in the experiences of former Sheriff Randall Liberty in Kennebec County, Maine. He

---

Six Unresolved Issues Bearing on the Development of Veterans Treatment Courts

1. Do veterans have different penal and post-release needs versus the general inmate population?
2. Could this be linked to military experience, injuries, character of discharge, penal treatment needs, pre-release planning, and service coordination?
3. Do veterans diagnosed with PTSD and/or Traumatic Brain Injury have a propensity to offend more than veterans not diagnosed?
4. Is there a causal effect between military service and criminal behavior in some veterans? In addition, some veterans claim there is a connection to their homelessness and substance abuse to PTSD.
5. What are the policy, practice, and financial implications for corrections and other parties?
6. Could some of this be linked to the relaxed recruitment posture and/or moral waiver since the Operation Enduring Freedom/Operation Iraqi Freedom conflict?

Figure 22. Source: Schaffer (2009, p. 46).

established a veterans dormitory in his jail to address the treatment needs of incarcerated veterans well before the county opened its veterans treatment court. Not only did Sheriff Liberty accept veterans transferred from other county jails, but his efforts were instrumental in the development of the county's veterans treatment court (see Chapter 9). Some may suggest that further evidence is required on a host of scholarly questions to justify the creation of court interventions, as evident in psychologist Bradley Schaffer's identification of six "veteran-specific issues and underlying themes," in Figure 22.

Due to the variance in the veteran population, none of these questions is easy. However, the experience of most of the nation's 461 veterans treatment courts and the 86 veterans' dormitory programs in county jails and state prisons (Crime Sider Staff, 2018) reveals the immense value of developing practical solutions to immediate problems, rather than delaying intervention for the sake of *paralysis by analysis*.

As the challenges presented by veteran readjustment became clear, correctional professionals supported diversion alternatives, veterans treatment courts, and corrections-based interventions for veterans. At the Summer 2005 Large Jail Network Meeting, the director for the Bureau of Justice Assistance's Jail and Work Industry Center discussed the impact of federal bars to benefits for incarcerated veterans (Miller, 2005, p. 5). Later, at the Winter Large Jail Network Meeting, psychiatry professor Joel A. Dvoskin presented on mental health services in jails, identifying adult combat veterans and combat veterans who were also victims of child abuse as "special populations" with particular "clinical needs" (2005, p. 23). In 2008, the same year that Judge Russell created the nation's first prototype for a veterans treatment court, participants in the September 2008 Large Jail Network Meeting identified the following topic as an issue to be covered at subsequent gatherings: "Returning veterans: disabilities, post-traumatic stress disorder, and early assistance programs" (National Institute of Corrections, 2008, p. 44).

By March 2010, the Large Jail Network Meeting minutes extensively covered "Programs for Veterans/Homeless Vets," with discussions ranging from:

- diversion programs intended to assist veterans with PTSD who would otherwise lose their benefits in South Carolina jails;
- the grass-roots development of a veterans court in Wisconsin;
- methodologies for identifying veterans in Kansas during the intake process; and
- the expansion of a Minnesota Mental Health Court into a separate docket for veterans; to
- the manner in which Operation Iraqi Freedom/Operation Enduring Freedom veterans are less likely than World War II and Vietnam veterans to engage the VFW for assistance because "veterans' issues today are different"

Source: National Institute of Corrections (2010, pp. 47–48).

Subsequently, at the 2012 Large Jail Network Meeting, veteran-specific issues ranged from:

- the "sticking point that [Veterans Administration] benefits have been lost when military veterans find themselves in jail";
- the ability of the jail to provide information to the Veterans Administration for the purpose of helping veteran find housing to avoid homelessness;
- booking rates of 200 veterans per month in one facility; and
- the $140,000 per year cost of dialysis for veteran inmates whose termi-

nated benefits cannot be used for their treatment; to, importantly,
- news of the development of a "specialized housing unit for veterans" in Shelby County, Tennessee "where Veterans Administration staff members come into the unit to provide services"

Source: National Institute of Corrections (2012, pp. 40–41).

The progressively expansive discussion of issues involving justice-involved veterans signals a clear desire to assist this population.

The culmination of this increased interest in justice-involved veterans was the National Sheriffs' Association's Resolution 2012-7, the "National Sheriffs' Association supports veterans treatment courts and Justice for Vets—the national clearinghouse for veterans treatment courts" (National Sheriffs' Association, 2012, p. 19). The resolution echoed other existing supportive statements from criminal justice associations, including the National District Attorney's Association, the Conference of Chief Justices, and the Conference of State Court Administrators (Seamone, 2011, p. 35). The sheriffs' endorsement is especially noteworthy because they run the very jails that are the source of diversion efforts for veteran offenders. This mounting of support has led to a fertile ground for collaboration and sharing of ideas. In some cases, participation in the Large Jail Network Meetings or exposure to articles in corrections trade publications led to the establishment of veterans housing units (see Chapter 9).

Responses to Criticisms of Veterans Treatment Courts

Even though veterans treatment courts raise some issues that do not arise in the corrections context, given that veterans treatment courts exist to *prevent* incarceration, a rich dialogue has emerged from critics' attacks on veterans treatment courts and the justice system's responses. Correctional professionals can still benefit from considering the varied positions on veterans treatment courts because some of the arguments apply to any justice-system intervention specifically tailored to veterans' needs, wherever it occurs. Beyond this, it may help veterans' advocates and cost-conscious urban planners to consider responses to potential criticisms that could occur in response to the implementation of a veteran-centric program in a given prison or jail. With that said, Figure 23 summarizes the eight most common attacks on veterans treatment courts:

Some of the attacks are based on shaky ground. For example, the position that veterans treatment courts unfairly stigmatize veterans by focusing on mental health disorders linked to crime "refuse[s] to acknowledge that such wounds do exist or that some offenders return from war as changed

---

Eight Common Objections to Veterans Treatment Courts

1. Creation of a separate court system for veterans represents preferential treatment solely based on military status;
2. Special treatment for veterans with mental health disorders but no similar assistance to nonveteran offenders with mental health disorders, thereby denying needed help;
3. Absence of consideration for victims' interests in targeting veteran offenders for special services;
4. Veterans' treatment courts represent a "free pass" that condones offending behavior, such as by attributing the offense to PTSD;
5. Veterans with mental illness and substance abuse problems are served by existing mental health and drug courts and do not require a veterans' court based solely on their occupation;
6. Veterans' courts' focus on offending by veterans with mental illness promotes the Wacko-Vet Myth and stigmatizes all veterans, especially among potential employers; and
7. Veterans treatment courts are inconsistent with the principles of the 14th Amendment's equal protection clause by providing privileges based on "who they are rather than what they are accused of doing or what problems they have" (Schaller, 2012, p. 208).
8. In veterans' courts that require guilty pleas prior to participation, there is concern that they are forfeiting various rights accorded by traditional due process safeguards simply so they can benefit from needed treatment.

Figure 23. Source: Kavanaugh (2011); Holbrook (2011); Holbrook & Anderson (2011); Schaller (2012); McCormick-Goodhart (2013).

people" (McCormick-Goodhart, 2013, pp. 924–925). Similarly, the suggestion that veterans treatment courts privilege veterans over other offenders simply by providing targeted services ignores the universal truth that "it is impossible to serve every similarly situated criminal defendant equally." The objection would apply to any specialized court, not just ones for veterans (McCormick-Goodhart, 2013, p. 922). One critic recently condemned veterans treatment courts, suggesting that all programs exist solely based on the status of the offender as a military veteran (Collins, 2017). On this view, veterans treatment courts should not be considered as problem-solving courts because there is no "systematic 'problem' to 'be solved'" in that when the veterans are finished with the court process they will not stop being veterans (Collins, 2017, pp. 1484, 1494). Such a broad attack totally glosses over the fact that the veterans' cultural transformation in the military often poses obstacles to successful readjustment without assistance in the transition back to civilian society and problems occur when veterans are influenced by combat and operational stress injuries. Based on their nuances, other positions seem to have more salience. The remainder of this section considers three of the most common responses that apply to several objections simultaneously.

1. The Issue of Special Treatment Denied to Other Individuals with Mental Health Needs

Individuals who are concerned about different treatment for nonmilitary defendants with PTSD often fail to recognize that Veterans Administration benefits come by virtue of military service. Veterans are qualified for certain benefits because they earned them by assuming duties that very few Americans undertake, placing themselves at substantial risk during the term of their service. Furthermore, in many cases, military service caused or contributed to the veteran's mental health condition. As a result of these considerations, assistance from the Veterans Administration, whether financial or medical, comes by virtue of law and is not a matter of preferential treatment. The Veterans Administration's cumbersome system for determining benefit eligibility is the best example of the Veterans Administration's strict adherence to legal standards in providing compensation and healthcare (see Chapter 5). With separate sources of federal funding to address criminally involved veterans' mental health and readjustment needs, it is of tremendous benefit to the state or local criminal justice entity to encourage full use of those benefits. In 2005, a Department of Justice report concluded:

> [A]rranging for severely ill offenders to qualify for Federal entitlements not only facilitates access to community-based care but can also 1) reduce the financial burden on the state and local governments that fund indigent health care systems and 2) allow community-based service providers to increase the number of disabled offenders served (Conly, 2005, p. 25).

Consequently, rather than detracting from non-veterans, specifically targeted Veterans Administration interventions for justice-involved veterans accrue to the benefit of nonveteran inmates and defendants by freeing up more local and state resources. It is also noteworthy, as Chapter 4 shows, that as a result from combat-related PTSD and other operational stress injuries, treatment of veterans is measurably different from treatment for other sorts of trauma, requiring the specialized types of interventions that the Veterans Administration has perfected over the years. As noted by attorney Tiffany Cartwright, "for combat veterans, their underlying problem is not their substance abuse, or even their PTSD—it is their combat trauma, and that is something that cannot be addressed effectively in a traditional drug treatment or mental health court" (2011, p. 303).

2. The Creation of a Separate Court System for Veterans

The earlier discussion in this chapter highlighted the manner in which veterans treatment courts represent rearranging of the docket to target concentrated efforts on specific types of offenders. None of these dockets detract from adjudication of other cases, but they do make management of specific types of offenders far more efficient. With specialized dockets for cases ranging from domestic violence to prostitution in some court systems, the veterans treatment court is not an exception but rather a primary example of a problem-focused approach to criminal justice (McCormick-Goodhart, 2013).

Importantly, different treatment for war-traumatized offenders is not necessarily preferential treatment (Pentland, 1979, p. 526). Although each of these specialized programs has some unique factors, specialized interventions in any of these programs may be necessary to facilitate treatment of the underlying problem. For example, while the inclusion of veteran mentors from the community is a *different* aspect of veterans treatment courts that may not occur in any other specialized treatment court, it is particularly necessary to facilitate treatment because the military culture results in a situation where veterans are unlikely to share their experiences and concerns with anyone who has not had similar experiences.

Military culture also distinguishes veterans from other inmates. Their training makes them more disciplined and capable of adhering to the orders of authority figures such as judges (Cavanaugh, 2011, p. 481). Veteran mentors are necessary to this end because they can help to identify issues that a veterans treatment court participant might even withhold from a judge or mental health provider due to this veteran-specific experience (Russell, 2009).

3. Moral Obligation

Despite a variety of explanations, it is still important to recognize the simplicity of the response that veterans sacrificed something for the nation and deserve additional opportunities to live productive lives in society. In McCormick-Goodhart's study of veterans treatment courts, he notes the Supreme Court's *Porter v. McCollum* as strong support that veterans, especially combat veterans, are deserving of leniency based on their military service (2013, p. 921). The Court's opinion addressed the importance of a defendant's right in a capital case to present evidence of military service during sentencing, recognizing the long history of leniency accorded to veterans, especially who served on the frontlines (*Porter v. McCollum,* 2009). In April of 2000, the United Kingdom codified this obligation in the form of a *Military Covenant* between society and ex-service members, which had formerly existed only as "an unspoken pact" (Howard League on Penal Reform, 2011, p. 14). The U. K. *Covenant* holds that:

> **[I]n putting the needs of the nation before their own, servicemen forego rights enjoyed by other citizens and submit to laws not applicable to civilian life. In return, they are entitled to fair treatment, to be valued and respected as individuals, and that they and their families will be sustained and rewarded by commensurate terms and conditions of service (Howard League on Penal Reform, 2011, p. 14).**

Although a continent away, it is not uncommon to find U.S. veterans treatment court judges and legislators defending veterans treatment courts on the basis of the unwritten rule that the government bears a responsibility to return the combat veteran and his or her family at least to the position they were in prior to military service (McCormick-Goodhart, 2013). The fundamental assumption underlying all veterans treatment courts is that the veteran's criminal involvement is related in some way to readjustment difficulties in transitioning back to society. The significant number of veterans with readjustment difficulties is profound. When divorced from diagnostic categories, large studies indicate that more than half the population of returned Operation Iraqi Freedom and Operation Enduring Freedom veterans "was struggling with anger control problems, and nearly one-third had engaged in behaviors that put themselves or others at risk since homecoming" (Sayer et al., 2010, p. 594).

The connection between these common problems in readjustment and criminal justice involvement is quite evident. Ultimately the moral obligation of courts is not to avoid the imposition of severe criminal sanctions, but rather to use to court as a point of intervention to deliver services that the veterans might otherwise fail to obtain on their own. The distinction is an important one because, in many instances, there may be no other way besides court-supervised and leveraged efforts to ensure that the veteran follows-through with treatment (Seamone, 2011).

4. Free Passes

The final response dovetails with the moral obligation to deliver effective treatment that will significantly improve the veteran's quality of life and read-justment to society. Namely, critics argue that the veterans, based on their status, obtain a "free pass" to avoid the types of punitive response that non-veteran inmates experience while incarcerated or in the absence of targeted and comprehensive treatment. However, veterans participating in treatment courts must endure program requirements far more demanding than supervision in the community. For example, program duration may require twelve-to-twenty-four months of regular appearances by the judge and a full regimen of programs to target various co-occurring problems related to debt, unemployment, and family disharmony. Further, there is the potential that termination from a veterans treatment court will lead to imposition of a sentence and far greater consequences (McCormick-Goodhart, 2013).

An additional, overlooked but significant, factor is the discomfort many veterans face when undergoing treatment for PTSD and other mental health conditions. Some of the most effective evidence-based treatment techniques that the court will inevitably mandate through the Veterans Administration are exposure therapies, which require the patients to repeatedly revisit their most distressing trauma to fully process the event (see Chapter 8's discussion of re-experiencing components and voluntariness in program participation).

Over the course of such treatment, most veterans will experience adverse symptoms to the point that they outwardly appear to be getting worse. For these reasons, participation in a veterans treatment court not only requires a more significant commitment of time and submission to various requirements that affect one's freedom of choice and behavior, but it may be extraordinarily painful as well. A 2012 study of seventy-four veterans treatment courts revealed that "one in five eligible veterans opt out, primarily because they consider the veterans treatment court program to be too rigorous or they do not want treatment" (Baldwin, 2013, p. 6), suggesting that jail or probation through the regular justice system might be more of a "free pass" than a veterans treatment court.

Concluding Remarks

This chapter provided a number of considerations regarding the decarceration movement and the function of veterans treatment courts as a salient aspect of the Sequential Intercept Model. Recognizing distinct differences between diversionary courts and confinement facilities, other chapters of this book provide additional insights. Chapter 7's discussion of veterans groups, Chapter 8's discussion of institutional programs for veterans, and Chapter 9's discussion of veterans' dormitories reveal the manner in which correctional professionals have responded to concerns over interventions for incarcerated veterans. Further, Chapter 10 concludes this book by introducing a threat-mitigation paradigm in response to varied criticisms.

Appendix

Ten Key Components of Veterans' Treatment Courts

Key Component One: Veterans treatment court integrates alcohol, drug treatment, and mental health services with justice system case processing.

Key Component Two: Using a non-adversarial approach, prosecution and defense counsel promote public safety while protecting participants' due process rights.

Key Component Three: Eligible participants are identified early and promptly placed in the veterans treatment court program.

Key Component Four: The veterans treatment court provides access to a continuum of alcohol, drug, mental health and other related treatment and rehabilitation services.

Key Component Five: Abstinence is monitored by frequent alcohol and other drug testing.

Key Component Six: A coordinated strategy governs veterans treatment court responses to participants' compliance.

Key Component Seven: Ongoing judicial interaction with each veteran is essential.

Key Component Eight: Monitoring and evaluation measures the achievement of program goals and gauges effectiveness.

Key Component Nine: Continuing interdisciplinary education promotes effective veterans treatment court planning, implementation, and operation.

Key Component Ten: Forging partnerships among the veterans treatment court, the Veterans Administration, public agencies, and community-based organizations generates local support and enhances the veterans treatment court's effectiveness.

Source: Russell (2009, pp. 365–367).

Chapter 7

BASIC ATTRIBUTES OF VETERANS' GROUPS IN CONFINED SETTINGS

This chapter has two aims. First, it provides insight on the variety of veterans' organizations that have developed within confined settings, including the characteristics that have consistently proven the effectiveness of these programs. Second, it discusses eleven discrete features of veterans' groups and institutional programs that can be replicated in any facility for specific benefits to the veteran inmates and the institution. Although the attributes of veterans in confinement have long been recognized as benefits to the institution (Bennett, 1954), the majority of veterans' prison groups evolved mostly due to a lack of traditional support from veterans' service organizations during and following the Vietnam War (MacPherson, 1992).

As a consequence of self-sufficiency, the emergent framework included groups of inmate veterans staffed by elected peer officers, according to bylaws, with the sponsorship of an institutional staff member and oftentimes a community organization, such as the Vietnam Veterans of America (VVA). While these groups often provide *informal* methods of treatment, such as group counseling or "rap sessions," most do not exist for the primary purpose of treatment. Most do not have residential dormitory components. And, most must comply with the institutional standards applicable to other non-veteran organizations, such as religious or cultural groups in the facility. In some cases, prison groups intended for veterans must be "all-inclusive"—open membership to inmates with no prior military experience (Hubert, 2009). The veterans' groups discussed in this chapter can be distinguished from more intensive institutionally sponsored programs for veterans that exist primarily to address the veterans' special needs, such as an underlying mental health condition or to ensure optimal reentry following release.

I. "Veterans Incarcerated": The Proliferation of Veterans Groups in American Prisons

Incarcerated veterans enjoy shared cultural experiences, which make them prime candidates for being organized into productive groups during their time behind bars (*see* Chapter 1). At the General Session of the Congress of Corrections in 2013, Secretary of Veterans' Affairs, General Eric Shinseki, mentioned the benefits of organizing veterans in their own segregated dorms, especially because veteran "inmates tend to take care of each other when they have shared experience" (Shinskei, 2013). This lesson resonates most, not only in the more contemporary prison programs, but also in the prison veterans' groups that have existed in the nation, some for more than a generation (Edelman, 2018). While there is a trend of veterans' housing units forming in at least twenty-nine states (Arkansas, Arizona, California, Colorado, Connecticut, Delaware, Florida, Georgia, Illinois, Indiana, Kentucky, Massachusetts, Maine, Michigan, Mississippi, Missouri, North Carolina, Nebraska, Nevada, New York, Ohio, Pennsylvania, South Carolina, Tennessee, Texas, Virginia, Washington, Wisconsin, and West Virginia), their number pales in comparison to nonresidential veterans' organizations within prisons. Although there have been informal veterans' groups in custodial settings in the aftermath of most wars, a major change occurred in the advent of Vietnam, which led veterans to seek formal recognition of their association while in custody.

Following World War II, and in the face of overwhelming community support, veterans service organizations, including the American Legion and Veterans of Foreign Wars, rallied to the defense of veterans who committed criminal offenses. There was a special effort to avoid the perception that the war had turned veterans into unpredictably violent threats to society (Burkett & Whitley, 1998, pp. 64–65). Notably, in a few short decades, the same organizations avoided incarcerated Vietnam Veterans. Researcher Myra MacPherson cites the Vietnam era as the impetus for most contemporary veterans' groups in jails and prisons.

Comparing Vietnam veterans to veterans of prior wars, MacPherson explains that veterans service organizations avoided confined Vietnam veterans, with their most conservative members believing that widespread accounts of their drug addiction and atrocities committed overseas were tarnishing their reputation as the prior wars' Greatest Generation (MacPherson, 1992). Inevitably, in the face of an unpopular war, as support waned, inmates had to form their own prison organizations to address their pressing needs. Forming these organizations was little different from the manner in which they assembled to accomplish their military duties, complete with a hierarchy of elected officers, defined duties, and mission statements.

The largest known group of veteran inmates in the 1970s was the Veterans Incarcerated at Angola, the Louisiana State Penitentiary, which had more than 400 members (May, 1979). Separated from the Veterans Administration's regional offices by hundreds of miles and confused by the lack of consistent information on the types of benefits they could obtain, Angola's veterans began to seek out information and training from the Veterans Administration. In this period, before legislation stripped the inmates of cash stipends that accompanied G.I. Bill benefits, the incorrect assumption that an honorably discharged inmate was not entitled to benefits would cost that inmate more than $388 per month, which often assisted his family members (Rideau, 1976, p. 167). Beyond this, inmates learned that, even armed with the right information about benefit eligibility, "[i]t becomes dysfunctional to quote benefits but provide [no] help obtaining them" (Pentland, 1979, p. 525).

Thus, Angola's program evolved to a point where "a core of about thirty inmates . . . received special instruction from Veterans Administration counselors in advising other veterans of the benefits they [were] entitled to" (May, 1979, p. 13). In some cases, the penitentiary's correctional officers even sought assistance from the "Inmate/Counselors" regarding their own Veterans Administration entitlements given the skills and capabilities that group members had developed. Based on the success of programs like Angola's, and the reality that trained veterans may be necessary to effectuate governmental outreach efforts, a vocal proponent of "onsite incarcerated veterans affairs offices" testified to the following at a Senate hearing in 1979:

> [N]ot until incarcerated veterans affairs offices are established within prisons, staffed and operated by incarcerated veterans, or some variants thereof, will the little assistance that the Veterans' Administration and penal officials are giving to incarcerated veterans be of any significance in the Veterans Administration outreach to incarcerated veterans. (Merretazon, 1979, p. 179)

In the late 1970s, a similar prison office of veterans' affairs "staffed by incarcerated Veterans Administration work-study students, under the supervision of a Veterans Administration employee" also operated at a prison in Columbia, South Carolina (Cranston, 1979, p. 127). Although less popular today, two veterans who are serving life sentences, have continued this tradition in one state prison, assisting other veterans in the recovery of more than $5 million in Veterans Administration disability compensation since they began their efforts in 2005 (Rosenthal & McGuire, 2013, p. 360). Other states, besides Louisiana, with large veterans' groups in prisons in the 1970s included Ohio, Maryland, the District of Columbia, and New York. Over time, some of the programs represented such a success that veteran inmate leaders testified before Congress and informed President Jimmy Carter about their key issues (Kirkland, 1984).

Evident in the General Accounting Office's discovery of severe shortfalls in prison outreach programs of the 1970s (Comptroller General, 1974), this also meant that incarcerated veterans largely had to educate themselves, and each other, about applying for disability compensation benefits, upgrading discharges, and navigating the Veterans Administration system. In some cases, incarcerated veterans with unanswered requests for PTSD treatment help each other endure the hardships of managing their stress reactions with the mutual support provided by veterans' groups.

According to the testimony of Pennsylvania veteran inmate Comer Glass at a class action lawsuit in Philadelphia, "We started a little stress group on our own. We cried on each other's shoulders. We helped each other out. We listened to each other's stories. We started putting in paperwork for delayed stress disability" (*Carter v. Jeffes,* Settlement Hearing Transcript, 1987, pp. 323–324). Mental health treatment issues were addressed through different vehicles than the inmate groups, as institutions perceived more of a stake in the mental health of inmates. Yet, there were some notable exceptions.

In those prisons where groups of veteran inmates were able to obtain assistance from local mental health providers and secure counseling services, these relationships probably arose from the inmates' efforts to count the number of veterans within a facility. Self-initiated counts were similarly persuasive with correctional staff, who watched as the population of Vietnam veterans grew. Some groups, such as Project Base Camp in Florida, made it part of their mission to assess how many veterans were incarcerated, not only within specific institutions, but within the entire department of corrections. They did this through an intricate system of communication across facilities. A Vet Center employee who participated in the program testified to a congressional committee, "The unique aspect of this project is that this is an effort of incarcerated veterans to locate other incarcerated veterans" (Cohen, 1990, p. 100).

When veteran inmates were lucky enough to garner the support of mental health professionals, usually based on letter-writing campaigns to nearby Veterans Administration clinics, counselors sometimes used the structure of these prison self-help groups as an expedient to provide limited forms of group treatment. The Auburn Correctional Facility in Cayuga County, New York, represents one example where a Veterans Administration Vet Center psychologist, Dr. Peter Hayman, networked with the institution's VVA chapter to provide group readjustment counseling to war-traumatized inmates on a bi-monthly basis (LaRue, 1985; Sheridan, 1985). July 1985 marked the first time the facility's administrators permitted readjustment counseling within its walls. Even though the program was subject to national policy changes within the Veterans Administration, this innovation stemmed from the existence of a well-organized and receptive veterans' group at the institution and the statistics the group helped to assemble, which revealed that 450 out of 1,600 inmates at the maximum-security facility were veterans.

In response to the lack of institutional support, veterans' groups took hold in many large prison systems mostly during the Vietnam era. In January of 1979, a major grant from the Department of Labor to the National Council of Churches provided the impetus to solidify many self-help groups as a method to assist incarcerated veterans (Salerno, 1979, p. 56; May, 1979, p. 13). With the establishment of the Vietnam Veterans of America in 1978, the organization's constitution featured an Incarcerated Veterans Committee to address the needs of incarcerated veterans. Much to its credit, through its Projects and Programs Subcommittee, the Vietnam Veterans of America has helped to create chapters and replicate this program across the nation (Vietnam Veterans of America, Veterans Incarcerated Committee, n.d.), establishing some veterans groups as the only inmate organizations with national sponsorship (Wills, 2012, p. A3). As of August 2013, there were twenty-five active Vietnam Veterans of America chapters in confined settings within the United States (Vietnam Veterans of America Membership Department, personal communication, August 19, 2013).[9]

Although incarcerated veterans' groups existed in many shapes, forms, and sizes, and inmates joined them for a great many reasons, it is important to note the results of a study by the Veterans Administration, which estimated the existence of more than 227 prison groups devoted to veterans as of 2010, broken out into 23 informally recognized veteran groups within federal prisons, 57 formally recognized veterans groups within state prisons, and 147 informally recognized veterans groups within state prisons (Rosenthal & McGuire, 2013, p. 359).

According to a VA report, there were over 227 active veterans' groups in state and federal prisons across America as of 2010. Many of these programs grew during the Vietnam era when traditional veterans' organizations rarely visited or advocated for veteran inmates.

---

9. These groups include single chapters in Alabama, California, Louisiana, Montana, New Hampshire, and Virginia, two chapters in Florida and Pennsylvania, four chapters in Michigan and Missouri, and six chapters in Ohio.

An exploration of the Vietnam Veterans of America chapter at the Mark W. Stiles Unit in Texas in 2012 reveals why these programs still function today. These programs provide a method for veterans to share their pride at having served the nation and an opportunity to re-embody the same values that characterized that collective experience (Wills, 2012). This same attribute of working together for a greater cause in the spirit of prior honorable service is the hallmark of the most successful veterans' groups and explains why they have endured throughout the years.

In 1954, after consultation with the twenty-nine federal prison wardens, the Director of the Federal Bureau of Prisons, explained, "by and large the ex-GI made a better adjustment, profited more by the rehabilitation program, and generally found it easier to adjust than the man who had no military experience." For this reason, he concluded, "generally speaking, we would rather deal in our institutions with men who have had military background than with those who never had to get along in close quarters with other men or had to follow a military order" (Bennett, 1954, p. 42).

At the 1979 congressional hearings on incarcerated veterans' readjustment needs, Robert L. Carr, the Chief Psychologist of the U.S. Penitentiary at Lewisburg, similarly testified, "veterans are a different breed of cat . . . [t]hey are more flexible. They receive fewer incident reports. They are not into contraband and various other things that are illegal" (Carr, 1979, p. 177). Importantly, Dr. Carr testified about the shared attributes of incarcerated veterans from studies conducted at federal correctional institutions in Pennsylvania, Texas, Illinois, and Wisconsin, displayed in Figure 24 (Carr, 1979, p. 262).

Even though more than a generation has passed since Dr. Carr's observations of Vietnam veterans in selected U.S. prisons, the findings ring true today. Consistently, the studies of the Bureau of Justice Statistics and others reveal that the nation's incarcerated veterans are more likely to be first-time offenders than non-veterans (May, 1979; Mumola, 2000, p. 1) (reporting that veterans in state prison were 30 percent more likely than non-veterans [23 percent] to be first-time offenders). Noonan and Mumola (2007, p. 4) report nearly a third of incarcerated veterans as first-time offenders in comparison to a quarter of non-veterans (Bronson et al., 2015, p. 6). Unsurprisingly, they do not represent the typical offender, and they are extremely resistant to the gang culture in confined settings (J. Murphy, personal communication, August 5, 2013).

In a very authentic way, incarcerated veterans still maintain the distinction of "the cream of the crop—at the bottom of the barrel," to repeat the words of Pennsylvania Secretary of Education John C. Pittenger (MacPherson, 1992, p. 579). Due to consistency in numbers, there is little reason to doubt multiple studies in the 1980s that revealed "a 20 percent higher

---

Common Attributes of Incarcerated Veterans at Federal Correctional Institutions in the Late 1970s

1. Veterans generally do not have extensive criminal histories.
2. Veterans generally are classified as and conduct themselves as "outsiders" to the criminal subculture while in prison.
3. Veterans generally received fewer incident reports and generally do not engage in assaults, work stoppages, or contraband and drug usage while incarcerated.
4. Veterans generally have a higher degree of narcotic involvement surrounding their crimes than do non-vets.
5. Veterans are generally more cooperative with authority figures and accept guidance and direction from staff while incarcerated.
6. Veterans suffer less anxiety about group living, and thus learn prison routines quickly. They are more flexible in their life style.

Figure 24.

chance for rehabilitation than non-veterans" (Roth, 1986, p. 3C). Apart from self-help and self-managed veteran groups, these same characteristics have also accounted for the historical success of programs offered by correctional institutions targeting veteran inmates. In line with the veterans' collective potential, the remainder of this chapter highlights major attributes of veterans' groups and institutionally operated veterans' programs.

II. The Eleven Distinguishing Characteristics of Veteran-Specific Programs

There are at least eleven major distinguishing characteristics of veterans' programs in jails and prisons, summarized in the textbox on the following page.

Each of these factors is important because it permits the veteran to retain a positive identity, separate from the impersonal and suppressed existence of an inmate. Membership in any group, when authorized and directed toward productive goals, may be the most vital measure for resilience and recovery in an incarcerated setting.

Eleven Characteristics of Veteran-Specific Programs

1. Distinctive Uniforms
2. Awards for Merit
3. Veterans' Memorials at the Institution
4. Military Environments and Regimens
5. Military- or Veteran-Focused Work Duties
6. Public Service (Inside Institutional Walls)
7. "Cadre" and Leadership Positions
8. Public Service (Outside Institutional Walls)
9. Military-Themed Illustrations, Seals, and Flags
10. Visits from Veterans and Veteran Mentors from the Community
11. Specific Values-Based Standards of Conduct

Those wardens and sheriffs who have instituted faith-based dormitories and other specialized programs have recognized the value of providing inmates with a constructive framework in which they perceive a group identity and self-worth (G. Cranor, personal communication, May 23, 2013; N. Richardson, personal communication, December 4, 2013). With incarceration representing a profound removal of privacy, personality, and choice (Dvoskin & Spiers, 2004), the ability to reconnect with an existence defined by personal values and a sense of accomplishment cannot be understated. This is especially true for veterans who all share a strong cultural identity with clear values and standards (see Chapter 1). Although no single program for confined veterans encompasses all eleven distinguishing characteristics, consider each factor that might independently contribute to the emergent cultural identity of the incarcerated veteran. Faced with shrinking budgets and manpower resources, correctional administrators can achieve significant gains by replicating certain features in the programs they develop.

1. Distinctive Uniforms

Veteran-specific confinement programs may feature distinctive uniforms, which, depending upon the institution, can include everything from hats and berets to specially designed shirts. Although incarcerated veterans who are members of color guards might be permitted to wear special uniforms for the presentation of the nation's colors, some facilities permit uniforms and accessories for other occasions. At the Roxbury Correctional Institution in Hagerstown, Maryland, inmates who are members of Incarcerated Veterans

Figure 25. Depicted above are the left and right sleeves of the I.V.O.R. polo shirt worn by members of the organization. While the right sleeve is generic, the left sleeve uses black bars to signify the number of years the veteran served in the U.S. military. © 2013 Evan R. Seamone.

of Roxbury (I.V.O.R.) wear distinctive uniforms for attendance at organizational events and during inmate visits with family and others. I.V.O.R. uniforms have individualized features, which contrast starkly with the common impersonalized garb of most inmates in the correctional culture. These veterans wear machine-generated Polo shirts depicting personal information and various tributes to the memory of those veterans who served the nation and those who made the final sacrifice (see Figure 25).

On the left arm, black bars indicate the veterans' number of years serving in the military, like the service bars an active service member displays on a service uniform. On the right arm is the image of an eagle and the American flag, with the inscription, "All Gave Some; Some Gave All." Notably, the back of the shirt depicts the seal for the organization, which prominently displays an illustration of the institution's veterans' memorial, encircled by the statements, "Standing Proud" and "A Tribute to All Veterans: Incarcerated Veterans of Roxbury." The front of the button-down polo shirt features the veteran's branch of service and his full name.

Other facilities have adopted less elaborate methods by which incarcerated veterans can distinguish themselves and let others know of the Armed Force in which they served. In one of Florida's five veterans' dorms, for example, "each man's bunk displays a card with his photo, branch of service, and years served" (Alvarez, 2011, p. A14). Veterans at California's San

Figure 26. Depicted above is the back of the I.V.O.R. polo shirt for all members of the organization. © 2013 Evan R. Seamone.

Quentin penitentiary have developed a custom of being among the only forty-one inmates out of 5,400 who wear powder blue ball caps with their work shirts and denim pants. Accordingly, "The officers know that if they see a blue hat, that guy is on the up and up" (Rowe, 2005, p. E-1) (citing William Waltz, Staff Sponsor for the San Quentin Veterans' Group).

In the final analysis, distinctive uniforms provide inmates with the ability to be recognized apart from non-veterans, and can reflect their name, their status as veterans, their branch of service, and their years of meaningful service to the nation. Such recognition "gives inmates a sense of ownership and control of their lives that is rare in the prison system" (Griggs, 2011, p. 10A).

2. Awards for Merit

Where inmates can adorn distinctive uniforms, the issue of decorations for merit necessarily arises. Within the Mark Stiles Unit, for example, inmates serving in the Color Guard wanted the opportunity to present themselves for official functions in the most distinguished manner possible. For a brief time, the organization experimented with the idea of permitting the inmates to wear replicas of their official service ribbons created using popsicle sticks painted with dye and other materials permitted for inmate use. According to Gary Cranor, the Treasurer of the North Texas Vietnam Veterans of America Chapter 292, who has sponsored the Stiles chapter as a supporting veteran citizen from the community since 1995, the replicas were virtually indistinguishable from official service ribbons. After a short time, this practice was discontinued over concerns that it would be necessary to verify which awards had been issued to each veteran to prevent medals' inflation or inaccuracy. Growing problems with incomplete military records and discrepancies in awards listed on official paperwork led to the extinction of the practice. This short chapter in the Stiles Unit's history signals the value of recognition for prior achievements, which, evident in the interest of the participating inmates, can serve as an incentive for program compliance and further achievement among veteran inmates.

At the Roxbury Correctional Institution, a different philosophy emerged regarding the issuance and display of awards for merit. Rather than focusing upon past achievements in the military, as the Stiles Unit proposed, medals and awards issued by I.V.O.R. reflect current contributions to the program, the institution, and the public in general.

Figure 27. Depicted above is the I.V.O.R. polo shirt of a more decorated veteran officer within the organization, who had prior service in the U.S. Army. © 2013 Evan R. Seamone.

Much can be gleaned from the development of polices permitting such uniforms and awards at the facility. The framework for issuance and display of awards came to fruition in 2012, shortly after Corporal John J. Worgul, Jr., assumed the role of staff liaison for the I.V.O.R. program. Worgul established a vision for the program based on his prior experience as an active duty Marine, an Army military police reservist, a drill instructor for a youth offender boot camp, and, notably, his recent attendance at a seminar involving Veterans Justice Outreach (J. J. Worgul, personal communication, September 20, 2013). In this regard, awards and decoration represent the embodiment of a salient cultural feature of military service that can easily be replicated within institutional walls—the shared experience of public recognition for individual accomplishment.

Corporal Worgul was explicit that the medals depicted on the shirts "represent service to I.V.O.R.," such as participation in the color guard, the flag detail, a specific leadership role held in the organization including committee membership. A different medal denotes community service work, like the Walkathon for charitable organizations, especially wounded warriors, car washes, and so forth (J. J. Worgul, personal communication, September 20, 2013). Another medal signifies participation in the monthly newsletter. Although the operational realities of confinement limit the nature in which such awards can be displayed, each year, I.V.O.R. members can order new shirts, on which they can add the new decorations. Under a carefully planned agreement, the inmates print the shirts in accordance with prison policy by using inmate industries, Maryland Correctional Enterprises. One of the youngest members of I.V.O.R. serves in the graphics department and inks the I.V.O.R. polo shirts.

A carefully developed plan permitting the display of awards in a similar manner as I.V.O.R. can enhance an institution's ability to replicate more positive aspects of military service with little expenditure of resources. While Napoleon's famous observation may be true in some cases that "[a] soldier will fight long and hard for a bit of colored ribbon" (Grice, 2011), such sentiments fail to reflect the fact that medals signify the values displayed independent of a service member's desire for recognition. Awards and decorations have a special intrinsic value for many reasons and are a defining characteristic of military culture. In the words of Marine Lieutenant Colonel Michael D. Grice: "The military is a truly unique profession in that we wear our resume upon our breast; a glance at a Marine in a service dress uniform tells a story of his career that succinctly articulates where he has served, and, to a large extent what he did when he was there" (2011). Usually awarded in very public ceremonies, medals and awards represent only one of the few vehicles that distinguish the individual from the team, even despite pervasive demands for uniformity throughout the services. As the Roxbury Correctional Institution has learned through experience, this exceptional practice may take the role of a tremendous incentive in programs tailored to veterans and is worthy of special consideration in any veteran-based confinement program.

3. Veterans' Memorials at the Institution

Currently, there are two completed memorials built from scratch by incarcerated veterans on institutional grounds. One exists in the Muskegon Correctional Facility in Michigan (Leepson, 2002) and the other at Roxbury Correctional Instituttion ("Prison Monument Completed," 1989, p. C-12). Another memorial is the first permanent monument to veterans on the Louisiana State Penitentiary (Angola) grounds. This grew from a former warden's donation of a Vietnam-era Armored Personnel Carrier (APC) to the incarcerated veterans' group, Camp F Veterans Incarcerated. For months, the inmates repainted and restored the vehicle to near-military museum quality conditions. After using free time following work details to build a concrete slab base, paint and finish the vehicle, and construct a site with landscaping and flagpoles to best display the APC, the group held a ceremony dedicating the memorial to demonstrate to the veterans that they were not forgotten (Myers, 2009). Many hundreds of hours of inmate labor were devoted to the perfection of this monument, like the construction of the monuments in Maryland and Michigan, which all exist as testaments to the coordination and determination of these prison groups.

In Maryland, I.V.O.R. members began construction of the Roxbury monument with the donation of approximately 4,200 bricks and materials from local businesses and community organizations ("Inmates Building Memorial to Vets," 1988, p. A3). The project was completed by Veteran's Day of 1988, as memorialized on its main dedicational plaque, featured on the following page.

The Roxbury memorial has provided the basis for several community events over the years. It sustains a three-man flag detail, which presents and retires the nation's colors daily along with the traditional musical accompaniment provided by a boom box, even in the most inclement weather (J. J. Worgul, personal communication, September 20, 2013). It marks the location where Roxbury holds its annual POW/MIA ceremony, which was attended by Maryland's Secretary of Veterans Affairs on its September 20, 2013 five-year anniversary (Maryland Department of Public Safety and Correctional Services, 2013) (see Figure 29).

The walkway leading to the colors lies between two parallel gardens. Since the unveiling of the Veterans' Memorial, I.V.O.R. members have raised the funds to dedicate a number of plaques to memorialize the veterans of

Figure 28. Depicted above are various views of the Memorial to Veterans and Their Families, which was built entirely by incarcerated veterans at Roxbury Correctional Institute in Hagerstown, Maryland. © 2013 Evan R. Seamone.

specific military campaigns, including the War of 1812, devoted 2009; World War I, devoted May 28, 1995; World War II, devoted November 9, 2007; the Korean War, devoted November 9, 2007; the Vietnam War, devoted November 9, 2007; Lebanon/Grenada, devoted November 9, 2007; the Persian Gulf War, devoted 2009; and World Peacekeeping and Humanitarian Efforts since 1916, devoted 2009, some of which appear in Figure 30.

Evident in Figure 31, additional spaces are reserved plaques memorializing other campaigns. I.V.O.R.'s President, inmate John Ricketts, continues to lead efforts to fund such efforts (Ricketts, 2013).

Elsewhere, there were plans to construct a veterans' memorial to veterans of all wars more recently at California's Correctional Institution at

Figure 29. Depicted above, the members of I.V.O.R. stand at parade rest during Roxbury Correctional Institution's Fifth Annual POW/MIA Memorial Ceremony. © 2013 Evan R. Seamone.

Tehachapi (Leepson, 2002). Other Vietnam Veterans of America efforts contributed to the dedication of a Vietnam Memorial in Carson City, Nevada, for which two chapters of incarcerated veterans in the state sculpted the rocks that constitute a monument outside of institutional walls (Leepson, 2005). The Roxbury monument stands-out as an institutional monument. In the words of past I.V.O.R. President George Lewis, "It [is] nice to walk out of your cell and see the American flag" ("Inmates Build War Memorial," 1988, p. 11). As the epicenter of so many public ongoing activities for incarcerated veterans, it provides the best example of what might be gained from similar efforts at other institutions.

4. Military Environments and Regimens

Programs for incarcerated veterans aim to remind veterans of earlier times in their lives when they felt pride, self-worth, and part of something greater than themselves. While all programs benefit from these reminders, they have diverse ways of achieving this result. In some cases, such as in Florida and Virginia's dormitory programs, institutions attempt to create a familiar military "regimen" and "environment," holding the inmates to similar standards as the military. In Florida, for example, the inmates attend out-

Figure 30. Depicted above are two of several plaques memorializing different campaigns since the Revolutionary War.. © 2013 Evan R. Seamone.

door formations each morning, rendering proper courtesies to the nation's colors during rise and revile (Alvarez, 2011; Vergakis, 2012).

Figure 31. Depicted above is one of the spaces reserved for additional dedications. ©
2013 Evan R. Seamone.

After viewing fifty Florida inmates who conducted a formation inside of
one of the state's veterans' dorms, Chief of Security, Major Torrey Johnson,
explained, "You should have seen these guys' faces. That intensity. It's like
being in formation was taking them back" (Griggs, 2011, p. 1A). Those
inmates are also subject to regular inspections of their living quarters where
clothing and equipment must be laid out in an orderly manner (Alvarez,
2011). These efforts are not a replication of the boot camp approach to corrections, as all these inmates already attended the real thing. Rather than
replicating boot camp, some suggest that the dorms serve to create a similar
"formative boot camp moment where all the group pulls together and over-
comes all challenges" (Griggs, 2011, p. 1A).

The effect of military routines and environments is noticeable in these
programs. In the words of a former Marine Gunnery Sergeant in Florida,
"The dorm and its rituals 'are bringing up these old memories of being an
upstanding citizen'" (Alvarez, 2011). Institutions can recognize these benefits without such great formality, however. Although the New York Veterans
Residential Therapeutic Program (VRTP) did not elect to conduct military
formations, it did adopt common terminology within its disciplinary structure, assembling veterans. There, veterans are organized in "companies"
within the dorm structure (Groveland Correctional Facility, n.d., p. 16). The
VRTP also provides a series of graduated sanctions that include both verbal
and written "pull-ups" (Groveland Correctional Facility, Program Conduct
Guide, n.d., pp. 17–18).

5. Military- or Veteran-Focused Work Duties

Jails and prisons sometimes develop work details or duties for veterans that have the objective of contributing to veterans or active military members outside the institution to instill additional purpose in the inmate's daily activities. The Maryland Department of Corrections instituted the first program in the nation in which incarcerated veterans live in specialized housing units where they train puppies to be service dogs for wounded warriors. The program exists as a result of at least fourteen donated Labrador Retrievers from America's VetDogs and free services from local veterinarians. It is open to veteran inmates who agree to raise the puppies and live with them in their cells.

The participants in the working dog training program often find the experience to be life-altering from the combination of the companionship of the animals and the knowledge that the dogs will be assisting fellow warriors who made tremendous sacrifices (Maryland Department of Public Safety and Correctional Services, 2012; Demetrick, 2013). Even without access to adorable puppies, other Maryland facilities enable confined veterans with honorable discharges to work in support of the state's veterans' cemeteries as part of an agreement with the Maryland State Department of Veterans Affairs, with the prospect of potentially continuing the work following their release. In FY10, for example, inmates from one institution devoted more than 9,000 hours to tending the veterans' cemeteries (Maryland Department of Public Safety and Correctional Services, n.d.).

To a lesser extent, the veterans' dorms in Virginia have made significant headway by instituting military-affiliated duty positions:

> At Indian Creek, each inmate is given a job that harkens to terms many learned in their military service. The sergeant at arms is in charge of enforcing the rules like making sure everyone's shirts are tucked in and making sure no one reads magazines in therapy. The mess crew services as the kitchen staff, the hazmat team is responsible for waste clean-up and the intel coordinator provides news and information from the outside world. (Vergakis, 2012; Hixenbaugh, 2012, p. A1)

Notably, the "Inspiration Coordinator" provides quotes from famous military leaders to start each day at mandatory morning briefings (Kamal, 2013). Although duties may differ, as well as the ability to contribute to military personnel or their families beyond institutional walls, these forms of work provide a sense of purpose and meaning in the veterans' daily activities. This can increase the inmates' sense of responsibility and the capability to hold similar roles as they had during prior periods of time when they were respected and recognized for their contributions.

6. Public Service (Inside Institutional Walls)

It is often the case that inmate veterans are recognized within institutional walls by non-veteran inmates for the leadership roles they play in the correctional setting. According to a former Superintendent at New York's Arthur Kill Correctional Facility, "[t]he veterans also tend to be leaders in the prison, teaching courses on aggression and substance abuse" (Marks, 2001, p. 3). Within some institutions, the veterans have color guard units. Although these teams may be visible during Veterans' Day and other military remembrances, they may also be found presenting the colors at G.E.D. graduations for non-veterans (G. Cranor, personal communication, May 23, 2013). Veterans also participate in fundraising activities in which they might be permitted to sell items desired by other inmates, such as Subway sandwiches or pizza (S. M. Verbecke & J. P. Strollo, personal communication, September 16, 2013).

Figure 32. Depicted above, Vietnam Veterans of America members participate in an elaborate color guard ceremony for fallen veterans from the community while simultaneously celebrating the organization's 14th anniversary at the Texas Mark W. Stiles Unit. © 2013 Sandra Womack, Reprinted with permission.

These activities in which veterans are visible within institutional walls have a definite impact on other inmates. In New York's VRTP, after the veterans beautified their dorm areas, other non-veterans who observed the improvements, in turn, beautified their own areas (Marks, 2001, p. 3). Perhaps the greatest testament to this effect is recognized in the Mark Stiles Unit in Texas, which has an auxiliary of non-veterans who participate in the veterans' group. As noted by one of the auxiliary members Robert Williams, "joining was a way to move forward. 'It helps to interact with people who can help me better myself'" (Wills, 2012, p. A3).

Attitudes from other inmates have changed markedly over time with the nation's continued involvement in combat operations. When the VRTP dorm program was first instituted at Groveland Correctional Facility in the late 1980s, it had the distinction of being "the program everybody loved to hate" (S. M. Verbecke & J. P. Strollo, personal communication, September 16, 2013). However, as time progressed, a palpable respect grew among other inmates who appreciated veterans' service in the nation's wars. Some non-veteran inmates were appreciative that they too were among the citizens that the incarcerated veterans sacrificed to protect. When veterans visibly contribute to the prison or the jail, such activities are reminders of these points.

7. *"Cadre" and Leadership Positions*

According to Reverend Neil Richardson, the Chaplain for the Muscogee County Jail veterans' dorm, even in the absence of a formalized leadership structure, groups of veterans will naturally develop their own leadership positions to fill the void (N. Richardson, personal communication, December 4, 2013). Other programs have learned that there can be tremendous value in developing specific positions of responsibility for incarcerated veterans. An observer of one of Virginia's two veterans' dorms explains, "The veteran[s'] dorm emulates the army structure with a chain-of-command and inmates given responsibilities like facility maintenance and keeping areas in compliance" (Kamal, 2013).

The most comprehensive inmate veteran leadership program exists at the New York State Department of Correctional Services, within the VRTP. There, inmate veterans can fill one of at least ten different positions. They range from the program director, who does everything from overseeing curriculum to managing a staff of up to ten other inmates, to the dorm superintendent, who "[i]nforms program participants of the rotational duties to be performed [and] holds participants who may have been given any extra details accountable for [their] completion" (Groveland Correctional Facility, *Dorm Positions and Responsibilities*, n.d., p. 7). The senior cadre in that program are expected to mediate disputes within the dorm, to propose or determine the type of discipline for infractions (depending upon their nature), and to manage other inmates with staff positions (Groveland Correctional Facility, *Program Conduct Guide*, n.d., pp. 17–18). Within the VRTP, there are at least sixty hours of training per cycle specifically for the peer cadre, which consist of "train-the-trainer classes, practice teaching, and advanced staff development programs" (New York State Department of Correctional Services, 1994, pp. 5–6).

By approaching management in this way, peer staff leadership positions contribute to the cost saving of the program's operation (Groveland Correctional Facility, n.d., p. 6). New York is not alone in formally capitalizing on veterans' leadership ability. To a lesser extent, Florida's veterans' dorms have leadership positions, such as the "Veterans Dorm Chairman" (Griggs, 2011, p. 1A). And, even without such a formalized leadership structure, the San Francisco Sheriff's Community of Veterans Engaged in Restoration (COVER) also recognizes that it helps to have inmates appointed as pod chairman, dorm vice-chairman, sergeant at arms, and secretary with the responsibility of coordinating regular meetings in the pod and setting a tone conducive to group participation.

8. Public Service (Outside Institutional Walls)

Incarcerated veterans' groups have traditionally contributed to public charities, which often, but do not necessarily, have a military focus (Rosenthal & McGuire, 2013, p. 360). A recent article demonstrates how veterans in prisons across the country are "paying it forward" with charitable contributions ranging from donating calfskin wallets to Veterans Administration hospitals in New York and Massachusetts to supporting church ministries and even an orphanage in Costa Rica (Davidson, 2013). Others, such as the Vietnam Veterans Group of San Quentin, have sponsored college scholarships for relatives of veterans who submit essays on the topic "How has your parent being in the military affected your life?" (Rowe, 2005, p. E-1). Through inmate contributions over the years, the San Quentin Group's fund has exceeded $36,500, permitting functions such as a banquet in which the inmates recognize the scholarship recipients (Rowe, 2005, p. E-1).

At one such ceremony, Warden Jill Brown remarked, "When you are at Cal State Long Beach next year, I want you to know—look around the room—every one of these men will be supporting you" (p. E-1). Whether through scholarships, walk-a-thons, or similar activities, many incarcerated veterans believe that these contributions outside the walls of confinement signify their individual and collective ability to make contributions to a civilian society that many will rejoin after their release. The programs likewise echo the theme of continuing service.

9. Military-Themed Illustrations, Seals, and Flags

Several veterans' dorms adorn prison walls with military-themed murals and statements. It is not uncommon to see eagles, the American Flag, the POW/MIA memorial image, or seals of the Armed Services. In one Florida Dorm, for example,

> One mural shows a group of Marines in combat gear running across the desert with a helicopter in the background. Another shows the Blue Angels flying in formation on the ceiling. On the rear wall of the dorm, what started as a small American flag painting sprawled into a massive two-story mural, which dominates the room with waiving red and white stripes. (Griggs, 2011, p. 1A)

In the San Diego County Jail's N-Module-3 Housing Wing, "[b]rightly colored paintings now hang on the walls: one of the Statue of Liberty, another of the U.S. Flag, and one of a screaming eagle landing with talons outstretched. Hanging on the ceiling are the service flags of U.S. military branches and the POW/MIA flag" (Perry, 2013). At the Los Angeles County Jail *circa* 2005, a painting by the occupants of the Veteran's Wing featured "images of war—paratroopers leaping from planes and a soldier carrying a wounded comrade" (Leonard, 2005, p. B1).

Although these images may invoke the same types of feelings as Roxbury's brick memorials and real flags, memorials provide something more. Evident at Roxbury, from inmates who pass by on their way in the yard, the entire inmate population experiences memorials. Contrarily, only a select few veterans might interact with the murals on the walls in specialized housing units. Of benefit, if funds and lack of resources prevent the erection of a monument to veterans, murals are easy to create, and it is likely that veteran inmates with artistic acumen would find great honor in contributing such works to their dedicated living quarters.

At the Indian Creek Correctional Institution in Virginia, the veterans' dorm murals are accompanied by "reminders of the program's goals on the walls . . ., such as remembering to deal with stressful situations and learning how to cope with major losses." Program administrators married the statements with the patriotic service-related images "to create a sense of community, trust, and accountability" (Vergakis, 2012). Perhaps the greatest benefit of these murals and decorations is the constant reminder of the positive qualities for which the veterans stood during their service to the nation, as opposed to dreary walls, which remind them of the contrast in their current role as inmates or detainees. Blake Chester, an inmate who graduated from Muscogee County Jail's Veteran's Dorm remarked on the motivational effect of the military crests that line the wall, "It was still jail, of course. But it was comforting—a feeling in yourself that your service does matter" (Kamal, 2013). In 2005, Arthur, a detainee in the Los Angeles County Jail's veterans' wing remarked, "We have camaraderie. The flags—sometimes you look up at them and it makes you proud of what you once were" (Leonard, 2005, p. B1).

10. Visits from Veterans and Veteran Mentors from the Community

Reminiscent of Indiana State Farm's Short-Term Incarceration Program for Veterans in 1946, which had the salient feature of teaming incarcerated veterans with mentors from community veterans service organizations for the period following release (Virgil & Hawkins, 1946), a few current programs for incarcerated veterans feature contact with veterans in the community during the course of incarceration. As a notable example, the Oklahoma Department of Corrections has developed a "Battle Buddies" program as a major component of its reentry planning. Retired Major General Rita Aragon, Oklahoma Secretary of Military and Veterans Affairs, combined forces with a focus group of wardens and security officers to implement this initiative to follow and support veteran inmates from confinement into the community following release. The resulting program "is staffed completely by volunteer veterans . . . at no cost to the state . . . and assigns a veteran volunteer who will be a 'battle buddy' to the offender veteran" (Jones & Castleberry, 2013, p. 46).

Like Indiana's rationale, with mentorship from the same individual during and after incarceration, the released inmate finds a source of constant support, and is expected to join a veteran's organization following release for additional community supports. While the program certainly seeks to help the veteran find employment and housing, it, more importantly, places the veteran in a community environment in which he is "surrounded by others who have served and understand what the veteran offender has gone through" (Jones & Castleberry, 2013, p. 46).

Veteran visitors might, for example, discuss strategies they used to deal with popular readjustment challenges or innovative methods to overcome them. To this end, the Center for Strategic Military Excellence is working with the Florida Department of Corrections to create a "mentorship program with the veterans dorm to take local veterans into the prison to speak with inmates nearing release" (Griggs, 2011, p. 10A). In Georgia's Muscogee County Veterans' Jail Dorm, it is vital that the mentor assigned to the inmate during incarceration "will be the mentor they have when they get outside" (Prann, 2012) (citing Chaplain Neil Richardson). Notably, the program introduces the veterans to community mentors up to three years prior to the inmates' projected release date, specifically because such planning "has the tendency to reduce the shock for someone being released" (Griggs, 2011, p. 10A).

The same effect can be found in the San Francisco County Jail, where the average inmate stay is only two months. There, every other week, the COVER program brings veterans who have successfully transitioned from incarceration to productive community life to share their stories with the dorm participants as part of a speakers' component. Representative topics include "dealing with friends, abuse of alcohol, what they did to reestablish their lives after deployment" (S. Schwartz, L. Levitas, & I. McCray, personal communication, October 15, 2012). This value of peer mentor involvement is most clear in veterans treatment courts and draws on the same vital concept.

11. Specific Values-Based Standards of Conduct

Veterans' dormitories throughout the nation have a shared reputation for inmates who hold themselves to higher standards than the general population. This is a major reason many sheriff's deputies and correctional officers volunteer to perform duties in the dorms. In the Groveland Correctional Facility's *Transitional Services Orientation Guide for the Veterans Residential Therapeutic Program,* the document specifically references the "higher standard of living in the dorm," which it is the responsibility of each participant to uphold (Groveland Correctional Facility, n.d., p. 10). Such elevated codes of conduct ensure that the dorm environment is conducive to treatment and self-exploration, rather than the typical inmate troubles. Thus, in Florida's veterans' dorms, "[t]o qualify for placement . . . and to remain there, the veterans are expected to behave better than the general prison population. Honesty and respect are paramount. Profanity and racial slurs are frowned down upon. The men must remain drug free" (Alvarez, 2011, p. A14).

Groveland further requires strict adherence to a confidentiality policy, which could result in punishment beyond removal from the program if violated (Groveland Correctional Facility, n.d., p. 20). Many observers recognize how a return to a sense of pride and the values displayed during earlier periods of service often motivates veteran inmates to care more about how they are viewed; not just as a representation of themselves, but the entire veterans' community within the institution. Accordingly, the same higher standards will usually emerge whether or not there is specialized housing for veterans. For example, in Texas, even without an exclusive dormitory, the 120 members of Vietnam Veterans of America Chapter 292 agreed to abide by very strict requirements. Not only must they remain free of disciplinary citations within the facility, they must also regularly attend scheduled meetings and hold themselves to higher standards than inmates in the general population (Wills, 2012, p. A3).

Concluding Remarks

The eleven attributes of veteran-focused programs in corrections settings underscore that it is not necessary to implement separate dormitories for veterans to benefit from any of these interventions. Even though characteristics such as murals on walls, military-style equipment layout, and drill and ceremonies may be more appealing in a housing unit dedicated to veterans, prisons and jails can still benefit from allowing or enabling all the features for veterans in the general population if separate housing arrangements are not possible. As will be evident in the following chapter, most of the programs in confined settings developed specifically to deal with combat veterans' PTSD were instituted in facilities without specialized veterans' dorms. Those programs still succeeded based upon the institutions' other allowances for veteran status. Alone, or in combination, these features all underscore the attributes that make veterans different from other inmates and which can provide for a ready-made supportive, facilitative, and purpose-oriented environment in which to address the underlying reasons for their incarceration.

Chapter 8

INSTITUTIONALLY-BASED PROGRAMS FOR VETERANS

The prior chapter described major lessons from jail- and prison-based veterans' groups and organizations. Such programs can be distinguished from institutionally based treatment programs for veterans. While, at times, the dividing line may be blurry, such as the case where visiting mental health providers used the structure of an existing veterans' group to conduct group counseling sessions with the goal of treating mental conditions (Sheridan, 1985; LaRue, 1985), this book distinguishes the institutional treatment program on the basis that the content of programming is not determined by the self-governance of the inmate participants like a group, but, instead, is mandated by the institution or an outside entity and usually evaluated for effectiveness.

For example, a residential dorm devoted to veterans requires the institution to designate necessary space and place members of the general population elsewhere. The necessary involvement of the facility makes it an institutional program, rather than a veterans' group/organization. In the normal course, institutions implement programs for veterans for several reasons, including comprehensive treatment of mental health conditions, preparation for reentry, and protection of vulnerable populations. While, traditionally, veterans have been a hidden population of "forgotten warriors" in prisons and jails (Boivin, 1986, p. 112), with their needs largely "neglected" and unrecognized by institutions (Gideon, 2013, p. 11), there have been significant historical exceptions.

Although many self-governed veterans' groups grew from the lack of an institutional response to veterans' unique concerns (Chapter 7), the programs that did emerge recognized that veterans constitute a special needs population within the corrections setting (Gideon, 2013). For the handful of institutions adopting this view, the development of such programs was an outgrowth of institutional responsibilities. These efforts also delivered benefits for the institutions. As criminologist Lior Gideon has noted, "When special needs are met, facilities can better manage the inmate population, and at times may even do so with less expense" (2013, p. 15).

This chapter provides an overview of the diverse types of intensive programs for confined veterans. Some key attributes are shared by non-residential programs and specialized housing units alike, as well as ones that target PTSD and service-related trauma and those that do not. Although the programs are separated by many years, in some cases, each of them offers valuable insights about the way a specialized program can be developed today within the jail or prison setting, especially when combined with any of the eleven features of incarcerated veterans' organizations described in the previous chapter.

This chapter is also sensitive to the fact that *jail* programs are necessarily limited in duration and may make programming more unpredictable as a result of the limited time available to address veterans' underlying issues. Consequently, the section describes six different models of organizing a veteran-specific program and discusses how each of the overarching thematic philosophies can both yield specific benefits and result in specific consequences. By exploring an array of programs—some long forgotten—the chapter offers comprehensive insight and distills the salient lessons from each program with the hope that correctional administrators can pick the ones most adaptable to their own institutional culture and immediately develop the metrics to measure program outcomes and effectiveness.

THE SIX MAJOR THEMES OF INSTITUTIONALLY-BASED PROGRAMS FOR VETERANS

Although some intensified programs may include aspects common to prison groups, they generally adopt *formalized* methods of counseling veterans on issues such as combat trauma and suppressed military experiences. These programs are usually funded at a level far greater than the veterans' groups/organizations and are often evaluated for effectiveness by the Veterans Administration, state, or local department of corrections/or county sheriff and other community groups. Although the programs are intensive and subject to formal evaluation, they are not homogeneous among institutions. From among the different variations, these programs take on six basic themes.

It is surely possible for programs to adopt multiple themes simultaneously. However, depending upon the theme embraced, veterans' programs take different shapes. Slight variations in these themes can affect everything from the physical accommodations of the participants, benefits available to

---

Six Basic Themes for Development of
Intuitionally Based Veterans' Programs

1. Programs developed to promote successful readjustment following deployment;
2. Programs developed to address combat-related trauma and PTSD, specifically;
3. Programs developed to address trauma, primarily, with some adaptability to veterans;
4. Programs developed to prepare the veteran for community reentry;
5. Programs developed to instill discipline or *Esprit de Corps*; and
6. Programs instituted to reward past service.

---

the participants during and after participation, the values promoted by the program, the priorities set by the program, non-veteran/nonparticipant perceptions of inmate participation in the program, to, most importantly, eligibility for program participation. For correctional professionals who are considering the establishment of a veterans' program, it is vital to recognize what can be gained—and lost—by adopting specific themes and related assumptions. Programs seeking to promote all themes equally may suffer.

I. Programs Developed to Promote
Successful Readjustment Following Deployment

Many observe how some veterans have physically—but not mentally—returned from combat. Marine Corps veteran Clint VanWinkle aptly described this experience as he sat in a Veterans Administration clinic's waiting room:

> My thoughts drifted in and out of the present, jumped between various places and events. I was at the Veterans Administration hospital, but also in a Virginia Beach hotel room my first night home, and somewhere in Iraq. Just another day of time travel. I told myself to concentrate, think about the present, live. Don't look for a meaning in all of the madness. But there was no subduing it: The past wanted the present. (VanWinkle, 2009, p. 27)

At the most basic level, programs that focus on this theme target these emotionally distant warriors. They recognize that the military experience represents a major life change and that the veteran may be in a confined setting for lack of tools to successfully acclimate to the role of civilian once again.

In recognizing the magnitude of the basic training experience and continual conditioning during subsequent training exercises, these programs will target even those veterans who did not deploy to combat on the basis that military service is transformative in any capacity.

While such programs may seek to learn about the veteran's military history and certain events that occurred during combat, the programs do not condition program admission on a specific diagnosis of a combat-related mental health condition. Similar to many veterans treatment courts, they assume that *all* military members may need the opportunity to relearn basic community life skills that will make them more employable, more capable of productive lives with significant others, and methods to remain calm and relaxed as opposed to hypervigilant and threat-anticipating. By providing these services to a broader group of veterans than those with specific diagnoses, the program opens itself to a variety of military experiences. Furthermore, in group settings, the program might permit peers to assist in detecting and pointing out the types of cognitive distortions that are typical in those veterans with mental conditions and severe symptomatology. A downside of these programs would be the inability to address a majority of specific mental health issues in the group setting due to incompatible concerns, which may alienate those with more serious treatment needs. The programs explored below highlight attributes of a focus on readjustment in the confined setting.

A. The Indiana State Farm at Greencastle's Short-Term Program for Delinquent Veterans

Like the State of Wisconsin, which elected to address the problems of incarcerated World War I veterans in the 1920s, the Indiana State Farm at Greencastle recognized that many veterans of World War II were returning with adjustment difficulties that contributed to law violations. In 1946, 20 percent of inmates admitted into custody were veterans, some of whom had only been back in the United States for a matter of days before committing offenses (Virgil & Hawkins, 1946, p. 16).

With veterans engaging in a range of misconduct, Indiana judges thought it best to reduce charges to misdemeanors, when possible, and sentence veterans to confinement at the State Farm so they could take advantage of a special program tailored to their needs. The State Farm developed a program for veterans on the realization that, as a group, they were distinctly different from other offenders. They were more educated, scored higher on intelligence tests, came from more stable home backgrounds, and, for the most part, had clean criminal records prior to their incarceration. Because the veteran "is more adaptable than his delinquent forerunners and represents considerable more insight into his problems," the State Farm's Administration concluded that "[t]he veteran seems to be a 'special' person who requires a 'special' type of treatment and appeal" (Virgil & Hawkins, 1946, pp. 16, 28).

The specialized treatment program for incarcerated veterans established at the Indiana State Farm had five components, all of which could be facilitated within the period that inmates were housed in this short-term facility:

- Immediate identification as a veteran during the classification process and designation for a special program of treatment;
- Scheduled participation in regular discussion groups with other veteran inmates led by a staff member who was also a veteran to address issues including "military and civilian attitudes, community integration, social resources at the disposal of the ex-servicemen, benefits, health and opportunities for worthwhile training and living";
- Individual counseling to plan for post-release employment, education, or vocational training, such that each veteran can "work[]-out in specific detail the exact steps to be taken in the post release program";
- Advance notice of a veteran's release to the American Legion or Veterans of Foreign Wars' rehabilitation committee to aid in post-release transitional mentoring and assistance, usually by "an older man in the home community pay particular attention to the welfare problems of this released inmate"; and
- Liaison with the county branch of the Red Cross to help provide for short-term living and subsistence expenses immediately following release.

The entire program existed as a form of "non-military basic training" aimed at teaching the veteran to recognize that he was a civilian once again and overcoming a common sense of superiority as though one was still in the military even though he had left it. The involvement of local veterans' organizations provided a sense of "belongingness" that is vital to positive adjustment to civilian roles. Furthermore, explicit planning for "exactly where he is to go, to whom he is to report and what assistance is to be his" provided the type of schedule to which he had become accustomed during military service, enhancing the chances of follow-through with related commitments (Virgil & Hawkins, 1946, pp. 28–29).

Take-Home Point

Some key aspects of the Indiana program may be found in existing programs for confined veterans, such as the prominence of community-support liaisons. By drawing on community veterans' groups to mentor inmates,

Indiana's program in the 1940s featured a similar peer mentoring component as the "Battle Buddies Program" now operating in the Oklahoma Department of Corrections (see Chapter 7).

Importantly, Indiana's program for veterans was not a diversion from incarceration. Although some judges who used it reduced charges from felonies to misdemeanors, thereby limiting the amount of incarceration, confinement was a very necessary component of the program. In considering modern options, the reason for confining these veterans is perhaps the most valuable to remember: they were incarcerated to provide them with the structure to undergo basic training to become a civilian. Implicit in the program description was that incarceration served a coordinating purpose and represented, perhaps, the first time that these veterans had the opportunity to address their lives in a constructive way since they were many steps separated from the civilian life to which they had so many problems adapting.

Through the mechanics of the program at the Indiana State Farm, inmates regained a predictable schedule similar to their military experience and others with a common background. As a group, they rallied together and received a new collective mission—only this time the goal was to reprogram their lives in a conscious manner. In this way, the State Farm recognized that jail and prison stays create a captive audience for genuine life change.

Modern programs for confined veterans also operate on this captive-audience philosophy, such as the programs for treatment of traumatized women inmates who often feel as though jail is the safest place they have been in comparison to their very challenging lives with abusive individuals on the outside. As Professor Bill Lousie observes, "ironically [confinement] serves as one of the few places where many of these women haven't been afraid, they haven't been brutalized, they remain drug free" (1998, p. 111). While there are some differences between veterans and survivors of sexual trauma and/or interpersonal violence, for members of these two groups, the effect of confinement-based trauma treatment is much the same. As recognized by Sunny Schwartz and Leslie Levitas, who helped to implement the Community of Veterans Engaged in Restoration (COVER) program in the San Francisco County Jail:

> **"While offenders are still in custody, we have an opportunity to seize the moment by providing programs that address the underlying causes of crime and violence" (2011, p. 59).**

Above all things, Indiana's civilian boot camp represents the continuing vitality of this philosophy.

The Indiana State Farm incorporated many of the same considerations as the Veterans Administration's current reentry programs. Similar to a major factor that distinguishes veterans treatment courts from other problem-solving programs, this post-World War II-era program relied on veteran mentors as a necessary component for the program's overall success. It also capitalized on staff members who were themselves veterans. While the program administrators doubted that any program would limit the number of recent veterans from engaging in criminal behavior, success of this veteran-specific program would be measured, instead, in "a small number of repeaters among those of the veteran group" (Virgil & Hawkins, 1946, p. 29).

Although additional programs would be instituted for veterans in the years to come, many of them emulated key aspects of Indiana's program implemented in the 1940s, likely without having any knowledge of it. The State Farm is a testament to the continuing applicability of these timeless lessons for veterans of any war. The only thing that Indiana's program did not account for was mental health conditions sustained by combat veterans during their service. It would not be until more than a generation passed, in the 1980s and 1990s, that formalized combat PTSD programs for incarcerated veterans would exist with this additional capability.

B. The Federal Correctional Institution Phoenix "Second Tour" Model

In the early 1990s, while he was serving as a correctional psychologist, Dr. Chester Sigafoos observed common behavior among veterans who were confined in the Federal Correctional Institution at Phoenix, Arizona. He watched as many of the Vietnam veterans adopted a highly defensive posture in the yard and their comings and goings, reminiscent of troops on patrol in the jungles of Vietnam (Sigafoos, 1994, p. 121). Although a PTSD treatment program existed for a brief time in the late 1980s at California's Lompoc Federal Penitentiary (Quinlan, 1990, p. 44), Dr. Sigafoos knew of no existing PTSD programs in the federal correctional system when he encountered veterans with special needs.

In 1993, Dr. Sigafoos implemented his own PTSD treatment program for incarcerated veterans. It was a voluntary program for all veterans, and ultimately included veterans from the Korean War, not just Vietnam (Sigafoos, 1994, p. 119). The only prerequisite was combat experience. Out of several program components, the preliminary phase addressed combat experience, independent from PTSD symptoms or PTSD treatment.

Dr. Sigafoos reasoned that it was essential to educate veterans about the way incarceration is likely to induce their prior conditioned behavior from combat so that they could recognize the phenomenon and address it prior to PTSD-specific instruction and individual therapy. This prerequisite grew from the recognition that incarceration is functionally equivalent to a *second tour* in hostile territory, little different from the *first tour* in a war zone. A description of the Second Tour component of the FCI-Phoenix model appears in this section and not the PTSD program section because of its fundamental relevance to all incarcerated combat veterans, and specifically because it targets behavioral symptoms related to combat, which remain distinct from operational stress injuries—even though combat-survival symptoms can certainly aggravate operational stress injury symptoms.

Like several programs addressed in this chapter, the FCI-Phoenix program and its Second Tour philosophy grew from the dedicated efforts of a single deeply interested professional. When Dr. Sigafoos left the institution after its second year, the program ceased operation. Because it had slightly more than a dozen participants and lasted for a short duration, some have noted the lack of a "full evaluation of the program" and thorough study of its effectiveness (Department of Veterans Affairs, 2013, p. 37). However, while there may be some caution from an academic research perspective, Dr. Sigafoos' program, like the others mentioned in this chapter, emphasize the dangers of *paralysis by analysis*; few if any of the programs would have emerged in the face of such strict demands. Fortunately, in recent times, the veterans treatment court in El Paso County, Colorado, has used Sigafoos' model as the basic framework for delivering treatment to veterans diverted from confinement (Ungvarsky, Conaty, & Bellflower, 2012). This chapter's discussion of programs in confined settings begins with Sigafoos' model as well because the Second Tour applies to every incarcerated combat veteran and highlights the reason correctional institutions should account for inmate's combat experience—in addition to veteran status—for planning effective treatment and reentry interventions, at the very minimum.

Contours of FCI-Phoenix's Second Tour Program

1. The Inevitable Activation of the Survivor Mode

Enduring the daily realities of combat operations requires the military member to adopt a personal coping style to remain "combat-ready" always. Dr. Sigafoos calls this the "survivor mode" and recognized that, even for those combat veterans who are able to deactivate this mode of existence following their return to civilian life, profound environmental stresses can easily reactivate the same conditioned response. On this theory, he defined the second tour as "the re-experiencing of a hostile environment in which it was necessary to rely on survivor skills just to be able to exist" (Sigafoos, 1994, p. 120). While caution for potential threats is necessary among all inmates, survivor mode has the risk of overestimating danger, often to the point where the veteran will take the offensive in response to nonexistent threats. This theory is consistent with the contemporary view of the American Psychiatric Association's practice guidelines for PTSD, which observe that some individuals "have an increased expectation of danger, resulting in an 'anticipatory bias' toward their environment and an increased readiness for 'fight, flight, or freeze' responses" (Grieger et al., 2011, p. 205).

On this theory, a necessary first step to reduce the risk of violence and symptom aggravation in incarcerated veterans is for these inmates to acknowledge the similarities of incarceration to combat. As Sigafoos points out: "As in Vietnam, you never know where or who your enemy is. You are always in a state of possible danger. There is no front line. You are told what to do. Your life is not totally in your control, and you have a set amount of time you must serve. There is no such thing as 'total relaxation'" (1994, p. 120). In the Second Tour program, the inmates thus explored these similarities as a group and then identified the characteristics of the individual combat-ready mode that each inmate developed as a matter of necessity. In making this comparison between incarceration and combat, the inmates considered their behavior along the categories of "affect, behavior, and cognition" (Sigafoos, 1994, p. 120).

Through the process of considering their conditioned responses to combat stress, and how it may have manifested in society following one's homecoming, it was hoped that inmates would be capable of recognizing the maladaptive nature of the combat mode in response to civilian stressors. Dr. Sigafoos emphasizes that the risk of reverting to the veteran's innate survival mode is a self-fulfilling prophecy of sabotage in which the veteran does not seek fulfilment, advancement, or progress of any kind but rather sets his or her sights on merely surviving from day-to-day: "If life starts going good for them, they may sabotage it so as to return to the survivor mode" (Sigafoos, 1994, p. 121).

> In prioritizing day-to-day survival in confinement, the combat veteran constantly expects harm and often sabotages his or her progress to return to the "combat-ready" mode that was engrained during deployment. This can impede the prospects for recovery and reentry unless it is addressed explicitly early in the course of incarceration.

While overanticipation of harm is detrimental to an incarcerated veteran, the aim of the Second Tour program was not to totally disarm the veterans or paralyze them from being cautious altogether. "[B]y breaking the veteran out of this mode, the therapist takes away the only defense they have to survive in prison" (Sigafoos, 1994, p. 121). The goal of the program was accordingly to make the veteran aware of this innate state so that the veteran can control it and respond to it in more constructive, alternative ways. Careful examination of threat-perception and response prior to combat, during combat, and after combat in a group setting can help expose the cognitive patterns of the survivor mode (Sigafoos, 1994, pp. 121–122).

Take-Home Point

The undeniable parallels between combat and confinement are extremely vital for correctional professionals to understand. It should be a primary goal to ensure that combat veterans are not perpetually in a "combat-ready" state during confinement, because activation of this conditioned response can potentially activate an arsenal of related undesirable behaviors, shaped by the veteran's training in hand-to-hand combat, use of weapons, survival skills, search and destroy, infiltration, area studies, and intelligence gathering (Sigafoos, 1994, p. 117).

As explored in Chapter 1, survivor mode is a result of overtraining in the military, instituted to encourage the behaviors of the innate in combat settings, to decrease casualties, and to increase the potential for mission accomplishment. Because actual experiences in combat conditions served to cement these behaviors, it behooves correctional professionals to identify combat service, beyond simply identifying veteran status and to take additional measures to note any of these specialized warfighting skills.

Based upon the reality that roughly 260,000 contractors were serving in Iraq and Afghanistan in 2010, which exceeded the numbers of U.S. troops deployed to those regions (Huffman, 2013, p. A28), and at least 3,400 U.S. contractors lost their lives in Iraq alone (Editorial, 2013, p. 4), it is similarly prudent to identify whether inmates have been in a combat zone even if they do not profess any military experience. The contribution of the Second Tour model is that, ultimately, any persons forced to endure combat for a prolonged time necessarily develop their own style of coping and response, which is at tremendous risk of emerging during confinement.

Another lesson from the Second Tour philosophy is the necessary extension of the comparison to the reentry process, beyond mere conditions of confinement. Beyond the similarity of incarceration to combat, Dr. Sigafoos emphasizes that discharge from confinement is also similar to discharge from the military: "Being released from prison is similar to the returning veteran's entrance back into American society. If prison is analogous to a 'second tour,' then release from prison is analogous to being 'ETS'd to the United States' (Enlisted Termination of Service)—discharge from the military to return to the United States" (1994, p. 127). These parallels may be useful for prisons and jails to adopt in programming for veteran inmates based on the inmates' familiarity and experience. It may help inmates to view their confinement experiences in tandem with their military experiences as long as the two are not confused or the negative attributes of military experience are not superimposed on the inmate's concept of confinement. The next section explores the benefits of drawing a key parallel to the combat experience.

2. The Squad Orientation as an Optimizer for Incarceration

As wardens and other correctional administrators have consistently noted, veteran status brings many advantages to the incarcerated veteran and the institution. In developing a program to address incarcerated veterans' special readjustment needs, Dr. Sigafoos recognized that combat experience also provides an intrinsic measure to mitigate survivor overreactions: the concept of a squad of interdependent team members. Traditionally, a squad containing twelve troops with an assault, support, and security element, has been the staple of military operations and explains much of the success in urban operations in Iraq and Afghanistan (Catagnus, Edison, Keeling, & Moon, 2005, p. 86). Sigafoos recognized that, in combat, "the squad became the soldier's sole defense against the enemy" (1994, p. 119). Consequently, the squad orientation can help inmates rely upon one another for a more satisfactory level of safety and protection without having to revert to the survivor mode. Namely,

> In prison, the group becomes the veteran's new squad. The squad is the only group of men the veteran feels he can trust in prison. The bond between squad members is more than the common experience they shared in Vietnam, that only provides for the *bona fides* of joining. Once their *bona fides* is validated, then the real reason why they bond in prison is acted upon. The fellow group member takes on the same role as the squad member, providing protection against the elements and the reassurance that they will make it out of prison. (Sigafoos, 1994, p. 120)

Sigafoos observed several ways in which the squad orientation promoted successful rehabilitation during the course of incarceration. Not only did the members of the veteran squad candidly and honestly participate and support one another during group sessions, he provides a telling example in which a "buddy team" of squad members enabled relaxation exercises with a system of rotating periods on "watch" in the face of safety concerns for letting one's guard down to engage in relaxation exercises for PTSD stress response (1994, p. 122).

Take-Home Point

The squad orientation is a major optimizing factor for veterans' programs in confined settings and provides the framework for the type of social network that enables readjustment and recovery from PTSD. Combat veterans are hotwired to be contributing members of an interdependent group based on the fact that "[t]he soldier lived with his squad 24 hours a day sharing the same experiences, the same bunker, the same food, the same misery, and the same success" (Sigafoos, 1994, p. 119). While this cannot easily happen with members of the general population, it can easily occur among groups of veterans. Based on this factor alone, it is advisable, wherever possible, to group and house veterans together as much as possible. In the experience of the various residential dorms, even if there is no explicit assignment to squads, veterans almost always form their own hierarchies and distribution of assignments should be based on the strengths and capabilities of the members owing to their combat experiences and the skills they acquired. Whether this ability comes through rehearsed or actual battle drills, teams of veterans necessarily rely upon their component parts on the theory that the collective members of the team will always accomplish much more than even the most skilled, talented, or fit individual. In this context as in others, "Veterans don't give up on veterans" (Harden, 2001, p. 1F).

Summary of Programs to Optimize Combat Readjustment

If the objective is to assist veterans in readjusting to civilian society after relying upon maladaptive coping strategies developed in combat:

1. Screen for combat experience during the classification process. Do not settle only on veteran status. Furthermore, recognize that civilian contractors with experience in Iraq and Afghanistan face the same readjustment issues even though they may lack prior military service.

2. Recognize that all combat veterans, by necessity, adopt a personal "combat-ready" mode as a default to ensure their survival. This survival mode traditionally overestimates threats and innately prioritizes survival from day-to-day over personal accomplishment. The profound similarities between combat and incarceration are likely to activate the survivor mode, even if the veteran was able to turn it off following the deployment.

---

continued

Summary of Programs to Optimize Combat Readjustment—*Continued*

3. Implement training that alerts combat veterans to the operation of the survival mode and illustrate the maladaptive nature of survival mode in civilian, as opposed to combat, environments.

4. Recognize that confinement provides an unmatched opportunity for the inmates to critically evaluate their life course free from many of the traditional distractions that have interfered with recovery.

5. Implement a program of "basic training" in how to be a civilian open to all veterans, regardless of mental health diagnosis, and which is open to contractors who lived in combat conditions, even if they never served in the military.

6. Recognize that the squad orientation to participation in veteran programs will substantially optimize the effects of such programming based on the veterans' prior experience. Even where it is not feasible to house veterans in the same units, pods, wings, or dorms, the squad orientation during formal treatment and informal periods of association will achieve far more.

II. Specific Programs Developed to Address Combat-Related Trauma and PTSD

A. The Pennsylvania Department of Corrections' Vietnam PTSD Treatment Program

Beginning in 1982, Vietnam veterans in three separate Pennsylvania prisons who were aware of recent initiatives to promote readjustment counseling for their non-incarcerated peers repeatedly requested clinical assessment for Agent Orange exposure and treatment for symptoms of PTSD. In September of that year, after denial of their requests, these inmates filed a class action lawsuit in the federal court claiming that their civil rights had been violated by the Department's deliberate indifference to a serious medical need posed by their combat-related conditions. Brad Carter, the lead plaintiff shared his experience during a multiple-day hearing, explaining in pertinent part:

> When I came into Graterford to get treated, to get classified, to get placed
> somewhere in the correctional system, nobody asked me if I ever been to
> Vietnam. Nobody asked me if I had special problems. 2,500 combat mis-
> sions, [nine] tunnels, shot once, 48 medals, and I went to Vietnam because
> I was trying to get in the mainstream of America. And guess what, I am still
> trying today. (Carter, 1987 [Day Three], p. 455)

The legal complaint specifically alleged that "prison officials violated the
constitutional rights of the inmates who were Vietnam veterans in failing to
provide diagnosis and treatment for veterans suffering from" PTSD and
Agent Orange exposure, and that "there was essentially no treatment being
provided for PTSD in any of the state correctional institutions" (Plaintiffs'
Memorandum in Support of Motion for Final Approval of Stipulation, 1987,
p. 3). Although the Pennsylvania Department of Corrections vigorously resisted the suit, in December of 1982, the federal court appointed a law firm
to represent the inmates, and on July 20, 1983, certified as a singular class
of plaintiffs "all present and future inmates of Pennsylvania correctional institutions who are veterans of the Vietnam War and who claim that they suffer from PTSD [or Agent Orange exposure] as a result of their service"
(Plaintiffs' Memorandum in Support of Motion for Final Approval of Stipulation, 1987, p. 3).

The court denied the Department of Corrections' motion to dispose of
the 42 U.S.C. § 1983 cause of action through summary judgment, enabling
the class of inmates to proceed to a jury trial in 1984. In the face of this
unprecedented case with potential national ramifications, the Pennsylvania
Department of Corrections began a series of years-long negotiations for a
settlement of the suit, which included the development of a Department-
wide PTSD program specifically for incarcerated Vietnam veterans. For a
time, it appeared as though the Department would approve conditions of a
consent decree imposing various responsibilities on the Department to be
monitored by the court. However, Pennsylvania's Governor rejected the
terms of the decree. On July 22, 1986, the Department elected for an option
that would eliminate the need for continuing court supervision, and promptly instituted a statewide policy that met most of the proposed standards, except for the requirement that the Attorney General revisit the sentences of
those convicted veterans who were diagnosed with combat-related PTSD
through the institutional program (Flournoy, 1987 [Day Three], p. 379).
When the case was finally settled, the Department had developed the most
extensive program known to diagnose and treat incarcerated Vietnam combat veterans for service-connected PTSD.

Pennsylvania's program is quite remarkable, even today, because of the
careful and serious manner in which the Department sought to construct an

effective program targeting combat trauma. Many of the concerns raised by Mr. Carter and his peers were highlighted in the Pennsylvania State Senate's own hearings on Vietnam readjustment difficulties. Through years of negotiations, the lawsuit resulted in the recruitment of some of the nation's leading PTSD experts who had been instrumental in the development of national policies to implement Veterans Administration treatment programs based on the newly created 1980 diagnostic criteria for PTSD. Because of the sense of immediacy for developing an effective treatment regimen, the potential for nationwide consequences if the Department lost at trial, and court-supervision, which ultimately led the court to order inspections of programs by the plaintiff's experts and production of regular statistical reports, the testimony from the case offers insights that would not easily be obtained elsewhere. As only one example, experienced Veterans Administration psychologist Michael Edward Flournoy appeared to speak as an expert on the "development and implementation of a PTSD program and the contents of which that program should have" (Flournoy, 1987 [Day Three], p. 395).

Beyond being the only program in the nation to target incarcerated veterans with PTSD, Pennsylvania's treatment program successfully operated until it was changed by two major events which led to its extinction in the mid-1990s: a large riot within the prison system and the Veterans Administration's sea change in policy, which led to the withdrawal of clinical counseling support by its staff within the walls of the nation's correctional institutions (O. Nash, personal communication, August 15, 2013). Although the program has not functioned in recent years, the efforts and compromises that led to its development, especially about eligibility criteria, program completion requirements, treatment planning considerations, and collaboration between Veterans Administration and departmental mental health providers, offer lessons that are as vital to prison and jail administrators today as they were in the early-to-mid-1980s. The subsections below describe some of the key take-home points of Pennsylvania's program, including its most salient feature as outlined in Commissioner Glen Jeffes' Administrative Memorandum, the *Program Manual,* and the corresponding testimony of mental health professionals who explained the bases for major program attributes.

Contours of Pennsylvania's PTSD Treatment Program

1. The Department's Policy

It is apt to begin with the policy that the Department adopted for the PTSD treatment program:

"It is the policy of the Department of Corrections that inmates diagnosed as suffering from PTSD be offered appropriate treatment by trained staff for their disorder within the ability of the Department to provide such services" (Jeffes, 1986, ¶ 2).

Thus, capability to treat PTSD was measured by the resources of the Department of Corrections, rather than the Veterans Administration. Although the policy statement did not directly reference combat-related PTSD, this implied term is evident in the subject title of the memorandum, addressing "Post Traumatic Stress Disorder (PTSD) Identification and Treatment *for Vietnam Veterans*" (Jeffes, 1986, p.1). The Department's policy was not simply to provide counseling to alleviate undesirable symptoms in general, but to treat the underling origins of these combat-related conditions. To this end, the *Program Manual* stated, "[i]n accordance with staff training, emphasis will be placed upon reliving and dealing with the Vietnam experience as well as related personal adjustment problems" (Commonwealth of Pennsylvania, 1986, ¶ IV-02. A).

Even though most mental health professionals in the Department lacked knowledge of and exposure to treatment techniques for combat-related disorders, one hallmark of the program was that Department mental health providers were designated to provide treatment services rather than Veterans Administration employees. On this view, the Veterans Administration served a significant role in consulting the Department on the incorporation of leading PTSD treatment protocols. With the recognition that numerous inmates might require treatment and the Department of Corrections was the entity being sued for failing to provide the treatment, it was incumbent on the Department to assume this primary responsibility.

It did not seem feasible to expect that the Veterans Administration would be willing to send its practitioners to the state prisons on a regular basis for daily treatment. During the hearing, the comments of the Chief Deputy Attorney General Maria Vickers revealed that, prior to the litigation when the Department had adopted the practice of transporting inmates to medical centers, the Veterans Administration directed the Department to stop sending inmates to their hospitals for medical evaluations (Vickers, 1987 [Day Three], p. 375). Consultancy was more feasible for the Veterans Administration and took the form of "four days of in-service training for the Department of Corrections at Camp Hill" (Flournoy Testimony, 1987 (Day 1), p. 28), "liaisons between the Vet Center nearest the institution[s] that have a PTSD program whereby V. A. can provide technical assistance on an ongoing and regular basis to those particular projects" (Flournoy Testimony, 1987 (Day 1), p. 29), and, more generally, initial and periodic follow-up training.

The *Program Manual* described the overall process for training departmental staff. Under "general considerations," it advised that the department had responsibility for training staff in "the recognition of PTSD signs and symptoms, diagnosis, and treatment" (Commonwealth of Pennsylvania, 1986, ¶ VI-00). Yet, in the discussion of "training resources," the *Manual* clarified that "[t]he primary source for the initial training will be the Veteran's Administration. The Veterans Administration training staff will, in cooperation with the Department of Corrections, designate trainers with expertise in PTSD and develop a training course." Following initial training, the "Veterans Administration will provide ongoing consultation on an as needed basis. The Program Coordinator and PTSD trained institutional staff involved in the follow-up programming may have access to the Veterans Administration consultants and training sources through the Psychology Division" (Commonwealth of Pennsylvania, 1986, ¶ VI-001. A-B).

These measures were reinforced through a system of periodic visits where Veterans Administration experts audited the treatment program. Although this practice had its origin in motions filed by the plaintiffs and a court order from the federal judge, as the program developed, and a settlement neared, the program embraced voluntary site inspections and audits. In 1987, there were plans to "provide training on a regular basis for each class of correctional officers that go through the academy [and] consultant, technical assistance to each one of the treatment facilities on an ongoing basis" (Flournoy, 1987 (Day 1), p. 30). The record suggests that mental health personnel at the Department faced several challenges learning the new and unfamiliar methods that the Veterans Administration had developed to treat this new combat-related disorder. But through ongoing interaction with Veterans Administration providers, and oftentimes the purchase of books on the subject with their own funds and the devotion of additional hours of their own free time, correctional mental health staff rose to the challenge (Ream, 1987 [Day Three], p. 428).

Take-Home Point

Chapter 5 highlights how, since the 1990s, there has been no prospect of obtaining direct treatment support from Veterans Administration clinicians for incarcerated veterans with PTSD or other operational stress injuries. Pennsylvania's approach is noteworthy for its use of the Veterans Administration in other ways to meet the treatment needs of its inmates. The Pennsylvania program is a testament to the value of Veterans Administration augmentation for services provided by a corrections department, whether this takes the form of periodic training, audits or other site inspections, or ongoing consultations, as needed. With a greater presence of Veterans Administration personnel in prisons and jails as a result of reentry programming, correctional administrators have the necessary linkages to explore such options.

Dr. Joel Rosenthal, through his responsibilities for Veterans Justice Programs related training, at least five California prison facilities where the Veterans Administration arranged for contracted clinical trainers to provide guidance to correctional mental health professionals. (J. Rosenthal, personal communication, November 13, 2018). Although there is no formalized procedure applicable to all Veterans Administration Medical Centers and all departments of correction, Dr. Rosenthal recognizes the potential for additional agreements along similar lines. Importantly, the prison correctional staff in this instance reached out to the Veterans Administration and asked how it would be possible to receive specialized training in the treatment of combat PTSD. In this case, for a modest fee, 25 clinicians were able to attend a two-day Cognitive Processing Therapy course for Veterans Administration practitioners. Beyond this, they were able to take part in an additional day of training on implementation of the intervention in groups, followed by weekly telephone consultations. While the trainers will not be providing treatment to inmates through the correctional staff, they will serve as an ongoing resource to assist the clinicians in developing their skills. Through collaborations such as these, correctional professionals seeking to address underlying causes of inmates' symptoms can indeed stay abreast of combat-PTSD-specific advances in the field.

2. Identifying Service-Related PTSD

The specific focus of the program on combat-related PTSD sprang from the legal requirement to develop sensitivities to the unique treatment needs of military veterans as opposed to survivors of non-military trauma. In the opinion of Dr. Flournoy, this evaluation necessitated "distinguish[ing] between trauma that recurs as a result of military service versus a trauma that could have occurred during the developmental stages of childhood, adolescence and young adulthood" (Flournoy Testimony, 1987, p. 357).

In a practical sense, the department learned early on that it must first require proof of prior military status, usually in the form of the DD214 form, which could take some time to request through official channels if the inmate lacked a ready copy. Based on the considerable time lag, Dr. Flournoy recommended individual treatment for self-identified veterans in the period after they identified a military history but still awaited service documentation (Flournoy Testimony, 1987, p. 358). Proof of service "up front" was necessary due to the initial trial of the program in which some inmates falsely claimed veteran status in attempts at admission (Ream, 1987, p. 421).

To accomplish the goal of linking current symptoms to military experiences, the department developed the *Military Experience Scale* as "an instrument utilized to record an individual's level of experience in Vietnam" (Jeffes Memorandum, 1986, ¶ IV. B). The Scale contained seventeen questions on the full range of experiences, such as: "Did you fire land based or naval artillery on the enemy?"; "Did you engage in hand-to-hand combat?"; "Did you encounter mines, booby traps or pongee pits?"; and, "Did you kill or think you killed the enemy?" The full *Scale,* reprinted in Appendix A of this chapter, has features which are useful to consider today.

Take-Home Point

The take-home point for correctional professionals is that Pennsylvania recognized the importance of going beyond the simple question of whether the veteran served, or even whether the veteran deployed to combat. The PTSD treatment program sought to understand the nature and magnitude of specific experiences during an individual's wartime service. There are many ways that veterans perceive war zone stress (King, King, Gudanowski, & Vreven, 1995). Some stressors in a deployed setting may not relate to combat at all. In examining stresses in the Gulf War, for example, researchers developed a thirty-one-item list of common stressful events, including heat injuries and exposure to "smoke from oil well fires," with only nine items devoted to combat type experience (Carney et al., 2003, p. 655).

In the advent of Operation Iraqi Freedom/Operating Enduring Freedom, newer scales have been updated to address the characteristics of counterinsurgency, such as roadside bombs and Vehicle-Borne Improvised Explosive Devices (VBIEDS). Thus, contemporary treatment programs in confined settings should incorporate a recent scale tailored to the types of combat stressors common to the Global War on Terrorism, in addition to preserving unique stressors specific to Vietnam and other past campaigns. It may be useful to review the 2012 *War Experiences Inventory* (Katz et al., 2012, pp. 69–70, app.). For comparison, this chapter includes a number of deployment-specific portions of the *Deployment Risk and Resilience Inventory-2,* located in Appendix B (King et al., 2009).

Any quick survey can still leave some room for confusion. For example, in considering more recent measures, some researchers have noted a phenomenon in which mortar and rocket fire in Iraq and Afghanistan have been so common that veterans who experienced these events regularly would answer "No," to the question "Were you ever under enemy fire?" because they perceived that the question related only to extremely close calls (Novaco,

Swanson, Gonzalez, Gahm, & Reger, 2012, p. 663 n.2). Despite some inherent possibility of imprecision, these scales are imminently useful for quickly identifying the types of experiences that can substantially increase veterans' risk for behavioral symptoms of disorders related to military service.

As highlighted in Chapter 4's discussion of Moral Injury, very recent research indicates the value and necessity of surveying veterans for their experience of ethical challenges during military service—in addition to the classic life-threat experiences presumed to cause PTSD. Clinicians warn that it is a "disservice to . . . veterans if [mental health providers] fail to conceptualize and address the lasting psychological, biological, spiritual, behavioral, and social impact of perpetrating, failing to prevent, or bearing witness to acts that transgress deeply held moral beliefs and expectations" (Litz et al., 2009, p. 697).

The nine-item *Moral Injury Event Scale,* shows promising potential to provide these important insights with targeted prompts, such as: "I feel betrayed by leaders who I once trusted"; "I am troubled by having witnessed others' immoral acts"; "I am troubled by having acted in ways that violated my own morals or values"; and "I violated my own morals by failing to do something that I felt I should have done" (Nash et al., 2013, p. 651 fig.).

3. Defining a Qualifying Mental Condition

Commissioner Jeffes' administrative memorandum explained that inmates who served in Vietnam would be eligible for participation in the PTSD treatment program if they "may have PTSD":

> To meet this requirement, there had to be "documentation that the inmate is demonstrating at least some of the symptoms listed as diagnostic criteria for PTSD in [the *Diagnostic and Statistical Manual of Mental Disorders*]" (Jeffes, 1986, ¶ IV. B. 5(b)).

The distinction that inmates needed only to show *some* PTSD symptoms, rather than *all* PTSD symptoms, was intentional and serves as a vital lesson for correctional administrators today.

Even though the diagnostic criteria for PTSD had been developed only two years before the *Carter* litigation began, and there remained much to be learned about the nuances of PTSD assessment, the architects of the program appreciated the fact that PTSD is a diagnosis that often lacks perfect precision. This is why, to the PTSD Program Director, "[a]s far as the program itself, we don't see it as PTSD. . . . We as professionals do not see PTSD as a single entity" (Ream Testimony, 1987, p. 428). This view hasn't changed and is bolstered by the mental health profession's rocky reception of the revised PTSD criteria in the 2013 *DSM-5*. Today, the term PTSD is still, at best, a "heuristic, functioning as a simplified communication device . . . about the nature of an individual's range of clinical symptoms related to an event perceived as traumatic" (Young, 2007, p. 148). As a consequence, "adopting a uniform approach to the diagnosis, etiology, causality, and treatment of PTSD does not do justice to the research or the individual" (Young, 2007, p. 148).

In approaching the task of treating Vietnam veterans' military trauma, the Department decided to liberalize the criteria and cast "a much broader net to scoop up veterans with PTSD" than the thresholds applied by the Veterans Administration in its disability compensation evaluations (Flournoy, 1987 [Day Three], p. 395). Dr. John H. Ream, III, the Department's PTSD Program Director, testified that the correctional program did not seek to conduct four-hour interviews and develop lengthy histories of potential stressors over the life course like the Veterans Administration did because, "[t]he more history we get we will cut [more] people out" (Ream, 1987 [Day Three], p. 422). He recognized that Veterans Administration disability compensation standards for assessing mental conditions were very strict and not geared toward treating the symptoms of mental illness.

In Dr. Ream's estimate, if the Department had applied the Veterans Administration's more stringent diagnostic criteria for PTSD diagnosis, thirty-seven of the fifty inmates who had been treated by 1987 for Vietnam-related symptoms ultimately would have been rejected from the program (Ream, 1987 [Day Three], p. 421). Ream further estimated that between one-half to two-thirds of all inmates suffering some combat PTSD symptoms would not qualify for treatment (Ream, 1987 [Day Three], p. 422). Accordingly, the Department still admitted inmates in the Vietnam PTSD program if they suffered from adjustment disorders or other sub-threshold conditions, but not full-blown PTSD (Flournoy, 1987 [Day Three], p. 396).

Based upon the existing state of PTSD research and the very first iteration of the diagnostic criteria from the *DSM-III*, the architects of the Pennsylvania Combat PTSD Treatment Program developed and used a twenty-eight-item *Vietnam Veterans Scale* as "a self-report scale regarding physical and emotional feelings currently being experienced" (Jeffes, 1986, ¶ IV. C). The Scale included several questions tailored to the diagnostic criteria, with five items mentioning military experiences, such as, "I react negatively to reminders of Vietnam"; "I have nightmares and/or flashbacks about Vietnam"; and, "I am preoccupied with thoughts about Vietnam." The entire *Scale* is reprinted in Appendix C of this chapter. In evaluating the results of this measure, program administrators had two goals. First, they confirmed the existence of at least one PTSD symptom. Second, they classified such symptoms based on severity (Flournoy, 1987 [Day Three], p. 358), and used the results in combination with the scores from the combat experience measure to identify treatment needs (Ream, 1987 [Day Three], p. 421).

Take-Home Point

In the final analysis, the position adopted by the Department intentionally strayed from a "classic" disability compensation model of PTSD assessment. When the goal of a correctional program is PTSD treatment, the measure must be more flexible so that it can address a range of emotional and physical problems. The guiding philosophy for PTSD treatment of incarcerated veterans was "to get as many people that needed some help into the system [even if they suffer from] low levels of stress in their system" (Flournoy, 1987 [Day Three], p. 396).

Today, some assessment tools function like the *Vietnam Veterans Scale*, but are tailored to revised *DSM* criteria. As explored in Chapter 4, the PCL-M is one such tool that is reprinted in Appendix A of Chapter 4. Earlier scales do aid. As noted in Chapter 4, and reprinted in Appendix B, Dr. Jonathan Shay's *Combat Stress Barometer* is a detailed measure that captures several symptoms relevant to the veterans' current responses to combat-related trauma (1996).

4. PTSD Program Duration

While Commissioner Jeffes' memorandum was clear that "[t]reatment programming will run in 90-day cycles," it also indicated that a participant could develop a new treatment plan to cover additional periods beyond the initial three months if needed (Jeffes, 1986, ¶ V.C.3). Like the other aspects of the program, careful planning went into this provision as well. The settlement hearing established that the national PTSD expert consultant had recommended 180-days as the ideal duration of the residential PTSD treatment program for combat veterans. The Department rejected the idea, and it halved the term to three months for instilling in participants the desire to recover sooner.

On this point, Dr. Ream testified, "if you are given an indefinite time to come to grips and face a problem[,] some individuals won't come to grips." Contrarily, "[i]f you put them in 90 days it may make a person think and say, 'I have got to do it.' And then we give you the option with you and the therapist to re-negotiate" (Ream, 1987 [Day Three], p. 424). Importantly, even for those participants who did complete the PTSD treatment within the initial ninety-day period, a salient feature of the program was the capability of aftercare treatment, which could ostensibly continue through the Veterans Administration following the participant's eventual release from confinement in recognition that "ongoing counseling may be a necessity in some cases" (Commonwealth of Pennsylvania, 1986, ¶ III-05. G). By September 8, 1987, seventy Vietnam combat veterans "completed a primary ninety-day treatment cycle," fifty of them were in the "after-care" treatment phase," and twenty-five more awaited enrollment upon receipt of their service documentation (Stipulation of Settlement, 1987, ¶ 9).

Take-Home Point

The key lesson regarding program duration is the ability to temper the incentive for expedient program completion with the ability to extend program duration when necessary to meet the ends of effective treatment. It is noteworthy that Pennsylvania enrolled its inmates into the PTSD program for the duration of their period of treatment, emphasizing the importance to provide comprehensive services focused on PTSD treatment. In veteran readjustment programs not specifically created to address PTSD, or which may indirectly address PTSD as one of many facets of their programming, there is often tension between the PTSD program and other required programs with residential components. At the New York Department of Correctional Services' Veterans Residential Therapeutic Program dorms, participants are often pulled from the residential setting to complete everything from sex-offender treatment to narcotics and alcohol abatement programs. This disruption of continuity can have tremendously negative impacts on the veteran's overall adjustment and oftentimes can impede their progress in the program that inherits them after an abrupt transition (S. M. Verbeke & J. P. Strollo, personal communication, September 16, 2013).

For those prisons, especially, which seek to develop programs targeting the special needs of incarcerated veterans with some symptoms of PTSD, Pennsylvania's planning philosophy and New York's opposite experience show that efforts should be made to permit completion of the full course of a veteran's program—however long—prior to enrollment in other residential programs. Based on their extensive experience in New York, Veterans Guidance Specialists Susan M. Verbeke and James P. Strollo recommend that corrections programs identify veterans at the point of reception, place them in residential treatment to address readjustment concerns and military-specific issues first before any other residential program, and permit them to complete the program before they are transferred to the general population or other offense-based programs (Personal communication, September 16, 2013).

They estimate that such a model would provide the veteran inmate with essential skills that can enhance their own experience, the experience of other inmates, and the experiences of correctional staff and equip them with the ability to approach reentry in a more effective manner. FCI Phoenix's Second Tour program also echoes these sentiments by aiming to provide the veteran with a view of existence in the corrections setting that does not default to the mode of combat survival they relied upon to endure similar challenging circumstances. If such veterans are unable to learn an alternative viewpoint prior to their transfer from a veteran-specific program, some will inevitably bring the survival mentality with them to the new residential program.

5. Pre-Enrollment Trial Period

A defining feature of Pennsylvania's PTSD Treatment Program was the ability to test a given inmate's suitability for the program, including a trial period prior to enrollment. The *Program Manual* specified:

> The purpose of [a Decision Group] is to allow the inmate and staff to establish communications and get to know one another. The intent will be to draw out the inmate's experiences and feelings about his/her military service and its effects upon his/her lifestyle, emotional functioning, and if he/she wants to pursue a course of intensified treatment. (Commonwealth of Pennsylvania, 1986, ¶ 111-05. A)

The Commissioner's memorandum further explained that "[s]taff may choose to hold three or four 'decision group' sessions with interested inmate veterans to see what the program is like and for treatment staff to get to know and evaluate them before proceeding with diagnostic evaluations" (Jeffes, 1986, ¶ V. A.5). These decision groups helped to conserve resources by evaluating the inmate's interest in and compatibility with the program.

In his testimony, Dr. Flournoy discussed some key considerations about PTSD treatment in a confined setting that justified this trial period. One aspect of suitability for program participation was compatibility with group counseling. The "primary counseling approach" in Pennsylvania was three sessions per week for sixty-to-ninety minutes in groups of ten-to-twelve veterans (Commonwealth of Pennsylvania, 1986, ¶ IV-02. A-B). Dr. Flournoy noted that group treatment of PTSD symptoms simply will not work the same for every participant. Some will have to "learn" how to participate optimally. Others "do not do well in group treatment. So, the therapist should be aware that this may not be the appropriate environment in which to treat this individual" (Flournoy, 1987 [Day Three], p. 362). An inmate in the class of plaintiffs raised similar concerns about his own PTSD symptoms being triggered by an inmate with more severe symptomatology: "If you put us in the same group he will be going through some of his events and the next thing you know it might make my stress worse . . . so rather than help me it intensifies my stress and it might not help him at all" (Glass, 1987 [Day Three], p. 338).

To address those inmates with individual counseling needs, the PTSD program offered the option of individual counseling by departmental mental health providers or some combination of both individual and group therapy (Jeffes, 1986, ¶ V. D. 2). It seemed unlikely, however, that a veteran could successfully complete treatment in isolation. Despite options for individual counseling, the program's very structure emphasized the importance of group treatment for veterans, specifically. Not only were participants transferred to one of four residential housing units at State Correctional Institution (SCI) Pittsburgh, SCI Camp Hill, SCI Graterford, and SCI Muncy (for female veteran inmates) to undergo the three-month treatment regimen, but the department committed to "make good faith efforts to house PTSD therapy group participants as close as possible to each other" during the course of treatment (Plaintiffs Memorandum in Support of Their Motion for Final Approval of Stipulation of Settlement, 1987, p. 19). Accordingly, potential participants and program administrators alike required the ability to gauge how well the inmate would fit into the treatment setting *prior* to commitment of resources and transfer into the program.

Separate from compatibility with group treatment for combat PTSD, the trial period also emphasized the voluntary nature of program participation. Dr. Flournoy, while acknowledging a contrary view, testified unequivocally that it is possible to successfully treat combat PTSD in a confined setting:

> My sense is that individuals have . . . recovered and manage[d] PTSD after being in a confined setting. Whether or not more people would have satisfactorily completed adjustment if they had not been there is another question . . . I do know as a matter of record, we have successfully treated individuals for [combat] PTSD within a correctional setting. (Flournoy, 1987 [Day Three], p. 365)

However, he also emphasized that this is not an easy task because in group treatment, particularly the initial stages, the participant will necessarily be forced to confront unsettling emotions and memories that have often been bottled-up for years. This too commonly evokes "very, very bad feelings in which clients have a tendency to go into states of depression" (Flournoy, 1987 [Day Three], pp. 365–366). Along these lines, in its recommendation for treatment professionals to "bring out feelings and develop emotional awareness" regarding combat experiences, the *Program Manual* cautions that "[a]ttempts of the inmates to skirt the main issues and/or discuss prison concerns must be kept to a minimum" (Commonwealth of Pennsylvania, 1986, ¶ IV-02 A).

Many inmates with PTSD symptoms may not desire to endure this type of hardship in addition to the existing hardships confinement life, which have been known to cause adjustment problems even among inmates without prior mental health conditions (Dvoskin & Spiers, 2004, p. 44). For these reasons, program architects strayed from the strict participation requirements of residential programs at the Veterans Administration, which normally required completion unless one was ejected for misconduct (Ream, 1987 [Day Three], pp. 424–425). In Pennsylvania's Vietnam veterans PTSD program, "[w]hen it is a voluntary process, if it becomes too painful, you can withdraw" (Ream, 1987 [Day Three], pp. 424–425).

Take-Home Point

The useful lesson from Pennsylvania's PTSD Treatment Program is to make participation in veteran-focused programs completely voluntary and to build the capacity for prospective participants, program administrators, and already enrolled veterans to test the waters in a preliminary non-committal manner. The experience of veterans treatment courts is a testament to the need for careful vetting and selection of participants because enrollment of an individual who is not committed to the goals of the program or who is attending primarily for anticipated secondary gain can stifle the treatment progress of those inmates in the program who are committed to their own betterment. In states such as Texas, judges have bemoaned the statues, which have mandated enrollment of all similarly-situated veteran offenders into the Treatment Court Program, stripping them and the other members of the treatment team of the choice to deny enrollment (Merten, 2010). Contrarily, the highly-selective programs have been the ones with the best rates of completion and recidivism abatement (Seamone, 2011).

6. The Need for *Some* Confidentiality

Combat in Vietnam often involved exposure to atrocities, and sometimes participation in them. Of course, this is not to say that wartime atrocities are unique to Vietnam. Notably, during the trial of Lieutenant William Calley for the murders and rapes at My Lai, a group of World War II and Korean War veterans who protested the charging decision in that case attempted to surrender themselves to local police authorities "on the grounds that, 'If this man is guilty, he is guilty for the things we did. We shot up civilians under orders and killed civilians too'" (Bourke, 1999, p. 184). Collectively, they asserted that war often leads faithful warriors to do unspeakable acts for survival or stemming from a survival mentality. Chapter 4 points out the mili-

tary's own official recognition of this connection in its doctrine on misconduct stress behaviors. With a mandate to unearth the veteran's most troubling combat experiences, the architects of Pennsylvania's PTSD program
anticipated the possibility that the treatment might lead to admissions that
the veteran participated in morally objectionable and illegal behavior while
deployed in harm's way. To address the likely resistance against discussing
criminal and unappealing behavior for which the veteran might be culpable,
the program implemented a compromise of sorts in the form of a "confidential journal." Commissioner Jeffes' Memorandum concisely explained
this concept:

> Inmates may be required to maintain a personal daily journal and/or com-
> plete readings of materials recommended by the program staff, counselor,
> and V.A. consultants. The personal journal will be a confidential document
> to be used in the treatment process with the treatment staff, in group and
> individual counseling, and in peer interactions when deemed appropriate.
> The journal should include but not be limited to the inmate's daily interac-
> tions, feelings, attitudes, and reflections. The journal will not become a part
> of the inmate file. (Jeffes, 1986, ¶ V. D.2)

On confidentiality, in general, the *Program Manual* further described, that,
consistent with applicable ethical codes, treatment professionals would
endeavor to maintain confidentiality on matters not raising imminent danger and refrain from including sensitive information in inmates' permanent
records (Commonwealth of Pennsylvania, 1986, ¶ IV-02. G).

Take-Home Point

While the concept of confidentiality may seem at odds with promotion
of order and safety within a correctional setting, there may truly be an
exception in the case of veterans' traumatic wartime experiences. In varied
surveys of Global War on Terrorism veterans by the Mental Health Advisory
Teams, the studies conducted between 2003 and 2008 suggest that as many
as 27 percent of respondents "faced ethical situations during deployment in
which they did not know how to respond," 20 percent perceived that they
were responsible for the death of a non-combatant, 11 percent endorsed
unnecessary damage to property, and 5 percent stated that they had mis-
treated civilians (Litz et al., 2009, p. 696). These are the types of events that
commonly lead to moral injuries, which can be as, if not, more "profound
and long-lasting" than traditional life-threat trauma in the war zone (U.S.
Navy and U.S. Marine Corps, 2010, ¶ 4–16).

The inability to discuss these experiences for fear of disclosure or rejection only hampers recovery and perpetuates negative symptomology and its

corresponding risks of harm and even suicide. For this reason, clinicians propose careful attention to the development of a trusting relationship between the combat veteran counselee and the treating mental health professional (Litz et al., 2009, p. 174). While many aspects of the correctional setting limit the ability to replicate treatment attributes in the community, measures like a confidential journal may help achieve some of the most desired goals to this end in those programs that are brave enough to take on treatment of the underlying conditions that cause many of the more serious combat-related disorders.

Summary of Lessons Learned from the Pennsylvania Model

Pennsylvania Vietnam Veteran
PTSD Treatment Program Summary

If the objective is to treat underlying combat-related conditions that are responsible for symptoms of PTSD and combat and operational Stress:

1. Optimize existing contacts with the VA to coordinate for training and consultation regarding the treatment of combat and operational stress injuries, which does not run afoul of the prohibition on direct treatment.

2. Do not condition admission on strict adherence to all of the *DSM*'s diagnostic criteria. Rather, assess for the presence of some of the more troubling symptoms. Permit those with adjustment disorders or sub-threshold PTSD for the full treatment regimen.

3. Require outside confirmation of prior military service but provide individual counseling for the time it takes to obtain such confirmation.

4. Set a fixed time period for program completion, but always include the option of extending the time when treatment needs remain.

5. Ensure that the qualifying veteran inmate is able to participate in the combat trauma program first in order among other residential programs and that he or she is not prematurely transferred to a different residential program. Skills to address combat trauma will transfer to other programs if there is enough time to cement them.

---

continued

**Pennsylvania Vietnam Veteran
PTSD Treatment Program Summary**—*Continued*

6. Make program participation completely voluntary because intensive treatment can become too painful.

7. Develop the capacity for a trial period to gauge the individual inmate's fit with existing group and facilitator dynamics prior to expenditure of assessment and other resources.

8. Provide the option for individual, group, or combined therapy to address underlying issues but recognize that a participant should not entirely divorce himself or herself from the group setting.

9. Provide residential treatment and transfer veteran inmates to a central location for program participation.

10. Even where veteran participants are not housed in program-specific dorms, make every effort to ensure that they reside close to one another.

11. Offer some measure of confidentiality for discussions or writings related to stigmatizing traumatic material, such as the confidential journal. Otherwise, suppressed moral injuries from deep-seated ethical conflicts may result in persistent symptoms.

B. The Southern California Veterans in Prison (V.I.P.) Self-Help Model

In the late 1970s, shortly after the Veterans Administration increased its outreach efforts in response to the General Accounting Office's scathing 1974 report, employees of the Brentwood Veterans Administration Hospital in West Los Angeles, California, estimated many benefits of a program tailored specifically for incarcerated veterans. Estimates from the period placed this population at 25 to 33 percent of California's incarcerated (Pentland & Scurfield, 1982, p. 21). There was growing concern at the time that a substantial portion of this subpopulation might be suffering from a condition then known as Post-Vietnam Syndrome. Veterans Administration counselor Bruce Pentland spearheaded the initiative to develop veteran self-help groups in prisons, supported by a network of community programs orchestrated under his coordination and consultation. The overall program can be summarized as:

> **[A] peer, self-help model of organization [including] elected officers of the group who facilitate the self-organization of veteran inmates through regularly scheduled meetings where veterans discuss areas of mutual concern, organize recreational/social activities, and facilitate attendance and participation of interested veterans with the VIP community resource team that visits the facility [monthly]. (Pentland & Scurfield, 1982, p. 22)**

This was not simply a prison group. A key component included addressing combat experiences in a methodical manner and another major staple was the "consultancy" of Veterans Administration mental health provider, which regularly included individual and even family therapy (Pentland, 1979, p. 523). The basic goal of the program was to "help the veteran to help themselves" by changing attitudes and connecting inmates with needed resources and services (Pentland & Scurfield, 1982).

While this may describe any number of programs for inmates, V.I.P. recognized that veterans constituted "a sizeable group who are potentially in need of specialized understanding and interventions" (Pentland & Scurfield, 1982, p. 21). An effective response to veterans' combat readjustment difficulties would require a coordinated effort with multiple layers of organizational involvement. Over numerous negotiations with jail and prison administrators, in which Mr. Pentland conducted trial runs of the program to gain support, he laid the groundwork for a comprehensive system. The "precedent-setting" program, operated with tremendous success (Scurfield, 2004, p. 72, n.45), to the point where it was frequently praised for its results. In 1979, Veterans Administration's Director of Mental Health and Behavioral Science, Department of Medicine and Surgery, revealed plans to expand the program across the country (Ewalt, 1979, p. 130).

Although some contemporary programs in prisons and jails may use the term "Veterans in Prison Program," there are two major reasons why this early program would be difficult to replicate today. First was the unmatched dedication of Mr. Pentland, who personally sustained the program through his individual initiative. By 1982, this program was running in six long-term incarceration facilities, two central jails, and two civil commitment facilities, including two programs run for women veterans (Pentland & Scurfield, p. 21). As its primary director, Mr. Pentland not only coordinated the activities of several community organizations, which provided services at each of these institutions, he personally visited 200 to 300 incarcerated veterans per month—150 who had Post-Vietnam Syndrome issues—whom he either "consulted" or treated under extremely liberal interpretations of the Veterans Administration's regulations (Pentland, 1979). This last point dovetails with the second reason V.I.P. cannot exist under an identical framework today. This difference relates to the state of the Veterans Administration's rules prior to the early 1990s. While Chapter 5 of this book describes the gradual erosion of Veterans Administration treatment in confined settings, treatment providers had some capabilities in 1977 when this program began.

Notably, in the 1970s, Veterans Administration policies authorized continued medical and mental health outpatient care to incarcerated veterans who were already under Veterans Administration treatment at the time they were initially confined (Pentland & Scurfield, 1982). Thus, if an incarcerated veteran was either in outpatient or inpatient treatment just before confinement, the Veterans Administration could continue care so long as the confinement facility enabled the veteran to be transported to an outpatient facility and did not make it the Veterans Administration's responsibility to ensure discipline and correctional control during the treatment (Pentland & Scurfield, 1982, p. 21). In a 1979 hearing, Veterans Administration Administrator Max Cleland described the basis for this rule requiring non-veterans administration security: "We operate a medical care system, and it would be most unfortunate and anti-therapeutic if our facilities were used as an adjunct to the correctional system" (Cleland, 1979, pp. 463–464).

By 1990, congressional hearings on a proposed law to provide direct care to incarcerated veterans exposed the Veterans Administration's sentiment that the Veterans Administration did not desire to provide treatment services to incarcerated veterans because this would pull services away from other groups of veterans with dire needs that could more easily be fulfilled without the effect of certain statutory limitations on benefit eligibility and utilization (Chapter 5). Thus, a robust program of a nature that Mr. Pentland had developed would run contrary to the precedent that the Veterans Administration desired to set. Although the Veterans Administration had begun removing Veterans Administration personnel from rendering services for incarcerated veterans throughout the early 1990s, the position solidified in October 1999 when the Veterans Health Administration expressly prohibited the duplication of any medical or psychiatric services that a prison or jail would be responsible for providing. Although this means that Veterans in Prison programs exist today only in name, correctional professionals have much to gain from considering at least eight of its major lessons learned.

Contours of the Southern California V.I.P. Program

1. Incarcerated Veterans are Especially Disadvantaged by the Operation of Veterans Administration Laws and Regulations

The V.I.P. program recognized the manner in which various laws and regulations within the Veterans Administration benefits framework detrimentally affected incarcerated veterans and, by extension, any family members who depended upon such benefits. The consequence of incarceration for veterans undergoing mental or physical treatment at the time of confinement is a disruption in their continuity of care. Beyond this, educational benefits may decrease dramatically, and disability compensation might stop altogether or become substantially reduced depending on various circumstances (Chapter 5). While the collateral consequences of incarceration surely create challenges for all inmates, the effect of incarceration on Veterans Administration benefits plays an entirely different role with the capacity to seriously harm many veterans' prospects for successful reentry and for addressing the underlying problems that often contribute to incarceration.

Because the V.I.P. program was foremost a Veterans Administration program, even though it included community and local resources, it was essential to address incarcerated veterans' concerns over the manner in which their benefits were reduced or entirely disallowed. For many, it appeared as though the Veterans Administration had entirely written them off, and, even worse, devalued any of the sacrifices they made in military service to gain eligibility for the benefits in the first place.

> **For veterans receiving VA benefits at the time of incarceration, the benefits represent "tangible proof that society indeed had not abandoned them" (Pentland & Scurfield, 1982, p. 23). Limits on those benefits as a result of incarceration often lead incarcerated veterans to perceive abandonment by the VA, which can have detrimental consequences for readjustment and reentry.**

Over years of coordinating the program, Pentland heard numerous sentiments, such as "I served my country, and now they are taking away what I was told I would get by successfully completing my obligation" (Pentland & Scurfield, 1982, p. 23). In responding to these concerns, he found that the best way to approach the issue was to ensure that incarcerated veterans understood the temporary nature of the limits on their entitlement: "The VIP approach emphasizes to the incarcerated veteran that he/she has not permanently 'lost' Veterans Administration benefits by explaining the reasoning behind these laws, but in effect that they are in a situation where they must defer temporarily taking advantage of such benefits until release from prison" (Pentland & Scurfield, 1982, pp. 23–24).

He used the concept of "double-dipping" to put these temporary handicaps in perspective, essentially that it would constitute waste to provide funding or services when "the incarcerated veteran is already receiving food, clothing, housing and medical care at the expense of a governmental entity— either local, state, or federal" (Pentland & Scurfield, 1982, p. 22). Importantly, these experiences also alerted Mr. Pentland to the significant risk facing veterans who assume the Veterans Administration has written them off:

> Unless the veterans understand the rationale for these laws . . . and have an opportunity to vent their feelings regarding these new restrictions, incarcerated veterans can become so turned off to "the system" that they will refuse to take advantage of their benefits at a later time, even though still entitled to them. (Pentland & Scurfield, 1982, p. 23)

Take-Home Point

Due to the severe statutory and regulatory limitations on Veterans Administration benefits during incarceration, the primary focus of many prison- and jail-based programs has been on reentry. One byproduct of this has been concern over veterans who have not yet applied for Veterans Administration benefits. The V.I.P. program emphasized the necessity of addressing the impact of these laws on those inmates who have already received disability ratings or those who are otherwise already relying upon the Veterans Administration to meet their life needs at the time of entry into confinement.

For those who are not capable of attaining sufficient ongoing employment or who may need medical care as an alternative to services provided by the Veterans Administration, disability compensation may be the major factor sustaining the veteran and his or her family (Sayer et al., 2011). For these reasons, especially the risk that a veteran will disengage from Veterans Administration services after having established eligibility, the ability to constructively address the impact of these lost benefits and the perception of discarding one's prior honorable service is vital. It may be more vital, in fact, than introducing inmates to the Veterans Administration system for the first time.

2. The Instrumental Value of Applying for Veterans Administration Benefits *During the Course of Incarceration*

While the V.I.P. program certainly recognized the potential consequences of severe restrictions on those veterans whose existing benefits are disrupted by incarceration, the program simultaneously distinguished those veterans who have no existing dependence on the Veterans Administration. For this group of potentially eligible veterans, there is immense value in applying for benefits, even if these entitlements might never be paid or obtained until after the veteran's release. Although a veteran may not expect full receipt of benefits until release, other incremental steps in the process have specific value to the veteran. The key is to do more than provide pamphlets and reading material about benefit eligibility, as "[i]t becomes dysfunctional to quote benefits but provide [no] help obtaining them" (Pentland, 1979, p. 525).

Meaningful steps include expressed willingness to address inmates' questions and issues, "active follow up when necessary outside of prison walls," realistic responses, and timely feedback (Pentland & Scurfield, 1982, p. 26). It also helps to make persons available to consult veterans who have a degree of "insider knowledge" on the workings of the Veterans Administration's various administrative procedures for benefits adjudication (Pentland & Scurfield, 1982, p. 26). When the veteran sees these results:

> The very "process of obtaining [VA] benefits [becomes] more important than the benefits themselves" (Pentland & Dwyer, 1985, p. 413).

The inmates have "[t]he opportunity to experience some measure of success that has been attained through following the rules and procedures of the system" (Pentland & Scurfield, 1982, p. 25). And, for those who may have readjustment issues related to distrust of the Veterans Administration and the military (for example, drafted into Vietnam service, involuntarily extended service in Iraq or Afghanistan, or receipt of a stigmatizing discharge), each one of these small gains permits the veteran to "redevelop some faith in the system" (Pentland, 1979, p. 525). For this reason, assistance with discharge upgrading was a primary goal of the V.I.P. program (Pentland & Scurfield, 1982, p. 23).

Take-Home Point

At face value, it might appear that the receipt of Veterans Administration benefits is no different from the receipt of other medical or compensatory benefits, regardless of the state or federal agency that administers them. There are major differences, such as the fact that the quality of care at Veterans Administration facilities consistently rates above civilian medical institutions and the Veterans Administration's programs are collectively more comprehensive than any other federal benefits program. In fact, Dr. Jim McGuire, who led the Veterans Justice Programs office, explains, "No other system is able to address the types and quality of services needed by reentering inmates as they try to make the best of a new chance at living successfully in the community" (McGuire, 2007, p. 397).

Beyond this, however, even if some dollar amounts paid or services rendered may be comparable to public programs for non-veterans, Veterans Administration benefits are distinguishable because they relate back to the veterans' service in the military, and they provide another way for the veterans to perceive the government assigning value to their service. For the survivors of military sexual trauma, even if they were disbelieved or even retaliated against by superiors, Veterans Administration benefits for a mental condition relating to the trauma provide a way to recognize what the veteran sacrificed (Seamone & Traskey, 2014).

For the servicemember who received an Other-than-Honorable Discharge but receives a subsequent decision from a Veterans Administration character of service evaluation that his or her service was still sufficiently meritorious to be seen as something other than dishonorable, this determination lends value to the veteran's service (Chapters 2 and 6). Establishing qualifying entitlements for benefits whether available inside or outside of a confined setting can have immediate positive effects during the period of incarceration. Thus, it should be a priority of any jail or prison program to build the capacity to apply for Veterans Administration benefits and discharge upgrades during the term of incarceration. Given the lengthy period time that the Veterans Administration requires to process claims and the additional difficulties imposed by conditions of confinement (for example, securing evidence in support of filed claims), the veteran should get started on the process as early as possible, rather than waiting a certain period prior to release (Pentland, 1979, p. 23).

3. A Sufficient Program Must Incorporate Established Community Resources Beyond the Veterans Administration

Although Mr. Pentland's involvement as Coordinator of the V.I.P. program represented an unprecedented Veterans Administration commitment, even he recognized the necessity to involve multiple community organizations, which included the Center for Veterans Rights, the UCLA Educational Opportunity Center, a local career planning center, the California State Department of Veterans Affairs, and the Disabled American Veterans (a congressionally chartered Veterans Service Organization) (Pentland & Scurfield, 1982, p. 22, n.6). A major function of the V.I.P. program was "organization of community resources into a team that brings services into the prison system" (Pentland & Scurfield, 1982, p. 21). In addressing this wide range of participants, Pentland emphasized that the V.I.P. program did not aim to do anything *new*; instead, it aimed to leverage the proven resources of existing agencies. This also made sense from a fiscal perspective, as such programs permitted a "broader scope of services" in prisons and jails than any one program or the Veterans Administration could ever provide (Pentland, 1979, p. 525). While the goal of diverse community agency involvement was clear, a method to practically attain it within prisons and jails required significant planning that would respond to concerns over preferential treatment for veterans as well as the fit of a multi-organizational program within a specific jail or prison culture.

"Special" versus "Preferential" Treatment of Veterans

Transporting community programs into the confinement setting for veterans, specifically, would require approval of correctional administrators who were rightfully concerned over the perception of special privileges. The concern here is that "[m]any prison administrators do not want veterans to be treated 'special.' They fear that if the veteran receives money for attending educational programs, or any other attention which sets him apart [from] the rest of the yard, this will lead to attitude problems with the veteran or the other inmates" (Pentland, 1979, pp. 525–526). To address these concerns Mr. Pentland seized every opportunity to emphasize that "special attention" does not mean "preferential attention." Namely, incarcerated veterans face extraordinary circumstances that do not exist for non-veterans.

As emphasized throughout this book, not only do veterans share a distinctly different culture, combat trauma is significantly different from trauma experienced by civilians, and the operation of Veterans Administration laws creates a benefit-eligibility status that derives exclusively from military service. These are the factors that make incarcerated veterans' needs "different and unique"—and worthy of focused attention (Pentland, 1979, p. 526). However, none of these differences adopt or imply value judgments on whether a particular veteran is better than a nonveteran inmate.

As Mr. Pentland testified to a Senate committee, to ignore irrefutable differences based on prior military status is to "ignore reality"; "if we truly want to work a positive change in their lives, we must recognize the reality of their position and program accordingly. This group will not . . . respond to 'business as usual'" (Pentland, 1979, p. 524). Reality here also represents the

improved ability to treat the veteran inmate's underlying problems and thereby promote order in the institution, as well as successful reentry and recidivism abatement.

Effective Administrative Controls from Within the Program

The V.I.P. program combined the resources of several different entities,
each with its own respective mission statement. This was important because,
when community organizations effectively contribute services to prisoners
and detainees, correctional staff are less likely to be accused of preferential
treatment toward a particular group of inmates (Salierno, 1979, p. 361).
Incorporation of multiple organizations within confined settings necessitated
a level of coordination and regular visitation schedules that would guarantee
minimal disruptions to the daily operations of correctional staff. The program required "viable administrative controls" implemented from within,
the foremost of which was a Community Resources Liaison position in which
a single representative would interface with the correctional staff as an inter-
mediary for all the different entities (Pentland & Dwyer, 1985, p. 406; Pentland & Scurfield, 1982, p. 22).

Because the program represented an unprecedented assortment of organizations across the spectrum from local grassroots groups to federal bureau-
cracies, Mr. Pentland also used trial periods in which he would operate a
V.I.P. group for a brief time to demonstrate that the program would function
optimally and add value within a particular correctional institution's culture.
In many cases, this included "one-on-one services with individual inmates
. . . in order to establish a good track record" (Pentland & Scurfield, 1982,
p. 22 n.5). These trial runs were as necessary for the incarcerated veterans,
who doubted whether self-help programs would be valuable in addressing
their concerns. Realistic expectations developed through effective coordination and trial periods will hopefully avoid the possibility that correctional
professionals will view these outside services as a ***replacement for***, rather
than a supplement to, their own health services (Pentland, 1979, p. 526). Regardless of the success of a given program, ensuring the health and wellbeing
of inmates remains a non-delegable function of the correctional institution.

Take-Home Point

Prisons and jails cannot afford to ignore the characteristics of incarcerated veterans that make them different from inmates with no history of military service. A recent revealing study underscores some of these recurring
dynamics, regardless of the war in question. While most incarcerated veterans are older and have more education than their non-veteran peers, the

most telling difference is always that the majority of incarcerated veterans are eligible for a range of statutory benefits, as opposed to zero percent of the non-veteran population. The complication is that the Veterans Administration is neither the only nor the viable source to provide services to meet incarcerated veterans' special needs, particularly in readjustment services and mental health treatment tailored to combat experiences.

Beyond regulatory restrictions, even for veterans who are not incarcerated, the mounting demand for treatment of combat-related mental health conditions is currently outpacing the Veterans Administration's ability to provide effective services (Rubin, 2013, p. xxvi). When considering the severe legal limits imposed on incarcerated veterans, these inmates must necessarily rely upon entities other than the Veterans Administration to meet their special needs. In the right conditions, much like the experience in contemporary veterans treatment courts, a combination of community organizations can offer an "onsite comprehensive, one-stop range of services readily accessible to inmates that no single agency could adequately provide" (Pentland & Scurfield, 1982, p. 22). Thus, prisons and jails will benefit immediately by supporting the involvement of diverse organizations in programs designed for incarcerated veterans. Implementation of "viable administrative controls," such as the appointment of a single coordinator as point person and trial periods to determine the suitability of a program are factors that will assist in developing the most effective interventions.

4. Combat Trauma May Result in Violent Behavior in Confined Settings When Unaddressed

As a program developed to address the special readjustment concerns of incarcerated veterans, V.I.P. coordinators had significant exposure to the symptoms exhibited by veterans with mental health conditions and aggravated by the conditions of confinement. Although the FCI Phoenix program addressed the manner in which the combat "survival mode" manifests during incarceration, Mr. Pentland and his colleague described an additional risk of PTSD symptomatology. The condition, which he labeled as "action junkies'" behavior, involves the attempts of veterans to induce and replicate a state of excitement to which they had grown accustomed during combat. In Dr. John P. Wilson and Sheldon D. Zigelbaum's acclaimed article on the different manifestations of combat PTSD, they called this same phenomenon "Sensation Seeking Syndrome," in which the veteran "only feels happy, alive, and whole when engaging in thrill and adventure-seeking activities analogous to those performed in Vietnam" (1983, p. 72, tbl. 1). It has likewise appeared in recent descriptions of "the adrenaline rush during combat that the vet may miss and seek to re-experience after returning home" (Rubin,

2013, p. xxv). Although the use of the term "junkie" suggests thrill-seeking behavior as a desire of the veteran, along the same lines that some combat veterans report "they never felt so high as when in combat" (Pentland & Dwyer, 1985, p. 408), the V.I.P. program's experience with such behavior underscored a different manifestation of this destructive behavior.

> **For some veterans with this particular symptom of combat trauma, without a method to alleviate stress symptoms triggered within the confinement setting, "seeking out danger is a form of self-medication that defends the veteran against experiencing stress symptoms" (Pentland & Dwyer, 1985, p. 408).**

Take-Home Point

It is vital to remember that not all combat veterans have PTSD, and even among those who do, not all will engage in violence-related behavior. With this in mind, the V.I.P. program's recognition of sensation-seeking syndrome as a method to alleviate aggravation of stress in confinement is still noteworthy. It signifies that the very symptoms that contributed to some veterans' incarceration may put them at risk of continued misconduct in confined settings. Moreover, this observation highlights the fact that confinement can produce additional variations of symptoms, in other words, violent acts to self-medicate other symptoms. Accordingly, correctional professionals have even more reason to identify combat veterans in confined settings who are potentially at risk of these symptoms. Beyond identification, the V.I.P. experience also highlights the need for a program that has the capability to respond to particular manifestations of combat trauma. Although a trauma-focused program is certainly better than a generic behavior-modification program for offenders, if the program avoids dwelling on the combat experience and its transformative nature, the interventions may not be sufficient to reduce symptoms that may increase the potential for violent behavior in incarcerated settings. Ultimately, there is an ongoing need to keep in mind that combat veterans have special needs and different issues, even among the subset of all inmates who suffered nonmilitary traumatic experiences, such as survivors of sexual assault, torture, or interpersonal violence.

5. The Necessity to Target and "Work Through" Traumatizing Military Experiences

Although the V.I.P. program's group and individual counseling had many facets, one of the major components is the mandate for all members of the program to carefully examine their traumatic experiences in the military, and specifically in combat. Mr. Pentland recognized that this was a major reason standard programs for career criminals are dysfunctional as applied to the common experiences of traumatized veteran inmates; not only did the program have to examine traumatic experience, but it had to address combat trauma. Given that many of the inmates had suppressed their war experiences for over a decade, sometimes at the insistence of family members, friends, and civilian employers who did not desire to hear about Vietnam, it was necessary to unearth those experiences (Pentland & Scurfield, 1982, p. 27). He explained that until incarcerated veterans "work through" their combat experience, many "will remain the 'outlaw casualties' of the war" on account that criminal behavior is too often a form of "coming home" for those without the tools to undertake proper readjustment (Pentland & Dwyer, 1985, pp. 405–407). Given the limitations of any therapeutic intervention in the corrections setting,

> **The objective was to place combat experience in context so that the inmate could understand how experiences related to current behavior, attitude, and state of mind (Pentland & Dwyer, 1985, pp. 412–413; Pentland & Scurfield, 1982, p. 27).**

Thus, "[t]he focus [was] on taking care of the 'unfinished business' relating to the Vietnam or homecoming experiences, accomplished at least partly through ventilation of repressed feelings and memories" (Pentland & Scurfield, 1982, p. 27). While this may not enable the veterans to assign a meaning to the traumatic experiences they suffered, it did help the majority of participants in the V.I.P. program to take the "first steps on their individual journeys home" toward recovery through a reasoned appraisal of motivations for behavior (Pentland & Dwyer, 1985, p. 415).

Importantly, similar to the experiences of Pennsylvania's PTSD Treatment Program, the necessary process of confronting suppressed and unsettling war experiences inevitably resulted in unsettling feelings and re-trauma. As Mr. Pentland noted, the process of dealing with "unresolved issues related to past traumatic experiences" sometimes required "referral for more in depth psychotherapy" (Pentland & Scurfield, 1982, p. 27). Importantly, it was a cost worth bearing to break the cycle of unexplored influences on the veterans' appraisal of their actions in life.

Take-Home Point

An extremely valuable lesson from the V.I.P. program, which echoes the experience of Pennsylvania's PTSD Treatment Program, is the necessity to address combat trauma head-on, even if such examination will produce adverse reactions and unpleasant symptoms in some of the participants. While a simplistic view might counsel against potentially invoking undesirable feelings in a group that is prone to greater risk factors than other inmates, it must be remembered that all of the evidence-based treatments for PTSD—which mainly require some form of exposure therapy—have identical or greater undesirable consequences. On any view, combat trauma is simply the type of experience that cannot be discussed without some level of discomfort and risk of depressive or other adverse symptoms. The V.I.P. program's success in addressing these issues reveals that specific program features, especially the creation of supportive peer discussion groups, can help to minimize such consequences, although it remains impossible to avoid them entirely.

6. Reality Therapy as the Means to Prevent Externalization

Largely as a result of the draft, many Vietnam veterans in the V.I.P. program faced common sentiments that the military—particularly undesirable experiences in combat—was to blame for postwar problems and offending. Mr. Pentland described this sentiment as a primary example of "externalization," described as "the tendency of veterans to place responsibility for their actions on outside forces" (Pentland & Dwyer, 1985, p. 411). Although externalization is common in *any* inmate population, the general concept has veteran-specific variants, which include: (1) the position that all veterans are "victims" of the War, and consequently that the War or the draft is responsible for any of their life problems; (2) that veterans were no more than a "tool to be used and discarded" after being robbed of their best years at an early age (Pentland & Dwyer, 1985, p. 412); and (3) the notion that adverse War experiences are "proof that [the veteran's] actions are futile and that he has no 'importance'" (Pentland & Dwyer, 1985, p. 412).

When veterans position themselves against society and blame society or the military for all of life's hardships following discharge, they might adopt a "façade of goodness," characterized by a completely innocent intent in all prior behavior (Pentland & Scurfield, 1982, pp. 25–26). Further, these sentiments can manifest into oppositional defiance in which the veterans seek to prove their own worth and value by demonstrating the capability to make an impact on someone or something. Although such defiance can result in positive contributions, it can also assume the form of "revenge," in which attempts at proving one's value and worth are measured by the level of disruption to order and discipline (Lifton, 1992, p. 142).

The V.I.P. program recognized that an effective intervention for veterans, specifically, would require reversal of the effects of externalization. The primary way to do this is to emphasize personal responsibility at all times (Pentland & Scurfield, 1982, p. 25). Thus, in both group and individual counseling, the program implemented a form of modified reality therapy, which sought to emphasize the veteran's own agency in making life decisions. Modification of this model was necessary to address those events during the course of war that were truly attributable to outside forces. The goal was thus to help the veterans "focus on their own actions during [Vietnam] and the distinctions between what war experiences they could and could not control" (Penland & Dwyer, 1985, p. 411).

A staple of this counseling approach was a standardized method for discussing wartime and homecoming experiences whether in group or individual counseling:

> Discussion of combat experiences proceeds along a chronological line. Counseling usually begins at the feelings and events surrounding induction into the military, and proceeds through basic training to Vietnam and post-military experiences. General questions about feelings, emotions, and so forth are not asked nor are they gone into. The same is true of motivational issues. What is discussed are the acts themselves, and the accompanying experiences. A perspective is placed on the time and place in which the acts occurred and how they affect the veteran's current life. (Pentland & Scurfield, 1982, pp. 27–28)

In the experience of the V.I.P. program, "as these individuals accept responsibility for their thoughts, feelings, and actions, the [Vietnam] experience is put into perspective. It is better understood and is not viewed as an all-powerful controlling force in their lives" (Pentland & Dwyer, 1985, p. 411).

Take-Home Point

Many inmates may be tempted to blame their offending on societal conditions that were out of their control, such as poverty, a history of abuse, and so forth. Those who experienced trauma may have even more incentive for externalization, which is indirectly bolstered by the legal process in the mounting of a defense that seeks to assign blame or responsibility elsewhere. This true of mitigation, where the law is required to consider past adversity, such as emotional and physical abuse and mental illness, as a prospect for a lighter sentence (Vick, 1995, p. 366, n.147). This also applies in the names of some current defense theories, such as "lack of mental responsibility" or "partial mental responsibility" (Hayes, 2006–2007, pp. 85–100). In the after-math of Vietnam, a "victims' movement" emerged in the nation, in which some antiwar activists and veterans with adjustment difficulty advocated that the Vietnam War was responsible for ruining the lives of veterans and result-ing in any postwar misdeeds (Burkett & Whitley, 1998, p. 65). With such popular sentiments, incarcerated Vietnam veterans had greater incentive to invoke this theory to externalize responsibility for their crimes and the predicaments that led to them.

Arguably, the Operation Iraqi Freedom/Operation Enduring Freedom experience has been quite different for veterans. Given the absence of a draft, and recent veterans' conscious choice to deploy to combat, most vet-erans, even those with PTSD and combat trauma believe that their military service represented the greatest accomplishment in their lives, or at least was a valuable experience that evokes pride and a sense of accomplishment.

This does not mean that the risk of externalization is gone, especially if the veteran mounted a defense in court that focused on his or her lack of responsibility based upon combat factors. Nor does it mean that all veterans have the same sentiments about Operation Iraqi Freedom/Operation Endur-ing Freedom participation. Remnants of the Vietnam Era's pattern of exter-nalization may still emerge where a current veteran experienced involuntary extension of obligated service as a result of the Stop Loss orders in the mid-2000s (Brown, 2005), and instances where the veteran was discharged under less-than-honorable circumstances (Chapter 2). Consequently, it is important to recognize that, based on various experiences of individuals, incarcerated veterans may have more incentive to externalize responsibility than other inmates without military experience

Aside from alerting correctional professionals to the potential for greater externalization among some veteran inmates, the V.I.P. program emphasized the value of specific interventions for combat trauma. Although modified reality therapy may share a number of common attributes with contempo-rary programs by different names, such as SAMSHA's "Seeking Safety" model, the major difference is the special care with which combat experi-ences were targeted and addressed. While more recent programs are adapt-ing generic therapeutic interventions to veterans by keeping the programs in tact but adding "veteran-centric examples and stories rather than changing the content of the treatment" (Department of Veterans Affairs, 2013, p. 63), this may not be enough. The V.I.P. program offers support for the position that further programming is necessary to effectively address combat and homecoming from war, as opposed to other variations of trauma experi-enced by nonmilitary inmates.

7. The Necessity of Adopting a Peer-Based Model of Self-Help

Not unlike most therapeutic programs in confined settings, the V.I.P. program depended upon a peer-based self-help group orientation, because, arguably, "[a]ny successful treatment approach in prison depends heavily upon engaging inmates in mutually supportive relationships" (Pentland & Dwyer, 1985, p. 412). Unlike other group programs in jails and prisons, however, the V.I.P. program recognized the necessity of peer involvement specifically because "Vietnam veterans themselves are prone to put up barriers and be reluctant to discuss Vietnam or its aftermath with anyone—except perhaps another Vietnam veteran" (Pentland & Scurfield, 1982, p. 27). Even today, this factor is so important to the effective treatment of veterans that education programs for mental health clinicians are attempting to develop skills for counselors without military experience who will undoubtedly face obstacles in developing trusting relationships (Hassan, 2013, p. xiv).

The V.I.P. program also teaches that other characteristics enhance the effectiveness of veterans' therapy groups within confined settings. Much like the New York Department of Correctional services "Cadre" concept, and the FCI Phoenix notion of "squad organization" for confined veterans' therapy groups, the V.I.P. program incorporated elected officer leadership components in the organization of their groups (Pentland & Scurfield, 1982, p. 22). While Mr. Pentland took a pragmatic approach to group orientation, recognizing that there remained potential for "group sabotage" within groups of veterans, he underscored how, leadership positions, the requirement for a non-judgmental orientation for information revealed, and "[c]areful screening and tangible rewards for participation" were all factors that overcame these potential obstacles (Pentland & Dwyer, 1985, p. 410).

Take-Home Point

Peer support is one of the major reasons why the veterans treatment court model has succeeded as an alternative for diversion of veterans from confinement (Russell, 2009; Mullen, 2011; Russell, 2015). Moreover, even for veterans who are not incarcerated, group therapy has distinct advantages of brotherhood/sisterhood and shared experience that individual therapy lacks (Lifton, 1992, p. 80). The V.I.P. program underscored these essential points in the corrections setting. Beyond this, the program also emphasized that there is value in elected leadership positions within therapeutic programs for veterans. Leadership roles undoubtedly give leaders additional reason to be concerned for the wellbeing of their subordinates. These positions also promote the corresponding value of followership—the subordinate's responsibilities to the group over one's self and respect for the objectives of a leader with the ability to view issues on a grander scale by increased responsibility. When oriented toward therapeutic roles, as represented by New York's program, these capacities permit inmate veterans to assist one another outside of group sessions in manner that may be even more effective than what occurs within the group setting. While the V.I.P. program did not have an element that required separate housing for veterans within the program, it is a logical extension of the model that greater contact with those in the same "squad" promotes increased motivation to meet common objectives and extend mutual support, as a result of the recurrent reminders that close and sustained contact provides.

8. Veterans Administration Input as a Method to Improve Classification Decisions

As the V.I.P. program grew in success and popularity within the Southern California corrections community, July 1980 marked the program's unprecedented expansion into the Forensic Mental Health Unit at the Los Angeles County Central Jail (Pentland & Scurfield, 1982, p. 22). A full-time Veterans Administration employee joined the Forensic Mental Health Unit for two primary purposes. The first objective was to identify those veterans with immediate treatment needs that might result from disruptions to ongoing healthcare that had formerly been provided by the Veterans Administration. The second related objective was to enhance the process of inmate classification by informing correctional administrators of the veteran's treatment history and special needs (Pentland & Scurfield, 1982, p. 22). Much of this goal was accomplished with access to Veterans Administration records and liaison with Veterans Administration personnel.

Experience proved that "[m]any times the information possessed by a staff person at one of the Veterans Administration Medical Centers can be most useful in effecting an appropriate decision" (Pentland & Scurfield, 1982, p. 22). As part of the formalized role, this V.I.P. program counselor would also make recommendations to the classification boards as well as the court regarding the propriety of diversion from confinement in the case of an individual veteran. Due to the short duration of detention in comparison to confinement in a prison, officials clearly benefitted from the insights of a full-time Veterans Administration resource. Importantly, while current regulations and the structure of the Veterans Justice Outreach program might limit the ability to fully replicate these services, the V.I.P. program emphasizes the value of considering a range of factors at the earliest point possible besides simply veteran status in the development of effective planning.

Take-Home Point

The value of input from the Veterans Administration (or a veterans service organization) in the classification and diversion planning process was underscored as early as the 1920s in the great "Prison Clean-Up" following the First World War (Chapter 5). Despite the significant passage of time and evolution of warfighting tactics out of the trenches, the V.I.P. program's incorporation of Veterans Administration employees in the framework of the jail detainee classification process is a modern reminder of the value of this practice. While access to complete Veterans Administration case files may require the veteran's informed consent so as not to violate medical privacy standards, the procedures adopted by veterans treatment courts to ensure adequate treatment planning for diversion purposes are testaments to the viability of the idea.

Along the same lines, in 1979, Veterans Administration Administrator Max Cleland recognized a similar point: "One of the ways we are trying to assist the criminal justice system is by making available, with appropriate consent, Veterans Administration medical records in connection with care and treatment provided to veterans by the Veterans Administration prior to a period of incarceration." He further noted that this information could be particularly "useful in determining how best to meet the veterans' needs" (Cleland, 1979, p. 463).

Southern California V.I.P. Program Summary

If the objective is to treat underlying combat-related conditions that are responsible for symptoms of PTSD and combat and operational stress:

1. Recognize the special hardships imposed by the operation of law on veterans who are already receiving benefits at the time of incarceration. Acknowledge the risk that the veteran's reaction to these hardships may impede successful reintegration. Implement interventions to address these veterans' concerns.

2. Recognize the instrumental value of applying for *new* VA benefits as a means of successfully participating in society. Provide the ability to apply for benefits and discharge upgrades as soon as possible following incarceration. Confinement time can make the VA's notorious administrative delays less burdensome if the veteran starts early. Discharge upgrading is an example of a claim, which does not require extensive physical evaluation for adjudication.

---

continued

Southern California V.I.P. Program Summary—*Continued*

3. Involve as many community organizations as possible to supplement VA support and capitalize on their existing proven resources rather than seeking to develop a new program. In the incorporation of community organizations, use "administrative controls" to minimize disruption of operations, such as a single group coordinator as a liaison and trial periods to test the fit of the program in a particular institution.

4. Target and provide a context for addressing suppressed combat experiences in any program for incarcerated veterans. Recognize that failure to "work through" such issues may impede reentry and can, in some cases, increase the risk for violence during incarceration.

5. Consider a modified reality approach for its effectiveness in providing a framework specifically for discussing combat trauma in a group setting, but recognize that there will necessarily be some degree of discomfort in discussing these issues under *any* therapeutic method designed to address them.

6. Understand that veterans may be more likely to externalize responsibility for their actions based on war experiences. Although the draft is long gone and this was common among Vietnam draftees, recent veterans who were Stop Loss'd (i.e., involuntarily extended) or discharged under less-than-honorable conditions may have similar perceptions of being victims of the system.

7. Embrace the maxim that the greater the opportunity for peer involvement in addressing military-related issues, the greater the chances of fostering an ideal support network for recovery from combat trauma. In this context, leadership positions (whether elected or otherwise determined) enhance program effectiveness by replicating familiar military attributes of leadership and followership in accomplishing the mission.

8. Incorporate VA treatment histories and the recommendations of VA mental health professionals to enhance correctional classification and treatment planning at the outset of a veteran's incarceration. If VA personnel are unable or unwilling to provide these services, consider the state department of veterans affairs or veterans service organizations as an alternative classification insights.

C. The FCI-Phoenix PTSD Program for Combat Veterans

Earlier in this chapter, the section on programs targeting readjustment from combat introduced Dr. Chester Sigafoos and his concept of the Second Tour necessarily experienced by all combat veterans while confined following their first tour in the war zone. On this view, awareness of one's "combat-ready" mode and recognition of the potential for overreaction to perceived threats and maladaptive responses is the first of multiple stages of a program designed to treat combat PTSD.

The PTSD treatment program operated out of drug treatment program facilities recognized that the overwhelming majority of the veterans had co-occurring substance abuse issues (Sigafoos, 1994, p. 119). Even though the program had specific objectives regarding PTSD awareness and treatment, every effort was made to "view the veteran as an integrative whole," rather than on the basis of a particular disorder or combination of disorders (Sigafoos, 1994, p. 119).

The program was developed to equip the veterans with techniques to recognize and de-escalate stress symptoms prior to any in-depth work on traumatic experiences (Sigafoos, 1994, p. 122). After the Second Tour and stress management instruction, the program progressively moved into the following four components:

1. *Handling Symptoms of PTSD* . . . returns the veteran to the traumatic stressor. The events of the past are recast using the knowledge of today. The PTSD symptom picture is examined on how it has impacted the veteran's life.

2. *Veterans, PTSD, and Crime* examines the veteran's mechanisms for coping with the stressors of Vietnam, and whether those mechanisms were active during the commission of their criminal acts.

3. *Conflict Resolution* . . . continues the examination of the veteran's behaviors and stresses the need for self-acceptance. It provides alternative ways of handling stressful situations by being assertive instead of being assaultive. It examines how veterans could have handled life problems in diverse ways, which could have resulted in a more positive outcome.

4. *Effects of PTSD on the Family* . . . uses the techniques learned above, and places them within the context of family problems. By this time if dysfunctional interpersonal relationships exist, they will have been shown. The family becomes the support group for the veteran. Source: Sigafoos (1994, pp. 125–126)

Some aspects of this program are noteworthy. Notably, the explicit search for connections between combat trauma and offending is a hallmark of the FCI-Phoenix program. Although, as addressed in the V.I.P. program, such connections could potentially be used to externalize blame for offending, the goal of the FCI-Phoenix Program was not to search for excuses for offending behavior, but instead to recognize the manner in which maladaptive coping strategies contributed to the commission of the offense.

During participation in the program, some veterans detected how dissociation from society, survivor guilt, and thrill-seeking with roots in Vietnam experiences contributed to their criminal behavior (Sigafoos, 1994, p. 124). Additionally, with respect to the last prong, Dr. Sigafoos took special note of the manner in which combat PTSD symptoms influenced families and led to disharmony and divorce in a number of confined veterans. Although not explicit in this description, this special focus emphasizes the effect of deployment cycle and unique challenges facing military families as a necessary component of a PTSD program for incarcerated veterans.

The FCI-Phoenix PTSD treatment program did not emerge overnight. Dr. Sigafoos estimates that it took two-to-four months of building rapport before a sufficient level of trust existed in the group to undergo the formalized training program (1994, p. 120). An extensive discussion of each phase of the program would duplicate a number of the lessons from both the V.I.P. and Pennsylvania PTSD treatment programs and is beyond the scope of this chapter. There are, however, two stand-out attributes of the FCI-Phoenix model that are worthy of consideration for any confinement-based program targeting veterans' PTSD, specifically. One component included analysis of the history of the Vietnam War, including studies of social and political forces at play, which the veterans may have missed based on their focus as warfighters (Sigafoos, 1994, p. 126). The other component of the PTSD treatment program included a review of movies depicting the Vietnam War from several perspectives, which would inevitably induce some level of re-experiencing wartime trauma and unearthing suppressed content (Sigafoos, 1994, p. 127).

Contours of the FCI-Phoenix PTSD
Program for Combat Veterans

1. Combat Veterans Undergoing Treatment for PTSD Need the Ability to Understand the Historical Context of the Campaign(s) in which they Served

A noteworthy feature of the combat PTSD program at FCI-Phoenix was the historical review of the Vietnam conflict. This insight was necessary owing to the fact that "[m]ost of the veterans entered the Vietnam conflict as young, immature men" (Sigafoos, 1994, p. 126). Once the veterans enlisted, they were provided with very simple justifications for their involvement that contributed to instantaneous compliance with the orders they received. With pressure to report high body counts during Vietnam and to match the military's metrics for defining success, it was not likely that they were encouraged to consider alternative points of view while they served. If anything, the warriors were distanced from critical perspectives of U.S. military involvement as much as possible during their service (MacPherson, 1993). While this may have assisted the troops during the course of their deployments, it was particularly counterproductive during their homecoming.

A number of the participants at FCI-Phoenix had negative encounters with antiwar protestors upon their return from Vietnam in the airports, which left indelible marks on them (Sigafoos, 1994, p. 123). Despite this, most of them "were not totally familiar with the rationale of the antiwar protest" (Sigafoos, 1994, p. 123). By learning about the social and political issues that surrounded the Vietnam War at the same period when they served, the participants became better able to interpret their past experiences. This had a direct relationship to PTSD in that "[e]xamining the war from an older, more mature perspective, provided a necessary element to understand the condition" (Sigafoos, 1994, p. 127). More specifically,

> In most instances, a contrast was created; knowledge of the war as a young man versus knowledge of a world situation in broader perspective. When the narrow and the broader perspectives were compared, the narrow schemas, the throwbacks in time, took on a different meaning. The Vietnam conflict could be understood utilizing a more logical, historical interpretation. (Sigafoos, 1994, p. 127)

Take-Home Point

Certainly, there are differences in public attitudes regarding Vietnam and the Global War on Terrorism. In contrast to Vietnam, historians emphasize the American public's widespread support of the lethal response to an unprecedented attack that took the lives of thousands of innocent American civilians on American soil. The attack on 9-11 was, in fact, a motivator for the entry of many recent veterans into the military, with many leaving well-paying jobs for a chance to defend the nation. While this explains Afghanistan, it does not so as neatly describe military involvement in Iraq, which members of the public attribute to official lies and misrepresentations regarding Iraq's alleged possession of weapons of mass destruction (Ramsay, 2009). For Iraq veterans, specifically, and for veterans who experienced involuntary extensions of their obligated service to fight in the Global War on Terrorism as the conflicts became less popular over time, there is a similar value to critical analysis of the historical and social backdrop surrounding military operations. If the veteran has adopted a revenge perspective, perceiving society as the enemy based on negative experiences, additional perspectives can help to expose the dysfunctional nature of those positions. The inability to explore their experiences in historical and social context increases the potential for the veterans to reach inaccurate assumptions about the meanings of noteworthy events in their lives.

2. War-Themed Movies Can Provide a Basis for Re-Visiting Wartime Trauma in a Confined Setting

Apart from the setting of ongoing professional treatment, display of war-themed films to veterans with combat and operational stress injuries might appear to be a recipe for disaster or a cruel and demeaning trick. But context is vitally important when considering the inherent limitations of therapeutic alternatives in a confined setting. In 1993 and 1994, using existing movies, Dr. Sigafoos was able to develop a variety of media resources that enabled meaningful group discussions regarding traumatic war experiences. Today, two decades later, there are doubtless many more options available for optimal incorporation of this same approach, with a series of fictional accounts and documentaries that explore Vietnam, the Gulf War, and the Global War on Terrorism.

As Dr. Sigafoos explained, "[i]t was important to allow sufficient time for processing of fears and feelings of anger, rage, and guilt. The movies allowed for a cathartic release, revitalizing old memories" (Sigafoos, 1994, p. 127). While this led some inmates to require additional individual therapy, the consequence was little different from the V.I.P. program's reality therapy approach to the chronological discussion of combat and homecoming from it or the Pennsylvania program's necessary element of re-experiencing the trauma in the group setting. Exposure to the media was a method that allowed inmates to "identify those external stimuli, originally experienced in Vietnam, that trigger combat reactions in the veteran," but in the context of a supervised, mutually supportive, safe environment (Sigafoos, 1994, p. 123).

Take-Home Point

Fictional or documentary films can easily be incorporated into therapeutic programs by trained mental health practitioners to enable veteran-specific interventions for PTSD and other operational stress injuries. While it has become a widespread practice to adapt existing trauma-focused programs to veterans, this practice strikes a balance that preserves the focus on combat veterans, not all trauma victims.

Summary of the FCI-Phoenix
PTSD Program for Combat Veterans

If the objective is to treat underlying combat-related conditions that are responsible for symptoms of PTSD and combat and operational stress:

1. Provide participants with a historical, social, and political perspective on the campaigns in which they served so that the veterans may approach their experiences with a richer contextual foundation. Their assumptions about society and the underlying motivations for negative experiences may be mistaken and reconciliation of these harmful impressions can relieve symptoms of PTSD.

2. Recognize the ease with which simple resources like films and documentaries about war can help maintain a sufficient focus on veterans' unique experiences, over generic approaches to trauma.

3. Recognize the need to address the family dimension of combat PTSD, which raises issues separate from other trauma survivors and their families given the unique effects of the deployment cycle and other factors unique to the military.

4. Recognize the need to explore the connections between combat trauma and commission of charged (or uncharged) offenses when the exploration seeks to prevent recidivism, rather than excuse criminal offending.

III. Programs Developed to Address Trauma, Primarily, with Some Adaptability for Veterans

Even without the aim to completely resolve an inmate's trauma-related mental health condition, many prisons and jails have recognized the value of developing trauma-informed approaches to the needs of such inmates. "Seeking Safety" is a trauma-informed program that was initially developed in 1993 by Lisa M. Najavits as an intervention to deal with the impact of Posttraumatic Stress combined with Substance Use Disorders (Najavits, 2002). Within community treatment settings, the program usually has twenty-five hour-long components, which mental health clinicians can reorder and match in a flexible manner to meet the needs of a given population. The program is recognized as a cognitive-behavioral therapy and, though it can be augmented with exposure therapy, it generally seeks to avoid participants "describing traumatic experiences in detail" (Lynch, Heath, Mathews, & Cepeda, 2012, p. 89) or asking clients "to delve into the painful details of their trauma" (Najavits, 2002, p. 141).

As opposed to typical programs in corrections settings, the Seeking Safety program integrates treatment for substance use, trauma, and PTSD with a priority on establishing and maintaining safety (Lynch et al., 2012, pp. 89–90). Its components address "anticipating danger situations, setting boundaries, anger management, and affect regulation" (McCauley, Killeen, Goss, Brady, & Back, 2012, p. 293). The inherent flexibility of the program, including deployment in individual or group therapy, has made the program popular in various community mental health treatment settings including combat veterans (Landes, Garovoy, & Burkman, 2013, p. 529). Although there are open questions regarding the generalizability of outcomes in community as opposed to incarcerated settings, continuing research with incarcerated populations suggests that Seeking Safety does help to reduce PTSD symptoms and result in satisfaction among participants (Wolff et al., 2012, p. 708; Lynch et al., 2012; Zlotnick, Johnson, & Najavits, 2009; Zlotnick, Najavits, Rohsenow, & Johnson, 2003).

In 2008, the Substance Abuse and Mental Health Services Administration (SAMHSA), through its Center for Mental Health Services (CHMS) National Gains Center Forum on Combat Veterans, Trauma, and the Justice System, convened a team of multidisciplinary experts to develop a national policy for veterans entangled in the criminal justice system. The result of this historic meeting was the establishment of grants for various community-based pilot programs to identify veterans, provide integrated treatment, and keep them out of confinement (Center for Mental Health Services National Gains Center, 2008). Since 2008, through its *Jail Diversion and Trauma Recovery Services for Veterans Initiative*, SAMHSA has been awarding grants to public agencies in thirteen pilot states, including jails and prisons that have implemented Seeking Safety and similar trauma-informed programs[10] as part of its veteran-specific jail and prison interventions (Center for Mental Health Services National Gains Center, 2011a, pp. 2–4). Ultimately, SAMHSA has identified Seeking Safety among the primary evidence-based trauma-specific interventions for veterans, noting that it is supported by the greatest

10. Aside from Seeking Safety, SAMHSA favorably mentions Trauma Affect Regulation: Guide for Education and Therapy (TARGET), Trauma Recovery and Empowerment Model (TREM) as psycho-educational evidence-based models (Center for Mental Health Services National Gains Center, 2011b). While these programs all seek to provide additional coping skills and to promote a greater sense of safety, they do not profess to fully process suppressed traumatic experiences, which may be a task for later stages of in-depth therapy after release from confinement.

amount of research, which found the program to "effective in a wide variety of settings" (Center for Mental Health Services National Gains Center, 2011b, p. 2). A sample of grants for 2008 and 2009 may be located on the website: *Jail Diversion and Trauma Recovery Program-Priority to Veterans*, available at http://gainscenter. samhsa.gov/grant_programs/jdtr. asp#.

Among the nations' veterans' dorms in correctional settings, the San Francisco Sheriff's Department instituted Seeking Safety as the group-therapy approach for war-traumatized participants since the unveiling of the Pod (ABC News Radio, 2013). According to Leslie Levitas and Sunny Schwartz, who helped to implement it, the program is, at best, a form of "quasi-therapy," which helps to "reduce the baggage they have to carry," but this is a significant improvement that helps to alleviate symptoms of veterans and enable them to focus on their recovery during their stays, which usually last two months on average (S. Schwartz, L. Levitas, & I. McCray, personal communication, October 15, 2012).

Although Seeking Safety avoids re-experiencing trauma, and some of the programs, such as V.I.P., Pennsylvania's PTSD Treatment Program, and FCI-Phoenix all embraced exposure elements and "working through" the trauma, Seeking Safety may still alleviate some current symptoms and provide an alternative for those institutions that question whether they have the capacity or mental health resources to deal with the aftermath of exposure-based therapies. When addressing the utility of the program for prisons and jails, Dr. Najavits explained how it adequately replaces trauma processing components, which can "destabilize" inmates and lead to "unsafe" conditions in correctional settings (2002, p. 137). While these risks are minimized, no intervention will remove them all, and other programs still did well in addressing exposure components for years in some cases.

Seeking Safety may also have particularly enhanced benefits for veterans, as opposed to other groups. Program facilitators frequently recognize that veterans adapt to it differently, in a manner that taps into the same team approach that has led to the success of veterans dorms and reinforcing communities:

> [W]hen it goes well, they bond like a symbolic combat unit; they are supportive of each other, and connect almost like a fire team [a group on a military mission]. The recovery of these men is like a different version of combat, it's a real love for their comrades and they get to re-live it. A lot of Seeking Safety groups directly express [the] notion of being combat veterans *on a mission to recover* (emphasis added). (Najavits et al., 2009, p. 41)

As long as veterans can learn to detect their own "cognitive biases with respect to environmental threats and the detection of disconfirming evidence," this can be done with a cognitive-behavioral modality of treatment and may help address some of the core reasons why the veteran is incarcerated (Moore et al., 2009, p. 70). While the same may be said of any veterans group, whether self- or institutionally-organized, these benefits are certainly preferable when delivered in an optimally integrated modality with a trained professional.

Take-Home Point

Jails and prisons can implement trauma-focused programs like Seeking Safety to alleviate veterans' PTSD symptoms and address the dual challenges of PTSD and substance use. While these interventions avoid the types of re-experiencing components that many would argue are necessary to fully recover from combat-induced mental conditions, these programs exist as alternatives for those institutions that want to provide a constructive environment, but do not desire the possibility of adverse reactions to more intense treatment. Considering the immense value of dormitories for veteran inmates, it is quite possible that the combination of a program like Seeking Safety with specialized housing may provide overall effects that achieve better results, given the unparalleled opportunity that veterans have to share stories with one another and process much of their trauma at an informal level through safe and constructive interactions with trusted peers.

IV. Programs Developed to Prepare the Veteran for Community Reentry

Some programs for confined veterans may exist as an effort to prepare the veteran for a forthcoming release date. On this theory, the institution will wait until the veteran has a certain amount of time remaining before offering targeted services, which usually include transitional planning for housing, Veterans Administration benefits, and employment. Such time-sensitive policies exist in the Virginia Department of Corrections' requirement of less than two years (Hixenbaugh, 2012, p. A1), the Florida Department of Corrections' requirement of "no more than 36 months until their release and no less than six" (Kamal, 2013), the Ohio Department of Rehabilitation and Correction's veterans' dorm requirement of "less than two years of release" (DeFrank, 2012), and the Ohio Incarcerated Veteran Outreach Program's non-dorm requirement of "6 months or less remaining on their sentence" (Hammond, 2010, Ch. 21).

A major benefit of this time-sensitive model is that it embodies the mission of the Veterans Administration's Healthcare Reentry for Veterans and Veterans Justice Outreach (VJO) initiatives, which help incarcerated veterans plan for transition back to the community with the full array of services for which they are eligible (Rosenthal & McGuire, 2013, pp. 365–366). To this end, the Veterans Justice Outreach program permits direct counseling and other services upon release available from more than 120 specially trained specialists who regularly visit prisons and jails and consult with incarcerated veterans (currently, over 300) (Rosenthal & McGuire, 2013, p. 366). Although more recent initiatives permit Veterans Justice Outreach personnel to conduct in-depth transition work earlier in an inmate's period of confinement, outreach counselors have operated for years under a rule that limited their contact to a six-month period prior to release (Department of Veterans Affairs, 2010, ¶ 1). In Indiana's INVET program, a major benefit of the transitional service is that "Veterans Administration appointments are scheduled before release, which would otherwise take substantial time if one waited until release for scheduling (Dean, 2012, p. 8). While such planning would be effective within a few months of release, it would be difficult to institute years before release.

When institutions wait until a certain period before entry into veteran-specific programs, they can use participation as an incentive for good behavior, which is evident in the admission prerequisite requiring inmates to have a record of good behavior for a certain period of time. Delay of entry into the program may similarly aid in vocational rehabilitation by helping the inmate prepare for the type of daily schedule that is more consistent with life in the community as a release date approaches. However, as inmates and institutions have learned through experience, many ex-service members require substantial time to apply for Veterans Administration benefits and obtain disability ratings, especially those with less-than-fully-honorable discharges.

Certainly, with the average processing times for initial Veterans Administration disability determinations taking 312 days to process nationally, *for claimants who are not even incarcerated* (States News Service, 2013), confinement will add further delay to the process. Thus, a competing consideration for a delayed model of program participation is the need to ensure that veterans have the opportunity to begin learning about and applying for Veterans Administration benefits as soon as possible during the term of confinement to increase the chances of securing the benefits that will aid in the eventual reentry process.

Take-Home Point

For those veterans who never applied for Veterans Administration benefits, the claims process takes a substantial amount of time and the Veterans Administration may have to reach a determination on whether the ex-service member is even considered to be a "Veteran," eligible for any of the Veterans Administration's services, under the legal definition of the term. As a result,

> It is vital to begin the VA eligibility determination process and educate veterans about VA services as early as possible during the course of their incarceration. Delaying these services until such time as the veteran is closer to a release date may ultimately deny access to the special transition and reentry services that are most desired.

V. Programs Developed to Instill Discipline and Develop *Esprit de Corps*

Discipline is an essential component of correctional culture and military culture, which features "regimentation, universally applied rules, implicit authority of security staff, and punitive sanctions for violations by inmates" (Appelbaum, Hickey, & Packer, 2001, p. 1344). Military culture is not much different in this regard and emulates identical qualities (see Chapter 1).

Accordingly, it is beneficial when a program can replicate attributes of military discipline in the correctional setting. Among the approaches for incarcerated veterans, some prison and jail administrators have developed targeted programs to revive a sense of discipline from past eras of military service. In Ohio, for example, the Veterans' Unit at the Belmont Correctional Institution exists to "reinforce and re-instill the core values of military service in the inmates" (DeFrank, 2012). The same was true in the Los Angeles County Jail's program, in which administrators hoped "that by rekindling the pride and discipline that veterans learned in the military, inmates will find the resolve to turn their lives around" (Leondard, 2005, p. B1).

In San Diego, Sheriff Bill Gore explains the basis for the Veterans Moving Forward housing module this way: "We're trying to instill that *esprit de corps* back in them, build that sense of responsibility and accountability back in their character" (Repard, 2013, p. B-1). For some programs, this means creating a "military environment" (Vergakis, 2012) or "barracks behind bars" (Griggs, 2011) within prison or jail walls. This includes drill and ceremonies, morning formations (Alvarez, 2011, p. A14), and being "dressed, pressed and not just the standard" (Griggs, 2011, p. 1A).

Despite different iterations of institutional veterans programs, the notion is two-fold, in that, by requiring certain standards of conduct similar to the military: (1) the program should give the veterans something to be proud of once again, sometimes after many, many years; thus (2) making them feel as if there is worth to life and potential to succeed in the mission of recovery. Virginia's Secretary of Public Safety, Marla Decker, sees the department's program as a way of "morph[ing] . . . all the good things they learned in the service, all the discipline and structure," and positively channeling these attributes toward recovery (Vergakis, 2012). The programs share an element of time travel, evident in the "drill sergeant routine" performed by Lieutenant Terry McCarty, the director of the Veterans' Wing at the Los Angeles County Men's Central Jail in 2005. After a lecture "on the honor the military instilled in them and the respect it earned them":

> We try to bring them back when they were 18 years old and that someone in their family, their mom, their grandma, still has that photo of them in their uniform. We try to stress "Remember the pride when you got that picture. We want to return that pride that you had in yourself." (Leonard, 2005, p. B1)

Even without hearing such a speech, Virginia inmate Brian Pits explains the nature of his experience at the Haynesville Correctional Center's Veterans Dormitory: "What this program tries to promote is that at one time, we were responsible not just for ourselves but for our country and we have to understand that—what we once upon a time represented" (Kamal, 2013).

As Florida Re-Entry Administrator Nichole Landrum observes, "[t]he hope is that the military environment and camaraderie with other veterans will help inmates recover the pride and motivation they had before running afoul of the law" (Griggs, 2011, p. 1A). In many cases, participants' feelings that result from being part of a veteran-specific program will revive "the only thing in their lives of which they are proud" (Harden, 2001, p. 1F), making participation extremely "energiz[ing]" for participants as a consequence (Repard, 2012, p. B-1). Programs that aim to instill the same feelings as past military service often point out that they are not intended to be like boot camp models of incarceration (Griggs, 2011 (discussing Florida's dorm program); DeFrank, 2012 (discussing Ohio's dorm program)).

The difference is aiming to replicate the military sense of being an accountable and responsible member of a supportive team who contributes to an effort that is greater than any single member (Griggs, 2011). While it remains debatable which attributes are the most successful in decreasing recidivism and helping incarcerated veterans obtain the treatment and readjustment support they need, one thing remains indisputable: feelings of camaraderie, especially among veterans with similar experiences of service to the nation, will "dissipate [the] sense of hopelessness" that pervades correctional institutions (Harden, 2001, p. 1F) (comments of veterans' advocate Daniel Thomas).

Take-Home Point

All veterans who made it through basic training, experienced a formative period in their lives when they had to shed their familiar civilian values
and routines and adopt far more disciplined standards. Military service in
times of combat reinforces the lesson, many times over. Regardless of service or period of service, military indoctrination requires recruits to believe
in their value as members of a team and their importance to a military mission. For many, passing the standards was considered the most important
achievement; one they never believed they could have attained prior to
undergoing the actual experience (U.S. Department of the Army, n.d.).
Correctional facilities are learning how this experience provides a renewable
source of purpose, motivation, and determination to jump-start rehabilitative
efforts. It does not require morning formation or drill to invoke the sense of
pride that came with prior service to the nation. Rather,

> **Through regular reminders of the responsibility they had, the
> pride they invoked in others, the importance of the duty they ful-
> filled, and the value of adhering to requirements of a given mis-
> sion, incarcerated veterans can emulate the same qualities in con-
> fined settings. This effect becomes greater when veteran inmates
> engage in activities as a group, whether in dorms, group therapy,
> educational classes, or other settings where they have the ability
> to interact both formally and informally.**

VI. Programs Instituted to Reward Past Service

While veteran-specific correctional programs exist for different reasons,
some exist to recognize the sacrifices of former service members who were
either drafted or volunteered to serve their country. As only a small percentage of Americans who wore the nation's uniform, these inmates share
experiences and sacrifices that distinguish them from other inmates. San
Diego Sheriff's Deputy, Corporal Dean Hardy, explains the philosophy
underlying his veterans' module: "We owe it to help them. They volunteered
to help our country. They've been down and out a little bit and now it's our
turn to help them. We owe it to them and we also owe it to the nation" (San
Diego Sheriff's Department, 2013). Former Sheriff Randall Liberty of Kennebec County, Maine likewise sees it as a ***moral obligation*** as a uniquely posi-
tioned public servant to use the jail's resources to meet these veterans' pressing needs. He explains, "Morally, I can't just walk away. I can't say, 'You're

broken and I know it's a result of your service, but you're on your own'" (Schroeder, 2013).

In an authentic way, it is an appeal to patriotism to recognize such service and want to help, especially when offenses can be traced to combat service, even in criminal justice systems (Wilson et al., 2011b, p. 320). Notably, in December 2013, while serving as Maricopa County's Sheriff, Joe Arpaio, then known as the nation's "toughest" sheriff based on his overtly punitive jail conditions, instituted a program to house veterans separately in a dormitory suited toward rehabilitation. His open letter to over 100 veteran inmates explained, "This program is our way of letting you know that we have not forgotten your commitment, despite whatever circumstances in your life have landed you in the custody of the Maricopa County Sheriff's Office" (ABC News Radio, 2013). A similar sentiment is evident in the Library of Congress' American Folklife Center, which recently recorded the oral histories of incarcerated veterans in Maryland and New Jersey prisons in recognition that the inmates should be included in the Veterans History Project; they have important experiences to offer that are just as valuable as those of the many thousands of non-incarcerated veteran participants selected for memorialization by the program (Dishneau, 2008).

There is special intrinsic value to positive recognition of past service. Historically known for being ignored and forgotten populations (May, 1979; Boivin, 1986; Gideon, 2013), incarcerated veterans appreciate efforts to recognize their past service and periods of great honor and sacrifice to the nation. This lesson rings true on occasions when community organizations visit incarcerated veterans. But something very different occurs when the correctional institution recognizes the veterans and creates special programs for them.

In the words of Indiana Air Force veteran William Dickerson, "Setting aside a dorm for incarcerated veterans lets me know that I am not forgotten about, that I am not excommunicated from society. For the Department of Correction to recognize military veterans means more than words can express" (Holmes, 2011). This effect is particularly important considering that veterans often experience great turmoil when they are incarcerated because their misconduct so starkly contrasts with the values they upheld during service. As former Los Angeles County Sheriff Lee Baca recognized, "The people who go to the military are taught the right things—about leadership, about sacrifice, about what is important to character. All the more reason a fall for a vet is a great fall" (Leonard, 2005, p. B1).

Take-Home Point

Perhaps, the least complicated reason to institute a veterans' program at a prison or a jail is the most persuasive: It is the right thing to do simply based upon the infusion of a greater number of military personnel into society, who are leaving the service, many involuntarily, after having experienced severe and repeated stress of a nation at war for over a decade. The problems faced by Iraq and Afghanistan veterans are complex, as are the problems faced by Vietnam veterans, but for distinct reasons (Bay City News Service, 2012). What unites these groups is a shared tradition of service, uncommon to non-veteran inmates. With PTSD and TBI linked both to combat and greater risk of violent behavior, even the most cautious researchers inevitably conclude that *some* portion of veterans will come in contact with the criminal justice system as a result of their military experiences after serving faithfully, loyally, and honorably (Moore et al., 2009; Brown, 2010). As recognized by those institutions that have implemented special programs for incarcerated veterans, a net to catch these warriors at their lowest point, while they are confined for the inability to conform their conduct to societal standards, is literally the most important intervention of them all.

Having reviewed the six leading themes for instituting veteran-specific interventions in prisons and jails, the following chapter will explore a small but growing trend to implement specialized housing units as a method of addressing veterans' special treatment and rehabilitation needs.

Appendix A

Pennsylvania Department of Corrections
Vietnam Veteran Experiences Scale

MILITARY EXPERIENCE OF VIETNAM VETERANS

Below are listed some assignments and experiences you may have had while in Vietnam. Please read each item and indicate if it applies to you. **RARELY** means three times or less; **OFTEN** means from four to ten times; **VERY OFTEN** means over ten times. Your replies will be kept confidential and will be very helpful in planning your treatment.

	Never	Rarely	Often	Very Often
1. Did you fire land based or naval artillery on the enemy				
2. Were you in aircraft over South or North Vietnam				
3. Were you at forward observation posts				
4. Did you receive incoming artillery, rockets or mortars				
5. Did you encounter mines, booby traps or pongee pits				
6. Did you receive sniper or sapper fire .				
7. Were you in an ambush				
8. Were you in a firefight				
9. Did you see Americans killed or wounded				
10. Did you see NVA or VC killed or wounded				
11. Did you see or have to handle body bags				
12. Did you kill or do you think you killed the enemy				

continued

	Never	Rarely	Often	Very Often
13. Did you provide medical care to the wounded				
14. Did you engage in hand-to-hand combat				
15. Did you lose anyone close to you in Vietnam				
16. Were you wounded				
17. Were you hospitalized because of illness (not wounds)				

Name_____

Appendix B

Deployment Risk and Resilience Inventory-2
Government Work in the Public Domain
(U.S. Dep't of Veterans Affairs, n. d.)

DRRI-2

SECTION D: COMBAT EXPERIENCES

The statements below are about your combat experiences during your most recent deployment. As used in these statements, the term "unit" refers to those you lived and worked with on a daily basis during deployment. Please mark how often you experienced each circumstance.

While deployed…	Never	Once or twice	Several times over entire deployment	A few times each month	A few times each week	Daily or almost daily
1. …I went on combat patrols or missions.	1	2	3	4	5	6
2. …I took part in an assault on entrenched or fortified positions that involved naval and/or land forces.	1	2	3	4	5	6
3. …I personally witnessed someone from my unit or an ally unit being seriously wounded or killed.	1	2	3	4	5	6
4. …I encountered land or water mines, booby traps, or roadside bombs (for example, IEDs).	1	2	3	4	5	6
5. …I was exposed to hostile incoming fire.	1	2	3	4	5	6
6. …I was exposed to "friendly" incoming fire.	1	2	3	4	5	6
7. …I was in a vehicle (for example, a "humvee", helicopter, or boat) or part of a convoy that was attacked.	1	2	3	4	5	6
8. …I was part of a land or naval artillery unit that fired on enemy combatants.	1	2	3	4	5	6
9. …I personally witnessed enemy combatants being seriously wounded or killed.	1	2	3	4	5	6
10. …I personally witnessed civilians (for example, women and children) being seriously wounded or killed.	1	2	3	4	5	6
11. …I was injured in a combat-related incident.	1	2	3	4	5	6
12. …I fired my weapon at enemy combatants.	1	2	3	4	5	6
13. …I think I wounded or killed someone during combat operations.	1	2	3	4	5	6
14. …I was involved in locating or disarming explosive devices.	1	2	3	4	5	6
15. …I was involved in searching or clearing homes, buildings, or other locations.	1	2	3	4	5	6
16. …I participated in hand-to-hand combat.	1	2	3	4	5	6
17. …I was involved in searching and/or disarming potential enemy combatants.	1	2	3	4	5	6

DRRI-2

SECTION E: POSTBATTLE EXPERIENCES
Next are statements about your exposure to the consequences of warfare during your most recent deployment. Please mark how often you experienced each circumstance.

	Never	Once or twice	Several times over entire deployment	A few times each month	A few times each week	Daily or almost daily
1. I saw people begging for food.	1	2	3	4	5	6
2. I saw refugees who had lost their homes or belongings.	1	2	3	4	5	6
3. I observed homes or communities that had been destroyed.	1	2	3	4	5	6
4. I took care of injured or dying people.	1	2	3	4	5	6
5. I saw civilians after they had been severely wounded or disfigured.	1	2	3	4	5	6
6. I saw enemy combatants after they had been severely wounded or disfigured.	1	2	3	4	5	6
7. I saw Americans or allies after they had been severely wounded or disfigured.	1	2	3	4	5	6
8. I saw the bodies of dead enemy combatants.	1	2	3	4	5	6
9. I saw the bodies of dead Americans or allies.	1	2	3	4	5	6
10. I saw the bodies of dead civilians.	1	2	3	4	5	6
11. I interacted with detainees or prisoners of war.	1	2	3	4	5	6
12. I was exposed to the sight, sound, or smell of dead or dying animals.	1	2	3	4	5	6
13. I was involved in handling human remains.	1	2	3	4	5	6

DRRI-2

SECTION F: EXPOSURE TO NUCLEAR, BIOLOGICAL, OR CHEMICAL AGENTS
Next are statements about nuclear, biological, and chemical agents (NBCs) that you may have been exposed to when you were preparing for your most recent deployment or during your most recent deployment. Please mark "Yes", "No", or "Not sure" for each question below.

Either in preparation for or during my deployment...

1. ...I took preventative pills (for example, to protect against nerve gas).	Yes	No	Not sure
2. ...I received preventative vaccinations by injection (for example, to prevent anthrax or botulism).	Yes	No	Not sure

While I was deployed, I was exposed to...

3. ...nerve gas agents (for example, sarin).	Yes	No	Not sure
4. ...mustard gas or other blistering agents.	Yes	No	Not sure
5. ...government-issued DEET-containing insect repellents.	Yes	No	Not sure
6. ...other pesticides (for example, in flea collars, uniforms, or the environment).	Yes	No	Not sure
7. ...smoke or other air pollution.	Yes	No	Not sure
8. ...diesel or other petrochemical fuel on my skin.	Yes	No	Not sure
9. ...fumes or exhaust from heaters or generators, including heaters in tents.	Yes	No	Not sure
10. ...depleted uranium in munitions.	Yes	No	Not sure
11. ...burning trash or burning feces.	Yes	No	Not sure
12. ...chlorine gas.	Yes	No	Not sure
13. ...nuclear, biological, or chemical weapons.	Yes	No	Not sure

DRRI-2

SECTION G: DEPLOYMENT CONCERNS
The statements below are about the amount of danger you felt you were exposed to during your most recent deployment. Please mark how much you agree or disagree with each statement.

	Strongly disagree	Somewhat disagree	Neither agree nor disagree	Somewhat agree	Strongly agree
1. I was concerned about getting an infectious disease.	1	2	3	4	5
2. I was concerned that my health might suffer due to exposure to nuclear, biological, or chemical (NBC) agents.	1	2	3	4	5
3. I felt I was in great danger of being wounded (for example, losing a limb).	1	2	3	4	5
4. I was concerned that the medicine I was given to protect me from illness would make me sick.	1	2	3	4	5
5. I was concerned that I would encounter an explosive device (for example, a roadside bomb, mine, or booby trap).	1	2	3	4	5
6. I feared that I would become sick from pesticides (for example, bug spray) or other routinely used chemicals.	1	2	3	4	5
7. I was concerned that a rocket or mortar would hit our living quarters.	1	2	3	4	5
8. I was concerned that I might be exposed to depleted uranium in munitions.	1	2	3	4	5
9. I thought I would never survive.	1	2	3	4	5
10. I was concerned that I might be taken hostage.	1	2	3	4	5
11. I was concerned that the locals who were supposed to be helping us were actually working against us.	1	2	3	4	5
12. I was concerned about being trapped in the crossfire of rival factions.	1	2	3	4	5

DRRI-2

SECTION H: TRAINING AND DEPLOYMENT PREPARATION
Below are several statements about how well-prepared you were by the military for your most recent deployment. As used in these statements, the term "unit" refers to those you lived and worked with on a daily basis during deployment. Please mark how much you agree or disagree with each statement.

	Strongly disagree	Somewhat disagree	Neither agree nor disagree	Somewhat agree	Strongly agree
1. I had all the supplies and equipment needed to get my job done.	1	2	3	4	5
2. The training I received made me feel confident in my ability to use my equipment.	1	2	3	4	5
3. The training I received prepared me to deal with the region's climate.	1	2	3	4	5
4. I was accurately informed about the role my unit was expected to play in the deployment.	1	2	3	4	5
5. I had enough gear to protect myself in case of an attack.	1	2	3	4	5
6. I received appropriate training for the nature of the deployment I experienced.	1	2	3	4	5
7. My military duties and assignments were what I expected.	1	2	3	4	5
8. My unit was well-prepared to operate as a team during deployment.	1	2	3	4	5
9. The training I received made me feel confident in my ability to perform tasks assigned to me during deployment.	1	2	3	4	5
10. The training I received taught me everything I needed to know for deployment.	1	2	3	4	5

Appendix C

Pennsylvania Department of Corrections Vietnam Veteran Scale

VIETNAM VETERANS SCALE (your replies will be kept confidential)

	Never	Rarely	Often	Very Often
1. I feel anxious or tense				
2. I feel irritable or short-tempered				
3. I have sudden attacks of fear or panic..........................				
4. I react to loud noises and/or the sound of helicopters				
5. My heart beats very fast				
6. I sweat a lot				
7. I have problems with my stomach and/or headaches				
8. I have rages or fear the loss of control				
9. I have difficulty dealing with people in authority				
10. I am preoccupied with thoughts about Vietnam				
11. I react negatively to reminders of Vietnam				
12. I react negatively to the sight of Vietnamese here				
13. I have nightmares and/or flashbacks about Vietnam				
14. I have feelings of guilt				
15. I have trouble falling asleep, staying asleep, or over-sleeping				

	Never	Rarely	Often	Very Often
16. I have a problem trusting people				
17. I avoid getting close to people				
18. I am bothered by crowds				
19. I feel tired, or have no energy				
20. I forget things, get confused, can't make decisions				
21. I feel sad, depressed, or blue				
22. I don't have confidence				
23. I don't seem to care about anything .				
24. I feel numb, or don't seem to have any feelings				
25. I have thoughts of taking my life				
26. I use alcohol and/or street drugs to control my tension				
27. I have difficulty with my sex life				
28. I talk about Vietnam				

Name_____ SS#_____ Date_____

Chapter 9

VETERANS DORMS: "PURPOSE-DRIVEN INCARCERATION" AS THE COUNTERPART TO PROBLEM-SOLVING VETERANS' COURTS

I. The Small but Significant Trend

The concept of housing incarcerated veterans separately from other inmates for promoting their treatment and readjustment dates back 1921 and Wisconsin psychiatrist William F. Lorenz. He observed the importance of housing combat traumatized veterans apart from the general population and granting them additional liberties to meet therapeutic recovery objectives (Casey, 1923, p. 27). It took more than fifty years for this notion to come to fruition, when the Arthur Kill Correctional Facility in Staten Island, New York, instituted the first veterans dorm in 1987 (Marks, 2001, p. 3). In contemporary times, veterans' dorms operate in a number of jurisdictions. By May 2018, research for this book identified twenty-nine states with specialized housing programs devoted to incarcerated veterans in a total of eighty-one institutions. Approximately twelve states have both jail and prison units for incarcerated veterans, while eight states have only prison units and eight states have only jail units. Florida boasts units for veterans in its state prisons, county jails, and Federal Correctional Institutions. Table 9.1 provides a breakdown for the estimated 86 programs in prisons and jails as of January 2018 (Crime Sider Staff, 2018).

With knowledge of these developments, and the manner in which sheriffs and wardens are sharing information, some commentators have suggested that these units are becoming a "national trend" (Shepherd, 2017; Crime Sider Staff, 2018).

Although numerical estimates vary, different names are used such as "module," "unit," "block," "pod," "floor," or "wing" (Edelman, 2018, p. vii), or "Veterans Service Unit" (Tasi & Goggin, 2017, p. 45). These differences might prevent the researchers from obtaining an accurate count. However, a

Table 9.1. Housing of Incarcerated Veterans by Jurisdiction and Venue

Jurisdiction	Jail	Prison	Federal Correctional Institution
Arkansas	X	X	
Arizona	X	X	
California	X	X	
Colorado	X		
Connecticut		X	
Delaware		X	
Florida	X	X	X
Georgia	X	X	
Indiana		X	
Illinois	X		
Kentucky		X	
Massachusetts	X		
Maine	X		
Michigan	X		
Missouri	X		
Mississippi		X	
Nebraska	X		
North Carolina		X	
Nevada		X	
New York	X	X	
Ohio	X	X	
Pennsylvania	X	X	
South Carolina	X		
Tennessee	X	X	
Texas	X	X	
Virginia	X	X	
Washington	X	X	
Wisconsin			
West Virginia			X

noteworthy point is the emergence of many programs in roughly the same time. Between 2010 and 2012, at least five programs materialized in Maine, Georgia, Florida, Ohio, and Virginia—some quite distant from the others (Schroeder, 2013). According to at least one account, the Virginia Department of Corrections was inspired to create its own veterans' dorms based on learning of Florida's veterans dorms (Kamal, 2013). More recently, Arizona modeled its program after one in Massachusetts (Shepherd, 2017). While this inescapably signals a trend, the trend is still quite small.

Given that there were 1,223 state prisons in America in 2012 (American Correctional Association, 2013) 3,313 jails in 2012 (American Correctional Association, 2012), and 182 federal prison facilities in 2013 (Federal Bureau of Prisons, 2013), it is unrealistic to say veterans dorms are pervasive in American correctional institutions. Nor have the programs been unanimously adopted within states. In fact, it appears as though *either* jails *or* prisons have assumed the responsibility for instituting such dorms, but not both. In West Virginia, for example, while sheriffs and the state department of corrections have not instituted veterans dorms, one Federal Correctional Institution has charted its own course (National Institute of Corrections, n.d.).

In New York, since March of 2013, Erie County has operated a veterans dorm in its jail entirely separate from the veterans dorms developed by the New York State Department of Correctional Services (Lionti, 2013). Although the programs are understandably different given the longer duration of prison terms, they ultimately share common recognition for specialized residential services to this vulnerable population. Erie County's program is also noteworthy for operating in the same jurisdiction as the Buffalo Veterans Treatment Court, credited with starting a national movement. In fact, the jail dorm was a direct outgrowth of the effectiveness of the Buffalo Veterans Treatment Court (Lionti, 2013). If diverted veterans benefit from therapeutic interventions, surely similar benefits would accrue to veterans awaiting trial or serving jail terms.

Stressing the same form of peer support that is credited for the success of Buffalo's innovative program, Erie County Sheriff Tim Howard observes that the dorm allows participants to lean on each other the same way that they did in the military based on "peer support, similar backgrounds, [and] similar experiences" (Lionti, 2013). While there are numerous reasons why other jurisdictions have developed these programs, like Erie County, the Florida Department of Corrections developed veterans dorms "to compliment the effective use of specialized veterans' courts" (DeFoor, 2013, p. 3P).

The philosophies in both veterans courts and veterans' dorms are virtually indistinguishable. Former Kennebec County Sheriff (now Maine State Penitentiary Warden) Randall Liberty, a former Army senior noncommissioned officer, often trains first-responders on special methods to assist subjects experiencing PTSD symptoms during crisis-response. Liberty views the development of the county's veterans dorm as a prime example of "purpose-driven incarceration." Little different from the veterans treatment court problem-solving court philosophy of aiming at the underlying problem, rather than merely the criminal symptoms, "The philosophy of 'purpose-driven incarcerated' means we ask, 'Why are people here?' In this population, it's a result of trauma that was sustained in service to our country" (Schroeder, 2013).

Although Liberty often jokes, "that we're a veterans' advocacy organization that does some law enforcement," the dorm does not exist to dispense special treatment to veterans. Instead, it represents "different forms of treatment to address needs specific to their military background" (Schroeder, 2013). Liberty developed the veterans cellblock in his jail after realizing that incarcerated veterans might be suffering from the same PTSD symptoms that he experienced following combat as an Army Sergeant Major (Fitzpatrick, 2013). He joins the ranks of other sheriffs who were informed by their prior military service, such as Missouri Sheriff Glenn Boyer and former Los Angeles County Sheriff Lee Baca who both served in Vietnam (Carbery, 2013, p. 11B; Leonard, 2005, p. B1).

While the expansion of veterans dorms may not be as rapid as veterans treatment courts, which currently number over 461 (Tsai et al., 2018), it is quite possible that veterans dorms will gain momentum as veterans treatment courts continue to expand. Interestingly, the reverse is possible in terms of inspiration. This is particularly clear in the implementation of the Jefferson County Jail Veterans' Program in Saint Louis, Missouri, in which, after establishing the dorm in late 2012, Sheriff Glenn Boyer approached the local judge "about establishing a Veterans Court to deal with cases involving veterans" (Carbery, 2013, p. 11B). Likewise, in Kennebec County, Maine, Sheriff Liberty established the veterans cellblock in the period before the county had implemented its veterans' court, even offering to admit veterans convicted in distant locations.

An hour-long film, *A Matter of Duty: The Continuing War Against PTSD*, which depicts Sheriff Liberty's experience developing the Kennebec County Jail's Veterans Cellblock, and extended interview footage, is accessible at the following Web address: http://www.mpbn.net/Television/LocalTelevision Programs/AMatterofDuty.aspx.

II. Evolution of the Nation's First Veterans Dorms

Like veterans treatment courts, veterans dorms are extremely diverse in admissions criteria and structure. In Florida and Virginia, a military discharge under Other-than-Honorable conditions will bar an incarcerated veteran from admission to the program (Alvarez, 2011, p. A14; Hixenbaugh, 2012, p. A1). Accordingly, a dishonorable discharge is treated in a similar light as a history of "escape attempts in the last five years" for eligibility purposes in Florida's veterans dorms (Kamal, 2013).

Contrarily, the Indiana Department of Corrections admitted inmates with dishonorable discharges into its Indiana Veteran's Education and Transition Unit (INVET) Veterans Dorm (Dean, 2012, p. 6). In Los Angeles County, while the Veterans Wing at the Men's Central Jail had no problem admitting an Army veteran with a Bad-Conduct Discharge, its administrators automatically barred participation from those inmates whose civilian offenses included murder or rape (Leonard, 2005, p. B1).

Some of these policies clearly relate to different underlying purposes for operating a specialized housing unit. Programs that seek to help individuals recover lost pride from an earlier time by replicating familiar customs of military service have more reason to seek honorable periods of service; the embodiment of discipline and values is predicated on earlier success. In those programs, dishonorable discharge status might ironically suggest a return to the absence of values or integrity based on this ideological orientation.

While all veterans dorms, to some degree, use earlier periods of service to instill pride and self-worth in their participants (Edelman, 2018), discharge characterization matters far less for programs seeking to optimize treatment by creating a therapeutic environment. As in other institutions, a given dorm's underlying theme and mission will dictate various traits that are most desirable in that program's participants.

The following section uses the nation's first and longest running program to explore the basic tenets of veterans dorms, despite their numerous differences. The New York State Department of Correctional Service's Veterans Residential Therapeutic Program (VRTP) has been in continuous operation since the late 1980s and, unlike recent programs, enjoys a history of evaluation for more than two decades. While other states' newer programs may have evolved without any knowledge of New York's program, the VRTP shares enough basic commonalities to provide meaningful lessons to benefit any prison or jail that is considering the development of specialized housing units for veteran inmates. Similar to the newer programs, the VRTP represents a departure from the traditional view that populations of inmates should not be segregated by virtue of common experiences (Rosenthal & McGuire, 2013, p. 364).

A. The Genesis of the New York's VRTP

The VRTP began after prison administrators observed the value of rap groups for Vietnam veterans who faced similar readjustment difficulties from combat experiences, including trauma and PTSD diagnoses. The rap groups evolved from one session per week with the aid of a Vet Center specialist to four sessions per week. By 1987, with the facilitation of Mr. Don Little, New York's Arthur Kill Confinement Facility at Staten Island established the state's first veteran-specific dormitory (Marks, 2001). The program's success highlighted the common needs of veterans throughout the state, leading to the approval of the Veterans Residential Therapeutic Programs by the Commissioner of Corrections in February of 1990.

The most noteworthy facility is the Groveland Correctional Facility in Western New York's Livingston County (Groveland Correctional Facility & Veterans Administration, 1992, p. 58). In the initial stages of this program, from 1989 to 1991, it adopted a "primary focus on PTSD," mainly among incarcerated Vietnam veterans (New York State Department of Correctional Services, 1994, p. 3). In 1991, the Veterans Administration supplemented the program with a staff team from the nearby Veterans Administration Medical Center at Canandaigua, which included a core of "a staff counseling psychologist, a staff RN/therapist, a psychology technician, and two chemical dependency rehabilitation technicians," often supplemented by additional mental health clinicians and addiction specialists (Groveland Correctional Facility & Veterans Administration, 1992, p. 58).

The infusion of trained personnel permitted the VRTP program to implement the Veterans Administration's treatment interventions within the correctional setting, including replication of the updated behavioral-therapy interventions (New York State Department of Correctional services, 1994, p. 6). The additional staff saved funds and further enabled the program to concentrate on issues besides PTSD, including substance abuse and complex trauma. Moreover, the Veterans Administration staff also enabled additional individual counseling sessions. After this major transformation in 1991, it was not uncommon to see a division of labor between corrections mental health providers and Veterans Administration employees with the latter leading groups for "PTSD/Combat Stress" and providing input on the treatment and reentry plans developed by all inmate participants (Groveland Correctional Facility & Veterans Administration, 1992, p. 62). The collaboration, including the Veterans Administration's supply of "therapeutic content and direction of the program," was unprecedented and made the VRTP program the most unique operation in the entire New York State Department of Corrections (New York Department of Correctional Services, 1994, p. 2).

The mission of the VRTP has been consistent through the decades:

"Under the direction of professional staff, [VRTP] provides individualized, comprehensive and integrated services to veterans for the purpose of successful re-integration into society." In pursuit of this goal, the four components of the program (Chemical Dependency (60 hrs), Aggression Counseling (30 hrs), Personal Enhancement (120 hrs), and Community Re-Integration (90 hrs)) "all include a specific relationship to the veterans' military service" (Groveland Correctional Facility n.d., p. 1).

The program achieves these objectives with a full schedule of classes to occupy the inmates' time during two three-to-four-hour shifts per day, historically disbursed among eighty-two classes and groups per week instructed by veterans, Department staff, or Veterans Administration personnel (Groveland Correctional Facility & Veterans Administration, 1992, p. 58). The total program duration is twelve months, split into a six-month orientation program primarily devoted to substance abuse and general topics. This is followed by a more intensive six-month treatment component, with a graduated process designed to "build readiness for therapy," develop clear expectations of the program, and encourage a safe and trustful environment prior to the most sensitive and difficult self-exploration (New York Department of Correctional Services, 1994, p. 5). Over time, especially when the Veterans Administration staff contributed to the program, it was "not unusual for an individual veteran to have more than a thousand hours of classes and group therapy, as well as individual counseling" during the twelve-month term of participation (New York Department of Correctional Services, 1994, p. 11).

Notably, Dr. Terrence Keane, the Director of the Veterans Administration's National Center for PTSD, evaluated the program at the time of the Veterans Administration's most intense involvement and concluded, "[i]t is clearly among the very best psychological service delivery programs that I have observed in the public and private sector," further recommending replication of the program in other correctional facilities (New York Department of Correctional Services, 1994, p. 2).

B. Attributes of the VRTP Veterans' Dorms

The VRTP imposes high standards of personal conduct, which are reinforced by a participation contract (see Appendix A of this chapter) and a separate confidentiality policy, which can subject a violator to expulsion and punitive sanctions (see Appendix B of this chapter). The latter document relates to a number of disclosures in the dorm or therapy group setting, including:

- Any criminal behavior disclosed by the participant which might be used to deny him release.
- The nature of the Instant Offense—or of prior Instant Offenses.
- Personal and sensitive family issues; including names, addresses, and so forth.
- Potentially sensitive personal issues (such as being the victim of childhood sexual abuse, certain aspects of past military experience (such as behaviors during combat), personal financial or residential issues, and so forth.
- A good guideline is "common sense." If the disclosure of this information could be harmful, then it should be kept confidential!

Source: Groveland Correctional Facility, n.d., p. 20.

Evident in the observations of the veterans' dorm Chaplain in Georgia's Muscogee County Jail, confidentiality is particularly necessary for effective treatment because personal disclosures of ones "deepest darkests, even substance abuse histories, become weapons in jail, which can easily be used by other inmates" (N. Richardson, personal communication, December 4, 2013). While, in any program, including the VRTP, contractual safeguards encourage tranquility, respect, and secrecy, program success depends more on a number of different attributes.

Participants understand that, as dorm residents, they must be committed to the program not only in classes or group sessions, but around-the-clock in a mode where they are ready and able to learn at all times (Groveland Correctional Facility, Transitional Services Orientation Guide, n.d., p. 10). The dorms enable the inmates to "live and work as a unit," which provides a framework for more meaningful behavioral intervention (New York State Department of Correctional Services, 1994, p. 4). Work details and chores in the dorm highlight the inmates' responsibilities to one another, as does a higher level of behavioral expectations than the members of the general population (Groveland Correctional Facility, n.d., pp. 3–4). A full description of the various peer duties within the VRTP appears in Appendix C of this chapter.

Life in a veteran community environment further permits the cadre (inmate, peer, and staff) to detect, respond to, and mediate disputes within the dorm at the earliest possible time with the opportunity for graduated sanctions, rather than a more limited range of options if knowledge of the event follows a lengthy delay. This is notable in the peer intervention team leader's discretion to "address some problems behaviors through mediation rather than intervention" (Groveland Correctional Facility, n.d., p. 7) and the cadre member's discretion to institute a reprimand, learning experience, or a therapeutic assignment after the issuance of a written pull-up (Groveland Correctional Facility, n.d., p. 17).

Early on, the VRTP administrators recognized the tremendous value, and necessity, of grouping veterans in a specialized housing unit during their treatment rather than in the general population. A 1994 *Program Overview* explained that "[t]he common residential area is critical to the success of the program" because "[p]erhaps for the first time in their lives, the veterans are with other men their own age in an intensive and structured therapeutic setting" (New York State Department of Correctional Services, 1994, p. 7). Furthermore, the inmate peer staff who receive training in PTSD and combat stress issues "can be a safe and sympathetic listener—for they have shared many of the same problems themselves" (New York State Department of Correctional Services, 1994, p. 7). The current edition of the orientation guide to Groveland's VRTP additionally notes:

> Probably the most important reason for the housing is the need to provide a safe and supportive environment in which to address some very sensitive issues. For many of the program participants there are issues surrounding child abuse, sexual behavior, and other issues that a person would avoid in a setting of a general population. To make the changes needed, these issues have to be addressed. The housing environment provides both the security and the support to a program member to face these harsh and painful issues, and come to some resolution or closure. This allows for new behavior that is not influenced by past trauma, guilt, resentment, or insecurities. (Groveland Correctional Facility, n.d., p. 3)

Together, the various Groveland and VRTP program overviews highlight the following three major benefits of housing veteran inmates together in a residential dorm:

Three Major Benefits of Housing Veterans in a Specialized Unit

1. Provide a safe and trusting environment to discuss sensitive and potentially sensitive issues, thus enabling successful outlet of suppressed experiences and feelings.

2. Instill a sense of accountability in each member for the entire program's success. When every participant feels like they have a stake in the program, there is more incentive to follow the rules. There is also the notion of being a member of a community, which promotes effective reentry into the civilian community.

3. Provide inmates with increasing responsibility as they progress. This includes leadership positions, but also specific duties that can develop skills in special problem areas.

The current edition of Groveland's *Program Overview* advocates against mixed housing arrangements in which veterans might only share an area of a facility rather than an entire dorm, "The idea of splitting up the community by housing them only on one floor will undermine the entire goal of the community. The negativity that would come about from non-participants would pollute the entire dormitory" (Groveland Correctional Facility, n.d., p. 4).

The VRTP program is noteworthy because it consistently demonstrated significant success rates, measured in terms of decreased recidivism. By 1994, the reincarceration rate within the Groveland and Mt. McGregor VRTP Dorms was 6.1 percent with a projected sixty-six-month return rate of 8.89 percent, compared to New York State's recidivism rate many times greater at 40.57 percent of *veterans* in the general population, and 51.85 percent of *all* inmates (New York State Department of Correctional Services, 1994, p. 2). The most recent edition of Groveland's VRTP *Program Overview* notes continued success, including a 5–8 percent recidivism rate in addition to an exemplary disciplinary record for the program (Groveland Correctional Facility, n.d., p. 6).

Correctional administrators within the New York State Department of Correctional Services attribute these continued success rates to the housing arrangements at the stand-alone veterans' dorms: "The net effect of this arrangement is that the therapeutic process can focus more directly not only on symptomatic behaviors, but on causes" (New York State Department of Correctional Services, 1994, p. 7). These statistics are also important because the early-to-mid-1990s marked the Veterans Administration's withdrawal of its treatment professionals from prisons and jails. With increasing pressure to align with the policy positions expressed by Veterans Administration officials at congressional hearings in 1990, who believed that services to incarcerated veterans detracted from other needy groups and unnecessarily duplicated responsibilities of the institutions, the VRTP quickly suffered the prompt exodus of its Veterans Administration partners. In many cases, veteran inmates who had developed very close and productive relationships with particular clinicians experienced great turmoil at the prompt and unexpected discontinuation of their treatment (S. M. Verbecke & J. P. Strollo, personal communication, September 16, 2013).

While the program required necessary retooling and changes to accommodate the decrease in Veterans Administration expertise, the VRTP continued. Now operated mainly through three institutions at Mt. McGregor, Mid State, and Groveland Correctional Facilities (New York State Department of Correctional Services, n.d.), the program still maintains rigorous educational programs that prepare veterans for successful readjustment. The program is run by veterans' guidance specialists, themselves former military veterans with counseling backgrounds, who were heavily involved in the dorms since the early 1990s, through the transition following the Veterans Administration's departure (S. M. Verbecke & J. P. Storollo, personal communication, September 16, 2013). While the program currently provides a number of classroom hours on PTSD as a forum in which the veterans can address issues related to their symptomatology, the retreat of Veterans Administration treatment professionals resulted in the shift of responsibility for PTSD treatment from formal Veterans Administration programming to informal—primarily peer—assistance, including increased responsibilities on part of the trained peer cadre (S. M. Verbecke & J. P. Strollo, personal communication, September 16, 2013).

The VRTP's ability to sustain the same rates of success today, in the absence of the Veterans Administration's direct involvement, and in light of the increased reliance on fellow inmates' support, reveals two key points. First, even despite formal prohibitions on mental health or physical health treatment from Veterans Administration clinicians in confined settings (38 C.F.R. § 17.38(c)(5)), with the institution of specialized housing units, prisons and jails can address veteran inmates' needs and significantly impact recidivism rates. This is likely due to the creation of a shared space in which classic symptom aggravators are removed and in which veterans can enjoy peace, quiet, mutual support, and the ability to engage in relaxation and other introspective exercises without fear of being exploited in a vulnerable state. Second, it emphasizes the manner in which "treatment" in confined settings takes on a different form than treatment in the community.

The experience at Groveland, Arthur Kill, and other VRTP Dorms in New York underscores major points raised by Joel A. Dvoskin and Erin M. Spiers in their article "On the Role of Correctional Officers in Prison Mental Health" (2004). There, the authors explained that mental health professionals have a limited reach in addressing inmates' aggravated symptoms. Due to their inability to be with inmates around-the-clock, the greatest responsibility for meaningful intervention falls, instead, on those who are constantly present with the inmates, including correctional officers, sheriff's deputies, staff—implicitly peers—who can make a huge difference simply by talking to the inmates, showing concern, and helping in other ways. To Dvoskin and Spiers, such "treatment" in confinement by non-clinicians can often result in superior results when compared to clinical treatment after the fact.

Furthermore, "[t]ruly effective correctional mental health care can only be accomplished by employing both formal *and* informal intervention strategies" (Dvoskin & Spiers, 2004, p. 46). Groveland's experience is an ideal example of the way that veterans' dormitories, by the nature of their special attributes and the cultivation of staff, cadre, and peer relationships, provide high-quality "treatment" of combat PTSD and other conditions that normally heighten risks of self-harm and violence in populations of veteran inmates.

In sum, as the nation's first and longest continuously operated veterans' dormitories, New York's VRTP is a model for prisons and jails alike. Its message is so universal that, for more than a decade, Ohio veterans' advocacy groups pushed for a similarly modeled program for veterans in that state. In 2001, the advocates recognized that VRTP "took a group of men whose chief commonality was the shame of their crime and, instead, gathered them with brothers whose chief commodity was pride in their service to their country" (Harden, 2001, p. 1F). In December of 2012, the Belmont County (Ohio) Sheriff's Department instituted a veterans' dormitory, with an unveiling ceremony attended by notaries including an Ohio Supreme Court Justice. In fact, it is the only known program in the nation with a special military preparatory track that allows inmates to be selected for possible continued service in the Ohio Military Activation Task Force, a statutorily created organization designed to assist in the mobilization of Ohio's reserve and national guard forces in the case the President calls them to active service (DeFrank, 2012). While Ohio's county dorm is certainly different from the VRTP, it draws largely on the same underlying principles.

C. The Continued Lesson from the San Francisco Sheriff's Department Community of Veterans Engaged in Restoration (COVER) Dormitory Program

This section reviews the San Francisco County Sheriff's Department's Veterans' Pod, which complements the prison dorms in New York, and which has drawn on various community services in an unprecedented manner for the benefit of its participants. San Francisco is a county most populated by veterans. Not only does California rank as having one of the highest veteran populations, it also has the country's largest active duty (12.9 percent) and reserve (6.9 percent) populations (Institute of Medicine, 2010, p. 22). Unsurprisingly, the San Francisco County Jail booked between a low of fifty-seven veterans and a high of ninety-seven veterans *per day* in a year-and-a-half period between 2010 and 2012 (Stock, Wagner, Paredes, Escamilla, & Carroll, 2012). In August 2010, both community veterans' advocates like Michael Blecker, the Director of Swords to Plowshares in the Bay Area, and then-Sheriff Michael Hennessey and other deputies, noticed the growth of the veteran population in the County's jail facilities (Tyler, 2013).

While San Francisco is not a location with large active duty military installations, the higher number of veterans in California raised concern in combination with the fact that "prisoners with prior military service" constitute "one of the fastest growing segments of the criminal justice system" (Schwartz & Levitas, 2011, p. 48). These concerns developed into a concept called the Community of Veterans Engaged in Restoration (COVER), which has the following mission statement:

The Community of Veterans Engaged in Restoration (COVER) is a San Francisco Sheriff's Department program designed for veterans of all the branches of the U.S. Military. The COVER program provides veterans regardless of their character of discharge with an opportunity to address their obstacles for positive reintegration into society after serving in the military and its aftermath. COVER provides in-jail/post release case management services utilizing the multi-faceted departments of the San Francisco Sheriff's Department and its supporting agencies (San Francisco Sheriff's Department, n.d.).

The COVER program explicitly acknowledges that it exists in great part to help "repair the damage [veterans] suffered in war" because, for too many of the participants, "[t]hey didn't go into the service this way" (Ban, 2012) (citing Susan Fahey). More specifically, "[i]n developing COVER, [San Francisco Sheriff Department] leadership recognized that, as a society, we train military personnel to fight and even kill, but we do not provide the much-needed support for them to return home in a safe and healthy way, which will enable them to thrive in civilian life" (Schwartz & Levitas, 2011, p. 55). Accordingly, in COVER, as in Muscogee County's veterans' dorm, it does not matter whether inmates have a particular disorder or diagnosis. As Chaplain Neil Richardson puts it, "Rather than trying to ascertain whether this is due to the military or not, the fact is they are veterans" (Salahi, 2012).

Because the COVER concept evolved without an identified source of funding, the program necessarily relied upon the wealth of community organizations operating in San Francisco, which was an ideal setting to locate volunteers versed in meditation, acupuncture, yoga, and alternative medicine interventions. Increased involvement of non-Veterans Administration stakeholders permitted the program to address the needs of ex-service members with less-than-honorable discharges, who would otherwise be barred from receiving federal benefits. Reminiscent of the theories of community involvement first espoused by Bruce Pentland in the early iteration of Southern California's V.I.P. program (see Chapter 8), the COVER program has continued to achieve its broad goals, mainly through a mosaic of different agencies, including the following:

Organization	Role
Veterans' Administration	For those with honorable discharge there is a vocational outreach coordinator
Community Works	Man Alive (through RSVP)
San Francisco Vet Center	Weekly visits to assist in VA documents (i.e. DD-214)
NoVA Project	Visits those who need housing but do not meet VA criteria
Metropolitan Fresh Start	Weekly group facilitation
Salvation Army	Housing beds for veterans
Five Keys Charter School	Resource sharing (new program beginning to share computers during and after school)
Jail Psychiatric Services	Interns dedicated for counseling purposes
Coming Home Project	Provides information on community resources for veterans
I-Rest	Weekly meditation
Acupuncture	Volunteer services for weekly acupuncture
Swords to Plowshares	Case management, outreach

Source: San Francisco Sheriff's Department, n.d.

Within the framework of standardized classes, and electives, the program exists as a multimodal, milieu therapy approach, which has components addressing trauma-informed group counseling, victim restoration, and anger management (S. Schwartz, L. Levitas, & I. McCray, personal communication, October 15, 2012). The combined effort is all-the-more important because of the different, but unique, treatment needs of different generations of veterans. San Francisco Sheriff Ross Mirkarimi recently observed how the dormitory structure permits the jail to best address these diverse needs: "We're challenged by two distinct populations of veterans: the older, incarcerated veterans, who require a specialized level of care that they didn't get years ago, and the veterans returning from Iraq and Afghanistan whose health and welfare needs are unique from those of their predecessors" (Bay City News Service, 2012).

Operating with a forty-eight-member capacity, the COVER Pod boasts a waiting list from among the county's numerous veteran inmates. Not only does the program strive to identify veterans as quickly as possible upon booking with targeted questions and signs, but it also sends volunteers into the general population at post-booking stages to solicit for veterans who may not have initially stepped forward (S. Schwartz, L. Levitas, & I. McCray, personal communication, October 15, 2012). Given that the average stay in the San Francisco County Jail is two months, the program conducts regularly scheduled programs, which include recurring visits from veterans in the community every other week in a robust speakers' program. As time has progressed, with the support of innovative community partnerships, COVER has attempted to develop a greater capacity for reentry planning.

As a first of its kind in the nation, the San Francisco Veterans Administration Medical Center opened a Justice Clinic at its downtown location in May 2012 with a major goal of ensuring a seamless transition to the community for veterans exiting the county jail by serving as a "one-stop shop" for various forms of continued care (Mendonca, 2012). At base, despite the multitude of community supports, COVER still remains a peer-based program. While it shares a number of attributes with the nation's newer veterans dorms, COVER is a testament to the principle of broad-based community involvement beyond the Veterans Administration. The program offers numerous lessons to those institutions hoping to develop programming to meet the needs of all veterans, including and especially those who are harder to reach as a result of "bad paper" discharges, which have prevented quality care since the time of their discharge from the service.

III. Common Justifications for Instituting Veterans Dorms

Despite their differences, correctional professionals in diverse jurisdictions have developed specialized housing units for veterans for six primary reasons—above and beyond the general intention to replicate the success of nearby veterans treatment courts. A summary of these themes includes the following:

Six Basic Themes for Development of Veterans' Housing Units

1. Concentrating veterans in the same location permits more effective delivery of specialized services.

2. Specialized housing units for veterans represent the most cost-efficient intervention within a correctional institution.

3. Specialized housing units permit veterans to fully participate in their treatment without common distractions of the general population.

---

4. Specialized housing units enable better detection of behavioral changes and needs by correctional staff and fellow participants.

5. Specialized housing units for veterans increase officer safety and limit officer stress.

6. The jail is located near a military installation, which increases contact with active duty service members and veterans.

Role of Correctional Officers Within Treatment Teams

In exploring each of these motivations, the remainder of this chapter aims to address the function of correctional officers as vital members of the treatment teams within residential settings. While it stands to reason that correctional officers and deputies with prior military service are at an advantage for relating to, and being relied upon, by veteran inmates or detainees, it is important to understand the special function of *any* correctional officer in responding to veterans' mental health and other service-related conditions. The correctional officer's role extends beyond merely responding to crisis, but preventing it in the first place and, moreover, instilling in veterans a sense of purpose and respect.

A. Concentrating Veterans in the Same Location Permits More Effective Delivery of Specialized Services

This is a leading justification for the creation of any specialized dormitory, evident in the recent development of other dorms suited to special populations. In Florida's veterans dorms, correctional administrators observe that, "[b]y housing the men together, the state has an easier time in providing services" (Alvarez, 2011). This is a universal concept for all special needs inmates, not only veterans. In Muscogee County Jail, for example, after successful experiences with a GED dorm, the sheriff instituted the veterans dorm, and a fatherhood dorm, which offers a reading program for young children with the help of the local library and slogans, such as "To Become a Father is not hard. To be a father is" (Gierer, 2013). Muscogee County's separate faith-based jail dorm, which features visits from the clergy and illustrations of the Cross and Scripture, enjoys a 22 percent recidivism rate as of October 2013, a large improvement over the general population (Gierer, 2013, p. 1). Regardless of the focus, these specialized programs realize that more resources may be targeted to a population with similar needs when they are located in the same place. As noted by Jo Ellen Rackleff of the Florida Department of Corrections, the dorms permit the institutions to "congregate as many inmates as possible in one area where the V.A. could meet with them and discuss programs available to them" (Breen, 2011, p. A6). Apart from other groups, veterans, especially those suffering from combat and operational stress injuries, require the greatest devotion of resources from the most diverse sources to assist them in their recovery. Veterans dorms promote prompt consideration of "veteran-related issues" (Salahi, 2012). As observed by Dean Lachance of the Bread of Life Ministries, who recently opened a half-way house just for veterans in Maine, veterans' needs are very substantial:

> Veterans are twice as likely or more to be homeless. Veterans are two to three times more likely to have physical disabilities. Veterans are three to four times more likely to have a mental health disability or challenge. They are two to three times more likely to have substance abuse. There's absolutely no doubt in my mind our country, our communities, our nonprofits, our faith communities are absolutely not prepared for the epidemic that we face today. (*A Matter of Duty*, 2013)

To former Sheriff Darr, it was only "natural" to open the veterans dorm: "Where you have a group of inmates that share a characteristic like their military service, they often have a lot of similar problems, and it can be easier to provide programming to that group when they are all in the same place" (Ban, 2012).

Outside groups can do the most good for inmates when they can easily access the group with minimal disruptions (Pentland & Dwyer, 1985, p. 406; Pentland & Scurfield, 1982, p. 22). As observed by the INVET Dorm Reentry Specialist Alexis Dean, "having all the veterans together in one dorm will make it much easier for programs that come into the facility" (Holmes, 2011). Common features of veterans dormitories similarly put less pressure on correctional staff when outside organizations are forced to make multiple visits due to problems of coordinating visitation schedules for service delivery.

B. Specialized Housing Units for Veterans Represent the Most Cost-Efficient Intervention within a Correctional Institution

Ultimately, the greatest assets to any program targeting veterans in confinement are the correctional staff and the veterans themselves. When Veterans Administration clinicians retreated from the nation's prisons in the 1990s, the New York Department of Correctional Services proved this point by continuing their program even though they had lost the basis for expansive high quality mental health treatment. A key point repeated by sheriffs and superintendents is that the dorms impose little to no cost on taxpayers. As a result, the establishment of these cost-effective measures represents a "strategic justice investment" (DeFloor, 2013, p. 3P).

Thus, the allocation of space is the only true imposition of the program, which may require little more than "shuffling cell assignments to put the veterans together" (Ban, 2012). If there is no space, the creation of a dorm may be delayed, as evident in Las Colinas Women's Jail in Santee, California, which is waiting to institute a female-only veterans dorm for this reason (Repard, 2013, p. B-1). Once space is devoted, all that may be required is the price of "two or three gallons of paint," as Erie County Sheriff Tim Howard boasted upon the opening of his new dorm in October 2013 (Lionti, 2013). Chapter 7's discussion of common attributes of veterans' programs underscores how inmates have the capability of illustrating military murals that serve as additional motivation and veterans' organizations from the community can assist with seals, flags, plaques, and other iconic reminders of military service.

In terms of services, the veterans dorm programs in prisons and jails serve more to coordinate existing resources than to create new ones from scratch. As Florida Department of Corrections Re-entry Administrator Nichole Landrum remarks, "We're using facilities and resources that we already have. Nothing new is being built, and there's no additional staff for this" (Griggs, 2011, p. 1A). After the exodus of Veterans Administration professionals, the New York Department of Correctional Services learned the important lesson that highly trained peer counselors, many of whom provided group and individual counseling to inmates during weekends when clinical staff were gone and even wrote portions of the VRTP manuals, surely had the ability to shoulder greater responsibility. Within VRTP, peer counselors actually make the program "cost efficient" because the program is built on the notion of veterans assisting other veterans (Groveland Correctional Facility, n.d., p. 6).

Beyond this, Cook County Jail Sheriff Thomas J. Dart learned that his jail could capitalize on the productivity, determination, and reliability of the inmates in the veterans' dorm to replace the laundry services contract with veteran labor, saving 13 percent of the costs formerly paid for a two-year 1.5-million-dollar contract (Beggs, 2010). San Diego Sheriff Bill Gore noted a primary reason for instituting the veterans' dorm in San Diego County as the cheapest way to meet the goals of California State's realignment. Because programs targeting veterans substantially reduce recidivism, there is a more certain return to be expected from concentrated services for this population. To Sheriff Gore, dorms for veterans, as opposed to other special populations, are consequently, a "logical first step" for cost effectiveness (Repard, 2013, p. B-1).

C. Specialized Housing Units Permit Veterans to Fully Participate in Their Treatment Without Common Distractions of the General Population

Treatment of trauma requires a survivor to become vulnerable and address very painful experiences in a manner that has been described as "picking off an emotional scab" (*A Matter of Duty*, 2013). When the environment is "as comfortable as possible" in a dorm, "inmates can concentrate on rehabilitation" (Leonard, 2005, p. B1). Inmate Robert Nathaniel, a veteran of the Marine Corps, explains, that a veterans' dorm has a "more relaxed atmosphere" where "[y]ou can concentrate on getting your life in order" (Vitello, 2011, p. 1). For Nathaniel, the opportunity for self-examination was largely attributable to the lack of threats, violence, and gang culture (Vitello, 2011, p. 1).

Evident in the *Program Overview* for the Groveland Correctional Facility's VRTP in New York, inmates are generally reluctant to bring up sensitive topics in the general population. According to Sheriff Randall Liberty, who instituted the Veterans' Cellblock in Kennebec County, Maine, veterans will avoid discussions of sensitive issues even more than other members of the general population: "There is a culture of suffer in silence. You suck it up and take the pain. That's a behavior that serves us well in combat, but when you get out, that mentality ultimately continues to be adopted" (Schroeder, 2013) (see also Chapter 1 discussing aspects of military culture). Confidentiality policies, such as those instituted within the VRTP, assist in developing a more secure environment for the program participants. But, the most important thing is a dorm culture in which the participants embrace the notion that the special setting exists to facilitate healing and better address sensitive issues.

By promoting a trusting environment, veterans are able to open up to each other and share common issues and experiences. They understand the key point that "We are all working together to improve ourselves" (Buyer, 1992). In the observations of VRTP Veterans Guidance Specialists Susan Verbecke and Jim Strollo, the most powerful healing occurs more during informal time off in the dorms when the veterans are talking than during the course of the formal portions of the program (S. M. Verbecke & J. P. Strollo, personal communication, September 16, 2013). Sheriff Liberty makes a similar observation of the veterans' cellblock in Maine: "[O]ne of the reasons for housing veterans together is to encourage them to talk about their trauma, share knowledge about resources and mentor each other on coping mechanisms" (Schroeder, 2013). This was true for Indian Creek, Virginia's veterans' dorm participant Johnny Casiano, who was incarcerated for setting a fire in which he tried to kill himself. The Navy veteran explained, "My greatest fear on getting help was opening up to someone. Today, I'm not afraid to speak to no one. I can open up to anyone and get past that hurt" (Vergakis, 2012).

Veterans are more likely to develop informal supportive relationships because they form teams as an innate part of their military culture. They often search for other veterans in incarcerated settings and "meet[ ] on a regular basis to talk," even in the absence of formalized programs or shared living arrangements (Holmes, 2011) (comments of Re-entry Specialist Alexis Dean). And, within veterans' dormitory settings, they will establish shared responsibilities without being prompted. The nation's Dorm Czar, former Sheriff Darr of Muscogee County, Georgia, observed how once the veterans had their own jail dorm, "They kind of formed their own self-help group— that's really what this is" (Kamal, 2013). To create a "dorm culture" that was conducive to optimal rehabilitation, Darr's jail implemented a phased approach, in which administrators initially populated the dorm with Vietnam veterans, who could more readily appreciate the opportunity for peace and quiet and waited about two months before they opened the dorm to younger Iraq and Afghanistan veterans (N. Richardson, personal communication, December 4, 2013). The phased approach made a significant difference.

Drawing on aspects of military culture that promote teamwork and shared responsibilities is especially vital to recovery from combat trauma because these features promote the sense of community and trust that are often absent following the traumatic event. Even if discussions of trauma can be triggering for inmates in dorms, it is a necessary part of re-experiencing that can constructively address repressed emotion (*A Matter of Duty*, 2013) (Comments of Sheriff Randall Liberty). Such discussions are akin to a form of narrative therapy, which is valuable when it enables a trauma survivor to reappraise past events in recognition of his or her human dignity (Schauer & Schauer, 2010, p. 405). Importantly,

> [T]rauma tears the social fabric and the tissue of family life and saps the individual of a sense of continuity, finally destroying the sense that one is, after all, a part of a larger spiritual community. Linkage in human community is made in large measure through language. In this way, telling your story to a compassionate listener, someone who can truly listen—which means being able to hold part of the hurt—is how the self-narrative comes into play in the healing process. (Chalsma, 1998, p. 203)

Veterans' dorms similarly have components that are capable of treating underlying moral injury, which often exists apart from traumatic life-threat combat experiences. Research shows that, apart from a comprehensive clinical approach, an alternative treatment that is effective in addressing morally injurious experiences is "exposure to corrective life experiences," which "entails increasing the accessibility of positive judgments about the self by doing good deeds and positive judgments about the world by seeing others do good deeds, as well as giving and receiving care and love" (Litz et al., 2009, p. 701). For all these reasons, a dorm that concentrates communities of like-minded veterans maximizes opportunities for offline discussions with peers, which are often even more meaningful than formalized programming with clinicians.

D. Specialized Housing Units Enable Better Detection of Behavioral Changes and Needs by Correctional Staff and Fellow Participants

Dvoskin and Spiers (2004) make a persuasive case that correctional professionals provide far more meaningful "treatment" of offenders with mental illness than mental health providers are capable of giving. This is basically because clinicians have only limited opportunities to assess the inmates and correctional officers are able to observe them around-the-clock. On this theory, correctional officers and facility staff "play a central role in the care of psychiatric patients" (Appelbaum et al., 2001, p. 1344). They often provide unparalleled services because acts as simple as listening to and talking with inmates and demonstrating "basic human respect and concern" help to alleviate mental health symptoms (Dvoskin & Spiers, 2004, p. 47). These practices also serve to augment "the most therapeutic intervention . . . of clear boundaries and consequences" (Appelbaum et al. 2001, p. 1344). Within some veterans' dorms, the correctional officers participate more directly in therapeutic activities, such as Shift Supervisor Sergeant Alan Gregory, who teaches a very popular class in fly fishing tackles to assist PTSD afflicted inmates in maintaining a focus on a task (Schroeder, 2013).

In practically all veterans' dorms, the correctional officers and sheriff's deputies who supervise the participants frequently interface with mental health professionals as active members of a treatment team, which surely contributes to any clinical care the inmates ultimately receive from mental health providers. In the COVER program, for example, all of the correctional officers are considered to be equal members of the clinical treatment team (S. Schwartz, L. Levitas, & I. McCray, personal communication, October 15, 2012). Not only are correctional staff the first to respond, but they are often the first to help diagnose (Appelbaum et al., 2001, p. 1345). Beyond this, because the dormitories have concentrated individuals with many of the same types of needs, correctional professionals are able to detect negative symptomatology much sooner than they would in a general population raising more immediate safety concerns relating to non-veteran inmates (Salahi, 2012).

E. Specialized Housing Units for Veterans
Increase Officer Safety and Limit Officer Stress

Regardless of differences in veterans dorm themes or military service experience of correctional officers who staff the dorms, most programs unanimously report that the dorms are the safest, cleanest, and most positive places to be in the facility. Much of this owes to the inmates' increased levels of responsibility for the success of the program. In Florida, for example, the dorm may not be "perfect, but even on the worst days, it is civil, which is why everybody is careful with the rules" (Alvarez, 2011, p. A14). Kennebec County Cellblock member Anthony Gerard, an Army veteran with two Purple Hearts, explains, "Nobody wants to get in a fight. Nobody wants to get in trouble. We all have something to lose and the only reason we have something to lose is because they're giving us the opportunity to get our lives back" (Schroeder, 2013).

Muscogee County Jail Veterans Dorm graduate Blake Chester remarks, "It was still a jail, of course, but it was comforting" (Kamal, 2013). Such peace behind bars has a definite effect on correctional staff because, when inmates experience less symptoms of mental illness, correctional staff members experience less stress (Appelbaum et al., 2001, p. 1344). Unsurprisingly, in those institutions that do not use a rotational staff plan, the veterans dorms are places where correctional officers often volunteer to go (e.g., S. M. Verbecke & J. P. Strollo, personal communication, September 16, 2013; San Diego Sheriff's Department, n.d.).

In Florida's Santa Rosa Correctional Institution, Chief of Security, Major Torrey Johnson, watched in amazement as the fifty residents of the veterans' annex participated in a coordinated formation within the facility (Griggs, 2011, p. 1A). He noted the pride and determination in their faces and commented how it would simply be "unheard of" to coordinate cooperative inmates in the general population in the same manner (Griggs, 2011, p. 1A). Officers at that dorm "rarely ever have to raise their voice" in this environment, which makes it a pleasure to work there (Griggs, 2011, p. 1A). Given the threats that correctional officers face on a daily basis, there is great reward from the peace, tranquility, and positivity in veterans' dorms. Virginia dorm participant Brian Pitts notes how an environment populated by "a group of veterans who underwent military training is a stark contrast from . . . the general population where inmates are young and 'bouncing off the walls'" (Kamal, 2013). In this light, it rings particularly true that officer health and wellbeing is thus directly related to that of the inmates they supervise (Dvoskin & Spiers, 2004).

F. Corrections Officers Can More Easily Alter Common Practices in Specialized Housing Units to Limit Retrauma of Veterans, as Opposed to the General Population

Combat veterans suffering from posttraumatic stress are particularly susceptible to factors in confinement that can aggravate their condition and trigger stress responses. Loud and unpredictable noises, bright persistent lights, and crowding in close quarters are some inherent features of prison and jail that pose recurring problems for veterans. The lack of a safe place to participate in relaxation exercises is one of the major impediments to effective PTSD treatment in confined settings (Sigafoos, 1994).

Residential dormitories provide a location where it is possible to retool environmental factors on a small enough scale not to disrupt the general population but to make a meaningful difference. As recognized in the 1920s, additional liberties to move more freely with fewer impediments in living areas can help address common readjustment difficulties faced by incarcerated veterans (Casey, 1923). Many veterans require even more adaptive measures. In the New York Department of Corrections VRTP, correctional officers have modified the way they take count at night by shining lights at the veterans' feet rather than in their eyes (S. M. Verbecke & J. P. Strollo, personal communication, September 16, 2013). Similarly, at the Kennebec County Veterans Cellblock, correctional officers manually open and close the doors to prevent loud machinegun-like sounds normally produced by automatic locks on doors (*A Matter of Duty*, 2013).

The dorm participants value these attempts to surpass business as usual, as emphasized in the comments of Veterans Cellblock participant Joseph Harmon regarding correctional officers' efforts: "They don't just barge in on people, knowing we have needs and PTSD. They have caution and try to show respect and we give it to them in return" (Schroeder, 2013). Veterans dorms also address difficulties in being vulnerable when they offer a secure place in which to conduct relaxation exercises without the fear of attack (Sigafoos, 1994). This is a major component of the holistic approach adopted within the San Francisco COVER Pod (Schwartz & Levitas, 2011). Because the dorm environment is generally a place where participants recognize that they are working to mitigate individual stressors in their lives, the inmates, themselves, make a special effort to create an environment conducive to therapeutic intervention and self-improvement. In New York's VRTP, observers noted the sense of community in the dormitory was most evident in the fact that participants did not feel the need to safeguard their personal belongings due to a high level of trust (Buyer, 1992). As a Maine Veterans' Cellblock member observes, "It's better cohesion. We know everyone is stressed out so we try to look out for each other" (Schroeder, 2013).

G. The Jail Is Located Near a Military Installation, Which Increases Contact with Active Duty Service Members and Veterans

The San Diego County Jail's Veterans Module is located close to Camp Pendleton Marine Base and a booming military community. Similarly, the Muscogee County Jail is mere miles from sprawling Fort Benning, Georgia. In both locations, the sheriffs recognized that the increased numbers of active personnel and military veterans necessitated the development of a targeted approach to incarceration (Kamal, 2013; Repard, 2013, p. B-1). This does not suggest that veterans cannot be found in large numbers elsewhere.

Other research has established that Oregon county jails confined over 20,000 veterans between 2010 and 2012, with near doubling of this population in Salem's Marion County Jail between 2007 and 2011 (Brown et al., 2013, pp. 15–16). While large cities without military bases also boast larger military populations, the development of veterans' dorms in military communities is a proactive move. In light of the ever-intensifying reduction of the active Armed Forces following withdrawal from Iraq and Afghanistan, former Muscogee County Sheriff Darr estimated "a perfect storm of things that are coming" when he developed its veterans' dorm, noting, "you need to try to get ahead of a problem before the problem gets ahead of you" (Kamal, 2013). Because there will undoubtedly be an increase of veterans who become entangled in the criminal justice system as a result of the latest drawdown in forces, veterans dorms represent a vital precautionary measure to promote safety and targeted treatment.

Concluding Remarks

In New York's longest running specialized housing units for veterans, graduates of the dorms have substantially less recidivism than members of the general population, including veterans who are housed in the general population. This result is common to newer programs that have only recently created dorms, such as Cook County Jail's recidivism rate of less than 2 percent among the 161 veterans who participated in the program (Votello, 2011). Sheriffs and wardens who have instituted dorms have capitalized on veterans' common cultural attributes, which make them ideally suited for programs that restore a sense of purpose, dignity, and commitment to a cause greater than themselves.

Importantly, the more peaceful, orderly, and positive environment that results from a return to the realities of better times benefits correctional officers and staff by giving them refuge from the more common conditions in the general population. With the recognition that veterans dormitories also provide a more disciplined workforce for prison and jail industries, it is possible to direct these energies at budget deficits in the same manner as the "clean start" laundry program in Cook County.

Of course, there will still be inmates and correctional officers who do not fancy the idea of a specialized dorm for veteran inmates. Not all veterans will desire to enter or remain in a veterans' dorm, especially if they are in denial that they have issues to be addressed or perceive it that they will be forced to revisit their traumatic experiences or such tasks will be too painful to endure. Further, some officers may be hostile to the idea. In Muscogee County, Georgia, the veterans jail dorm opened without assignment of specially designated or hand-picked deputies. Rather, it became the responsibility of the squad that was responsible for the building in which the dorm operated. As an unexpected consequence, some of the guards who were veterans became offended at the idea of placing the military seals in the dorm and honoring the service of inmates who had committed crimes. Some responded with the perspective, "I served in the military, but I did not commit any offenses," and, as a result of this attitude, were perceptively harsher in their treatment of the veterans (N. Richardson, personal communication, December 4, 2013). In one instance, an officer was reassigned because of his conflicting philosophy.

Overall, however, these types of responses prove to be exceptions rather than the normative experience among correctional officers. Such experiences emphasize the importance of carefully planning the initiative and learning about inmate and staff perspectives before launching the program. The following chapter puts these considerations in perspective by addressing common considerations in planning, including common challenges and responses to criticism over special programs for veterans in the criminal justice system.

At the outset of this chapter, the question was posed whether purpose-driven veterans' dorms are the counterparts to problem-solving veterans courts. In fact, jail and prison programs may be even more vital and necessary given the fact that they will inevitably house those inmates who do not qualify for diversion from incarceration, for any number of reasons. To continue the analogy, the lesson learned by veterans treatment court Judge Steven Manley of Santa Clara, California, is entirely applicable here: "I've already seen young people coming back from Iraq and Afghanistan into our court system, and the very worst you can do is ignore them because these things don't go away" (Stock et al., 2012). The criminally involved veteran population is, after all, one in the same.

Appendix A

VRTP Participation Contract

> DO NOT SIGN THIS CONTRACT UNTIL YOU HAVE READ IT COMPLETELY,
> UNDERSTAND IT, AND AGREE TO ABIDE BY IT.

Name _____ Din#_____ Date_____

GROVELAND VETERANS PROGRAM
CLIENT PARTIOCIPATION CONTRACT

In exchange for the opportunity to participate in the Veterans Program, I agree to the following while an active program participant:

✓ I will make a sincere effort to change my behavior through the therapeutic process. This means I personally commit myself to active program involvement, which includes:

  ★ Being on time to all program activities.
  ★ Active participation in class (to include staying awake).
  ★ Handing in all written assignments, class work and homework, on time.
  ★ No absences, unless on a valid facility recognized call out.
      (I will return to group after the call out is complete)
  ★ Excessive tardiness for medical reasons may result in being removed from the dorm program until you are able to satisfactorily participate in program activities.

✓ **In order to fully participate in the group process I am willing to honestly discuss both my instant offen[s]e and the circumstances that may have influenced my past decisions. I understand that the group may question me on many issues.**

✓ I commit myself to the development of a written personal growth and goal oriented Relapse Prevention/Recovery Program, including a definite plan for re-entry into society. I will complete and turn in to the Counselor a Post Release Portfolio.

✓ I understand that the following behaviors may constitute removal from the program:

  ★ Physical contact with another participant (fighting, etc.)
  ★ Stealing from other members of the dorm/program
  ★ Verbal threats towards other members of the program
  ★ Excessive Interventions for negative behavior

✓ I agree to maintain strict confidentiality. This includes not discussing issues which are part of the therapeutic process with any one outside of the group/program.

✓
✓ I understand that the dorm I will be living on is maintained as a "Therapeutic Setting." I will be introduced to the rules of this dorm when I move onto it and I agree to abide by these rules. I also understand that Correction Officers have the final say in any matter and/or discrepancy on the housing unit.
Suspension, or termination, from the program can be for bre[a]ch of contract in any way. This will be made at the discretion of the Program Correction's Counselors, Director and Assistant Directors.

✓ Programs outside of the VRTP will not excuse you from the responsibility of the VRTP obligations (homework etc.). These programs will <u>only</u> be done with the permission of the VRTP Correction Counselor.

✓ **Any refusal of a state mandated program (A.R.T., A.S.A.T., Sex Offender) will be grounds for removal from VRTP.**

✓ **I understand that the Aftercare segment of the program is not automatic. My progress, attitude, commitment, and overall behavior will be assessed by the Program Counselor. The Program Counselor reserves the right to deny Aftercare for the overall benefit of the program without further explanation.**

✓ I have read and fully understand and agree to abide by the rules, standards, policies and procedures of the Department of Correctional Services Veterans Program. I understand that placement in the program is voluntary and that while I can be removed from the program for any violation of this contract I also have the option to leave on my own with no negative consequences to me for this decision.

✓ My signature on this contract indicates the validity of my military status. Any false statement in regards to my military status will subject me to disciplinary action by the security staff.

Witness _____

Date _____

Veteran _____

Date _____

SOBC _____

Mr. Strollo: OBC _____

Appendix B

VRTP Confidentiality Policy

<u>Confidentiality Policy</u>

The intent of this policy is to address **sensitive personal information** which may be disclosed in a group, class, or shared with another vet "in confidence." It does not apply to issues of lateness, tardiness, class participation, quality of insight displayed b[y] participants, or even the identification of so-called "core" issues which may be discussed among cadre with the sole intent of helping the participant make better therapeutic progress.

It **does** apply to the following:

- Any criminal behavior disclosed by the participant which might be used to deny him release.
- The nature of the IO (Instant Offense) – or of prior IOs.
- Personal and sensitive family issues; including names, addresses, etc.
- Potentially sensitive personal issues (such as being the victim of childhood sexual abuse, certain aspects of past military experiences (such as behaviors during combat), personal financial or residential issues, etc.)
- A good guide is "common sense." If the disclosure of this information could be harmful, then it should be kept confidential!

*No matter where you heard this information (class, group, dorm, in the yard with other participants) it is **inappropriate** to share this information with others! A good question to ask yourself before passing it on:* "Could this be harmful to a fellow veteran and program participant?"

BASIC GUIDELINES

1. What is stated in group stays in group.

2. Exceptions are made in the following situations:

   - Violence or threats of violence – or similar issues of personal safety
   - Suicide threats
   - Intent to violate major program rules (i.e., drug use or possession in the vets dorm, etc.)
   - Cadre may discuss participants' therapeutic issues—in an appropriate setting – when the entire intent is to help the participant make better therapeutic progress.
   [3]. If there is an issue of safety (violence, threats of violence, suicide, etc.) the first step is to discuss it with any of the following:

   - Cadre, Assistant Director, Director

They will attempt to deal with the problem on a person-to-person level. Certain issues, such as safety or violence, may be determined to be a clear violation of program rules. Under those circumstances, the individual may be removed from the program or the facility by the civilian staff.

4. Certain issues may involve referrals to Mental Health Staff. If appropriate, the permission of the participant should be sought before such a referral is made.

5. If you violate confidentiality, you may be subject to punishment. Depending on the nature of your violation, you may even be removed from the program or facility.

Appendix C

VRTP Peer Duties
V.R.T.P.
DORM POSITIONS AND RESPONSIBILITIES

1) <u>Program Director</u>: Oversees curriculum, scheduling, intakes of new participants. Interacts with outside Veterans Affairs Personnel. Manages staff up to 10 facilitators and 2 assistant directors. Works closely with Department of Corrections Counselors in all aspects of the program management. Involved with crisis intervention and individual peer – counseling. Facilitating classes using both cognitive and confrontational methods.

2) <u>Assistant Director</u>: Works closely with the training of facilitators, and working with the facilitators in groups with participants that are resistant to the material, the process, and/or the program on the whole. Works to keep the facilitators on schedule. Works closely with the Corrections Counselors to work with participants that are having problems adjusting to the program/dorm. Involved with crisis intervention and individual peer – counseling. Facilitating classes using both cognitive and confrontational methods.

3) <u>Office Clerk</u>: Works not only in the office but also may be assigned duties that are outside of office at the request of the Program Director, Assistant Director or Vet's Counselors. In office duties, include intakes of new participants, updating information files on the computer. Maintains daily attendance records for both groups and individuals. Edit and update current program manuals as assigned by the Program Director and/or Assistant Director. Responsible for developing and maintaining an office inventory. General upkeep of office appearance.

4) <u>Facilitator</u>: Act in the role of group leader for the therapeutic process. There are at least two facilitators assigned to a group. They also act as role models in the dorm setting, and make themselves available to the participants for answering questions and providing guidance.

5) <u>Intervention Team Leader</u>: It is the Team Leader's job to keep a written log of interventions for review by the counselors. IT is at the discretion of the Team Leader to address some behaviors through mediation rather than intervention. The Team Leader reports to the Program Director the incident and the decision of the intervention or mediation for review.

6) <u>Intervention Team Member</u>: Acts to address a participant[']s negative behavior by reviewing the incident that brought the behavior to light, and if necessary issuing a learning experience. The intervention team also acts as mediation in disputes between participants. . . . The intervention team consists of at least five members and the Team Leader.

7) <u>Community Relations Team Member</u>: Act as liaison between the program participants and the Program Director. By listening to suggestions and hearing complaints this team is responsible for smooth day to day interactions.

8) <u>Dorm Superintendent</u>: Informs program participants of the rotational duties to be performed. Holds participants who may have given any extra details accountable for [their] completion.

9) <u>Television Monitor</u>: Plans and writes up a T.V. schedule. Takes requests from program participants and makes sure that no inappropriate programs are viewed.

10) <u>Welcoming Committee</u>: Meet the new arrivals in the dorm. Introduces the rules and the contract. Answers questions that the new participants may have. Makes introductions to the senior cadre.

Chapter 10

CONCLUDING REMARKS: URGENCY IN PREPARATION FOR THE COMING "STORM" OF VETERAN OFFENDERS

I. The Small but Significant Trend

Sheriffs in communities with large veteran populations agree that they have only just begun to see a growing trend of offenders with military experience. Part of their concern relates to the downsizing of the force that has occurred after withdrawal from Iraq and Afghanistan. Additional complications arise from the recent enforcement of a policy that forces service members with health conditions out of the military if they are medically non-deployable for twelve months (Sisk, 2018). This measure alone could potentially lead to the involuntary separation of 286,000 military personnel with continuing healthcare needs (Sisk, 2018).

In a time of corresponding budget cuts within corrections, it is only natural to ask the key question, where will funding and resources come from to develop targeted programs for veteran inmates? Fortunately, the collective experience of the various wardens and sheriffs who have implemented veterans' dorms signals how veterans' programming is extremely cost efficient, with few demands other than commitment from the staff and the veterans to adjust living arrangements. In a 1989 *Corrections Today* article, Anthony Swetz, Jr. examined various programs within prisons for incarcerated veterans—even without the benefit of the new data from over two dozen new veterans dormitories, and concluded:

> **"Even if resources from outside the correctional system disappear, a strong continuing commitment within the correctional system can effectively continue this necessary work"** (Swetz, 1989, p. 186).

289

Today, despite some speculation that the era of the Operation Iraqi Freedom/Operation Enduring Freedom hero has come to an end with the gradual strain of ongoing warfare, the groundswell of public support for wounded warriors provides even greater hopes program development and program sustenance than Mr. Swetz could have anticipated prior to September 11th. If the exponential growth of veterans' treatment courts and expansive funding of other community diversion programs are not enough evidence of abundant community resources for this purpose, consider the growing number of legal services programs established by state bar associations, private law firms offering pro bono services, and law school clinical programs (Berenson, 2009), some of which operated at local VA medical centers.

Evident in the experience of confinement facilities with both self-governing inmate veteran groups and staff-initiated programs, all prisons and jails have the two most essential commodities for program success: (1) other veterans who can offer peer support and revive the values of a committed squad (Sigafoos, 1994); and (2) correctional staff who are either veterans themselves, or who have been trained in crisis intervention training with a veteran component. The greatest obstacles to program development are not fiscally based, but statistical and ideological.

A. The Illusion of Evidence-Based Programming

While there is a preoccupation with evidence-based approaches for virtually every correctional program, most of the current veterans dorm programs emerged from necessity in the absence of readily available data. Sheriffs and wardens consulted with existing programs, suggested modifications, and conducted trial runs of their programs mainly to see whether inmates would volunteer for participation before implementation. The implementation process was practical rather than scientific or academic. The suggestion that correctional professionals must be paralyzed until researchers can answer the most challenging theoretical questions about the nexus between offending and mental health conditions or specific types of treatment and reduction in recidivism ignores the reality of treatment programs in corrections settings. Jails and prisons cannot be held to the same standards as a community-based PTSD program. Reasonable goals for "correctional treatment" revolve around minimizing symptoms, ensuring that veterans can share their experiences, and help each other in a safe environment, and providing psycho-educational tools to detect and avoid their stress triggers (Dvoskin & Spiers, 2004).

Correctional professionals can meet most of these goals merely by reassigning veterans to a designated space, painting the walls, modifying staff rotations, and inviting community organizations to visit at a regular time to share information. Prior chapters provide lessons to help any prison or jail staff select specific features of a veteran-specific program based on the themes and objectives most suitable to a particular facility's unique correctional culture.

B. The Trouble with Generalized Statistics

This book has avoided a litany of unknowable statistics on the number of veterans with combat and operational stress injuries or the number of incarcerated veterans, and the effectiveness of veterans' treatment courts or dormitories in reducing recidivism. Such quest for a generalizable figure that applies to all-similarly situated offenders is futile. Certainly, some studies of smaller population subsets might be relevant for a given town, military installation, medical center, or correctional facility. While, perhaps, 15 percent of *all* veterans who deployed to combat may suffer from PTSD, many more will suffer from other mental conditions that do not meet the full diagnostic criteria. Furthermore, individuals who spent their deployed time in a fortified base without exposure to intense combat scenarios are likely to have the same PTSD rates as military members who never even left the United States (Castro, 2009, p. 252).

Contrarily, service members who engage in repeated missions "outside the wire" in high-intensity combat conditions are likely to suffer PTSD at rates of 50 percent, almost to the point where a PTSD diagnosis is the norm, rather than the exception (Castro, 2009, p. 252). Yet, if a service member was forced to act in a manner that violated deeply held moral beliefs and codes—say, for example, destroying an incriminating report of detainee abuse on orders from a commander—even if the service member never steps a foot outside the comforts of his or her heavily-fortified forward operating base, there may be an equivalent risk of developing PTSD as someone who experienced life threats in combat.

Along these same lines, the fact that a given prison program had a 9 percent recidivism rate hardly promises a similar result in a different institution. Just as a host of factors might result in greater incidences of arrest and incarceration, others might produce even better reductions. The VRSS program promises to improve on one of the most troublesome datasets to date. While the efforts of the Bureau of Justice Statistics have certainly provided various snapshots in time, many have treated these limited frames as definitive indications of reality. Until December 2015, researchers continued to apply the 2004 estimate of Iraq and Afghanistan veterans constituting only 4 percent of the state and federal prison inmates as though it applied to the prison population years later, despite the fact that the wars intensified over a decade thereafter infusing a host of veterans into the criminal justice system who survived multiple tours, extended combat deployments, and stop-loss orders, which forced many to serve beyond the initial term of their contractual service obligation. As of 2011–2012, an updated estimate for the period 2011 to 2012 placed Iraq and Afghanistan (and Operation New Dawn) veterans at 13 percent in prisons and 25 percent in jails, the percentage change representing a monumental increase from the earlier 2004 estimates (Bronson et al., 2015).

For a host of reasons, citations to the 2007 Bureau of Justice and Statistics Report are questionable, outdated, and cannot be taken at face value. Professor Brown and his colleagues further demonstrate that jails and prisons may very well be experiencing micro-doublings of their veteran inmates in the short span of a year while new national years-long studies are in the works (Brown et al., 2013). And, even back in 2007, following the release of the report, others had reason to doubt it because the sample population used for the study was represented only "1 percent of all state and federal prison inmates" (Gambill, 2011). The December 2015 Special Report on *Veterans in Prison and Jail, 2011–12* (Bronson et al., 2015) likely garners similar concerns given the universal problems affecting all studies of incarcerated veterans.

For all of these reasons, generalized statistics provide little help in the case of a given institution. Reliance on generalized statistics without considering individual cases runs the risk of faulty and inaccurate conclusions. VRSS is a helpful tool in identifying veterans so long as jails and prisons agree to use the program. However, some scholars suggest that there may be reasons why an elected corrections head may desire not to know the true number of veterans. As Professor William Brown observes, reluctance comes either from the position that "veteran status information is not a critical factor in the day-to-day operation of their jails" or that collection of such data "might be politically damaging" because it could suggest a lack of support for the troops (2008, pp. 7–8).

There is an important lesson from the U.K.'s recent examination of incarcerated veteran offenders. There, it is estimated that between 4 percent and 6 percent of the inmate population has prior military service. Whatever the actual number of incarcerated veterans is in the U. K., that number is considered to be "significant." Similar to the U.S., even if the figure is less than 10 percent in American facilities, as is currently estimated, veterans may actually be the largest subset of incarcerated adult male offenders when considered by former occupation (Howard League on Penal Reform, 2011, p. 17). With or without VRSS, correctional professionals must delve deeper than merely the number of veterans in their facilities to understand the needs and dynamics in their own veteran inmate populations.

C. The Nation's Gratitude Is a Poor Justification for Urgency

Supporting a shared vision for the institution of a veteran-specific correctional program may be difficult as opposition may arise even from staff members who are veterans. The VRSS program may assist in identifying veterans, but the basis for targeting them for treatment intervention must be more than their confinement in the facility. In considering objections and responses to veterans treatment courts, Chapter 5 identified three basic reasons, which included: (1) the fact that military service and combat place veterans at greater risk of sustaining the types of mental health conditions that put them in conflict with the law; (2) the fact that veterans are culturally disposed to being reluctant to share their experiences or needs with anyone except peers who have undergone similar life challenges; and (3) because they have earned statutorily conferred benefits by virtue of their service that not only promise to improve the quality of their lives upon release, but which simultaneously free up resources for nonveteran inmates' pressing needs when federal benefits are used.

These collective responses signal bases in cost efficiency and moral obligation to help veterans reintegrate back into society in at least as good a position as they were prior to entry into military service. As persuasive as these reasons may be, they may not amount to the sense of urgency that is required for sustained efforts. In San Francisco, for example, a Vietnam Veteran named Ron Perez, who was instrumental in developing Swords to Plowshares, lobbied for specialized treatment programming since 1975. In 2010, the COVER program finally resulted after more than a generation of persistent appeal to these same moral tenets. Likewise, after pointing to the success of New York's Veterans Residential Therapeutic Program, Ohio veterans' advocates pushed for the development of a similar incarceration-based program in 2001. The program finally came about in the form of a jail dormitory that was unveiled in 2013—over a decade later.

The major problem with gratitude and thanks for service is that these factors do not convey the sense of urgency that rightfully surrounds the issue of incarcerated veteran programming. Heightened suicide risk, increased veteran unemployment, the mounting ejection of medically unfit service members, the effects of multiple deployments on military families, and, most importantly, the stifling influence of 38 C.F.R. § 17.38's bar on inpatient or outpatient care to incarcerated veterans, threatens a "perfect storm" of havoc for those correctional professionals who fail to act (Brown et al., 2013).

Those sheriffs close to military installations who have instituted veterans' dorms in bustling military communities—El Paso County, Colorado; San Diego County, California; and Muscogee County, Georgia—have begun to see the first bolts of lightning and rupture of thunder in the distance. Yet, when the storm arrives, it will move beyond their jurisdictions tracing the patterns in which discharged veterans will inevitably migrate. Consequently, these remarks conclude with a different, more accurate paradigm than morality, sympathy, and gratitude in explaining the *imperative* to institute veterans' programs within prisons and jails—immediately.

D. The Precautionary Public Safety Mandate

Many of the key factors discussed in the prior chapters of this book highlight the nature of combat and operational stress injuries and violent or criminal behavior. While public planners may never be able to accurately estimate the number of veterans with combat and operational stress injuries who will commit criminal offenses as a result of their symptoms, it is fairly evident that there will inevitably be a population of offenders. We can also safely conclude that this unknown, but substantial, population is an extremely small fraction of discharged veterans, a very small fraction of discharged veterans who have served in combat, and still a relatively small proportion of combat veterans with a PTSD diagnosis.

Consequently, in threat-mitigation planning and hazard preparedness, it is appropriate to consider the risk of veteran offending as a "low probability, high consequence" event (Seamone, 2013a). After all, on that relatively rare occasion when the veterans do commit service-related offenses, their training and potentially combat experience, can easily make the symptomatic veterans' criminal conduct of a more significant magnitude (see Chapters 4 and 5). Since 9-11 and an increasing number of natural disasters and international disease threats, disaster planners have developed certain key principles to guide them in responding to other "low probability, high consequence," events, including: infectious disease, transborder forest fires, terrorist attacks, space debris, or asteroid strikes with the earth, and the eruption of volcanoes (Seamone, 2002; Seamone, 2003; Seamone, 2004).

Although it exists in various policy contexts, the precautionary principle is most evident in public law and policy relating to environmental-threat mitigation. It is here that the Rio Declaration on Environment and Development stands as the most vivid example:

> **"Where there are threats of serious and irreversible damage, lack of full scientific certainty shall not be used as a reason for postponing cost-effective measures to prevent environmental degradation" (United Nations Conference on the Environment and Development, 1922, Principle 15).**

The precautionary principle arises most often when the threat is one that is not easily predicted but is certain to be devastating when it strikes. This principle is not only a hallmark of international law, but one that is evident in U.S. emergency response provisions like Homeland *Security Presidential Directive Number 5,* the *National Response Plan,* and the *National Incident Management System,* which mandate that local, state, and federal government entities must work together to develop effective coordination and response plans, regardless of the nature or size of a community threat (Seamone, 2004).

Criminally involved combat traumatized veterans are in the same category of mitigation responsibility as other low, probability, high consequence threats—like transborder forest fires, the spread of infectious disease, and terrorist attacks. While we know that, as a conservative estimate, roughly 20 percent of combat veterans of the Iraq and Afghanistan wars suffer from PTSD, it will always be the case that each individual veteran will experience symptoms in a personalized way. Because we cannot predict precisely which veterans' symptomology will place them in conflict with the law, the criminal justice system becomes quite reactive to the problem. We do, however, have an idea of the great number of ways that PTSD and other combat and operational stress injuries contribute to criminal behavior (see Chapter 4).

Psychiatrist Hal Wortzel and his colleagues have applied the precautionary principle to incarcerated veterans as a basis to institute targeted suicide prevention interventions for this population. Recognizing that veterans have a higher likelihood of suicide and that incarcerated inmates also have a higher likelihood of suicide, they draw the reasonable inference that incarcerated veterans are a group with elevated suicide risk based on the cumulative effects of the dual status, demanding immediate intervention even though it remains impossible to calculate and quantify the associated risk. In support of this policy mandate, they use the following depiction in Figure 33.

Even though there is inherent uncertainty regarding the exact size of the population of at-risk veterans, and though it is not possible to estimate when suicidal acts will occur, the magnitude of the risk is great enough to warrant action, and these planners have accordingly suspended the requirement for more certain information due to the likelihood of significant harm.

In the case of targeted programs for incarcerated veterans with combat and operational stress injuries and the risk of recidivism, the precautionary principle is even more instructive, though it is worth noting that specialized housing and other measures will have an impact on suicide prevention as well. In the most general sense, emergency response personnel have obligations to analyze the nature of a threat and then determine the threshold for fiscal and other mitigation efforts. This is often described as a "limit of intolerability" (Bailey, 2011, p. 139) or the "community risk tolerance" limit (Canton, 2007, p. 140).

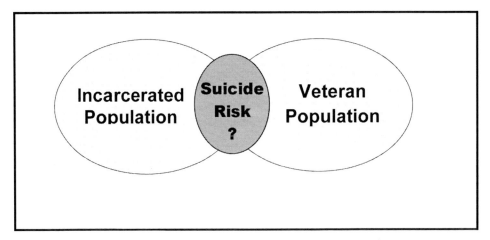

Figure 33. Source: Wortzel et al. (2009, p. 87, fig. 1).

Increasingly, in applying the precautionary principle, emergency managers employ an actuarial perspective. While the mechanics of this process are complex, the analysis usually begins with a hazard profile. Figure 34, below, shares a very basic one. By juxtaposing some facts, we know about veteran criminality, such as weapons-related violence, suicide, and tolls on

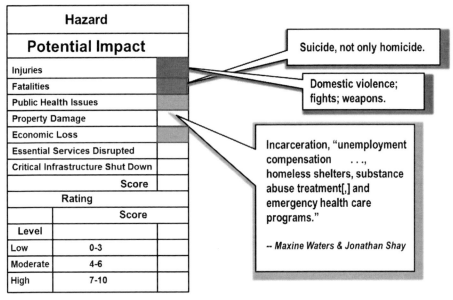

Figure 34. Thresholds for Risk Mitigation Evident in "All Hazards" Homeland Security Directives. Source: Canton (2007, p. 141, fig. 5.7); Seamone (2013a).

public services, the profile for criminally involved veterans suggests a significant risk level and need for concerted action and policy under any view.

Here, it is unnecessary to conduct the full actuarial analysis because the point of the hazard profile is simply to highlight the fact that no national agency has overtly addressed the problem of criminally involved veterans as a hazard in this manner, even though it would be quite reasonable and informative to do so. If such an attempt were made, the issue would impose definite duties rather than sympathy or unwritten appeals to patriotism. Evident in the hazard profile, correctional professionals must never forget what makes combat veterans different from other inmates and what similarly makes them a chief public safety concern: Their training and experience being lethal with rifles, bayonets, or bare hands. As British General Rose remarked, "No other group in society is required either to kill other human beings, or expressly sacrifice their lives for the nation" (Gleave, 2010, p. 19). Veterans with untreated mental health conditions, therefore, invoke an entirely different risk dynamic.

Returning to Wortzel's illustration of this hazardous interaction of known converging factors, each with independent risks that become additive in combination, the lack of veteran-focused interventions can be expressed through Figure 35's visual. For those veterans with combat and operational stress injuries who receive standardized criminal justice responses as a result of misconduct related to their condition, the compounded stress of criminal justice runs a substantial risk of exacerbating symptoms and increasing recidivism.

Sir General Rose's quote on unique characteristics of military veterans trained in lethal ways is apt to mention the experience of criminality among

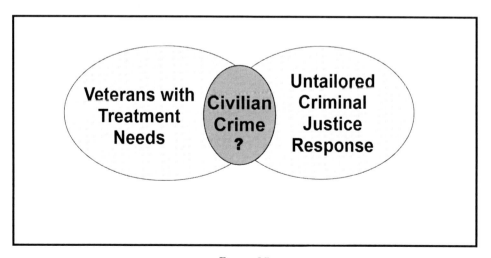

Figure 35.

untreated veterans of British campaigns. Estimates in the U. K. Parliament revealed that more veterans of the Falklands War and Gulf War had committed suicide following those campaigns than had been lost to battle in both instances (Renwick, 1999). Even more concerning, there was significant societal cost borne by those veterans who occupied Northern Ireland:

> As a consequence of not receiving any help for their rehabilitation back into Civvie Street, or treatment for conditions like PTSD, many of these ex-soldiers found themselves without a job, homeless, and often drinking in excess and/or taking drugs. A course that frequently led to trouble, violence and jail. Since 1969, probably more deaths and injuries have been inflicted on the civilian population in Britain by our returning soldiers than by IRA bombings. Like the US after Vietnam, the war has come home. (Renwick, 1999, p. 103)

The risk of inaction by our correctional professionals is simply too great. In recognition of this dynamic, Medal of Honor recipient Roger Donlon has urged veterans to obtain help not simply because it will alleviate symptoms, but because these particular untreated conditions essentially perpetuate the enemy's hostilities back home within America's neighborhoods, living rooms, and bedrooms. Donlon's public service announcement warns, "Don't let the enemy defeat you *at home*" (Donlon, 2010). If veterans are untreated and incarceration worsens their conditions, the surest victims will be the families and communities to which they return.

Secondary Traumatic Stress, which transmits combat trauma to family members, after all, has been called the "signature psychological effect" on military families, even where the traumatized service member is not physically abusive or violent (Herzog & Everson, 2011, p. 196; Seamone, 2012, pp. 326–327). When effective treatment is withheld for this small population, the magnitude of the risk reaches thus reaches future generations imposing a certain mandate beyond traditional motivations that have often failed to produce necessary urgency.

E. Conclusion

It is the author's hope that this book has provided the reader with the tools necessary to tackle the challenging but rewarding task of addressing the incarcerated veteran's special needs. The editors of the *Prison World* provided important insights when they emphasized how the new trend of institutional-based outreach to veterans (separate from the Veterans Administration) achieved an important service to the public, aside from just the veteran or just the institution ("Editor's note," 1949, p. 14).

Even without reliable statistics on a given veteran's rehabilitative potential, the lived experiences of wardens over time has consistently pointed to significant return on the investment of specialized veteran-specific programming. The precautionary principle emphasizes the need to think beyond the inmates to their families and the community, as well as the future generations that will be impacted by lost opportunities to address underlying causes. For those concerned with the lack of numbers and studies and understanding of causal connections, it is useful to revisit Wisconsin Governor Blaine's response to the critics who challenged his efforts to search out World War I veterans and treat their combat trauma both inside and out of the prisons:

"When I can pluck a thistle and plant a flower when I think a flower will grow, I am going to do it" (Severo & Milford, 1989, p. 240).

May you use the gardening tools in this book to design a bountiful recovery and reentry landscape.

REFERENCES

ABC News Radio. (2013, December 11). Arizona Sheriff Joe Arpaio to house jailed vets together. On *WFJA Classic Hits 105.5*. [radio station]. Retrieved from http://www. classichitsandoldies.com/v2/2013/12/11/arizona-sheriff-joe-arpaio -to-house-jailed-vets-together/

Addlestone, D. F., & Chaset, A. (2008). Veterans in the criminal justice system. In D. Addlestone & C. Kubey (Eds.), *The American veterans and servicemembers survival guide: How to cut through the bureaucracy and get what you need and are entitled to* (pp. 311–322). New York: Veterans for America. Retrieved from https://www.nvlsp .org/images/products/survivalguide.pdf

Advocates survey war veterans in penal institutions: Twenty thousand said to be mentally abnormal and suffering from wounds. (1923, May 18). *New Castle News* (Pennsylvania), p. 25.

Alvarez, L. (2007, February 14). Army giving more waivers in recruiting. *The New York Times*. Retrieved from https://www.nytimes.com/2007/02/14/us/14military .html

Alvarez, L. (2011, December 12). In Florida, using military discipline to help veterans in prison. *The New York Times*. Retrieved from http://www.nytimes.com /2011/12/12/us/veterans-in-prison-get-help-in-florida-program.html

American Correctional Association. (2012). *2011–2013 national jail and adult detention directory* (12th ed.). Alexandria, VA: Author.

American Correctional Association. (2013). *2013 directory of adult and juvenile correctional departments, institutions, agencies, and probation and parole authorities*. Alexandria, VA: Author.

American Legion notes. (1924, January 9). *Indiana Evening Gazette*, p. 7.

American Legion news (1923, December 8). *Sandusky Star Journal* (Oklahoma), p. 7.

American Legion and V.F.W. news. (1923, January 15). *Connersville News Examiner*, p. 4.

American Psychiatric Association (2013). *Diagnostic and Statistical Manual of Mental Disorders: DSM-5* (5th ed.). Washington, DC: Author.

Appelbaum, K. L., Hickey, J. M., & Packer, I. A. (2001). The role of correctional officers in multidisciplinary mental health care in prisons. *Psychiatric Services, 52*(10), 1343–1347.

Archer, D., & Gartner, R. (1984). *Violence and crime in cross-national perspective*. New Haven, CT: Yale University Press.

301

Aufderheide, D. (2011). The need for collaborative leadership in correctional mental health. *Corrections Today, 73*(5), 38–41.

Bailey, M. (2011). Risk and natural catastrophes: The long view. In L. Skinns, M. Scott, & T. Cox (Eds.), *Risk* (pp. 131–158). Cambridge, UK: Cambridge University Press.

Baillargeon, J., Hoge, S. K., & Penn, J. V. (2010). Addressing the challenge of community reentry among released inmates with serious mental illness. *American Journal of Community Psychology, 46*, 361–375.

Baldwin, J. M. (2013, June 4). *Executive summary: National survey of veterans treatment courts.* Little Rock, AR: University of Arkansas, Little Rock.

Baldwin, J. M. (2016). Investigating the programmatic attack: A national survey of veterans treatment courts. *Journal of Criminal Law and Criminology, 105*(3), 705–752.

Ban, C. (2012, May 7). County jail cellblocks cater to military vets. *County News, 44*(9).

Barger, D. (2012, October 3). Veterans rehab program planned at Jefferson County Jail. *Arnold Patch: Police and Fire News* (St. Louis, Missouri). Retrieved from http://arnold.patch.com/groups/police-and-fire/veterans-rehab-program-planned-at-jefferson-county-jail

Barnes, F. C. (1922, April 14). The veteran and crime. *The American Legion Weekly*, p. 22.

Baskir, L. M., & Strauss, W. A. (1978). *The draft, the war, and the Vietnam generation.* New York: Alfred A. Knopf.

Bay City News Service. (2012, November 12). Sheriff, rehab groups stress need for help for incarcerated veterans. *San Mateo Daily Journal.*

Bednar, R. (1962). Discharge and dismissal as punishment in the armed forces. *Military Law Review, 16*, 1–42.

Beeler, A. (2007, February). When Johnny or Jane comes marching home and changes one uniform for another. *Corrections Today, 69*(1), 60–63.

Bennett, J. V. (1954). The criminality of veterans. *Federal Probation, 18*(2), 40–43.

Berenson, S. K. (2009). Legal services for struggling veterans—then and now. *Hamline Journal of Public Law and Policy, 31*, 101–141.

Beggs, B. (2010, November 29). Veterans gain job skills, get "clean start" in jail program. *American Laundry News.*

Bernton, H. (2012, August 11). Troubled veterans left without health-care benefits. *Seattle Times.* Retrieved from https://www.seattletimes.com/seattle-news/troubled-veterans-left-without-health-care-benefits/

Bitzer, R. (1980). Caught in the middle: Mentally disabled veterans and the Veterans Administration. In C. R. Figley & S. Leventman (Eds.), *Strangers at home: Vietnam veterans since the war* (pp. 305–323). New York: Praeger.

Blaine orders survey of all vets in prison: Plans to protect rights of unfortunate ex-soldiers. (1922, November 22). *The Capital Times* (Madison, Wisconsin), p. 2.

Blum, B. (2017). *Ranger games: A story of soldiers, family and an inexplicable crime.* New York: Doubleday.

Boivin, M. J. (1986). Forgotten warriors: An evaluation of the emotional well-being of presently incarcerated Vietnam veterans. *Genetic, Social, and General Psychology Monographs, 113*(1), 109–125.

Bonds, T. M., Baiocchi, D., & MacDonald, L. L. (2010). *RAND Arroyo Center documented briefing: Army deployments to OIF and OEF.* Santa Monica, CA: RAND Corporation.

Bourke, J. (1999). *An intimate history of killing: Face-to-face killing in twentieth century warfare.* London, UK: Granta Books.

Breen, D. (2011, November 10). Several prisons open up special dorms that offer programs for veterans. *Orlando Sentinel,* p. A6.

Brignone, E., Fargo, J. D., Blais, R. K., Carter, M., Samore, M., & Gundlapalli, A. (2017). Non-routine discharge from military service: Mental illness, substance use disorders, and suicidality. *American Journal of Preventive Medicine, 52*(5), 557–565.

Bronson, J., Carson, A., Noonan, M., & Berzofsky, M. (2015). *Veterans in prison and jail, 2011–12.* Washington, DC: Bureau of Justice Statistics.

Brooker, J. W., Seamone, E. R., & Rogall, L. C. (2012). Beyond "T.B.D.": Understanding the VA's evaluation of a former servicemember's benefit eligibility following involuntary or punitive discharge from the armed forces. *Military Law Review, 214,* 1–328.

Brookes, M., Ashton, C., & Holliss, A. (2010). Assisting veterans at HMPs Grendon and Springhill. *Prison Service Journal, 190,* 3–9.

Brooks-Holliday, S., & Pedersen, E. (2017). The association between discharge status, mental health, and substance misuse among young adult veterans. *Psychiatry Research, 256,* 428–434.

Brown, D. C. (2005). Stop Loss: Illegal conscription in America. *American University Law Review, 54,* 1595–1634.

Brown, W. B. (2008). Another emerging "storm": Iraq and Afghanistan veterans with PTSD in the criminal justice system. *Justice Policy Journal, 5*(2), 1–37.

Brown, W. B. (2010). War, veterans, and crime. In M. Herzog-Evans (Ed.), *Transnational Criminology Manual* (Vol. 1, pp. 599–620). Nijmegen, The Netherlands: Wolf Legal Publishers.

Brown, W. B., Stanulis, R., Theis, B., Farnsworth, J., & Daniels, D. (2013). The perfect storm: Veterans, culture and the criminal justice system. *Justice Policy Journal, 10*(2), 1–44.

Bryant, C. D. (1979). *Khaki-collar crime: Deviant behavior in the military context.* New York: The Free Press.

Bryant, E. (2012, February 8). New program helps veterans in prison. *WSOCTV.com.* Retrieved from http://www.wsoctv.com/news/news/local/new-program-helps-veterans-prison/nHX2R/

Budd, F. C., & Harvey, S. (2006). Military fitness for duty evaluations. In C. H. Kennedy & E. A. Zillner (Eds.), *Military psychology: Clinical and operational applications* (pp. 35–60). New York: The Guilford Press.

Bureau of Investigative Journalism. (2018, January 7). Drone warfare. Retrieved from https://www.thebureauinvestigates.com/projects/drone-war

Burkett, B. G., & Whitley, G. (1998). *Stolen valor: How the Vietnam generation was robbed of its heroes and its history.* Dallas, TX: Verity Press.

Burkhead, M. D. (2007). *The treatment of criminal offenders: A history.* Jefferson, NC: McFarland & Company.

Buyer, B. (1992, July 19). Veterans find strength in self-help programs at Groveland: Intense counseling gives inmates second chance. *Buffalo News* (New York).

Callahan, P. (2013). *Military injustice.* Mustang, OK: Tate Publishing and Enterprises, LLC.

Camacho, P. (1980). From war hero to war criminal: The negative privilege of the Vietnam veteran. In C. R. Figley & S. Leventman (Eds.), *Strangers at home: Vietnam veterans since the war* (pp. 267–277). New York: Praeger.

Canton, L. G. (2007). *Emergency management: Concepts and strategies for effective programs.* Hoboken, NJ: John Wiley and Sons.

Carbery, K. (2013, November 7). Helping troubled veterans: Sheriff implements veterans program at county jail. *Jefferson County Leader* (St. Louis, Missouri).

Carden, M. J. (2009, November 3). Shinseki outlines plan to end veteran homelessness. *Armed Forces Press Service.* Retrieved from http://www.defense.gov/News/NewsArticle.aspx?

Carney, C. P., Sampson, T. R., Voelker, M., Woolson, R., Thorne, P., & Doebbeling, B. N. (2003). Women in the Gulf War: Combat experience, exposures, and subsequent health care use. *Military Medicine, 168*(8), 654–661.

Carpenter, A. (2010, January 12). Navy doctor warns: Misconduct may be symptom of stress disorder. *The Washington Times,* p. A1.

Carson, B. (2016, February 4). *Memorandum for secretaries of the military departments: Subject: Consideration of discharge upgrade requests pursuant to supplemental guidance to military boards for correction of military/naval records (BCMRs/BCNR) by veterans claiming Post Traumatic Stress Disorder (PTSD) or Traumatic Brain Injury (TBI).* Washington, DC: Office of Principal Deputy Under Secretary of Defense.

Carter, J. (1979, May 21). *Presidential review memorandum on Vietnam era veterans* (Released October 10, 1978). Washington, DC: U.S. Government Printing Office.

Carter, P. (2013, November 10). The vets we reject and ignore. *The New York Times.* Retreived from https://www.nytimes.com/2013/11/11/opinion/the-vets-we-reject-and-ignore.html

Cartwright, T. (2011). "To care for him who shall have borne the battle": The recent development of veterans treatment courts in America. *Stanford Law and Policy Review, 22*(1), 295–316.

Casey, R. J. (1923, September 28). The lost legion: 20,000 veterans are in prison—How many of them ought to be in hospital. *The American Legion Weekly, 7,* 24–27.

Castro, C. (2009). Impact of combat on the mental health and well-being of soldiers and marines. *Smith College Studies in Social Work, 79,* 247–262.

Catanese, S. A. (2010). Traumatized by association: The risk of working sex crimes. *Federal Probation, 74*(2), 36–38.

Catagnus Jr., E. J., Edison, B. Z., Keeling, J. D., & Moon, D. A. (2005, September). Infantry squad tactics: Some of the lessons learned during MOUT in the battle for Fallujah. *Marine Corps Gazette,* 80–89.

Cavanaugh, J. M. (2011). Helping those who serve: Veterans treatment courts foster rehabilitation and reduce recidivism for offending combat veterans. *New England Law Review, 45,* 463–488.

Center for Mental Health Services National Gains Center. (2011a, February). *Jail diversion and trauma recovery—priority to veterans.* Bethesda, MD: Substance Abuse and Mental Health Services Administration.

Center for Mental Health Services National Gains Center. (2011b, August). *Trauma-specific interventions for justice-involved individuals.* Bethesda, MD: Substance Abuse and Mental Health Services Administration.

Cetina, J. G. (1977). *A history of veterans' homes in the United States 1811–1930* (Doctoral dissertation). Retrieved from OCLC (Accession No. 3574753).

Chalsma, H. W. (1998). *The chambers of memory: PTSD in the life stories of U.S. Vietnam veterans.* Northvale, NJ: Jason Aronson.

Changes in Texas prison population. (1920, May 29). *Galveston Daily News,* p. 2.

Chiarelli, P. W. (2013). VCSA sends. In *Army 2020: Generating health and discipline in the force ahead of the strategic reset.* Washington, DC: U.S. Department of the Army.

Chiaramonte, N. Y. (2018, January 19). Discharge upgrades being offered to previously denied veterans. *The Legal Intelligencer.* Retrieved from https://www.law.com/thelegalintelligencer/sites/thelegalintelligencer/2018/01/19/discharge-upgrades-being-offered-to-previously-denied-veterans/?slreturn=20180420162311

Christensen, D., & Tsilker, Y. (2017, May 5). *Racial disparities in military justice: Findings of substantial and persistent racial disparities within the United States military justice system.* McLean, VA: Protect Our Defenders.

Claims "rip-off" in G.I. benefits (1976, May 8). *Syracuse Herald-Journal* (New York), p. 13.

Clark, S. (2010, July 14). *Veterans Administration programs for justice-involved veterans.* Washington DC: VHA Veterans Justice Outreach Program.

Clark, S., McGuire, J., & Blue-Howells, J. (2010). Development of veterans treatment courts: Local and legislative initiatives. *Drug Court Review, 7*(1), 171–208.

Cohen, L. W. (1990, April 24). Memorandum to Ms. Gayle Chisholm, Treatment Leader, Jacksonville Vet Center and Mr. O. J. Phillips, Jr., Superintendent, Baker Correctional Institution, Subject: 6-months progress report/proposal: Project Base Camp (Feb. 8, 1988). In *Hearing before the Subcommittee on Courts, Intellectual Property, and the Administration of Justice of the Committee on the Judiciary on H. R. 3453, Incarcerated Veterans Rehabilitation and Readjustment Act of 1989, House of Representatives,* 102d Cong. 2d Sess. Ser. No. 99. Washington, DC: Government Printing Office.

Collins, E. R. (2017). Status courts. *Georgetown Law Journal, 105,* 1481–1528.

Commonwealth of Pennsylvania, Department of Corrections. (1986, September). *Post traumatic stress disorder program manual* (No. OM-107.08). Philadelphia: Author.

Comptroller General of the United States. (1974, December 30). *Need for improved outreach efforts for veterans in prison or on parole* (No. MWD75-48). Washington, DC: U.S. General Accounting Office.

Conly, C. (2005, November). *Helping inmates obtain federal disability benefits: Serious medical and mental illness, incarceration, and federal disability entitlement programs* (Field Note. Revised and Final Report). Washington, DC: U.S. Department of Justice.

Connecticut Veterans Legal Center (2018, May 18). *Supplemental guide: Applying for a discharge upgrade when you have a mental health condition.* Retrieved from https://ctveteranslegal.org/wp-content/uploads/2018/05/18.04.16-FINAL -Discharge-Upgrade-Mental-Health-Supplement.pdf

Correia, K. M. (2001). *A handbook for correctional psychologists: Guidance for the prison practitioner.* Springfield, IL: Charles C Thomas.

Cosgrove, P. J. (2003). Foreword. In G. E. Kearney, M. Creamer, R. Marshall, & A. Goyne (Eds.), *Military stress and performance—The Australian Defence Force Experience* (pp. v–x). Australia: Melbourne University Press.

Costello, M. A. (2012). Heroes or hopeless? Homeless veterans caught in a dysfunctional system. *The Journal of Law in Society, 13,* 417–438.

Cramer, R. J. (2011). Prosecutor pretrial attitudes and plea-bargaining behavior toward veterans with posttraumatic stress disorder. *Psychological Services, 8*(4), 319–331.

Cranston, A. (1979, July 11). Statement as Chair of the Senate Committee on Veterans' Affairs.

Crime sider staff. (2018, January 10). Jails increasingly set aside cellblocks for veterans. *CBS News.* Retrieved from https://www.cbsnews.com/news/us-jails-cell blocks-for-veterans/

Custis, D. L. (1971, September). Due process and military discharges. *American Bar Association Journal, 57,* 875–878.

Davidson, M. (2013). Paying it forward: Veterans incarcerated paying back and paying forward. *Vietnow.com.* Retrieved from http://www.vietnow.com/incarcerated -veterans-paying-it-forward/

Dean, A. (2012, September 6). Indiana veteran's education and transition unit (INVET) at Indianapolis Re-Entry Educational Facility. *National Criminal Justice Association's Veterans Specific Reentry Webinar.*

Defense Manpower Data Center (2011, August 11). *Demographics of active duty U.S. military.* Washington, DC: Author.

DeFloor, A. (2013, November 10). Mass incarceration doesn't work. *Tampa Bay Times,* p. 3P.

DeFrank, R. (2012, December 11). Military unit opens at BCI. *The Times Leader* (Ohio).

Department of Veterans Affairs. (2010, April 9). *Health Care for Re-Entry Veterans (HCRV) Program: VHA handbook 1162.06 transmittal sheet.* Washington, DC: Author.

Department of Veterans Affairs, Center for Health Care Evaluation, Veterans Administration Palo Alto Health Care System. (2013). *A structured evidence review to identify treatment needs of justice-involved veterans and associated psychological interventions.* Menlo Park, CA: Veterans Administration Palo Alto Health Care System.

Department of Veterans Affairs. (n.d.). DDRI-2: A survey of experiences before, during, and after military deployment. Washington, DC: U.S. Department of Veterans Affairs.

DeFazio, V. J. (1984). Psychoanalytic psychotherapy and the Vietnam veteran. In H. J. Schwartz (Ed.), *Psychotherapy of the combat veteran* (pp. 23–46). New York: SP Medical and Scientific Books.

Demetrick, A. (2013, October 24). 3 pups complete Md. prison vet dog training. *CBS Baltimore.* Retrieved from http://baltimore.cbslocal.com/2013/10/24/3-pups -complete-md-prison-vet-dog-training

Dishneau, D. (2008, October 18). Imprisoned vets tell their war stories for history. *USA Today.*

Donlon, R. (2010, August 6). *Medal of Honor: Speak out! Save lives.* Retrieved from http://www. medalofhonorspeakout.org.

Dretsch, E. C. (2013). Chronically ill inmates. In L. Gideon (Ed.), *Special needs offenders in correctional institutions* (pp. 117–153). Los Angeles: Sage.

Duffy to aid of ex–service men (1924, January 31). *Moville Mail* (Wisconsin), p. 3.

Dvoskin, J. A. (2005, Winter). *Mental health services in jails: Identifying problems. Proceedings of the Large Jail Network Meeting.* Washington, DC: NIC Jails Division.

Dvoskin, J. A., & Spiers, E. M. (2004). On the role of correctional officers in prison mental health. *Psychiatry Quarterly, 75*(1), 41–59.

Edelman, B. (2018, May). *Barracks behind bars: In veteran-specific housing units, veterans help veterans help themselves.* Washington, DC: National Institute of Corrections.

Editorial. (2013, April 17). War could cost over $6 trillion in 40 years. *The Newberry Observer* (South Carolina), p. 4.

Editor's note. (1949). *The Prison World,* 11, 14.

Elbogen, E. B. (n.d.). *Criminal justice involvement among Iraq and Afghanistan war veterans: Risk factors and barriers to care.* Chapel Hill, NC: University of North Carolina at Chapel Hill, School of Medicine.

Elbogen, E. B., Fuller, S., Johnson, S. C., Brooks, S., Kinneer, P., Calhoun, P. S., & Beckham, J. C. (2010). Improving risk assessment of violence among military veterans: An evidence-based approach for clinical decision-making. *Clinical Psychology Review, 30,* 595–607.

Elbogen, E. B., & Johnson, S. C. (2009). The intricate link between violence and mental disorder: Results from the National Epidemiologic Survey on Alcohol and Related Conditions. *Archives of General Psychiatry, 66*(2), 152–161.

Elbogen, E. B., Johnson, S. C., Newton, V. M., Straits-Troster, K.S., Vasterling, J. J., Wagner, H. R., & Beckham, J. C. (2012). Criminal justice involvement, trauma, and negative affect in Iraq and Afghanistan war era veterans. *Journal of Consulting and Clinical Psychology, 80*(6), 1097–1102.

Etter, D., McCarthy, L. B., & Asken, M. J. (July 2011). Police negotiations with war veterans: Seeing through the residual fog of war. *FBI Law Enforcement Bulletin.* Retrieved from: http://www.fbi.gov/stats-services/publications/law-enforcement -bulletin/july-2011/police-negotiations-with-war-veterans

Emsley, C. (2013). *Soldier, sailor, beggarman, thief.* Oxford, UK: Oxford University Press.

Everson, R. B., & Camp, T. G. (2011). Seeing systems: An introduction to systemic approaches with military families. In R. B. Everson & C. R. Figley (Eds.), *Families Under Fire: Systemic Therapy with Families* (pp. 3–30). New York: Routledge.

Evigil, A. E., & Hawkins, H. L. (1946). The short-term institution and the delinquent veteran. *The Prison World, 8*(3), 16, 28–29.

Federal Bureau of Prisons. Federal prison facilities. Retrieved on December 8, 2013 from http://www.bop.gov/DataSource/execute/dsFacilityLoc

Feldmann, C. E. (2011). Effective defense strategies. In *Strategies for military criminal defense: Leading lawyers on understanding the military justice system, constructing effective defense strategies, and navigating complex cases* (pp. 7–22). Eagan, MN: Thomson Reuters/Aspatore.

Finlay, A. K., Stimmel, M., Blue-Howells, J., Rosenthal, J., McGuire, J., Binswanger, I., . . . Timko, C. (2017). Use of Veterans Health Administration mental health and substance use disorder treatment after exiting prison: The Health Care Reentry for Veterans Program. *Administrative Policy in Mental Health, 44,* 177–187.

Fitzpatrick, D. (2013, November 5). Documentary brings the reality of veterans' post-traumatic stress disorders to viewers. *Bangor Daily News* (Maine).

Flatley, B., Clark, S., Rosenthal, J., & Blue-Howells, J. (2017, March). *Veterans court inventory 2016 update: Characteristics and VA involvement in veterans treatment courts and other veteran-focused court programs from the Veterans Justice Outreach perspective.* Washington, DC: U.S. Department of Veterans Affairs, Veterans Health Administration.

Flournoy, M. E., Testimony (1987, December 1). *Richard Carter, et al. v. Glen R. Jeffes,* Civ. Action No. 82-3821, Hearing re: Settlement (First Day, pp. 1–152). Philadelphia: Eastern District of Pennsylvania.

Flournoy, M. E., Testimony (1987, December 3). *Richard Carter, et al. v. Glen R. Jeffes,* Civ. Action No. 82-3821, Hearing re: Settlement (Third Day, pp. 291–469). Philadelphia: Eastern District of Pennsylvania.

Frakt, A. (2017, April 24). Spend a dollar on drug treatment and save more on crime reduction. *The New York Times.* Retrieved from https://www.nytimes.com/2017/04/24/upshot/spend-a-dollar-on-drug-treatment-and-save-more-on-crime-reduction.html

Frisman, L. K., & Griffin-Fennell, F. (2009). Commentary: Suicide and incarcerated veterans: Don't wait for the numbers. *Journal of the American Academy of Psychiatry and the Law, 37,* 92–94.

Gabriel, R. A. (1987). *No more heroes: Madness and psychiatry in war.* New York: Hill and Wang.

Gamache, G. (2000). Military discharge status of homeless veterans with mental illness. *Military Medicine, 165*(11), 803–808.

Gambill, G. (2010, May 5). Justice-involved veterans: A mounting social crisis. *Los Angeles Daily Journal,* p. 6.

Gambill, G. (2011, August 16). Is data doing justice to our veterans? Retrieved from http://www.justicepolicy.org/news/2861

Garamone, J. (2013, December 4). Dempsey praises veterans' rehabilitation program. *CQ Federal Department and Agency Documents.*

General Accounting Office (1974, Dec. 30). *Need for improved outreach efforts for veterans in prisons or on parole* (No. MWD-75-48). Washington, DC: U.S. Government Printing Office.

Generous Jr., W. T. (1973). *Swords and scales: The development of the Uniform Code of Military Justice.* Port Washington, NY: Kennikat.

Gibbons-Neff, T. (2018, April 30). Reports of sexual assault in the military rise by 10 percent, Pentagon finds. *The New York Times.* Retrieved from https://www.nytimes.com/2018/04/30/us/politics/sexual-assault-reports-military-increase.html

Gideon, L. (2013). Introduction: Special needs offenders. In L. Gideon (Ed.), *Special needs offenders in correctional institutions* (pp. 1–20). Thousand Oaks, CA: Sage.

Gierer, L. (2013, September 21). Church recovery program helps those in need. *Columbus Ledger-Enquirer* (Georgia), 1.

Glass, C. Testimony (1987, December 3). *Richard Carter, et al. v. Glen R. Jeffes,* Civ. Action No. 82-3821, Hearing re: Settlement (Third Day, pp. 291–469). Philadelphia: Eastern District of Pennsylvania.

Gleave, A. J. (2010, May 24). *Failure of a nation? Ex service personnel experience of returning to a civilian life.* Lancaster, UK: Lancaster University.

Gold, S., Marx, B. P., Soler–Baillo, J. M., & Sloan, D. M. (2005). Is life stress more traumatic than traumatic stress? *Anxiety Disorders, 19,* 687–698.

Gould, M., Adler, A., & Zamorski, M. (2010). Do stigma and perceived barriers to mental health care differ across armed forces? *Journal of the Royal Society of Medicine, 103*(4), 148–156.

Governor to pardon all ex-service men in Wisconsin prison. (1922, July 4). *San Antonio Light* (Texas), p. 1.

Grice, M. D. (2011, October 27). For a bit of colored ribbon. *Marine Corps Gazette.*

Grieger, T. A., Benedek, D. M., & Ursano, R. J. (2011). Violence and aggression. In D. M. Benedek & G. W. Wynn (Eds.), *Clinical management of PTSD* (pp. 205–225). Washington, DC: American Psychiatric Publishing.

Griggs, T. (2011, October 23). Barracks behind bars. *Pensacola News Journal* (Florida), pp. 1A, 10A.

Grossman, D. (2009). *On killing: The psychological cost of learning to kill in war and society.* New York: Back Bay Books.

Groveland Correctional Facility. (n.d.) *Veterans Residential Therapeutic Program: Groveland Correctional Facility vets dorm overview.* Groveland, NY: New York State Department of Correctional Services.

Groveland Correctional Facility. (n.d.). *Program conduct guide.* Groveland, NY: New York State Department of Correctional Services.

Groveland Correctional Facility. (n.d.). *Dorm positions and responsibilities.* Groveland, NY: New York State Department of Correctional Services.

Groveland Correctional Facility. (n.d.). *Transitional services orientation guide for the Veterans Residential Therapeutic Program.* Groveland, NY: New York State Department of Correctional Services.

Groveland Correctional Facility and Veterans Administration. (1992, November 11). Overview: Veterans Residential Therapeutic Program. *NamVet, 5*(1), 57–65.

Gundapalli, A., Fargo, J. D., Metraux, S., Carter, M. E., Samore, M. H., Kane, V., & Culhane, D. P. (2015). Military misconduct and homelessness among US veterans separated from active duty, 2001–2012. *Journal of the American Medical Association, 314*(8), 832–834.

Hadley Jr., F. M. (1968, February–March–April). The exemplary rehabilitation certificate. *JAG Journal, 22,* 77–80.

Hafemeister, T. L., & Stockey, N. A. (2010). Last stand? The criminal responsibility of war veterans returning from Iraq and Afghanistan with posttraumatic stress disorder. *Indiana Law Journal, 85,* 87–141.

Hagel, C. (2014, September 3). *Memorandum for secretaries of the military departments: Subject: Supplemental guidance to military boards for correction of military/naval records considering discharge upgrade requests by veterans claiming post traumatic stress disorder.* Washington, DC: Office of Secretary of Defense.

Hager, J. (2009). Veterans Administration's duty to assist incarcerated veterans. *Veterans Law Review, 1,* 231–241.

Hall, L. K. (2008). *Counseling military families: What mental health professionals need to know.* New York: Routledge.

Hall, L. K. (2011). Social work with the military: Current practice challenges and approaches to care. *Social Work in Health Care, 50*(1), 4–18.

Hambling, D. (2017). Give them a medal. *New Scientist, 235,* 24–25.

Hammond, R. (2010). *Introduction to sociology, Chapter 21: Sociology of the military veterans and the criminal justice system.* West Virginia University. Retrieved from http://freebooks.uvu.edu/SOC1010/index.php/license.html.

Harden, M. (2001, August 24). Veterans Administration program could help save inmates—and tax dollars. *Columbus Dispatch* (Ohio).

Harding, S. (2016). Self-stigma and veteran culture. *Journal of Transcultural Nursing, 28*(5), 438–444.

Hartill, D. (2013, January 6). Jails working to help veterans. *Sun Journal* (Lewiston-Auburn, Maine).

Hassan, A. (2013). Foreword. In R. A. Weiss & J. E. Coll (Eds.), *Handbook of military social work* (pp. xvii–xx). Hoboken, NJ: Wiley and Sons.

Hayes, Jr., T. (2006–2007). Post-traumatic stress disorder on trial. *Military Law Review, 190–191,* 67–110.

Hearing before the Subcommittee on Courts, Intellectual Property, and the Administration of Justice of the Committee on the Judiciary on H. R. 3453, Incarcerated Veterans Rehabilitation and Readjustment Act of 1989, House of Representatives. 102d Congress, 2d Sess. (1990, April 24) (testimony of D. A. Brigham as Director of Veterans Assistance Service, Veterans Administration). Ser. No. 99. Washington, DC: U.S. Government Printing Office.

Hearing before the Subcommittee on Courts, Intellectual Property, and the Administration of Justice of the Committee on the Judiciary on H. R. 3453, Incarcerated Veterans

Rehabilitation and Readjustment Act of 1989, House of Representatives. 102d Cong., 2d Sess. (1990, April 24) (statement of Rep. G. E. Brown, Jr.). Ser. No. 99. Washington, DC: U.S. Government Printing Office.

Hearing before the Subcommittee on Courts, Intellectual Property, and the Administration of Justice of the Committee on the Judiciary on H. R. 3453, Incarcerated Veterans Rehabilitation and Readjustment Act of 1989, House of Representatives. 102d Cong., 2d Sess. (1990, April 24) (statement of J. M. Quinlan, Jr. as Director of the Federal Bureau of Prisons). Ser. No. 99. Washington, DC: U.S. Government Printing Office.

Hearing before the Subcommittee on Courts, Intellectual Property, and the Administration of Justice of the Committee on the Judiciary on H. R. 3453, Incarcerated Veterans Rehabilitation and Readjustment Act of 1989, House of Representatives. 102d Cong., 2d Sess. (1990, April 24) (statement of W. F. Smith as National Membership Director, Vietnam Veterans of America Inc.). Ser. No. 99. Washington, DC: U.S. Government Printing Office.

Hearing before the Subcommittee on Courts, Intellectual Property, and the Administration of Justice of the Committee on the Judiciary on H. R. 3453, Incarcerated Veterans Rehabilitation and Readjustment Act of 1989, House of Representatives. 102d Cong., 2d Sess. (1990, April 24) (factual findings of the U.S. House Judiciary Committee). Ser. No. 99. Washington, DC: U.S. Government Printing Office.

Hearing Before the Subcommittee on Courts, Intellectual Property, and the Administration of Justice of the Committee on the Judiciary on H. R. 3453, Incarcerated Veterans Rehabilitation and Readjustment Act of 1989, House of Representatives. 102d Cong., 2d Sess. (1990, April 24) (testimony of A. J. Woods as Executive Director, Veterans Service and Resource Center, Dallas, TX). Ser. No. 99. Washington, DC: U.S. Government Printing Office.

Herzog, J., & Everson, R. B. (2011). Secondary traumatic stress, deployment phase, and military families: Systematic approaches to treatment. In R. B. Everson, & C. R. Figley (Eds.), *Families Under Fire: Systematic Therapy with Military Families* (pp. 191–214). New York: Routledge: Taylor and Francis Group.

Hixenbaugh, M. (2012, December 27). Veterans say uniform treatment in own prison helps healing. *The Virginian Pilot* (Norfolk).

Hogan, P. F., & Seifert, R. F. (2010). Marriage and the military: Evidence that those who serve marry earlier and divorce earlier. *Armed Forces & Society, 36*(3), 420–438.

Hoge, C. W. (2010). *Once a warrior always a warrior: Navigating the transition from combat to home including combat stress, PTSD, and mTBI.* Guilford, CT: GPP Life.

Hoge, C. W., Goldberg, H. M., & Castro, C. A. (2009). Care of war veterans with mild traumatic brain injury—flawed perspectives. *New England Journal of Medicine, 360*(16), 1588–1591.

Holbrook, J. (2011). Veterans' courts and criminal responsibility: A problem-solving history and approach to the liminality of combat trauma. In D. C. Kelly, D. Howe-Barksdale, & D. Gitleson (Eds.), *Treating young veterans: Promoting resilience through practice and advocacy* (pp. 259–300). New York: Springer.

Holbrook, J., & Anderson, S. (2011). Veterans courts: Early outcomes and key indicators for success (Widener Law School Legal Studies Research Paper Series

No. 11-25). Retrieved from the Social Science Research Network http://ssrn
.com/abstract=1912655

Holmes, B. L. (2011, January 31). Veterans unit opens at IREF. *Hendricks County Flyer*
(Avon, Indiana).

Holyfield, L. (2011). *Veterans' journeys home: Life after Afghanistan and Iraq.* New York:
Taylor & Francis.

Hospital instead of jail: American Legion aims to secure liberty of many ex-service
men now in prison. (1923, November 1). *The Roland Record,* p. 2.

Howard League on Penal Reform. (2011). *Report of the inquiry into former armed service
personnel in prison.* London, UK: Howard League on Penal Reform.

Hubert, T. P. (2009, January/February). Angola veterans salute their own. *The
Vietnam Veterans of America Veteran.*

Huffman, J. F. (2013, October 21). Fall in line, readers. *Air Force Times,* p. A28.

Hughes, E., & Reichert, J. (2017, December 11). An overview of problem-solving
courts and implications for practice. Retrieved from http://www.icjia.state.il.us
/articles/an-overview-of-problem-solving-courts-and-implications-for-practice

Human Rights Watch. (2015). *Embattled: Retaliation against sexual assault survivors in
the US military.* Washington, DC: Author.

Human Rights Watch. (2016). *Booted: Lack of recourse for wrongfully discharged US military rape survivors.* Washington, DC: Author.

Hunter, M. (2007). *Honor betrayed: Sexual abuse in America's military.* Fort Lee, NJ:
Barricade Books.

*Incarcerated Veterans Rehabilitation and Readjustment Act of 1989: Hearing Before the
Subcommittee on Courts, Intellectual Property and the Administration of Justice,* 101st
Cong. (1990), Serial 101-99.

Inmates building memorial to vets. (1988, October, 25). *Altoona Mirror,* p. A3.

Institute of Medicine. (2010). *Returning home from Iraq and Afghanistan: Preliminary
assessment of readjustment needs of veterans, service members, and their families.*
Washington, DC: National Academies Press.

Integrated Mental Health Strategy IMHS#22. (n.d.). *Evaluation of the Veterans Affairs
Justice Outreach Program as a model for service members facing disciplinary and legal
problems.* Washington, DC: U.S. Department of Defense and U.S. Department of
Veterans Affairs.

Jacobs, G. A., & Meyer, D. L. (2006). Psychological first aid: Clarifying the concept.
In L. Barbanel & R. J. Sternberg (Eds.), *Psychological interventions in times of crisis*
(pp. 57–71). New York: Springer.

Jacobson, S., & Colón, E. (2009). *Coming home: What to expect, how to deal when you
return from combat.* Arlington, VA: Ceridian Corporation, Military One Source.

James, N. (2015, January 12). *Offender reentry: Correctional statistics, reintegration into the
community, and recidivism.* Washington, DC: Congressional Research Service.

Jeffes, G. R. (1986, July 22). *Memorandum to superintendents, regional directors, and
Central Office directors: Subject: Post Traumatic Stress Disorder (PTSD) identification
and treatment for Vietnam veterans: Administrative manual (Vol. VII, OM-107.08).*
Commonwealth of Pennsylvania: Department of Corrections.

Johnson, L. B. (1966, October 16). *529–Statement by the President upon signing bill
authorizing exemplary rehabilitation certificates for certain persons discharged from the*

armed forces. Retrieved from The American Presidency Project. http://www.presidency.ucsb.edu/ws/index.php?pid=27936.

Johnson, R. S., Stolar, A. G., McGuire, J. F., Mittakanti, K., Clark, S., Coonan, L. A., & Graham, D. P. (2017). Predictors of incarceration of veterans participating in U.S. veterans' courts. *Psychiatric Services, 68*(2), 144–150.

Jones, B. K. (1973). The gravity of administrative discharges: A legal and empirical evaluation. *Military Law Review, 59,* 1–25.

Jones, J., & Castleberry, C. (2013, September/October). Innovative evidence-based approaches to recidivism reduction and reentry. *Corrections Today, 75*(4): 44–46.

Justice for Vets. (n.d.). Veterans treatment court locations. Retrieved from http://www.justice forvets.org/veterans-treatment-court-locations

Kamal, S. (2013, May 1). Veteran prisons pave path to re-entry. *Columbia News Service.*

Kane, A. W. (2007). Basic concepts in psychology and law. In G. Young, A. W. Kane, K. Nicholson, & D. W. Schuman (Eds.), *Causality of psychological injury: Presenting evidence in court* (pp. 261–292). New York: Springer.

Karney, B. R., & Crown, J. (2007). *Families under stress: An assessment of data, theory, and research on marriage and divorce in the military.* Santa Monica, CA: RAND Corporation.

Katz, L. S., Cojucar, G., Davenport, C., Clarke, S., & Williams, J. C. (2012). War experiences inventory: Initial psychometric and structural properties. *Military Psychology, 24,* 48–70.

Kennedy, C. H., & McNeil, J. A. (2006). A history of military psychology. In C. H. Kennedy & E. A. Zillmer (Eds.), *Military psychology: Clinical and operational applications* (pp. 1–17). New York: Guilford Press.

Kensing, K. (2013). The 10 most stressful jobs of 2013. Retrieved from www.career-cast.com

Kidder, T. (1978, March). Soldiers of misfortune: A report on the veterans of Vietnam—and on the often disgraceful treatment they have received from their countrymen. *The Atlantic.* Retrieved from https://www.theatlantic.com/magazine/archive/1978/03/soldiers-of-misfortune/305723/

Killgore, W. D. S., Cotting, D. I., & Thomas, J. L., Cox, A. L., McGurk, D., Vo, A. H., . . . Hoge, C. W. (2008). Post-combat invincibility: Violent combat experiences are associated with increased risk-taking propensity following deployment. *Journal of Psychiatric Research, 42,* 1112–1121.

King, D. W., King, L. A., Gudanowski, D. M., & Vreven, D. L. (1995). Alternative representations of war zone stressors: Relationships to posttraumatic stress disorder in male and female veterans. *Journal of Abnormal Psychology, 104*(1), 184–196.

King, L. A., King, D. W., Vogt, D. S., Knight, J., & Samper, R. E. (2009). Deployment risk and resilience inventory: A collection of measures for studying deployment-related experiences of military personnel and veterans. *Military Psychology, 18*(2), 89–120.

Kirkland, F. R. (2003). Honor, combat ethics, and military culture. In *Military Medical Ethics* (Vol. 1, pp. 157–197). Washington, DC: U.S. Department of the Army.

Kirkland, H. T. (1984). Specialist 4 Haywood T. "The Kid" Kirkland (Ari Sesu Merretazon), Washington, DC. In W. Terry (Ed.), *Bloods: Black veterans of the Vietnam War: An oral history* (Mass Market Edition, pp. 89–108). New York: Presidio Press.

Korb, L. J. (2009). Introduction. In L. J. Korb, S. E. Duggan, P. M. Juul, & M. A. Bergmann (Eds.), *Serving America's veterans: A reference handbook* (pp. 1–14). Santa Barbara, CA: Praeger Security International.

Kraus, S. W., Martino, S., Potenza, M. N., Park, C., Merrell, J. D., & Hoff, R. A. (2017). Examining compulsive sexual behavior and psychopathology among a sample of postdeployment U.S. male and female military veterans. *Military Psychology, 29,* 143–156.

Kravetz, P. (2012). Way off base: An argument against intimate partner violence cases in veterans treatment courts. *Veterans Law Review, 4,* 162–205.

Kulka, R. A., Schlenger, W. E., Fairbank, J. A., Hough, R. L., Jordan, B. K., Marmar, C. R., . . . Grady, D. A. (1990). *Trauma and the Vietnam War generation: Report of findings from the national Vietnam veterans readjustment study.* New York: Brunner/Mazel.

Kurta, A. M. (2017, August 25). *Memorandum for secretaries of the military departments, Subject: Clarifying guidance to military discharge review boards and boards of correction of military/naval records concerning requests by veterans for modification of their discharge due to mental health conditions, sexual assault, or sexual harassment.* Washington, DC: Office of the Undersecretary of Defense.

Kuz, M. (2015, July 26). Veterans dorm in jail aims to restore sense of mission learned in military: Shared military experience can help inmates, often with PTSD, cope. *Houston Chronicle.*

Lance, C. E. (1978). A criminal punitive discharge—an effective punishment? *Military Law Review, 79,* 1–134.

Landes, S. J., Garovoy, N. D., & Burkman, K. M. (2013). Treating complex trauma among veterans: Three stage-based treatment models. *Journal of Clinical Psychology: In Session, 69*(5), 523–33.

LaRue, W. (1985, September 29). Inmates form Vietnam vets' group at Auburn. *Herald American* (Cayuga/Seneca, New York), pp. B1, B2.

Law changed on pension benefits for vets in jail. (1957, June 5). *The Vidette-Messenger* (Valparaiso, Indiana), p. 3.

Lawrence, Q., & Peñaloza, M. (2013, December 10). For veterans, "bad paper" is a catch-22 for treatment. *National Public Radio.* Retrieved from http://www.npr .org/2013/12/10/249739845/for-veterans-bad-paper-is-a-catch-22-for-treatment

Legion to seek survey of ex-service men confined in Iowa penitentiaries (1925, May 25). *Waterloo Evening Courier* (Iowa), p. 1.

Leepson, M. (2002, November). The last full measure of devotion. *The Vietnam Veterans of America Veteran.* Retrieved from http://www.vva.org/archive /TheVeteran/2002 special/devotion.htm

Leepson, M. (2005, July/August). A winning tribute: The Nevada Vietnam Memorial. *The Vietnam Veterans of America Veteran.* Retrieved from http://www.vva.org /archive TheVeteran/2005_07/NevadaVietnamMemorial.htm

Leonard, J. (2005, January 30). Helping vets in jail get a fresh start: Special county unit aims to re-instill sense of pride. *Los Angeles Times,* p. B1.

Levy, V. (1980, April 29). Jailed vets lack counseling: Federal bill would improve services. *Wisconsin State Journal,* p. 7B.

Lifton, R. J. (1992). *Home from the war: Learning from Vietnam veterans* (Revised ed.). Boston: Beacon Press.

Lionti, K. (2013, October 24). Holding center to help rehabilitate incarcerated veterans. *YNN Buffalo.*

Lithwick, D. (2010, February 11). A separate peace: Why veterans deserve special courts. *Newsweek, 20.*

Litz, B. T., Stein, N., Delaney, E., Liebowitz, L., Nash, W. P., Silva, C., & Maguen, S. (2009). Moral injury and moral repair in war veterans: A preliminary model and intervention strategy. *Clinical Psychology Review, 29,* 695–706.

Louise, B. (1998). The victimization . . . and revictimization of female offenders. *Corrections Today, 60*(7), 106–111.

Loveland, D., & Boyle, M. (2007). Inclusive case management as a jail diversion program for people with a serious mental illness. *Journal of Offender Therapy and Comparative Criminology, 51*(2), 130–150.

Lynch, S. M., Health, N. M., Matthews, K. C., & Cepeda, G. J. (2012). Seeking safety: An intervention for trauma-exposed incarcerated women? *Journal of Trauma and Dissociation, 13,* 88–101.

Lyons, J. A. (2007). The returning warrior: Advice to families and friends. In C. R. Figley & W. P. Nash (Eds.), *Combat stress injury: Theory, research, and management* (pp. 311–324). New York: Routledge: Taylor and Francis Group.

Lunding, C. H. (1973). Judicial review of military administrative discharges. *Yale Law Journal, 83,* 33–74.

Lunney, T. J. (1949). A veterans' counselor goes to prison. *The Prison World, 11,* 14–16, 28.

MacPherson, M. (1993). *Long time passing: Vietnam and the haunted generation.* New York: Doubleday.

Maguen, S., Metzler, T. J., Bosch, J., Marmar, C. R., Knight, S. J., & Neylan, T. C. (2012). Killing in combat may be independently associated with suicidal ideation. *Depression and Anxiety, 29,* 918–923.

Martin, J. A., & McClure, P. (2000). Today's active duty military family: The evolving challenges of military family life. In J. A. Martin, L. N. Rosen, & L. R. Sparacino (Eds.), *The military family: A practice guide for human service providers* (pp. 3–24). Westport, CT: Praeger.

Maryland Department of Public Safety and Correctional Services. (n.d.). Community revitalization. Retrieved on December 7, 2013, from http://www .dpscs.state.md.us/ initiatives/psw/index_PSW_cr-new.shtml

Maryland Department of Public Safety and Correctional Services. (2012, September 24). Western correctional institution inmates are training service dogs for wounded U.S. veterans. Towson, MD: Author.

Maryland Department of Public Safety and Correctional Services. (2013). Media advisory: Maryland Veterans Affairs Secretary Edward Chow Jr. to join Roxbury Correctional Institution incarcerated veterans for POW-MIA

Remembrance Day memorial service on the compound, 9/20 at 1 p. m., 18701 Roxbury Road Hagerstown, Maryland 21746. Towson, MD: Author.

Matsakis, A. (2007). *Back from the front: Combat trauma, love, and the family.* Baltimore: Sidran Institute Press.

Matter of duty, A: The continuing war against PTSD (2013, Nov. 10). Bangor, ME: Maine Public Broadcasting Network.

Mauldin, B. (1947). *Back home.* New York: William Sloane Associates.

Marks, A. (2001). Giving extra help to imprisoned vets. *Christian Science Monitor* (Boston, MA), p. 3.

May aid veterans in institutions. (1924, Oct. 27). *Tyrone Daily Herald* (Oklahoma), p. 12.

May, E. (1979, Mar.). Inmate veterans: Hidden casualties of a lost war. *Corrections Magazine, 5*(1), 3–13.

McCabe, K. (2013, November 10). A helping hand for veterans: Many behind bars are finding there's a network of services to help them rebuild their lives. *The Boston Globe.*

McCarthy, P. (2017, April 17). CT veteran sues to upgrade thousands of Army discharges nationwide. *Connecticut Health I-Team.* Retrieved from http://c-hit.org /2017/04/17/ct-veteran-sues-to-upgrade-thousands-of-army-discharges-nation wide/

McCaskill, C. (2015, June 18). Letter to General M. A. Welsh.

McCauley, J. L., Killeen, T., Goss, D. F., Brady, K. T., & Back, S. E. (2012). Posttraumatic stress disorder and co-occurring substance use disorders: Advances in assessment and treatment. *Clinical Psychology: Science and Practice, 19,* 283–304.

McCormick-Goodhart, M. (2013). Leaving no veteran behind: Policies and perspectives on combat trauma, veterans courts, and the rehabilitative approach to criminal behavior. *Pennsylvania State Law Review, 117,* 895–926.

McDonnell, T. M. (2017). Rule of law in the age of the drone: Requiring transparency and disqualifying clandestine actors—the CIA and the Joint Special Operations Command. *University of Miami Law Review, 72,* 34–111.

McGuire, J. (2007). Closing a front door to homelessness among veterans. *Journal of Primary Prevention, 28,* 389–400.

McLeod, A. M. (2012). Decarceration courts: Possibilities and perils of a shifting criminal law. *Georgetown Law Journal, 100,* 1587–1674.

Mendonca, K. B. (2012, May 18). San Francisco Justice Clinic—The first of its kind in Veterans Administration. San Francisco Veterans Administration Medical Center. Retrieved from http://www.sanfrancisco.va.gov/SANFRANCISCO /features/Justice_Clinic.asp

Mental aftermath, The. (1922, March 24). *The American Legion Weekly,* 12.

Merten, S. (2010, October 7). Running on "bubble gum and duct tape": A new court aims to keep damaged vets out of jail. *Dallas Observer.*

Military Benefits Info (2018). 2018 VA disability rates. Retrieved from https: //militarybenefits. info/va-disability-rates/

Miller, R. (2005, Summer). Inmate labor: Entitlements, benefits, and regulations. *Proceedings of the Large Jail Network Meeting.* Washington, DC: NIC Jails Division.

Moore, B. A., Hopewell, C. A., & Grossman, D. (2009). After the battle: Violence and the warrior. In S. M. Freeman, B. A. Moore, & A. Freeman (Eds.), *Living and surviving in harm's way: A psychological treatment handbook for pre- and post-deployment of military personnel* (pp. 307–327). New York: Taylor and Francis Group.

Morris, S. W. (2003). A survey of military retirement benefits. *Military Law Review, 177,* 133–161.

Mullen, M. G. (2011, February 15). Letter to Hon. Eric K. Shinseki, Secretary, Department of Veterans Affairs as Chairman of the Joint Chiefs of Staff.

Mumola, C. J. (2000, September 29). *Veterans in prison or jail* (Revised ed.). Washington, DC: Bureau of Justice Statistics.

Munetz, M. R., & Griffin, P. A. (2006). Use of the sequential intercept model as an approach to decriminalization of people with serious mental illness. *Psychiatric Services, 57*(4): 544–549.

Myers, K. (2009, May/June). Stayin' alive: Mission minded getting it done at Angola Prison. *The Vietnam Veterans of America Veteran.*

Najavits, L. M. (2002). Seeking safety therapy for trauma and substance abuse. *Corrections Today, 64,* 136–140.

Najavits, L. M., Schmitz, M., Johnson, K. M., Smith, C., North, T., Hamilton, N., . . . Wilkins, K. (2009). Seeking safety therapy for men: Clinical and research experiences. In *Men and Addictions* (pp. 37–58). Hauppage, NY: Nova Science.

Nash, W. P., Marino, T. L., Carper, M., Mills, A., Au, T., Goldsmith, A., & Litz, B. T. (2013). Psychometric evaluation of the moral injury events scale. *Military Medicine, 178*(6), 646–652.

National Center for Telehealth and Technology. (2012). *DoDSER: Department of Defense Suicide Event Report calendar year 2011 annual report.* Washington, DC: U.S. Department of Defense.

National Coalition of Homeless Veterans. (n.d.). *Planning for your release: A guide for incarcerated veterans.* Washington, DC: U.S. Department of Labor, Veterans Employment and Training Service.

National Institute of Corrections. (2008, September). *Proceedings of the Large Jail Network.* Washington, DC: NIC Jails Division.

National Institute of Corrections. (2010, March). *Proceedings of the Large Jail Network.* Washington, DC: NIC Jails Division.

National Institute of Corrections. (2018). Justice involved veterans: Prisons and jails with dorms for veterans. Retrieved from https://info.nicic.gov/jiv/node/27

National Institute of Corrections. (2018). Justice involved veterans: Veteran intercepts in the criminal justice system. Retrieved from https://info.nicic.gov/jiv/node/113

National Sheriffs' Association. (2012, July/August). 2012 National Sheriffs' Association Resolutions. *Sheriff Magazine, 19.*

New York State Department of Correctional Services. (n.d.). Incarcerated veterans programs.

New York State Department of Correctional Services. (1994, January). *Veterans Residential Therapeutic Program: Program overview.* Sonyea, NY: Author.

New York Times Editorial Board. (2017, October 22). America's forever wars. *New York Times*. Retrieved from https://www.nytimes.com/2017/10/22/opinion/americas-forever-wars.html

Newhouse, E. (2008). *Faces of combat, PTSD and TBI: One journalist's crusade to improve treatment for our veterans*. Enumclaw, WA: Idyll Arbor.

Nicholson, K., & Martelli, M. F. (2007). Malingering: Overview and basic concepts. In G. Young, A. W. Kane, K. Nicholson, & D. W. Schuman (Eds.), *Causality of psychological injury: Presenting evidence in court* (pp. 375–409). New York: Springer.

Noonan, C. J., & Mumola, M. E. (2004). *Veterans in state and federal prison*. Washington, DC: Bureau of Justice Statistics.

Noonan, C. J., & Mumola, M. E. (2007, May). *Veterans in state and federal prison*. Washington, DC: Bureau of Justice Statistics.

Novaco, R. W., Swanson, R. D., Gonzalez, O. I., Gahm, G. A., & Reger, M. D. (2012). Anger and postcombat mental health: Validation of a brief anger measure with U.S. soldiers postdeployed from Iraq and Afghanistan. *Psychological Assessment, 24*(3), 661–675.

Nydegger, R. (2013). Depression. In M. Shally-Jensen (Ed.), *Mental health care issues in America: An encyclopedia* (Vol. 1, pp. 167–174). Santa Barbara, CA: ABC-CLIO.

Odierno, R. T. (2013, May 17). *CSA sends: Sexual assault and sexual harassment*. Washington, DC: U.S. Department of Army.

Ogle, A., Reichwald, R., RuHand, J. B., & Thurman, C. (2017). *Remote combat stress impact and mitigation: ISR in the kill chain*. Joint Base Langley-Eustis, VA: U.S. Air Force 480th Intelligence, Surveillance, and Reconnaissance Wing.

Olson, J., & Rashid, M. (2013). Modern drone warfare: An ethical analysis. Retrieved from http://se.asee.org/proceedings/ASEE2013/Papers2013/157.PDF

Olusanya, O. (2012). Toward an integrated theoretical model of risk factors for post-deployment PTSD and its implications for justice-involved veterans. *Journal of Human Behavior in the Social Environment, 22*(4), 690–706.

Oversight on issues related to incarcerated veterans: Hearing before the Senate Committee on Veterans' Affairs, 96th Cong., 1st Sess. (1979, July 11) (testimony of B. Carr, Chief Psychologist, U.S. Penitentiary of Lewisburg, PA).

Oversight on issues related to incarcerated veterans: Hearing before the Senate Committee on Veterans' Affairs, 96th Cong., 1st Sess. (1979, July 11) (statement of J. J. Cox as Director, Veterans Assistance Service, Veterans Administration).

Oversight on issues related to incarcerated veterans: Hearing before the Senate Committee on Veterans' Affairs, 96th Cong., 1st Sess. (1979, July 11) (statement of A. Cranston as Chair of the Senate Committee on Veterans' Affairs).

Oversight on issues related to incarcerated veterans: Hearing before the Senate Committee on Veterans' Affairs, 96th Cong., 1st Sess. (1979, July 11) (written response of J. R. Ewalt).

Oversight on issues related to incarcerated veterans: Hearing before the Senate Committee on Veterans' Affairs, 96th Cong., 1st Sess. (1979, July 11) (statement of R.F. Lauve as Associate Director of Human Resources Division).

Oversight on issues related to incarcerated veterans: Hearing before the Senate Committee on Veterans' Affairs, 96th Cong., 1st Sess. (1979, July 11) (prepared statement of A.

S. Merretazon as founder and director of Incarcerated Veterans Assistance Organization).

Oversight on issues related to incarcerated veterans: Hearing before the Senate Committee on Veterans' Affairs, 96th Cong., 1st Sess. (1979, July 11) (prepared statement of B. Pentland as Coordinator, Veterans in Prison Project, Veterans Administration Medical Center, Brentwood, Los Angeles, CA), pp. 523–528.

Oversight on issues related to incarcerated veterans: Hearing before the Senate Committee on Veterans' Affairs, 96th Cong., 1st Sess. (1979, July 11) (statement of P. Salierno, Jr. as Director, Incarcerated Veterans Project, National Council of Churches).

Oversight on issues related to incarcerated veterans: Hearing before the Senate Committee on Veterans' Affairs, 96th Cong., 1st Sess. (1979, July 11) (statement of M. Cleland as Director of Veterans Administration).

Painton, F. C. (1922, January 27). Extra!! "War hero loots bank!": In the headlines he may be lawless but a prison head finds the veteran is really the reverse. *The American Legion Weekly,* 5–6, 18–19.

Parrish, R. (n.d.). PTSD and "bad discharges." Vietnam Veterans Against the War. Retrieved on April 6, 2012, from www.vvaw.org

Pavlicin, K. M. (2003). *Surviving deployment: A guide for military families.* St. Paul, MN: Elva Resa.

Paznoikas, M. (2014, March 3). Yale class-action lawsuit seeks redress for Vietnam vets. *Connecticut Mirror.* Retrieved from https://ctmirror.org/2014/03/03/yale-class-action-lawsuit-seeks-redress-for-vietnam-vets/

Pennsylvania Department of Corrections and Pennsylvania Board of Probation and Parole. (2013). *Serving Incarcerated Veterans.* Harrisburg, PA: Authors.

Pentland, B. & Dwyer, J. (1985). Incarcerated veterans. In S. M. Sonnenberg, A. S. Blank Jr., & J. A, Talhott (Eds.), *Trauma of war stress and recovery in Viet Nam veterans* (pp. 403–416). Washington, DC: American Psychiatric Press.

Pentland, B., & Scurfield, R. (1982). Inreach counseling and advocacy with veterans in prison. *Federal Probation, 46,* 21–28.

Perillo Jr., M. J. (2011). A primer for civilian criminal defense attorneys. In *Strategies for military criminal defense: Leading lawyers on understanding the military justice system, constructing effective defense strategies, and navigating complex cases* (pp. 23–36). Eagan, MN: Thomson Reuters/Aspatore.

Perry, T. (2013, November 18). Separate jail facilities seek to cut recidivism rates among veterans. *Los Angeles Times*

Pew Research Center. (2011, October 5). *The military–civilian gap: War and sacrifice in the post-9/11 era.* Washington, DC: Pew Social & Demographic Trends.

Pfeiffer, M. B. (2007). *Crazy in America: The hidden tragedy of our criminalized mentally ill.* New York: Caroll & Graff.

Philipps, D. (2010). *Lethal warriors: When the new band of brothers came home.* New York: Palgrave MacMillan.

Philipps, D. (2013). Other than honorable: Locked away, Army struggles with wounded soldiers. *The Gazette* (Colorado).

Pienciak, R. T. (1980, September 28). "Son of Sam": "I could detail every fact . . . I wasn't alone . . . It wasn't me." *Doylestown Intelligencer* (Pennsylvania).

Pinchevski, A. (2016). Screen trauma: Visual media and post-traumatic stress disorder. *Theory, Culture & Society, 33*(4), 51–75.

Plaintiff's Memorandum in Support of Their Motion for Final Approval of Stipulation of Settlement. (1987, November 18). *Richard Carter et al. v. Glen R. Jeffes,* Civ. Action No. 82-3821 (pp. 1–50). Philadelphia, PA: Eastern District of Pennsylvania.

Porter v. McCollum, 558 U.S. 30 (2009).

Prann, E. (2012, May 5). First exclusive jail dorm opens. *Fox News.* Retrieved from http://www.foxnews.com/us/2012/05/05/first-veteran-exclusive-jail-dorm-opens

Press Release. (2018, March 22). Murphy's "Honor Our Commitment Act" included in FY18 Omnibus Appropriations Bill. Retrieved from https://www.murphy .senate.gov/newsroom/press-releases/murphys-honor-our-commitment-act -included-in-fy18-omnibusappropriations-bill

Prison cleanup campaign being put on by vets: Plan survey of jails to find ex-service men confined. (1922, November 27). *Laurel Daily Leader* (Mississippi), p. 4.

Prison monument completed. (1989, Nov. 10). *The News (Frederick, Maryland),* p. C-12.

Psychotic vet care eyed by Utah unit. (1950, February 5). *The Salt Lake Tribune* (Utah), p. 2B.

Purkiss, J., Serle, J., & Fielding-Smith, A. (2017, December 19). U.S. counterterror air strikes double in Trump's first year. Retrieved from https://www.thebureau investigates.com/stories/2017-12-19/counterrorism-strikesdouble-trump-first -year

Ramsay, C. (2009). The Iraq War and U.S. public opinion. In J. S. Duffield & P. J. Dombrowski (Eds.), *Balance sheet: The Iraq War and U.S. national security* (pp. 132–157). Stanford, CA: Stanford Security Studies.

Ray, S. L., Haines, K., & Longo, M. S. (2013). The paradox of military training: Survival in the streets among homeless veterans. In A. B. Aiken & S. A. Bélanger (Eds.), *Beyond the line: Military and veteran health research* (pp. 291–306). Montreal, BC: McGill-Queen's University Press.

Ream III, J. H. Testimony (1987, December 3). *Richard Carter, et al. v. Glen R. Jeffes,* Civ. Action No. 82-3821, Hearing re: Settlement (Third Day). Philadelphia, PA.

Record of the fifth national convention, The. (1923, November 9). *The American Legion Weekly,* 10.

Reddington, E. C. (2011). Accounting for differences in the military justice system. In *Strategies for military criminal defense: Leading lawyers on understanding the military justice system, constructing effective defense strategies, and navigating complex cases* (pp. 71–82). Eagan, MN: Thomson Reuters/Aspatore.

Reed, T. J. (2009). Parallel lines never meet: Why the military disability retirement and Veterans Affairs department claim adjudication systems are a failure. *Widener Law Journal, 19,* 57–135.

Reger, M. A., Smolenski, D. J., Skopp, N. A., Metzger-Abamukang, M. J., Kang, H. K., Bullman, T. A., . . . Gahm, G. A. (2015). Risk of suicide among U.S. military service members following Operation Enduring Freedom or Operation Iraqi Freedom deployment and separation from the U.S. military. *Journal of the American Medical Association Psychiatry, 72*(16), 561–569.

Renwick, A. (1999). *Hidden wounds: The problems of Northern Ireland veterans in civvy street.* Nottingham, UK: The Russell Press Ltd.

Repard, P. (2013, November 16). Vets united behind bars: Authorities hope they can better rehabilitate service members by housing them together in unit at Vista jail. *San Diego Union-Tribune,* p. B-1.

Richard Carter, et al. v. Glen R. Jeffes, Civ. Action No. 82-3821, Hearing re: Settlement (1987, December 3) (testimony of R. Carter) (Third day, pp. 438–466). Philadelphia, PA: Eastern District of Pennsylvania.

Richardson, J., Thompson, J. M., Boswall, M., & Jetly, R. (2010, May). Horror comes home: Veterans with posttraumatic stress disorder. *Canadian Family Physician, 56,* 430–433.

Ricketts, J. (2013, July 12). [Letter to Whom it May Concern, Re: 5-Armed Forces Plaques]. Roxbury Correctional Institute: Hagerstown, MD.

Rideau, W. (1976). Veterans incarcerated. *Penthouse: The International Magazine for Men* 7(8), 162–166.

Rinkey, G. T. (2011). Successfully defending military criminal cases. In *Strategies for military criminal defense: Leading lawyers on understanding the military justice system, constructing effective defense strategies, and navigating complex cases* (pp. 37–52). Eagan, MN: Thomson Reuters/Aspatore.

Ritchie, E. C., Schneider, B., Bradley, J., & Forsten, R. D. (2008). Resilience and military psychiatry. In B. J. Luckey & V. Tepe (Eds.), *Biobehavioral resilience to stress* (pp. 25–42). Boca Raton, FL: CRC Press.

Robinson, J. P., & Tate, C. (2016, October). Veterans endeavor for treatment and support: The role the Army judge advocate general's corps should play in establishing federal veterans treatment courts in and around major Army installations. *The Army Lawyer,* 23–36.

Rogers, A., & Law, H. (2010). Working with trauma in a prison setting. In J. Harvey & K. Smedley (Eds.), *Psychological therapy in prisons and other secure settings* (pp. 150–175). New York: Willan.

Rogers, K. (2015, June 5). Charges dropped against Creech drone sensor operator with PTSD. *Las Vegas Review Journal.* Retrieved from https://www.reviewjournal.com/news/military/charges-dropped-against-creech-drone-sensor-operator-with-ptsd/

Rosellini, A. J., Monahan, J., Street, A. E., Heeringa, S. G., Hill, E. D., Petukhova, M., . . . Kessler, R. C. (2016). Predicting non-familial major physical violent crime perpetration in the U.S. Army from administrative data. *Psychological Medicine, 46,* 303–316.

Rosellini, A. J., Monahan, J., Street, A. E., Petukhova, M. V., Sampson, N. A., Benedek, D. M. ... Kessler, R. C. (2017). Predicting sexual assault perpetration in the U.S. Army using administrative data. *American Journal of Preventive Medicine, 53*(5), 661–669.

Rosen, L. N., & Durand, D. B. (2000). Coping with the unique demands of military family life. In J. A. Martin, L. N. Rosen, & L. R. Sparacino (Eds.), *The military family: A practice guide for human service providers* (pp. 55–72). Westport, CT: Praeger.

Rosenthal, J., & McGuire, J. (2013). Incarcerated veterans. In L. Gideon (Ed.), *Special needs offenders in correctional institutions* (pp. 345–376). Thousand Oaks, CA: Sage.

Roth, J. B. (1986, November 8, 9). Guilty conscience. *The Gettysburg Times (Pennsylvania)*, p. 3C.

Rotunda, K. M. (2013, March). National Defense Authorization Act and military sexual assault/harassment: Sweeping reform or just words? *Orange County Lawyer, 55*(3), 18–22.

Rowe, P. (2005, November 13). Prison break: Locked away in San Quentin, some Vietnam vets try paying back with college scholarships. *San Diego Union Tribune*, p. E-1.

Rubin, A. (2013). Introduction: Understanding and intervening with military personnel and their families: An overview. In A. Rubin, E. L. Weiss, & J. E. Coll (Eds.), *Handbook of military social work* (pp. xxiii–xxxi). Hoboken, NJ: John Wiley and Sons.

Rubin, A., & Weiss, E. L. (2013). Secondary trauma in military social work. In A. Rubin, E. L. Weiss, & J. E. Coll (Eds.), *Handbook of military social work* (pp. 67–78). Hoboken, NJ: John Wiley and Sons.

Russell, M. C., Shaubel, S. R., & Figley, C. (2018). The darker side of military mental healthcare, part two: Five harmful strategies to manage its mental health dilemma. *Psychological Injury and Law, 11,* 37–68.

Russell Jr., R. (2009). Veterans treatment court: A proactive approach. *New England Journal on Criminal and Civil Confinement, 35*(2), 357–372.

Russell Jr., R. (2015). Veterans treatment courts. *Touro Law Review, 31,* 385–401.

Salem, J. P. (2011). Turning to problem-solving courts: Veterans' courts are latest example. *Insights on Law and Society, 12,* 10–13, 28.

Sandel, C. P. (1984). Other-than-honorable military administrative discharges: Time for confrontation. *San Diego Law Review, 21,* 839–859.

San Diego County Sheriff's Department. (2013, November 1). *Veterans moving forward.* San Diego, CA: Vista Detention Facility. Retrieved from http://www .youtube.com/watch?v= baChRYdFiNM

Savitsky, L., Illingsworth, M., & DuLaney, M. (2009). Civilian social work: Serving the military and veteran populations. *Social Work, 54*(4), 327–339.

San Francisco Sheriff's Department. (n.d.). C. O. V. E. R. project: Dedicated to assisting our incarcerated veterans. Retrieved on December 15, 2013 from http: //sfsheriff. com/special_COVER.html

Sayer, N., Noorbaloochi, A., Frazier, P., Carlson, K., Gravely, A., & Murdoch, M. (2010). Reintegration problems and treatment interest among Iraq and Afghanistan combat veterans receiving Veterans Administration medical care. *Psychiatric Services, 61*(6), 589–597.

Sayer, N., Spoont, M., Murdoch, M., Parker, L. E., Hintz, S., & Rosenheck, R. (2011). A qualitative study of U.S. veterans' reasons for seeking Department of Veterans Affairs disability benefits for posttraumatic stress disorder. *Journal of Traumatic Stress, 24*(6), 699–707.

Schaffer, B. J. (2009, October/September). The jailed veteran and a challenging economy. *American Jails,* 41–48.

Schauer, M., & Schauer, E. (2010). Trauma-focused mental-health interventions: A paradigm shift in humanitarian assistance and aid work. In E. Martz (Ed.), *Trauma rehabilitation after war and conflict: Community and individual perspectives* (pp. 389–428). New York: Springer.

Schroeder, K. (2013, July 21). Kennebec County Jail program aims to help inmates who are veterans. *Kennebec County Journal* (Maine).

Schwartz, S., & Levitas, L. (2011). Restorative justice for veterans: The San Francisco Sheriff's Department's Community of Veterans Engaged in Restoration (COVER). *Washington University Journal of Law and Policy, 36,* 47–63.

Scurfield, R. M. (2004). *A Vietnam trilogy: Veterans and post traumatic stress: 1968, 1989, 2000.* New York: Algora.

Schaffer, B. J. (2016). Incarcerated veterans outreach program. *Journal of Evidence-Informed Social Work, 13,* 293–304.

Schaller, B. R. (2012). *Veterans on trial: The coming battles over PTSD.* Washington, DC: Potomac Books.

Schell, T. L., & Marshall, G. N. (2009). Survey of individuals previously deployed for OEF/OIF. In T. Tanielian & L. H. Jaycox (Eds.), *Invisible wounds of war: Psychological and cognitive injuries, their consequences, and services to assist recovery* (pp. 87–115). Santa Monica, CA: RAND Corporation.

Schmidt, M. S. (2016, September 6). Air Force, short of drone pilots, uses contractors to fight terror. *The New York Times.*

Schmidt, M. S., & Schmitt, E. (2016, October 12). ISIS is piloting simple drones rigged to kill. *The New York Times.*

Sheridan, J. (1985, November 11). Vets behind bars: Why have many turned to crime? *Syracuse Herald-Journal,* p. A6.

Scott, C. W. (2010, July). Shinseki's surge: Can it work? *Federal Lawyer,* p. 30.

Seamone, E. R. (2002). When wishing on a star just won't do: The legal basis for international cooperation in the mitigation of asteroid impacts and similar transboundary disasters. *Iowa Law Review, 87,* 1091–1139.

Seamone, E. R. (2003). The duty to "expect the unexpected": Mitigating extreme natural threats to the global commons such as asteroid and comet impacts with the earth. *Columbia Journal of Transnational Law, 41,* 735–794.

Seamone, E. R. (2004). The precautionary principle as the law of planetary defense. *Georgetown International Environmental Law Review, 17*(1), 1–23.

Seamone, E. R. (2011). Reclaiming the rehabilitative ethic in military justice: The suspended punitive discharge as a method to treat military offenders with PTSD and TBI and reduce recidivism. *Military Law Review, 208,* 1–212.

Seamone, E. R. (2012). Improved assessment of child custody cases involving combat veterans with posttraumatic stress disorder. *Family Court Review, 50*(2), 310–343.

Seamone, E. R. (2013a). Dismantling America's largest sleeper cell: The imperative to treat, rather than merely punish, active duty offenders with PTSD prior to discharge from the armed forces. *Nova Law Review, 38,* 73–117.

Seamone, E. R. (2013b, November/December). A historical touchstone for Nebraska in the mission to divert criminally involved veterans from confinement. *Nebraska Lawyer, 16*(6), 7–15.

Seamone, E. R., & Traskey, D. M. (2014). Maximizing VA benefits for survivors of military sexual trauma: A practical guide for survivors and their advocates. *Columbia Journal of Gender & Law, 26*(2), 343–487.

Seamone, E. R., McGuire, J., Sreenivasan, S., Clark, S. Smee, D., & Dow, D. (2014). Moving upstream: Why rehabilitative justice in military justice proceedings serves a public health interest. *American Journal of Public Health, 104*(10), 1805–1811.

Seamone, E. R., Sreenivasan, S., McGuire, J., Smee, D., Clark, S., & Dow, D. (2018a). A rehabilitative justice pathway for war-traumatized offenders caught in the military justice catch-22. *Armed Forces and Society, 44*(1), 139–155.

Seamone, E. R., Brooks-Holliday, S., & Sreenivasan, S. (2018b). Veteran non grata: Veteran sex offenders with service-related mental health conditions and the need to mitigate risk. *Virginia Journal of Criminal Law, 6*(1), 182–237.

Severo, R., & Milford, L. (1989). *The wages of war: When America's soldiers came home from Valley Forge to Vietnam.* New York: Simon and Schuster.

Shane, S. (2016, July 4). Drone strike data reveals limits of fighting terrorists from sky. *New York Times.*

Shay, J. (1996). Combat stress barometer—recording how bad and how often. In B. H. Stamm (Ed.), *Measurement of stress, trauma, and adaptation* (pp. 117–121). Lutherville, MD: The Sidran Press.

Shepherd, T. (2017, November 19). Separate housing for veterans in jail becomes a national trend. *Washington Examiner.* Retrieved from https://abcnews.go.com/Health/Wellness/special-jail-housing-military-veterans/story?id=16222008

Shepherd, W. G. (1923, November 30). Youth + dope = crime. *The American Legion Weekly,* pp. 7–8, 27–30.

Shinseki, E. (2013, December 2). Remarks to the National Association of Drug Court Professionals. *Targeted News Service.*

Shuker-Haines, T. (1995). Radio soap operas and domestic masculinity: The World War II veteran comes home. *Journal of Radio Studies, 3,* 149–161.

Sieleni, B. (2011). Addressing the mental health crisis in corrections. *Corrections Today, 73*(5), 10.

Sigafoos, C. E. (1994). Post-traumatic stress disorder program for combat (Vietnam) veterans in prison. *International Journal of Offender Therapy and Comparative Criminology, 38,* 117–130.

Sisk, R. (2018, February 15). Pentagon's new deploy-or-out policy could separate up to 286K. Retrieved from https://www.military.com/daily-news/2018/02/15/pentagons-new-deploy-or-out-policy-could-separate-286k.html.

Slovenko, R. (2004). The watering down of PTSD in criminal law. *Psychiatry and the Law, 32,* 411–438.

Smith, J. W. (2012). The Anchorage, Alaska veterans court and recidivism: July 6, 2004–December 31, 2010. *Alaska Law Review, 29,* 93–112.

Smith, P. H., Potenza, M. N., Mazure, C. M., McKee, S. A., Park, C. L., & Hoff, R. A. (2014). Compulsive sexual behavior among male military veterans: Prevalence and associated clinical factors. *Journal of Behavioral Addictions, 3*(4), 214–222.

Snowden, D. L., Oh, S., Salas-Wright, C. P., Vaughn, M. G., & King, E. (2017). Military service and crime: New evidence. *Social Psychiatry and Psychiatric Epidemiology, 52*(5), 605–615.

Stander, V., Merrill, L. L., & Thomsen, C. J. (2008). *Premilitary sexual assault victimization and perpetration in a Navy recruit sample* (Report No. 05-28). San Diego, CA: Naval Health Research Center.

States News Service. (2013, October 28). Meng legislation to help end massive backlog of veterans disability claims passed by house. *States News Service.*

Steadman, H. J., McCarty, D. W., & Morrisey, J. P. (1989). *The mentally ill in jail: Planning for essential services.* New York: The Guilford Press.

Stein, N. R., Mills, M. A., Arditte, K., Mendoza, C., Borah, A. M., Resick, P. A., & Litz, B. T. (2012). A scheme for categorizing traumatic military events. *Behavior Modification, 36*(6), 787–807.

Stipulation of Settlement (1987, September 4 and 8). *Richard Carter et al. v. Glen R. Jeffes,* Civ. Action No. 82-3821 (pp. 1–49). Philadelphia, PA: Eastern District of Pennsylvania.

Stock, S., Wagner, L., Paredes, D., Escamilla, F., & Carroll, J. (2012, August 9). Veterans behind bars: More Iraq War veterans are landing in jail, but most counties don't track soldier inmates. *NBC Bay Area.*

Stovall, J. G., Cloninger, L., & Appleby, L. (1997). Identifying homeless mentally ill veterans in jail: A preliminary report. *Journal of the American Academy of Psychiatry and Law, 25*(3), 311–315.

Strom, T. Q., Leskela, J., Thuras, P. D., Voller, K., Weigel, R., Yutsis, M., . . . Holz, K. B. (2012). An exploratory examination of risk-taking behavior and PTSD symptom severity in a veteran sample. *Military Medicine, 177*(4), 390–396.

Sun, I. Y., Sung, H. E., & Chu, D. C. (2007). Collateral gains from the military? A cross-national analysis of armed forces–crime relationship. *International Journal of Offender Therapy and Comparative Criminology, 51*(5), 599–614.

Swetz Jr., A. (1989, August). Post-traumatic stress disorder: Special problems of the incarcerated Vietnam vet. *Corrections Today, 51*(5), 184–186.

Taft, C. T., Pless, A. P., Stalans, L. J., Koenen, K. C., King, L. A., & King, D. W. (2005). Risk factors for partner violence among a national sample of combat veterans. *Journal of Consulting and Clinical Psychology, 73*(1), 151–159.

Task Force on Mental Health (2007). *An achievable vision: Report of the Department of Defense Task Force on Mental Health.* Washington, DC: U.S. Department of Defense.

Taylor, J., Parkes, T., Haw, S., & Jepson, R. (2012). Military veterans with mental health problems: A protocol for a systematic review to identify whether they have an additional risk of contact with the criminal justice systems compared with other veteran groups. *Systematic Reviews, 53*(1), 1–9.

Tayyeb, A. R., & Greenburg, J. (2017, June 20). *"Bad papers": The invisible and increasing costs of war for excluded veterans.* Providence, RI: Watson Institute for International & Public Affairs.

Teten, A. L., Schumacher, J. A., Taft, C. T., Stanley, M. A., Kent, T. A., Bailey, S. D., & White, D. L. (2010). Intimate partner aggression perpetrated by male

Afghanistan, Iraq, and Vietnam veterans with and without posttraumatic stress disorder. *Journal of Interpersonal Violence, 25*(9), 1612–1630.

Tharp, A. T., Sherman, M. K., Holland, K., Townsend, B., Bowling, U. (2016). A qualitative study of male veterans' violence perpetration and treatment preferences. *Military Medicine, 181*(8), 735–739.

Tilghman, A. (2016, January 6). DoD rejects "Nintendo medal" for drone pilots and cyber warriors. *Military Times.* Retrieved from https://www.militarytimes.com / 2016/01/06/dod-rejects-nintendo-medal-for-drone-pilots-and-cyber-warriors/

Treatment not punishment is the need of ex-service men in prison board finds. (1923, Feb. 16). *Sheboygan Press-Telegram* (Wisconsin), p. 3.

Tristam, P. (2017, March 6). Predator drones and other unmanned aerial vehicles (UAVs): History, uses, costs, advantages and disadvantages. Retrieved from https: //www.thoughtco.com/predator-drones-unmanned-aerial-vehicles-2353718

Trojano, M. L., Christopher, P. P., Pinals, D. A., Harnish, A., & Smelson, D. (2017). Perceptions of voluntary consent among jail diverted veterans with co-occurring disorders. *Behavioral Science and Law, 35,* 408–417.

Truscott, M. R. (1989). *Brats.* New York: Dutton.

Tsai, J., Flatley, B., Kasprow, W. J., Clark, S., & Finlay, A. K. (2017). Diversion of veterans with criminal justice involvement in treatment courts: Participant characteristics and outcomes. *Psychiatric Services, 68*(4), 375–383

Tsai, J., & Goggin, E. (2017). Characteristics, needs, and experiences of U.S. veterans on a specialized prison unit. *Evaluation and Program Planning, 64,* 44–48.

Tyler, C. (2011, March 8). Unique jail caters to veterans. *abc7News.* Retrieved from http://abc7news.com/archive/8002409/

Underhill, J. J. (2011, May/June). Up to the challenge. *Pennsylvania Lawyer,* 25–27.

Ungvarsky, J. J., Conaty, M., & Bellflower, S. (2012, March). Back on track: Life skills training for veterans in the criminal justice system. Paper presented at the 2012 American Counseling Association National Conference. San Francisco, CA.

United Nations Conference on Environment and Development. (1992). *Rio declaration on environment and development.* U. N. Doc A/CONF. 151/5/Rev. 1, reprinted in 31 I. L. M. 84.

United States v. McBride, 50 C.M.R. 126 (A.F. Ct. Mil. Rev. 1975).

U.S. Army Human Resources Command. (2017, November 9). C and R devices. Retrieved from https://www.hrc. army.mil/content/C%20and%20R%20devices

U.S. Comptroller General. (1974). *Need for improved outreach efforts for veterans in prison or on parole.* Washington, DC: U.S. Government Printing Office.

U.S. Court of Appeals for the Armed Forces (FY2001–FY2011). *Annual reports of the committee on military justice.* Washington, DC: Department of Defense.

U.S. Department of the Army. (1994). *Field manual 22–51: Leader's manual for combat stress control.* Washington, DC: U.S. Department of Army.

U.S. Department of the Army. (n.d.). *A sense of achievement: Recent graduates of basic training look back on their experiences.* Washington, DC: U.S. Department of Army. Retrieved from http://www.todaysmilitary.com/inside/view/a-sense-of-achievement

U.S. Department of the Army. (2006). *Field manual 4-02. 51 (FM 8-51): Combat and operational stress control.* Washington, DC: U.S. Department of the Army.

U.S. Department of the Army. (2011, September 6) (Rapid Action Revision). *Army regulation 635-200: Active duty enlisted administrative separations.* Washington, DC: U.S. Department of Army.

U.S. Department of Defense. (2016). *2016 demographics profile of the military community.* Washington, DC: Office of the Deputy Assistant Secretary for Military Community and Family Policy.

U.S. Department of Navy and U.S. Marine Corps. (2010, December). *Combat and operational stress control: NTTP 1-15M, MCRP 6-11e.* Washington, DC: Authors.

U.S. Navy & U.S. Marine Corps (2010, December). *Combat and operational stress control: NTTP 1-15M, MCRP: 6-11C.* Washington, DC: Department of the Navy and U.S. Marine Corps.

U.S. Department of Veterans Affairs. (n.d.). Health Care for Re-entry Veterans services and resources. Retrieved from https://www.va.gov/homeless/reentry.asp (manually counting specialists).

U.S. Department of Veterans Affairs. (2015, June). *Veteran-Re-Entry Search Service (VRSS) FAQs.* Retrieved from http://www.montgomerycountymd.gov/HHS -Program/Resources/Files/A%26D%20Docs/CVA/VRSS_FAQs_20150612.pdf

U.S. Department of Veterans Affairs. (2018). Veterans pension rate table – effective 12/1/17. Retrieved from https://www. benefits.va. gov/pension/current_rates _veteran_pen.asp

U.S. Government Accountability Office (2016). *Veterans justice outreach program: VA could improve management by establishing performance measures and fully assessing risk, GAO 16-393.* Washington, DC.: Author.

VanWinkle, C. (2009). *Soft spots: A marine's memoir of combat and post-traumatic stress disorder.* New York: St. Martin's Press.

Vasterling, J., Proctor, S. P., Friedman, M., Hoge, C. W., Heeren, T., & King, L. A. (2010). PTSD symptom increases in Iraq-deployed soldiers: comparison with non-deployed soldiers and associations with baseline symptoms, deployment experiences, and post deployment stress. *Journal of Traumatic Stress, 23*(1), 41–50.

Veitch, T., & Irons, G. (2008). The legion of Charlies. In D. Kendall (Ed.), *The mammoth book of best war comics: Over 25 of the greatest war comics ever, by Sam Glanzman, Keiji Nakazawa, Will Eisner, Raymond Briggs, Alex Toth, Pat Mills, John Severin, Greg Irons, and many more* (1971 ed., pp. 253–286). Philadelphia: Running Press.

Vergakis, B. (2012, November 25). Va. prison groups veterans together for support. *Associated Press.*

Veterans Administration to furnish data to jailed veterans. (1946, January 30). *Racine Journal Times* (Wisconsin), p. 5.

Veterans Benefits (1980, February 1). *The Paris News* (Texas), p. 4.

Veterans Benefits Administration, Benefits Assistance Service. (2012, August). *Fact sheet: Incarcerated veterans: Can a veteran receive Veterans Administration benefits while in prison?* Washington, DC: U.S. Department of Veterans Affairs.

Veterans Legal Clinic. (2016). Underserved: How the VA wrongfully excludes veterans with bad paper. Jamaica Plain, MA: Harvard Legal Services Center.

Vick, D. W. M. (1995). Poorhouse justice: Underfunded indigent defense services and arbitrary death sentences. *Buffalo Law Review, 43,* 329–460.

Vickers, M. P., Testimony (1987, December 3). *Richard Carter et al. v. Glen Jeffes,* Civ. Action No. 82-3821, Hearing re: Settlement (Day Three, pp. 291–469). Philadelphia, PA: Eastern District of Pennsylvania.

Vietnam Veterans of America, Veterans Incarcerated Committee. (n.d.). *Veterans Incarcerated Whitepaper,* http://www.vva.org/Committees/VetsIncarcerated /VeteransIncarcerated WhitePaper.html

Virgil, A. E., & Hawkins, H. L. (May–June 1946). *Prison World, 83,* 16, 28, 29.

Vitello, B. (2011, May 29). Veterans in Cook County Jail: Together, a second chance. *Daily Herald,* 1.

Waite, M. (2008, September/October). Houston lawyers helping local veterans. *The Houston Lawyer.* Retrieved from http://www.thehoustonlawyer.com/aa_sep08 /page10.htm

War veterans in prison. (1923, May 22). *Manitowoc Herald News* (Wisconsin), p. 2.

Waters, M., & Shay, J. (1994, August 2). Heal the "bad paper" veterans. *Baltimore Sun* (Maryland), p. 7B.

Welfare worker. (1922, March 24). Some examples of "shell shock." *The American Legion Weekly,* p. 6.

Wentling, N. (2017, August 29). Pentagon expands policy to upgrade vets' bad paper discharges. *Stars and Stripes.* Retrieved from https://www.stripes.com/news /pentagon-expands-policy-to-upgrade-vets-bad-paper-discharges-1.485038

Wheelock, R. J. (2011). The dos and don'ts of defending military clients in criminal cases. In *Strategies for military criminal defense: Leading lawyers on understanding the military justice system, constructing effective defense strategies, and navigating complex cases* (pp. 83–95). Eagan, MN: Thomson Reuters/Aspatore.

White, M. (2008, September/October). Houston lawyers helping local veterans. *Houston Lawyer,* pp. 11–15.

Wilde, M. L. (2007). Incomplete justice: Unintended consequences of military non-judicial punishment. *Air Force Law Review, 60,* 115–154.

Wilk, J. E., Herrell, R. K., Wynn, G. H., Rivere, L. A., & Hoge, C. W. (2012). Mild traumatic brain injury (concussion), posttraumatic stress disorder, and depression in U.S. soldiers involved in combat deployments: Association with postdeployment symptoms. *Psychosomatic Medicine, 74*(3), 249–257.

Will look after jailed veterans: Survey of World War men in penal institutions of New York is ordered by Forbes. (1922, November 3). *The Olean Evening Herald* (New York), p. 5.

Wills, T. J. (2012, Aug. 12). Building "a chance": Veterans incarcerated group celebrates 14th anniversary, honors fallen. *Port Arthur News* (Texas), p. A3.

Wilson, J. K., Brodsky, S. L., Neal, T. M. S., Alvarez, L. (2011a, December 12). In Florida, using military discipline to help veterans in prison. *The New York Times,* p. A14.

Wilson, J. K., Brodsky, S. L., & Neal, T. M. S. (2011b). Prosecutor pretrial attitudes and plea-bargaining behavior toward veterans with posttraumatic stress disorder. *Psychological Services, 8*(4), 319–331.

Wilson, J. P. (1980). Conflict stress and growth: The effects of war on psychosocial development among Vietnam veterans. In C. R. Figley & S. Leventman (Eds.),

Strangers at home: Vietnam veterans since the war (pp. 123–165). Portsmouth, NH: Greenwood.

Wilson, J. P., & Zigelbaum, S. D. (1983). The Vietnam veteran on trial: The relation of post-traumatic stress disorder to criminal behavior. *Behavioral Sciences and the Law, 1*(3), 69–83.

Wolfe, M. (2013, July 28). From PTSD to prison: Why veterans become criminals. *The Daily Beast.*

Wolff, N., Frueh, B. C., Shi, J., & Shumann, B. E. (2012). Effectiveness of cognitive-behavioral trauma treatment for incarcerated women with mental illnesses and substance abuse disorders. *Journal of Anxiety Disorders, 26,* 703–710.

Woollcott, A. (1922, March 24). Invisible wounds. *The American Legion Weekly,* pp. 5, 6, 18, 19.

Wortzel, H. S., & Arciniegas, David B. (2010). Combat veterans and the death penalty: A forensic neuropsychiatric perspective. *Journal of the American Academy of Psychiatry and Law, 38,* 407–414.

Wortzel, H. S., Binswanger, I. A., Anderson, C. A., & Adler, L. E. (2009). Suicide among incarcerated veterans. *Journal of the American Academy of Psychiatry and Law, 37*(1), 82–94.

Would pardon a host, 20,000 ex-service captives ought to be let out now. (1922, December 19). *Independent* (Helena, Montana), p. 1.

Would reopen cases of jailed veterans: Speakers declare many affected mentally. (1922, November 26). *The Boston Sunday Globe,* p. 6.

Young, G. (2007). Multicausal perspectives on psychological injury I: PTSD and MTBI. In G. Young, A. W. Kane, K. Nicholson, & D. W. Schuman (Eds.), *Causality of psychological injury: Presenting evidence in court* (pp. 137–164). New York: Springer.

Zlotnick C., Johnson, J., & Najavits, L. M. (2009). Randomized controlled pilot study of cognitive-behavioral therapy in a sample of incarcerated women with substance use disorder and PTSD. *Behavior Therapy, 40*(4), 325–336.

Zlotnick, C., Najavits, L. M., Rohsenow, D. J., & Johnson, D. M. (2003). A cognitive-behavioral treatment for incarcerated women with substance abuse disorder and Posttraumatic Stress Disorder: Findings from a pilot study. *Journal of Substance Abuse Treatment, 25,* 99–105.

Zogas, A. (2017, February). *U.S. military veterans' difficult transitions back to civilian life and the VA's response.* Providence, RI: Watson Institute of International and Public Affairs.

Zuchinno, D., & Cloud, D. (2015, May 24). U.S. military and civilians are increasingly divided. *Los Angeles Times.* Retrieved from http://www.latimes.com/nation/la-na-warrior-main-2

INDEX

About the Author: Evan R. Seamone, LL.M., J.D., M.P.P.

Evan R. Seamone is an attorney at the Veterans Legal Clinic of the Legal Services Center of Harvard Law School where he represents veterans in a variety of matters, including disability benefit appeals and military-discharge upgrades. Part of his duties include regularly visiting and providing legal and readjustment assistance to the veterans confined in the HUMV specialized housing unit at the Middlesex County House of Correction. Prior to joining the Clinic, Evan was a professor at Mississippi College School of Law where he directed the legal writing program and helped to start the school's monthly program to assist veterans with legal matters. In that capacity he assisted the Mississippi Department of Corrections in establishing its first-in-the-state veteran-specific housing unit. Evan also serves as a Major in the Army Reserve Component with duties as a senior defense counsel. In 2015, he ended a twelve-year career as an active duty judge advocate. His most recent assignment was service as a prosecutor in the Office of Chief Prosecutor of Military Commissions where he was responsible for cases involving terrorism and the acts of unprivileged enemy belligerents tried at Guantanamo Bay, Cuba, under the *Military Commissions Act of 2009*. In other military assignments, Evan supervised prosecuting attorneys and several civilian and military paralegals in some of the busiest criminal jurisdictions in the Army. During his tours in Iraq, Germany, and at domestic military installations, he has participated in sexual assault, complex death penalty, and other felony criminal cases involving PTSD as a prosecutor and defense attorney.

Evan has published more than twenty scholarly articles with law schools including Yale, Columbia, Georgetown, and New York University on topics including psychology, medical malpractice, national security, and international law, and court administration. His *Military Law Review* articles on enhanced legal counseling techniques for clients with suspected or diagnosed PTSD have been featured by state bar associations, the Arizona Public Defenders Association, and in training for military disability–evaluation attorneys. He has written extensively about treatment-based sentencing alternatives in military courts-martial, and the use of civilian veterans' treatment and mental health problem-solving courts by military organizations and commanders.

Evan has presented on numerous occasions at the Vet Court Con conferences addressing veterans treatment court trends and developments and has worked with the Bureau of Justice Assistance to assist veterans treatment court judges and treatment teams in developing their programs. Most recently, Evan was featured in the 2018 *Barracks Behind Bars* volume published by the National Institute of Corrections where he provided insights on the development of specialized housing units for veterans at jails and prisons across the country. Evan's interests extend to family courts as well as criminal courts. After publishing the first–ever article to assist custody evaluators and family court judges in improving their assessment of parents with PTSD, Evan edited a special edition of *The Family Court Review* devoted to military families and the courts. As the Vice Chair of the Military Committee of the National Council of Juvenile and Family Court Judges, he is involved in the development of a standardized curriculum to assist family court judges in better understanding the unique needs of military families.

Evan Seamone is a member of the Bar of the U.S. Supreme Court and the District of Columbia Court of Appeals. He is also licensed to practice in the U.S. Court of Appeals for the Armed Forces and the U.S. Court of Appeals for Veterans' Claims. His education includes a Bachelor of Arts from the University of California, Los Angeles (*Phi Beta Kappa, summa cum laude*); a Master's in Public Policy from the University of California, Los Angeles's School of Public Policy and Social Research; a Master of Science in Nonprofit Management from Northeastern University; a Juris Doctorate from the University of Iowa College of Law; and a Master of Laws from The Judge Advocate General's Legal Center and School, U.S. Army (Criminal Law Specialization).